Through the Sands of Time

THROUGH THE

Sands of Time

A History of the

Jewish Community of

St. Thomas, U.S. Virgin Islands

Judah M. Cohen

Brandeis University Press

PUBLISHED BY UNIVERSITY PRESS OF NEW ENGLAND

HANOVER AND LONDON

Brandeis University Press

An imprint of University Press of New England

www.upne.com

© 2004 Brandeis University

First Brandeis University Press paperback edition 2012

Manufactured in the United States of America

Designed by Mike Burton

Typeset in New Caledonia and La Bamba by Integrated Publishing Solutions

ISBN for the paperback edition: 978-1-61168-309-7

For permission to reproduce any of the material in this book, contact

Permissions, University Press of New England, One Court Street, Suite 250,

Lebanon NH 03766; or visit www.upne.com

This book was published with the generous support of Ms. Kathryn Petersen

and the St. Thomas Hebrew Congregation.

Library of Congress Cataloging-in-Publication Data

Cohen, Judah M.

Through the sands of time : a history of the Jewish community of

St. Thomas, U.S. Virgin Islands / Judah M. Cohen.—1st ed.

    p.   cm.—(Brandeis series in American Jewish history,

culture, and life)

Includes bibliographical references (p.) and index.

ISBN 1–58465–341–8 (cloth : alk. paper)

1. Jews—Virgin Islands of the United States—Saint Thomas—

History. 2. Jews—Virgin Islands of the United States—Saint

Thomas—Social life and customs. 3. Saint Thomas (V.I.)—Ethnic

relations.   I. Title. II. Series.

F2105.C64 2004

972.97'22—dc22   2003020486

Brandeis Series in American Jewish History, Culture, and Life

Jonathan D. Sarna, Editor
Sylvia Barack Fishman, Associate Editor

Leon A. Jick, 1992
The Americanization of the Synagogue,
1820–1870

Sylvia Barack Fishman, editor, 1992
Follow My Footprints: Changing
Images of Women in American Jewish
Fiction

Gerald Tulchinsky, 1993
Taking Root: The Origins of the Cana-
dian Jewish Community

Shalom Goldman, editor, 1993
Hebrew and the Bible in America:
The First Two Centuries

Marshall Sklare, 1993
Observing America's Jews

Reena Sigman Friedman, 1994
These Are Our Children: Jewish
Orphanages in the United States,
1880–1925

Alan Silverstein, 1994
Alternatives to Assimilation: The Re-
sponse of Reform Judaism to American
Culture, 1840–1930

Jack Wertheimer, editor, 1995
The American Synagogue: A Sanctuary
Transformed

Sylvia Barack Fishman, 1995
A Breath of Life: Feminism in the
American Jewish Community

Diane Matza, editor, 1996
Sephardic-American Voices: Two Hun-
dred Years of a Literary Legacy

Joyce Antler, editor, 1997
Talking Back: Images of Jewish Women
in American Popular Culture

Jack Wertheimer, 1997
A People Divided: Judaism in Contem-
porary America

Beth S. Wenger and Jeffrey Shandler,
editors, 1998
Encounters with the "Holy Land":
Place, Past and Future in American
Jewish Culture

David Kaufman, 1998
Shul with a Pool: The "Synagogue-
Center" in American Jewish History

Roberta Rosenberg Farber and Chaim
I. Waxman, editors, 1999
Jews in America: A Contemporary
Reader

Murray Friedman and Albert D.
Chernin, editors, 1999
A Second Exodus: The American Move-
ment to Free Soviet Jews

Stephen J. Whitfield, 1999
In Search of American Jewish Culture

Naomi W. Cohen, 1999
Jacob H. Schiff: A Study in American Jewish Leadership

Barbara Kessel, 2000
Suddenly Jewish: Jews Raised as Gentiles

Jonathan N. Barron and Eric Murphy Selinger, editors, 2000
Jewish American Poetry: Poems, Commentary, and Reflections

Steven T. Rosenthal, 2001
Irreconcilable Differences: The Waning of the American Jewish Love Affair with Israel

Pamela S. Nadell and Jonathan D. Sarna, editors, 2001
Women and American Judaism: Historical Perspectives

Annelise Orleck, with photographs by Elizabeth Cooke, 2001
The Soviet Jewish Americans

Ilana Abramovitch and Seán Galvin, editors, 2001
Jews of Brooklyn

Ranen Omer-Sherman, 2002
Diaspora and Zionism in American Jewish Literature: Lazarus, Syrkin, Reznikoff, and Roth

Ori Z. Soltes, 2003
Fixing the World: Jewish American Painters in the Twentieth Century

David Zurawik, 2003
The Jews of Prime Time

Ava F. Kahn and Marc Dollinger, editors, 2003
California Jews

Naomi W. Cohen, 2003
The Americanization of Zionism, 1897–1948

Gary P. Zola, editor, 2003
The Dynamics of American Jewish History: Jacob Rader Marcus's Essays on American Jewry

Judah M. Cohen, 2003
Through the Sands of Time: A History of the Jewish Community of St. Thomas, U.S. Virgin Islands

Seth Farber, 2003
An American Orthodox Dreamer: Rabbi Joseph B. Soloveitchik and Boston Maimonides School

Amy L. Sales and Leonard Saxe, 2003
"How Goodly Are Thy Tents": Summer Camps as Jewish Socializing Experiences

CONTENTS

Acknowledgments   ix

Invitation: Why St. Thomas?   xiii

Introduction: On Writing a Synagogue Narrative   xix

CHAPTER 1   Gathering   1

CHAPTER 2   Growth: 1796–1831   19

CHAPTER 3   Rebuilding: 1831–1833   43

CHAPTER 4   A Battle of Reforms: 1833–1848   51

CHAPTER 5   Development: 1848–1867   87

CHAPTER 6   The Hebrew Reformed Congregation: 1867–1875   112

CHAPTER 7   Changing of the Guard: 1875–1914   142

CHAPTER 8   Struggle: 1914–1946   164

CHAPTER 9   A Revival from America: 1946–1967   195

EPILOGUE   Sifting through the Sands of Time   221

Notes   227

Bibliography   273

Index   297

Illustrations appear after page 86

ACKNOWLEDGMENTS

I am immensely lucky to have had the support and interest of many people from the moment I first expressed interest in researching the history of the Jewish community of St. Thomas. Without them, this book would have been merely an experiment in futility.

This project began as my undergraduate senior thesis at Yale. Funded by a Richter Summer Research Grant, and supported by Rabbi Bradd Boxman, who was then spiritual leader of the congregation, I conducted my first summer of research in 1994. David Brener and Katina Coulianos (and her family, husband Douglas and children Lane and Nathan) immediately took me under their respective wings in St. Thomas, providing me housing and board throughout this time and enlightening me with their deep dedication to preserving and cataloging the congregation's history. Beverly Smith, librarian for the Von Scholten Collection at the Enid M. Baa Public Library, graciously provided me ready access to the books and microfilms I requested, and provided many valuable suggestions to guide me in my research. What I wrote as my senior thesis, created under the advisorship of Paula Hyman and read by Eli Lederhendler, would become an early draft of chapters 4, 5, and 6. I am grateful to all for their invaluable assistance in sending me on my way.

After graduating, I spent a year researching in archives throughout Europe, the Caribbean, and the United States. Thank you to the librarians, archivists, and scholars (in many cases, these designations can be used interchangeably) who provided me so much help as I tried to piece together a widely flung history: Jeanette Bastian, head librarian of the Enid M. Baa Public Library; Carol Wakefield at the Whim Plantation Archive in St. Croix; Kevin Proffitt at the American Jewish Archives in Cincinnati, Ohio; Michelle Feller-Kopman at the American Jewish Historical Society, then in Waltham, Massachusetts; Susan Tobin, curator of the Archives at New York's Spanish and Portuguese Synagogue Shearith Israel; Joseph Schwartz at the National Archives II in College Park, Maryland; Ellis Lopes at the St. Eustatius Historical Society; and the staffs of the New York Public Library Jewish Division (New York City), the University College of London and Jewish Historical Society of England (London, England), the University of Southampton Archives and Manuscripts (Southampton, England), the Gemeendearchief Amsterdam, the Bancroft Library at the University of California at Berkeley, and the Copenhagen Rigsarkiv.

Along the way, I received advice, encouragement, and friendship from numerous other scholars in the field, including Mordecai Arbell, Per Nielsen, and George Tyson. Arnold Highfield and Jonathan Sarna read parts (and in the latter's case, all) of the manuscript, and gave me much well-needed feedback. I have benefitted enormously from their input, ideas, and conversation.

I also have been blessed with the opportunity to meet many wonderful people along my journey, all of whom contributed to the project in their own ways. Thank you to Sita Likuski, whose Excel files of the St. Thomas birth, death, and marriage protocols were a tremendous help in finding and sorting out congregational data; Emita Levy, Sita's mother, who lent me some of her family's precious nineteenth-century documents; David Jacobs (and family), whose hospitality and prodigious connections with the Jewish community in London helped streamline my research process significantly. I am also grateful to those who housed me throughout my travels: Kaj and Inge Rasmussen (Copenhagen), Anita and Richard Marcus (Washington, D.C.), and my cousins Jesse Levin (Amsterdam), Alexander Gottlieb, and Jennifer Goldstein (Northern California). I hope that this work reflects the great extent of your generosity.

My parents, Richard and Treasure Cohen, were responsible for my interest in the Virgin Islands in the first place. At the end of the summer of 1975, they moved down to St. Thomas with their two-year-old son, intent upon spending the rest of their lives on a small, idyllic island. There, they found the synagogue and soon became instructors in the Hebrew school—with me as their mascot. Although they moved back up to the States after two years, I retained my fond memories of the congregation and its rabbi at the time, Stanley Relkin. Such memories (as well as my parents' suggestion) led me back down to the island nearly seventeen years later. Thus, even as I was searching for the synagogue's past, I was also exploring my own.

I wish to thank the members, past and present, of the St. Thomas Hebrew Congregation. Over the past eight years, I have had the honor of forging strong friendships with many congregants, which have enriched me as a person in addition to helping me along with my research. It is in large part through their generous contributions, moreover, that this book can come to light. The names are too numerous to mention here, but I must single out the Coulianos, Ogden, Blackhall, Wiebel, and Feuerzig families—many of whom had first come to know me during my first tour on the island in the 1970s—for their support and trust all through the research and writing process. I also wish to extend a special thank you to Isidor Paiewonsky, historian and eternal gentleman, whose approbation was a crucial step for this project. I can only hope that this history gives justice to the kindness with which you have treated me.

Phyllis Deutsch and Jessica Stevens, my editors at the University Press of New England, have been patient, encouraging, and supportive throughout the publication process. Their work has been invaluable in bringing this book from manuscript to finished product.

I also owe thanks many times over to Kathryn Peterson, an angel whose generous decision to fund my research and part of the publisher's subvention made the entire undertaking possible in the first place. Without her support, and her interest in a researcher just beginning his career, this project would have remained a pipe dream. I am grateful that you gave me the opportunity to explore, learn, and develop my skills as an academic author. It has been a wonderful process, and I have grown much from it.

Lastly, I dedicate this book to the memory of David Stanley Sasso, Amalia Mylner, and Gladys De Castro, who passed away during the making of this history. I hope that your voices, and those of your ancestors, will echo as clearly throughout these pages as they did to me when I first heard them from you.

INVITATION: WHY ST. THOMAS?

A tour group, huffing and puffing after negotiating a steep hill, appears before the synagogue gate. The visitors' eyes widen, acclimating to a large stone edifice with white plaster columns, pointed-arch windows, and a pointed-arch entrance. "How magnificent!" they might think. "How rare! Who could ever imagine a synagogue in the middle of St. Thomas!"

Often, visitors see the synagogue in Charlotte Amalie, the port city on the U.S. Virgin Island of St. Thomas, as a curiosity. Many Jewish travellers read about the building in their cruise booklets or digest the unending short travel articles in Jewish periodicals. Still others hear of this structure through word of mouth, and visit the synagogue to quench an air of skepticism. Most do not anticipate the steep incline leading to the structure, which does not appear in any of its publicity photographs.

Nonetheless, when the wrought-iron gate appears suddenly on the right, it is almost a beacon of hope to out-of-shape travellers. It leads to a stone plaza flanked by two sloping palm trees, and a set of steps ascending to the sanctuary entrance. A vestry on the left houses a gift shop with various Jewish objects and specialty items, including a T-shirt boasting "I climbed Synagogue Hill."

At this point, most tourists know to take out their cameras and video recorders. Others simply sharpen their eyes and proceed into the building.

Stepping past the threshhold into the sanctuary, a foot lands on a legendary carpet of sand, which flows past mahogany pews to the center of the room. "What does it mean?" many ask. The answers are numerous: exile, heritage, prophesy, practicality, history, memory, or any combination. One person looks up, and sees a beautiful bronze chandelier descending from the center of a vaulted ceiling, each of its fifteen arms touched by a cherub. Another sees the white walls, recently replastered after thirty years of exposure, climbing and surrounding twelve peaked and shuttered window casings. Many take snapshots, many request an explanation.

And then comes the inevitable question: "Do you still have services here?" To the visitor, time reverses inside the sanctuary. From foundation to pinnacle the structure evokes a different and forgotten era. Even after the tourists are directed to the large bronze plaque illuminating service times at the entrance gate, it is difficult for them to view the building as anything but an old antique.

Yet it is a living monument. On Friday evening, Jews gather from across the island to welcome the Sabbath. As the breezes cool, and the cruise ships whisper away from the docks, residents park their cars on or around Synagogue Hill and walk up to the sanctuary together. Greeting each other at the door, they receive their copies of *Gates of Prayer,* the official prayerbook of the American Reform movement, and enter into a sanctuary lit by electric bulbs, cooled by electric ceiling fans. They discuss the events of the week, make dinner plans, and relax. At 7:30 P.M., a congregant sits at the synagogue's spinet piano, nestled up to one of the corner supporting columns; on the adjacent pews, a few people assemble to take the role of an informal choir. The rabbi emerges from the back foyer with a *kippah* (skullcap) on his head and a *tallit* (prayer shawl) around his shoulders, and makes his way down into the center of the room before turning and rising into his pulpit. The service begins.

It is an American Reform service. The tunes are all recent: by Debbie Friedman, Jeff Klepper, Tzvikah Pik, and their contemporaries. There is not a word of Spanish or Portuguese, not a single hymn reminiscent of the older days. Not surprisingly, some visitors who come to services looking for the old Sephardic rite have trouble reconciling the old architecture with the new spirituality and harmonizing the Sephardic layout with the American Ashkenazic worshipers. But to the congregants who contribute regularly to the synagogue and its welfare, this service is the continuation of a long tradition.

Kabbalat Shabbat: Welcoming the Sabbath onto the island in awe and solemnity. Once in a while, a Rastafarian zips by the synagogue entrance in his car, blaring local island music as he disappears up the hill. Voices and sounds from the waterfront occasionally waft through and intermingle with the sounds of the service. And, a few times a year, the welcome splash of rain augments the prayers spoken and chanted inside.

The rabbi intones his sermon, alternating between subdued speech and impassioned rhetoric, sometimes banging his hand on the reader's desk for emphasis. The walls resound with his words, as they have so many times before.

Then the president of the congregation, a landscape architect by trade, takes the pulpit to announce upcoming events. Hebrew school. A Holocaust memorial service. A community interfaith Seder. A sisterhood meeting. A Sunday morning grave wash at the Jewish cemetery. An announcement of a special guest speaker. An appeal for an island charity. A meeting of the ritual committee. A living, dynamic community, centered in the synagogue, branching out to all walks of island life, involved in island politics, concerned about the island's welfare.

After the service, the synagogue is closed up. Wooden hurricane shutters seal the sanctuary from the outside world. Old wooden doors swing together, a metal crossbar protecting the main entrance from winds and city intruders. An electronic security system is activated. The wrought-iron street gates creak shut, and the synagogue is shrouded in history once again. The sanctuary remains still, dark, quiet, as memories of the recent service join those from a hundred and seventy years past, and settle back into the sand.

What is the importance of the St. Thomas Jewish community in the context of American and world Jewish history? Sociologist Albert A. Campbell, in his 1942 article, "A Note on the Jewish Community of St. Thomas, U.S. Virgin Islands," stated that the community was of "limited importance."[1] Published histories of American Jewry give the community no more than a few paragraphs, if any mention at all.

And who could blame them? The St. Thomas Jewish community organized at the end of the eighteenth century—late by Caribbean standards. Its numbers never rose above a few hundred. Its population shifted constantly and dramatically through the ages due to whim, weather, and economy. The synagogue had no real succession of rabbinic authority. And the diminuitive St. Thomas community seems to bear little impact on American Jewry today. Besides, if a person wanted to study a Caribbean Jewish community, then Curaçao, with a longer history, older building, and larger cemetery, would be more appropriate. There appears to be no reason to center upon St. Thomas.

Yet upon closer examination, some significant details begin to appear. Jews from St. Thomas were among the first to receive copies of the new West London Reform liturgy when it came out in 1841. In 1843, the St. Thomas congregation held the first known Jewish confirmation ceremony in this hemisphere. Two of the hemisphere's first rabbinic leaders to give sermons in English, Benjamin C. Carillon and Moses N. Nathan, took tenures on the island during the mid-nineteenth century. In 1867, a British-style Reform congregation broke off and existed independently from the synagogue for several years. And, as if in complicity with those looking for the exotic, the synagogue has produced its own unique religious literature relating to hurricanes.

Further searching brings out more details: The island's Jewish community brought into the world Impressionist painter Camille Pissarro, Florida senator David Levy Yulee, and United States politician Judge David Naar, not to mention several local heroes, including former Virgin Islands governors

Morris Fidanque De Castro and Ralph M. Paiewonsky. Long-term residents included British-Jewish historian Elias H. Lindo, nineteenth-century Jewish communal hero Aron Wolff, and more recently, Pulitzer Prize–winning author Herman Wouk.

Through such evidence, two preconceived notions about this population begin to disintegrate. The first, based on modern popular perceptions of the island, is that St. Thomas contained an exotic, isolated Jewish community living a self-satisfying, sedentary life on their little island. The other notion, based more on academic literature, shows the St. Thomas Jews as a small link in a closed web of Caribbean Jewish communities with little social and political influence outside their immediate area.

Instead, a picture emerges that shows the Jews of St. Thomas as dynamic and highly mobile members in a progressive, cosmopolitan society rivalling that of any in the world. The nineteenth-century St. Thomas Jewish community was well-connected, well-travelled, up-to-date, and internationally savvy. Many members subscribed to Jewish periodicals, and frequently used them to air their on-island religious debates. Articles would appear frequently in the British *Jewish Chronicle of London* and the *Voice of Jacob*, and the American *Occident and American Jewish Advocate;* updates on their condition would be published in the German *Allgemeine Zeitung des Judenthums*, and the French journals *Les Archives Israélites*, and *L'Israélite Universelle*. Their numbers, which seem so small today, actually were comparable with those of emerging Jewish communities in continental America well into the nineteenth century. Moreover, as a percentage of the overall population, they easily trumped their stateside counterparts: At times they comprised over twenty percent of the island's white inhabitants.

As traders in a mercantile culture, the Jews made their mark at one of the world's busiest harbors. Jewish businessmen and women played a considerable role in island trade, and took a substantial part in St. Thomas's nineteenth-century rise to prominence in the northern Caribbean. St. Thomas businesses owned by Jews gained international stature, maintaining offices in Curaçao, Santo Domingo, St. Croix, and northern Venezuela (Coro, Caracas, and Barcelona); Bordeaux and Bayonne, France; Hamburg and Altona, Germany; London, England; Charleston, South Carolina; and New York City. Frequent correspondence with these offices made St. Thomas a world hub for information and recent news. Thus, the Jews of St. Thomas kept up with world Jewish events and were often eager to add their own voices to the discussion.

The St. Thomas Jewish community was an intimate part of the larger island community as well, relating through family, business, and social interactions.

Far from an exclusive group, it never really ghettoized, as members worked instead to be model citizens in a highly tolerant Danish colonial society. Jews took positions in government, acted as representatives in the Colonial Council, served as licensed auctioneers, participated actively in the local Masonic lodges, and represented other countries as consuls in St. Thomas. Many Jews had non-Jewish business partners. Others had few qualms about keeping their stores open on the Jewish Sabbath. Still others allowed their children to marry non-Jews, held open extra-marital relationships with free black women, and had no problem placing their own Jewish identities up to question.

St. Thomas was also home to some of the most colorful Jewish characters in history. Gabriel Milan, a seventeenth-century *converso* governor of St. Thomas, quickly became a paranoid tyrant and was shipped back to Copenhagen for his execution. Reverend Benjamin C. Carillon turned the St. Thomas and Jamaica Jewish communities upside down through the unwanted institution of his own radical ideas and customs. Meyer H. Myers, a descendant of a British rabbinic family, had a youthful temper and passion that gained him entry to the island's criminal court books, preventing him from sustaining a longer tenure as a Jewish religious leader on the island. Morris B. Simmonds, a merchant and Jewish leader in St. Thomas and Venezuela, advocated American reform, and then mysteriously converted to Unitarianism. Reverend Moses Nathan Nathan, a vigorous opponent of the Reform synagogue on St. Thomas, subsequently moved to England and joined the Reform West London Synagogue. Together on one island, they knew the likes of Mexican General Santa Ana, composer/pianist Louis Moreau Gottschalk, African nationalist Edward Wilmot Blyden, New Orleans privateer Jean Lafitte, and a diverse host of rogues, heroes, and people of influence.

Yet, all this aside, one other important aspect of this Caribbean Jewish community makes it stand out: its continuity. As with many islands in the area, St. Thomas is a land of volatility. Beset with frequent fires, hurricanes, earthquakes, epidemics, economic depressions, and political upheavals, life was and remains a constant adventure for the island's residents. A hurricane temporarily dispersed the Jewish community of Barbados; a 1781 invasion by the British marked the beginning of the end for St. Eustatius Jewry; and Martinique's Jewish community ended by expulsion in the seventeenth century. Colonial Jewish communities in Nevis, St. Croix, and Aruba are also gone. Curaçao's Jewish community survived partially through its size and its status as an intellectual and religious center for Caribbean Jewry. St. Thomas, though frequently in danger of extinction, survived through a combination of faith, perseverance, timeliness, and luck.

Swayed by the winds of change, St. Thomas's Jewish population represents a blueprint of local and international migration. Jews arrived from Curaçao, St. Eustatius, and Europe in the late eighteenth century; from a politically unstable Venezuela in the 1850s to 1860s; from Eastern Europe in the late nineteenth century; from New York in the 1940s to 1950s; and from Israel today. Jewish families also left St. Thomas for Europe and America, and represented a significant part of St. Thomas's late nineteenth-century migrations to Panama and Costa Rica. And through this, for over two hundred years, St. Thomas continued to play host to a Jewish religious service every week. Without the rise of St. Thomas as a free port, without the late nineteenth-century Eastern European migration, without renewed American post–World War II interest in the Virgin Islands, such a claim would not be possible.

This continuous history shows us a community of survival; a community with adequate resources and impressive zeal, but sometimes lacking in knowledge and personnel; a community that never had the luxury of numbers, and, in the face of ideological secession, could not maintain a second body for more than a few years. It also shows a community of transformation facing constant struggles between traditional and reform Judaism, between Ashkenazic and Sephardic custom, between European and American styles of worship and organization.

For these reasons, the Jewish community of St. Thomas is special and significant; a story worth telling. This book intends to open up the doors of history on this population as it celebrated its highs, suffered its lows, worshipped God, and went about its business on a tiny but central Caribbean island. Unique within all of Jewish and Caribbean history, St. Thomas nonetheless shares the common bonds of unity, faith, and a love of life that link communities together around the world. It is the author's hope that through the pages of this book, the memories of this people will find life once again in the mind of the interested reader, the historian, and the world traveller.

INTRODUCTION

On Writing a Synagogue Narrative

In 1953, the pioneering American Jewish historian Jacob Rader Marcus published a pamphlet entitled *How to Write the History of an American Jewish Community*. Marcus noted in his preface to the work that America's Jews, buoyed by their country's rise to superpower status after World War II, were becoming "history-conscious."[1] Facing one of the most optimistic and prosperous environments in memory, they consequently desired to recount the events that had led them to reach such financial and cultural security. Marcus himself had taken part in this rising sentiment, having helped establish the American Jewish Archives two years earlier; the pamphlet was a continuation of his project, providing direction for amateur historians who wanted to chronicle the pasts of their local Jewish communities. To accomplish this goal, he wrote, researchers needed to consider approaches that brought together American Jewry's "dual past"—"[o]ur sense of identification with our American homeland and our age-old Jewish history and tradition." Marcus then provided a series of steps toward producing such a history, listing resources to examine, important conceptual categories to consider, and model histories to consult. He also provided a sample outline, inviting writers to arrange their community's local details within a large-scale narrative of the American Jewish experience. Through these efforts, Marcus encouraged the propagation of a literature that could simultaneously showcase local pride and contribute to larger scholarly discourses of Jewry in the United States.

Marcus's pamphlet helped the local Jewish community narrative become an important form in American Jewish historical writing. Histories were often inspired by a significant congregational anniversary or community event; they were frequently written by a member or close associate of the community; and many were published by a local press. Funding for research and publication tended to come from a synagogue grant or a donation from congregants, and occasionally even from the author him or herself. The local synagogue, in addition to housing much of the archival material, sometimes wielded a great deal of control over the contents and presentation of the publication: Since the work's main readership would be local, and the publication's proceeds would tend to benefit the congregation, the book needed to be a symbol of the congregation's legacy. Its main purpose, after all, was a popular one: to tell a success story rather than embark on meticulous analysis. The final product thus presented a unique confluence of "insider" lore, continuous narrative, biography, and cultural observation, couched within a framework of social, local, national, and religious history.

To the wider field of Judaic studies, synagogue histories were useful in bringing obscure and highly localized source materials to light. Moreover, each constituted what Marcus called "an important stone in building the story of the Jew in this land," shedding additional light on an undiscovered part of American Jewish history.[2] Potential historians thus came to view their works with an eye toward wider discovery, possibly following Marcus's instruction: "When you are writing, you are writing not only for yourself and your generation, but also for posterity, for the American people."[3]

In some ways, my approach to the history of the Jewish community on the island of St. Thomas, in what is now the U.S. Virgin Islands, follows in the same tradition as Marcus's vision from a half-century ago. It was originally intended to accompany the congregation's bicentennial anniversary in 1996, and still shares its title with the slogan created for that celebration. The research and publication were funded almost entirely by generous donations from an interested island merchant and from the St. Thomas Hebrew Congregation. Although the congregation had considered hiring a professional historian to complete the job, it ended up giving the opportunity to an unproven college student who had been a member of the congregation as a child. The history itself was intended to move chronologically, more or less from one event to the next. Moreover, there is a decent chance that the book you are reading now was purchased in the St. Thomas synagogue's gift shop, with proceeds going to assist the congregation's operating expenses.

Yet I did not have to present my research in this form. During the long tenure for this project, I became familiar with the literature surrounding cultural anthropology and critical theory, causing me to bring some of Marcus's assumptions into question. Through the study of postmodernist scholars such as Frederick Jameson, Michel Foucault, Hayden White, and Jean-François Lyotard, I learned about the biases that narrative structure holds in portraying the lives of a multi-faceted community of individuals. The works of Benedict Anderson, Homi Bhabha, and Arjun Appadurai taught me to question issues of nationhood and religious grouping. Joëlle Bahloul (1996) and Eric Hobsbawm (1983), meanwhile, informed me that memory and tradition, respectively, are often as much a reflection of present values as they are of the past. On top of this, recent studies on Caribbean Jewish topics by Carol Holzberg (1987) and Alan Benjamin (2001) used historical narrative only as a way of leading to in-depth ethnographic investigation. I even took the opportunity during my studies to examine the value, meaning, and reliability of my own St. Thomas sources (Cohen 1997b). Through such a course of training, how could I even consider using such a problematic literary form as the narrative: a genre whose use of time as a primary axis and whose tendency to cover a broad swath of material at the expense of detailed analysis sometimes relegated it to a second tier of academic integrity?

In the end, however, I decided to use the narrative form to present this history. My answers as to why I did this fall along several lines of thought, and, I believe, serve to clarify the place of this work within Jewish and Caribbean studies literature.

First, the broad narrative form best served to open up the history of a community that had long retained a certain historic yet unknown mystique, even to those comprising the current generation of congregants. After giving tours of the sanctuary for several months, and attending to questions and concerns posed by the synagogue's members, I came to recognize that the congregation had an immediate need to tell its own story and make its voice heard, both within the history and culture of the U.S. Virgin Islands, and within the theater of American Jewish history. Historical accounts were a form of currency on St. Thomas (as they were in many other places) for discussing political, moral, familial, and environmental issues; and the Jewish community, with its long and integrated past on the island, was occasionally used as a point of reference in these discussions.[4] More than once, for example, I was informed by non-Jewish islanders of their bloodline connections to former members of the Jewish community; and I will never forget the time when, during a tour of the synagogue I gave to a local summer camp, one Afro-Caribbean boy asked me the tribe from which I was descended. Within Jewish historical discourse, meanwhile, the paradigm of community history was easily understood and digested by Jewish readership, for reasons described above.[5] St. Thomas's existing fragmentary history had even been cited by innumerable travel articles published in Jewish-interest American periodicals (see Rovner 1994, inter alia); yet tourists were consistently unsure of how to "fit" St. Thomas into the overall narrative of American Jewry. All previous accounts of the St. Thomas Jewish community, additionally, had employed the same historical narrative paradigm (as can be seen in chapter 9) and thus provided a precedent for the form my own research needed to take in order to "improve" upon this project. While I aimed to retain high academic standards and levels of analysis whenever possible, I thus felt it appropriate to arrange my data in a manner readily comprehended by a general audience, and discussed within a familiar and frequently used framework.

A narrative treatment also seemed warranted due to the community's tiny size. Though significant in the course of American Jewish history, the colonial Sephardic communities established on such islands as Curaçao, Barbados, St. Eustatius, and Nevis never exceeded a couple thousand, and more often remained smaller than a few hundred. St. Thomas, for example, had a Jewish population of over five hundred for only a short time in the mid-nineteenth century; by the early part of the twentieth century, the community had dropped to fewer than one hundred. As a result, "trends" and other issues within the community were usually effected by no more than a handful of people, who continued to recur in the records. Such individuals could be relied upon to serve not only as a *representatives* of the community's positions and activities, but ipso facto as much of the community activity itself (such as was the case with the arrival of Eastern European Jews to the island, chronicled in chapter 8). With these issues in mind, I have attempted to provide a causative chronicle of events whenever the supporting materials would allow. The community's relatively late founding in Caribbean history, and its overall view of itself as a literate, cosmopolitan, and internationally active congregation, provided me many opportunities to take advantage of this luxury.

Finally, and perhaps most importantly, the narrative approach was well suited to covering one of the most unique and significant aspects of the St. Thomas community: its remarkable continuity. As opposed to the Jewish population of Curaçao, whose core Sephardic culture has been portrayed as ethnically consistent and enduring throughout history (and institutionally differentiated from a co-existing "Ashkenazic" population), the St. Thomas Jewish population could best be seen as a community of accumulative ethnicity. Throughout the eighteenth and nineteenth centuries, St. Thomas served as a land of refuge for Jews—mainly, but not entirely from Sephardic backgrounds—escaping from unstable political climates throughout the Caribbean region. When difficult financial times descended on the island in the late nineteenth century, the growth segment of the Sephardic population departed, only to be "replaced" by a new group of young, enterprising Jews from Eastern Europe. Decades later, as the Eastern Europeans aged and intermarried, a group of Reform Jews came down from the United States to invigorate the synagogue once again. In all these cases, both the community and the new arrivals were too small in number to assert their respective cultural heritages autonomously. Instead, over time, communal practices at the synagogue migrated from one *minhag* to the next—sometimes by mere inclusion of a new or different ritual, and in other cases by outright institutional affiliation. So dramatic has this change been that by 2001, the Sephardic family names so prevalent in the congregation from its founding through the mid-twentieth century had completely disappeared from the local Jewish community.

Despite the congregation's demographic transformation over the past century, however, the early Sephardic culture has not been completely erased. Instead, it has been maintained as a form of collective memory, taken on by all who join the congregation.[6] In the 1970s, for example, a member of one of the prominent Ashkenazic families on the island presented a brass seven-branched menorah to the congregation under the impression that it had been forged in medieval Spain. The synagogue accepted the gift, mounted it prominently on the wall behind the Reader's Desk, and enthusiastically included it in its tours and literature as a symbol of its Sephardic past. Congregants have also gone to great lengths to preserve the 1833 Sephardic sanctuary and its ornaments, completing long, costly, and meticulous renovations of the building in 1974 and 2001. Money is set aside every year for cleaning and clearing the congregation's two cemeteries, one of which has been full since the mid-nineteenth century. Since my research began in earnest in 1994, the St. Thomas Hebrew Congregation has staged "reenactments" of a "Sephardic" Chanukah service (in close consultation with Sephardic clergy in New York) and the sanctuary's original dedication ceremony. Such activities have been reinforced by descendants of the island's old Sephardic families, who would send notes of congratulations on synagogue milestones from their homes in Panama and Florida, occasionally even putting in guest visits. From these situations, it is thus clear that the congregation—a dues-paying member synagogue of the American Reform movement—perceives itself as being linked spiritually, if not genealogically, to its Sephardic forebears.

The connections made over time between one generation of congregants and the next are thus important to understanding the nature and concept of a religious community, and even more so in the complex case of St. Thomas. How did each immigration of new worshipers come to accept and understand the next immigration? What did each group see as important to maintaining and transmitting a spiritual Jewish identity? How did these numerous styles of worship and cultural life interact over time with the island's unique idea of "tradition"? Most importantly: How was it that such vast changes in practice, ideology, and population could be effected under a single organizational body? The answers to these questions are not easily revealed; but I hope that by presenting a detailed, sequential history of the congregation, I can begin to address them meaningfully.

A note here must also be given regarding the sources used for this study. Marcus, in his pamphlet, directs would-be Jewish community chroniclers to their local synagogue's minutes as a primary font for information. In the St. Thomas congregation's case, however, there was no such luxury. Perhaps due to devastating storms, political intrigues, temporary breakdowns of communication, or any of a number of possible reasons, the congregation's minutes from before the 1950s are lost.[7] Government records referring to the community, meanwhile, are scattered and difficult to access: Most material that survives from before 1917 has been removed to archives in Denmark and the United States, where it is interspersed among enormous unmarked collections of government documents. Thus, for the most part, the clearest chronicle of the congregation's practices, controversies, and correspondence was not available. Instead, it was necessary to rely on other materials to shed light on the congregation's life and activities.

Several extant on-island sources were invaluable in helping to reconstruct the community's history. Perhaps most important were the congregation's birth, death, and marriage records. Dating back to 1792—though with significant lacunae—these registers provided names, dates, and in many cases detailed and valuable notes about the circumstances surrounding the congregation's lifecycle events. When decoded in collaboration with other source material, these accounts provided a highly contextualized portrait of the congregation through the nearly two centuries.[8] The island's several newspapers, dating back to the 1770s, remarkably have been preserved on microfilm almost in their entirety. Stored in the Von Scholten Collection of the Enid M. Baa Public Library in Charlotte Amalie, these films could be combed with relative ease, revealing much about the Jewish community's business dealings and the island's perceptions of the Jews; they also showed a striking level of public coverage (both voluntary and involuntary) of the Jews' internal synagogue affairs. Also in the library were the mostly complete results of several nineteenth-century censuses of St. Thomas, providing decade-by-decade snapshots of the community, its familial groupings, birthplaces, and length of time on the island. Complementing this were the Jewish community's extant physical artifacts: two cemeteries, a synagogue building with original furniture and lamps, several Torahs, and various occasional items. None of these items could tell a story by itself. When combined and analyzed closely, however, the island materials provided a relatively strong, timebound framework for understanding the community's concerns and affairs, while hinting at key events and people that warranted further research.

Several more narrowly focused sources were invaluable in infusing segments of the St. Thomas synagogue's history with depth and significance. International Jewish periodicals opened a particularly vibrant window into the community from the 1840s through the 1860s. Especially the American and British publications *The Occident and American Jewish Advocate, The Voice of Jacob,* and *The Jewish Chronicle of London* were organs through which the island's Jews could provide updates to their home communities, report on their achievements, air their differences, and appeal to Jewish authorities for assistance.

The international stature of the Jewish community (and the West Indies in general) meant that a significant amount of material also turned up in off-island archives. In College Park, Maryland, the National Archives II stores hundreds of linear feet of records taken from the Virgin Islands after the United States acquired them in 1917. Included among these records are the St. Thomas Hebrew Congregation's first two sets of bylaws, as well as a significant but focused amount of correspondence between the St. Thomas government and the synagogue members dating from the 1860s and 1870s. Much of this latter material has been microfilmed by the American Jewish Archives.

Denmark's State Archives (Rigsarkiv) in Copenhagen held a number of administrative records pertaining to the Jewish community dating as far back as the mid-eighteenth century, including court cases, wills, merchant licenses, and tax records, in addition to scattered birth, death, and marriage registers from the nineteenth century. These provided insight into the earliest years of the Jewish community, as well as a rare glimpse into the Jews' dating and marriage habits outside the synagogue. The archives at New York City's Spanish and Portuguese Synagogue, meanwhile, illuminated in detail another important episode in the congregation's history, the 1924 to 1925 visit of the synagogue's Rabbi Emeritus, Reverend Dr. Henry Pereira Mendes.

Other archives, most prominently the American Jewish Archives, the American Jewish Historical Society, and the archives at the University of Southampton in England, yielded significant amounts of supporting information on related communities, with occasional discoveries of important St. Thomas documents or documents relating to individual St. Thomas Jews. The St. Eustatius Historical Society also provided important information on one of its most eventful episodes, the 1781 attack on the island by Admiral George Brydges Rodney, which had a direct impact on the years leading up to the founding of the St. Thomas congregation.

In addition to written sources, I was grateful to have the assistance and support of the island's veteran congregants, who related in personal interviews their own memories of Jewish life on the islands. Their valuable discussions helped bring to life St. Thomas's quietest, leanest years at the start of the twentieth century—when documentation was particularly lacking—as well as its years of revival after World War II.

Other pieces of the puzzle came from important secondary sources, most notably Isaac and Suzanne Emmanuel's encyclopedic work on the Jews of Curaçao (1959, 1970), and other smaller histories of the Jewish communities in St. Eustatius, Jamaica, Panama, and coastal Venezuela. All these materials, in addition to countless assorted documents, observations, and ephemera that I collected in visits to Amsterdam, London, California, St. Kitts and St. Croix, were evaluated, compared against each other, and then grouped according to time frame. In many cases, the combined materials helped decode important details otherwise hidden in individual documents, and aided me in deciding on discrepancies in date or political position. Quilted together, the documents came to hold the history before you now.

I have tried to be as complete as my efforts would allow, though undoubtedly there are more sources to uncover, more connections to be made. May this be seen, then, as a well-intentioned start.

Through the Sands of Time

CHAPTER 1

Gathering

$\mathcal{T}$he island of St. Thomas is a small, mountainous, twenty-eight square mile land mass located just off the eastern coast of Puerto Rico. It is the second-largest of the U.S. Virgin Islands in terms of area: about a third the size of St. Croix, thirty-five miles to the south, and around fifty percent larger than St. John, three miles east. Although its first European sighting came at the hands of Christopher Columbus during his second voyage in 1493, the island was generally left alone to continued migrations of native American tribes for more than a century and a half afterward.[1] In 1672, the kingdom of Denmark, looking to join Spain, England, France, and the Netherlands in expanding its influence into the New World, successfully colonized St. Thomas. Arriving on the island's hilly, wild shores, the settlers were official representatives of a business concern known as the Danish West India Company, and had received specific permission to transform St. Thomas into an agricultural colony and shipping post. Eighty-two years later, when the Danish West India Company folded and the island became a proper colony of Denmark, St. Thomas had been joined by St. John (acquired 1718) and St. Croix (1733) to create the territory that became known as the Danish West Indies. St. Croix, with its relatively wide, comparatively flat terrain, went on to become the agricultural center of the islands; St. Thomas, meanwhile, began to specialize in trade. Blessed with an advantageous location between the Greater and Lesser Antilles archipelagos and a naturally protected harbor on its south shore, the island slowly gained prominence as a haven for the mercantile industry. Denmark attempted to accelerate the process in 1756, when it declared St. Thomas a free port. In doing so, the ruling country opened up the island to the commerce of the world, hoping in the process to increase its profits.[2]

As with other parts of the Caribbean theater, Jews were taking roles in the commerce of the area. For the most part these individuals were of Iberian descent (popularly known as Sephardim), whose ancestors had been forced by the Spanish Inquisition to convert to Christianity in the late fifteenth century. By the seventeenth century, many of these "Converso" or "New Christian" families had moved to other cities such as Amsterdam, Bordeaux, and Hamburg (and, unofficially, London), where they had begun business interests. In their new environment—which was in most cases Protestant and hostile to Spanish interests—many began to practice their religion openly again to increasing tolerance by local governments.

It is likely that the Jews received such "favors" in part because the same local governments had stereotyped them to be good businesspeople, and thus ideal agents for establishing trade routes to the expanding colonial scene. Particularly in the Netherlands, which in 1636 allowed one of the first post-Inquisition Sephardic synagogues to be established in Amsterdam, Jewish merchants began to take advantage of colonization offers in partial exchange for religious tolerance. Exercising their new freedoms and "rights," hundreds of Jews eventually travelled to the Dutch Caribbean colonies of Recife (Brazil), Surinam, and Curaçao to open plantations and expand their businesses by the mid-seventeenth century. A similar situation took place in England in the second half of the century in terms of helping to develop Jamaica and Barbados; and Denmark as well held the perception that Jewish merchants would be of great assistance to its nascent colonies. In this manner, small Jewish communities were established in the Caribbean as early as the mid-seventeenth century, becoming the first in the Western Hemisphere.[3]

Although individual Jews were known to have lived on St. Thomas as early as the late seventeenth century, their presence was sporadic and never enough to create a community in any sense of the word. The fourth governor of St. Thomas, Gabriel Milan, was reported to have been a Jewish convert to Christianity. His increasingly erratic and despotic rule between 1684 and 1687, however, caused endless strife on the island and brought him infamy in Copenhagen, quickly resulting in his extradition and execution.[4] In the 1690s, a Jew named Jacob Franks was believed to have spent a short time on St.Thomas as a prisoner of privateer Captain Kidd; Franks's testimony, according to this account, would lead to the pirate's downfall.[5] Emanuel Vass, a resident of the island around the middle of the eighteenth century, took an intermediary role in the 1733 transfer of St. Croix from France to Denmark.[6] In the 1740s, Melchior Berents, Salomon Joseph Unna, and Abraham Rosette were identified as Jews in local business court cases.[7] From 1755 to

1758, a Jew named Emanuel Alvares Correa possessed a cotton plantation on the island.[8] And two merchants named Isaac De Leon and Isaac Lopez began paying taxes on St. Thomas in 1776 and 1777 respectively. These occurrences, however, appear to comprise most of the known Jewish activity on the island before 1780.[9] Most Jews who came during this time operated independently or in pairs, taking advantage of Denmark's tolerant policies to establish lives for themselves and their families, or simply to create a field office for their home base on another island.

An even sparser representation of Jews existed on St. John, with only two intriguing yet unconfirmed names from this time on the taxpayers' list. St. Croix did apparently enjoy a somewhat larger community during this time, which may have peaked around 1764 with the construction of a synagogue in Christiansted and the acquisition of a Torah.[10] The building is reported to have burned down two years later, however, and was never rebuilt; from this point, the St. Croix Jewish community waned, eventually becoming a satellite of what would soon be the rising St. Thomas Hebrew Congregation.[11]

In this chapter, I will recount the forces that brought the early members of the St. Thomas Jewish community together at the end of the eighteenth century. Most of these Jews had already lived on other islands and were beyond the issues the earliest Caribbean communities had faced, including readjustment to Jewish identity after over a century of suppression.[12] Instead, they landed on St. Thomas—from several places, and for several reasons—with clear ideas of how to organize and sustain a Jewish community. Together, they laid the groundwork for a congregation whose fortunes, in line with the island, would soon be on the rise.

Statia: The Jews and the Golden Rock

Saturday, February 3, 1781, was an uneventful day in St. Thomas's history. The sun likely shined from morning to night, warming the air well past the threshhold of human comfort. Traders continued to go about their business, waking up in the early hours of the morning to load and unload their ships; the Danish colonial government continued to see that all was well; slaves continued to labor on the plantations; and the few Jews living on the island at the time likely took the day off to observe their Sabbath.

In the city, people buzzed with the latest news, received from packet ships coming into port. Many discussed the developing saga of the North American colonies, which had begun to mount a successful rebellion in order

to gain their independence from England. The revolt, in its sincerity and re-
sourcefulness, surprised the British world power; despite all British efforts
to block shipments of war materials to the North American mainland, the
colonists continued to receive supplies of gunpowder, guns, and other ne-
cessities to further their efforts. Denmark intended to maintain its neutral-
ity throughout the conflict, and officially did not encourage any part in the
American weapons trade on St. Thomas. Many of the island's merchants,
however, were likely well aware of where much of the smuggling *did* take
place.

About two hundred miles east-southeast of St. Thomas, on the Dutch
"Golden Rock" of St. Eustatius, February 3 began in a similar fashion. Merchants and servants arose before sunrise, and went to their stores and warehouses. Many walked down a steep, snaking ramp leading from their dwellings
in the Upper Town to their waterfront businesses several stories below.
Dozens of ships bobbed quietly in the harbor, waiting to dispense or receive
cargo. The sun rose gracefully over the Quill, a dormant volcano that dominated the eastern third of the island. People exchanged the latest news. No
one knew that when the sun set that day, the island would be a part of the
British empire. When the British armada, commanded by Admiral Sir George
Brydges Rodney, pulled into the harbor at ten o'clock that morning, it sealed
the fate of St. Eustatius, as well as its Jewish community.[13]

St. Eustatius, or Statia for short, is a tiny, eleven-square-mile island in the
eastern Caribbean. Its volcanic emergence is manifested by the ashen sand
and fertile land that extend westward from the Quill's dormant caldara. Although claimed in absentia by the Spanish in 1493 (like the rest of the West
Indies), the island remained relatively untouched until the Dutch annexed it
in the 1630s as part of its expansion into the region.[14] Initially, St. Eustatius
was seen as an agricultural colony, and adventurous souls were drawn there
under the Dutch promise of land ownership. The island's role as a port of
trade, however, soon began to gain dominance. A small, three-garrisoned fort
named for the Netherlands' ruling House of Oranje was built on the southern coast of the island, overlooking its best harbor and providing a lookout
against privateers and warships. Its presence provided the colonists at least a
minimal sense of security during the bouts of landgrabbing and colonial in-
trigue that typified the region.[15] The town of Oranjestad, founded just to the
east of the fort, became the center of commerce. Perched on an imposing
sandstone cliff, an "Upper Town" contained most of the dwelling places;
down a steep pathway, a "Lower Town" would eventually contain warehouses
with direct access to ships in the harbor. Over the next hundred years, as the

island population grew in size to over one thousand, St. Eustatius would be poised to become one of the most powerful trading centers in the region. An increasing demand for European and African goods and labor combined with a permissive Dutch mercantile policy and a favorable position along international shipping routes made Statia an ideal location for commerce.

Jews moved onto Statia slowly at first, often making initial contact with the island via travels from Curaçao.[16] Although Jews had officially been granted legal protection and "freedom of conscience" in the Dutch colonies from the start of the country's West Indian conquests, their St. Eustatius presence remained tiny.[17] Their success on the island, moreover, was variable: In 1709, for example, a privateer raid from a neighboring island sent the few Jews who had attempted to settle on Statia packing back to Curaçao.[18] It seems some semblance of a Jewish community had developed by 1722, however, when a census counted four Jewish families, comprising twenty-one individuals, out of the 1,204 inhabitants of the island.[19]

It is likely the island became a more attractive destination for Jewish emigration in 1730, when the wardens of the Sephardic congregation in Amsterdam successfully petitioned the Dutch government to emancipate their Statian co-religionists.[20] The Dutch acceptance of this suit eased concerns for potential Jewish settlers. Jews were allowed to worship in public, maintain their own cemetery at the outskirts of town, and trade with the same rights as all other merchants; and they were exempted from Saturday militia duty. Within ten years, St. Eustatius became home to seventeen Jewish families, many of whom were Sephardic in origin, Dutch in allegiance, and Curaçaoan by birth.[21]

In 1737, the Dutch colonial government allowed the Jews to build a synagogue in town, provided their service "did not hinder the one of the Christians."[22] Accordingly, the Jewish community bought up a lot substantially recessed from the main roads, though within view of the Fort and the Dutch Reform Church. Here, during 1738 and 1739, they built their synagogue. Curaçao contributed resources to the effort, and the Amsterdam Jews presented the new congregation with a Torah dressed in a red silk mantle with black flowers.[23] Dubbed *Honen Dalim*, or "Generous to the Needy," the congregation likely reflected in its name the financial state of the community at the time, and the willingness of outside communities to provide support. Jews wishing to attend services gained access via a narrow dirt alley leading from Fort Oranje Straat to the sanctuary. Over decades, this route received the unofficial name *Synagogue Pad*, or "Synagogue Path," in recognition of its primary use.

St. Eustatius flourished over the next forty years, earning the title "the Golden Rock" as acknowledgement of the wealth amassed there through trade and its open port status. Over one hundred ships could rest in its harbor at once, loading and unloading through a complex system of shuttling boats. The Lower Town at the foot of the cliffs developed into a bustling entrepôt of storage areas, weighing houses, and dwelling places. Merchants of all nationalities kept busy closing deals, checking on inventories, and looking after ships. A woman viewing the scene for the first time in 1775 described it:

> . . . never did I meet with such variety; here was a merchant vending his goods in Dutch, another in French, a third in Spanish, etc. etc. They all wear the habit of their country and the diversity is really amusing. . . . From one end of the town of Eustatia to the other is a continued mart, where goods of the most different uses and qualities are displayed before the shop-doors. Here hang rich embroideries, painted silks, flowered Muslins, with all the Manufacturers of the Indies. Just by hang Sailor's Jackets, Trousers, shoes, hats etc. Next stall contains most exquisite silver plate, the most beautiful indeed I ever saw, and close by these, iron pots, kettles and shovels. Perhaps the next presents you with French and English Millinary wares. But it were endless to enumerate the variety of merchandise in such a place, for in every store you find every-thing, be their qualities ever so opposite.[24]

Ships came from and departed for numerous international locations, including New York, Boston, Philadelphia, and Providence; the west coast of Africa; numerous ports in Europe; and Curaçao, Santo Domingo, and St. Thomas. Pirates and privateers also conducted trade through Statia, illegally smuggling large quantities of supplies, arms, and slaves to willing buyers.

Jewish merchants contributed to and benefitted from the island's prosperity, and their numbers increased. As with other merchants, they forged business relationships with firms in the major port cities; subsequently they also formed ties with most of the major Jewish communities of North America. But although comfortable, most Statian Jews were not excessively well-off, and several times the congregation had to appeal to other Jewish communities (especially those in Curaçao, Amsterdam, and New York) for financial aid.

In early September 1772, a severe hurricane roared through St. Eustatius, causing reported damages of a million pieces of eight and levelling the synagogue, among other buildings. The Jews sent out letters of distress to the neighboring communities, asking for funds to help rebuild the structure. New York's Sephardic (and at the time only) synagogue, Shearith Israel, sent eighty dollars to help the cause. The congregations at Amsterdam and Curaçao contributed substantial amounts as well.[25] And a French Jew named Salomon de Georgé, who split his time between St. Eustatius and St. Croix, contributed 150 pieces of eight and ten hogsheads of lime to the cause.[26] Through these and other donations, the Statian Jews were able to rebuild their place of worship.

The new synagogue was a small structure (only 40 feet by 27.5 feet, about half the area of a regulation tennis court). Its builders constructed it of yellow brick, likely brought over (as with most bricks on the island) from Holland as ship ballast.[27] Steps built to the right of the front entrance led upward, around the outside of the building, to a women's gallery that overlooked the men's section. A wooden floor supported rows of benches, a reader's desk, and a holy ark, in a layout oriented toward the east.[28] Among other objects, the congregation likely had on display a bronze *hanukkah* oil lamp, received as a gift from the "home" Jewish population of Amsterdam the year before and reminding all those who gazed upon it of their own trans-Atlantic ties.[29] Together with other ritual objects such as Torahs and a shofar (ram's horn), the *hanukkah* lamp assisted the Jewish community in observing the feasts of their liturgical calendar in their new building. For eight years, the Jews lived and operated in peace alongside the rest of the population.

When the British fleet appeared on the horizon in February 1781, the Statian Jewish community was probably at its peak, with over three hundred members.[30] Names and genealogies of many of these merchants could be traced back to Curaçao: Benjamin, De la Motta, Levy, De Leon, Hoheb, and Abendanone; several of these would soon trace forward to St. Thomas. Enjoying full privileges, including the right to vote, those in the Jewish community served as lawful citizens and traders, going about their lives with the full respect of the rest of the island. Once the British landed, however, all would change.

The attacking fleet consisted of at least fourteen gunships containing over one thousand cannons, and a force of several thousand troops—absurdly overmatching the twenty-five guns and fifty soldiers stationed at Fort Oranje.[31] Led by Admiral Rodney, its mission was to take the island and cut off all trade with French and American ships. This, according to the thinking of the British leaders, would prevent supplies from reaching the North American colonies, and cripple their rebellion. Once stationed in port, Rodney quickly dispatched his men to the island, and then sent a note to the governor demanding immediate surrender of "St. Eustatius and its dependencies and everything in and belonging thereto . . ."[32] The governor enacted only symbolic resistance, realizing the long odds, and quickly capitulated to Rodney's command.

Once Rodney had conquered the island, he commenced an infamous occupation campaign.[33] According to Member of the British Parliament Edmund Burke, in his grandiloquent campaign against Rodney's activities three months later, the British soldiers went about gathering up, "the wealth of the opulent, the goods of the merchant, the utensils of the artisan, the necessaries of the poor," as well as all account books and private papers of Statia's inhabitants.[34] The troops also siezed 130 merchant vessels of all nationalities in the harbor, confiscating their goods as the spoils of war.[35] Rodney ordered lists of the island's merchants drawn up, and demanded that each produce inventories of their estates and warehouses.[36] Once he had these lists in hand, he locked up the warehouses in the Lower Town and began to loot the island.[37]

While all of Statia's inhabitants were stripped of their wealth and property in some form or another, the Jewish community received particular—and somewhat curious—attention. About a week after the British took over the island, Admiral Rodney resolved with a newly appointed Board to deport the Jews, seeming to accede to the community's desire to send them to St. Thomas.[38] The reality of the situation, however was somewhat harsher: on Tuesday, February 13, over one hundred Jewish men were taken from their families and held in the Lower Town customs house for transport. British soldiers proceeded to relieve them of any riches they happened to take with them. According to M.P. Burke, the searching and seam-ripping committed by the soldiers yielded upward of £8000.[39]

Many of the imprisoned Jews were actually transplanted British subjects; but Rodney, instead of easing the sentence on his Jewish compatriots, treated them even more harshly. He was convinced that on this island of free trade, its British subjects, "while they called themselves Englishmen, were not ashamed to disgrace themselves and their country, by assisting her enemies [i.e., the Americans and the French] with the means to wound her."[40] Chances are, several of these men did act as agents for the French and Americans. However, such an assumption painfully overlooked Jewish island merchants such as Jacob Pollack, whose devoted loyalty to the Crown had resulted in expulsion from the North American colonies, and may have hastened the deaths of both his brother and brother-in-law. Pollack's mere presence on St. Eustatius, however, transformed him in Rodney's eyes into the very character he had despised in the Colonies: an American sympathizer. The country for which Pollack had sacrificed life and property stripped him of his welfare in the name of war.[41]

On February 16, the Jews sent a petition to Admiral Rodney and General Sir John Vaughn, pleading for relief and mercy:

> For what reason, or from what motive, we are to be BANISHED from this island, we are at a loss to account. If any among us have committed a crime for which they are punishable, we humbly beg those crimes may be pointed out, and that such persons may be purged from among us. But if nothing can be alledged against us, but the religion of our fore-fathers, we hope that will not be considered a crime, or that a religion which preaches peace and recommends obedience to government, should point out its sectaries as objects of your Excellencies rigour, and merit exclusion from a British island, by the express orders of British commanders. A moment's reflection must discountenance the idea, and leave us in perfect confidence of your Excellencies favourable answer.[42]

Later that day, whether influenced by the petition or by some other force, the British soldiers opened the customs house and sent most of the merchants back to their families.[43] About twenty others, however, had been boarded on the vessel *Shrewsbury* along with thirty-five other alleged American prisoners. The ship, rather than heading to St. Thomas, sailed a few miles southeast, and pulled into the neighboring island of St. Kitts. There, the gunship let off its human cargo for what proved a short stay. The exiles received a humane reception at the hands of the St. Kitts residents, and soon received British permission to travel back to St. Eustatius.[44] Rodney, in a 1787 apologia for the entire St. Eustatius incident, later described the deportation episode as a "mistake."[45]

The victims of this mistake, however, hardly received an advantageous resolution apart from their freedom. Such was the case with Samuel Hoheb, an Amsterdam native and a twenty-five-year resident and merchant of St. Eustatius who may have been sent away because, according to his testimony, he had concealed thirty-six shillings in his coat lining. After being deposited in St. Kitts, Hoheb eventually was able to procure passage back home, only to witness his property sold at public auction for one third of its retail value.[46]

In regard to personal property, a similar fate met most of the island community, Jew and non-Jew alike. Once they were finally granted access to their dwellings and warehouses, distraught merchants often returned to find them empty or ransacked. The British troops, viewing the island's goods as easily won spoils, had carried everything to captured merchant ships anchored in the harbor. By the end of March 1781, Rodney had packed most of the island's wealth into a convoy of thirty-three vessels. These he sent off to England, accompanied by several gunships for protection.[47]

After this, the British had little problem with the island's population; rather, the leaders Rodney appointed to administrate the island had to deal with their own errors of judgment, continuing an ill-equipped and ill-prepared occupation for several months. Finally, on November 26, French forces benevolently recaptured St. Eustatius, issuing a quiet yet humiliating defeat to the British.[48]

For some of the island's Jewish merchants, the traumatic events wrought by the British proved temporarily overwhelming. It is likely that several relocated to St. Thomas on their own with the onset of the siege, waiting until the situation stabilized. The exact time frame of these moves within the sequence of events is uncertain, though it appears to have taken place after the deportation episode. By 1782, the St. Thomas tax lists recorded Solomon Benjamin, Isaac and Jacob de Solas, Jacob Robles, a "Hoheb," and Isaac Welcome as residents of the island. Most had apparently taken up transitory lodging in Kronprindsens Quarter, the westernmost section of town that typically accommodated the free black and middle income populations, as well as the Jews' cemetery.[49] When tax collection came around the following year, however, all except Benjamin had apparently left the island.[50] A few probably returned to Statia, where they continued to dwell for several years: In 1789, Jacob Robles was listed as the "reader" of the St. Eustatius Jewish congregation; and "Isaac Wellcome" was included on the same list of the community's members, though he was notably "absent" from the island at the time.[51] Whatever the case, their temporary relocation hinted at St. Thomas's desirability as a rising port of call in the Caribbean theater.

Meanwhile, purged of its riches, and no longer belonging to the British empire, Statia slowly returned to a semblance of normalcy. French efforts to restore the island's trade to its former days of glory led to some initial success. Yet St. Eustatius's golden days as the center of east Caribbean trade were numbered; other local ports, including politically neutral St. Thomas, began to gain prominence. The final straw came in 1795, when slavery, long seen as the most profitable of the Caribbean trades, was all but abolished on Statia. Much of the goods trading followed suit, disappearing as business ventures collapsed; and the island slowly drifted into a state of suspended animation.[52] Over two hundred years later, Statia's port would remain quiet, aging gracefully in the shadow of the dormant Quill.

Samuel Hoheb became one of several dozen Statian merchants who sued Rodney after his attack, demanding compensation for their losses during the siege. He obtained passage to England, carrying his ripped coat as evidence, and through petition convinced the Parliament to provide him with a lawyer gratis.[53] It does not seem, however, that his efforts were successful. Hoheb died in St. Eustatus on January 26, 1788; a simple tombstone marked his grave suggesting that he died in relative destitution.[54]

The Jewish population, meanwhile, revived somewhat by 1790; during that year, about 170 Jews lived on the island, running organized religious services at their synagogue in the same spirit as before the Rodney attack.[55] But this did not last long, as death and migration caused the community to diminish. The last remaining Jew on the island, Mrs. Anna Viera de Molina, died in 1846.[56] Over the following centuries, the synagogue and Jewish cemetery fell into ruins.

Escaping the Revolution: From St. Domingue to St. Thomas

In 1793, British forces invaded St. Domingue, a French colony comprising the western third of the island of Hispaniola, deepening the island's internal and international turmoil.[57] Mainly a privateer haven throughout the seventeenth century, St. Domingue had experienced explosive economic growth throughout the eighteenth century due primarily to the sugar industry: By the 1740s, the territory was producing over 40,000 tons of sugar per year— more than twice the quantity of its closest rival; fifty years later, production had almost doubled, thanks in great part to the toil of 480,000 African slaves.[58] Such a massive yield transformed St. Domingue's ports into lucrative trading and culture centers, giving rise to a thriving artisan class that supplemented the mercantile and sugar industries. At the same time, however, sugar helped to create dire economic and social inequalities among the population that would eventually destroy the island's welfare.

Interestingly, it was the humanist ideals of the French Revolution that would serve as a flashpoint for violence in St. Domingue. The island's free people of color, enamored of the values of equality and fraternity espoused by the French revolutionaries, began to identify with the cause and incited rebellions against the European planter/merchant classes in the early 1790s. White colonists split along class lines on how to temper the issue, and in the end provided little organized resistance. To compound the situation, the French government sent down a military force with the noble intent of emancipating the island's slaves. The force's leader, Léger Sonthonax, had a zealous view of the revolution that fashioned all the island's white nobility as infidels, however, and he used his power to terrorize the planter and merchant classes. Such infighting made the once-rich island seem vulnerable to attack. Spain saw its opportunity to intervene, and joined the fray in March 1793. Then, encouraged by what looked like a free-for-all, the British forces took their cue in November, sending 13,000 troops over to wrest St. Domingue from chaos and the French.

Although Jews had been considered by French revolutionists for full emancipation as well, on St. Domingue the small Jewish population could hardly be distinguished from the white population. Small Jewish communities had existed as traders (and, occasionally, as planters) in many of the region's port cities since at least the middle of the century. Yet the ensuing mess that effectively decimated the sugar industry, the government, and the white population, affected the Jews equally strongly. Many, as a result, felt forced to flee for other islands.

Among the Jewish families that escaped, at least two relocated to St. Thomas. Abraham Julien, his young wife Rachel, and their three-year-old son Moses were among the first to leave, around late 1791.[59] Probably involved in shipping in the south St. Domingue town of Aux Cayes, the Juliens picked up and moved to Charlotte Amalie, where they restarted their business affairs.

Five years later, St. Domingue had entered into a more serious state of siege. Although the coastal city of Aux Cayes remained outside the most violent fighting, it nonetheless came under the possession of the emerging liberator of St. Domingue, Toussaint L'Ouverture. The situation was insecure, yet it was apparently safe enough for another Jewish family—the Pomiés—to continue their ownership of a local plantation. All pretense of security disappeared, however, in 1796, when one of L'Ouverture's enemies beseiged the city in an attempt to take it over. According to family tradition, the attack was accompanied by an order for all French families to quit their homes. Moses Monsanto Pomié, the father, already owned property in St. Thomas, and quickly sent his children and pregnant wife onto a ship. Although men had supposedly been prohibited from leaving the island, Pomié hid himself in a clothes hamper and had his slaves smuggle him on board. In this way, the Pomiés were able to settle in Charlotte Amalie and soon become re-entrenched in mercantile life.[60]

On August 28, 1796, one of L'Ouverture's generals led an uprising of the black population and recaptured Aux Cayes. Fighting similar battles over the next eight years, L'Ouverture's forces would eventually capture all of St. Domingue and transform it into the independent state of Haiti.

From Morocco to St. Thomas: Flight and Freedom

Across the Atlantic Ocean in Morocco, Elijah Levy-Yuly held the comfortable position of "merchant of the sultan" for the port cities of Mogador (later known as Essaouira) and Tangier. A rich and successful man, Levy-Yuly came from a family well-favored in the eyes of the sultans. "Yuly," a title of honor believed to be derived from Psalm 86:9 (an acronym of "[They] shall come and prostrate themselves before Thee . . .") had been granted to his father, Rabbi Samuel Levy Aben-Yuly, who was *nagid* of Moroccan Jewry during the reign of sultan Moulay Abd-Allah (1672–1727).[61]

Elijah Levy-Yuly found grace under Sultan Muhammad b. Abd-Allah (who ruled 1757–1790). His business sense and experience in trade showed him to be an able leader and good administrator, and he was granted the position of courtier to the sultan.

According to family story, Levy-Yuly's luck changed drastically when he discovered the sultan's son, Moulay Yazid, plotting a coup against his father. Immediately Levy-Yuly jailed the son, and produced proof of the charges. The sultan, however, dealt lightly with Yazid, and soon released him. When Muhammad b. Abd-Allah died in 1790, his son took power; and holding a grudge, he immediately issued a death-sentence on Levy-Yuly.[62] Rather than remain to face his fate, the former courtier fled the country. With his family and his Jewish bondservant Elias Sarquy among others, Elijah Levy-Yuly boarded a boat bound for Gibraltar.

At his first stop, Levy-Yuly's set his bondservant Sarquy free, and sent him out to seek his fortune.[63] Probably familiar with the trade routes his master so skillfully manipulated as vizier, Elias Sarquy appeared to travel around for a while, seeing new places and exploring the New World. In 1793, he settled in the prospering port of St. Thomas and applied to the Danish authorities for permission to start a business. He obtained approval the following year, and founded what would soon be a lucrative and influential house of trade.

Levy-Yuly, meanwhile, died in Gibraltar around 1799.[64] Soon after this,

his son, Moses Elias, stripped the "Yuly" from his name, erased his Moroccan past, and followed his father's bondservant down to St. Thomas with his mother and sister.[65]

The Rise of St. Thomas

As St. Eustatius and St. Domingue fell into hibernation and chaos respectively, St. Thomas entered its ascent. Denmark made every effort to keep its islands neutral during these times of constant battles and piracy, receiving with open arms the refugee merchants who came to its shores. Thus, with time and increasingly petty wars, St. Thomas's free and protected harbor became the favorite place for many merchants. In this way, the community grew.

The St. Thomas population experienced a significant influx of Jews during the early 1790s. In 1789, the tax registers listed fewer than ten Jewish households on the island; by 1795, the registers revealed a community of about seventy-five.[66] These included three newly arrived families of Abendanons from St. Eustatius; five De Leon women, likely all related to the late St. Thomas merchant Isaac De Leon; French merchant Abraham Julien with his wife and son, who came from St. Domingue; David Leon Mears, a likely relative of Hannah and Samson Mears from St. Eustatius; Moses Pomié and his family, St. Domingue Jews who would eventually become the extended relatives of impressionist painter Camille Pissarro; and former Moroccan bondservant Elias Sarquy.[67] The group encompassed numerous nationalities, traditions, and backgrounds. For them, however, this was hardly a new condition; island trading communities in general presented a slice of the world, connected only by a common interest and occupation in trade. Together through fate, happenstance and convenience, these Jews coalesced into an organized religious community that would be respected and recognized by the island's population and the Danish colonial government.

Before 1792, the tiny Jewish population on St. Thomas prayed in private homes, as per religious regulation.[68] Chances are, this was not an easy feat in and of itself. St. Thomas's merchant population travelled about frequently; and even taking into account the Jewish merchants and ship captains who came in from other ports, a quorum of ten men (a *minyan*) was probably difficult to assemble.

Yet the Jews did provide their small community with the most basic need: a cemetery. Often the first established Jewish landmark in an area, it was also the easiest to clear with the local government, requiring only the purchase of land. The Jews in St. Thomas appeared to acquire and dedicate their lot around 1750.[69] Located on the western edge of town, in a flat region known as Savan, the new cemetery provided the Jews with a place for proper burial, and the opportunity to retain their community ties even after death. In the 1760s, a growing population caused Charlotte Amalie to lay out Savan as a designated area for free coloreds. It is possible, however, that many Jews came to live in this part of town as well; and perhaps for this reason, the street facing the cemetery received the name *Jøde Gade*, or "Jew Street."[70]

By the early 1790s, the Jews had become numerous enough to organize a burial society. This society, a benchmark of many of the contemporary Spanish-Portuguese Jewish communities, prepared the bodies of the recently deceased for burial (which traditionally included a ritual washing, dressing the body in a shroud, and keeping a prayer vigil over the body until interment), and then took responsibility for organizing the funeral. Looking to the communities in Surinam, Curaçao, and New York for inspiration, the group called itself *Gemilut Hasadim*, or "Deeds of Lovingkindness."[71] Founded around 1792 (the year when steady records of births and deaths began), the society, also known as the *Hebre* (literally, "society" in Hebrew), was essentially an informal congregation, complete with at least one religious leader (David Serano, who died on September 27, 1793), a secretary, and communal responsibilities that spanned from recording deaths to registering births to solemnizing religious life-cycle ceremonies.[72] St. Eustatius residents Samuel and Benjamin Hoheb set up part of their home as a sanctuary where the group could gather for Sabbath and holiday services.[73]

With burgeoning numbers from increasing arrivals, however, the congregation began to develop a more pressing need for a formally recognized body of worship, on the same level as the Christian churches on the island. The *Hebre*, though religiously oriented, was small, did not reflect the whole Jewish community, and apparently did not warrant the same rights as a full-fledged "church" on the island. Thus, in 1796, a group of potential congregants, led at least in part by the Hoheb brothers, applied to the Danish King and the Danish colonial government for the privilege of founding a synagogue on the island. On June 26, 1796, Danish sovereign Christian VII granted the request. Frederik Baltharzar von Mühlenfels, Commandant of St. Thomas and St. John, accepted the King's wish without issue.[74] With this decree, then, Jewish life on St. Thomas began in earnest.

Three months later, just before the Jewish New Year 5557, *Kahal Kadosh Beracha VeShalom*—the Holy Congregation Blessing and Peace—fulfilled its first responsibility by submitting a founding constitution to the Danish colonial government.

The document they presented was an interesting mix of politics and ambition, organization and ritual. Addressing the expectations of the colonial government, it exhibited a greater concern for practical function than religious substance, and revealed much about the social and religious practice of this congregation of merchants. According to the constitution, *Beracha Ve-Shalom* was to be a social group of co-religionists, with a heathcare system and a code of synagogue conduct; it would also be a watchdog organization that would look out for the civil rights of its members. As later events would bear out, the congregation cared enormously about the content of their services and rituals. This was not reflected in the constitution, however: For the government's purposes, the founders must have regarded such issues of ritual as incidental, focusing more on the practical concerns of keeping order among the congregants.

Following the model set by numerous Sephardic congregations, the affairs of *Beracha VeShalom* ran by committee. On St. Thomas, this committee (called a *Mahamade*) consisted of seven elected members, none of whom could be related to each other.[75] Five of the members took standard committee seats, and went by the accepted term adjuntos, or "wardens." The other two positions, elected in the last month of the Jewish calendar and announced in services on the final two weeks of the Jewish Year, were the treasurer (or *Gabay*) and president.[76]

The treasurer's position was meticulously defined, revealing the founders' occupational familiarity with financial dealings. Eight of the document's twenty-five articles focused on his responsibilities in great detail. The treasurer had to record the meetings of the *Mahamade*, write the synagogue's correspondence, keep all synagogue accounts current, discern and administer to the needs of the poor, and then publish his records at the end of each year for the scrutiny of the congregation. As the keeper of monies for the synagogue, his job was crucial and highly visible.

The president, an Americanized appellation for the more traditional term *parnas*, served primarily as the organization's chief disciplinarian.[77] His main responsibility was to ensure that "in Synagogue during service their [sic] shall be all Decency and Decorum observed by the Congregation."[78] This included ejecting troublesome congregants during services and selecting people for *Mitsvoth*, or "honors," such as being called up to the Five Books of Moses. The latter of these responsibilities, which typically included a financial contribution on the part of the honoree, was potentially quite a sensitive one, since it had led in other congregations to accusations of favoritism.[79] Aware of this, the constitution asserted that the president could not be questioned in public.

In addition to the treasurer and president, the congregation named two other positions, both under the treasurer's watch. One was the "samos," or sexton, who served primarily as a collection agent and messenger. When the treasurer, who settled accounts at the end of each month, faced a delinquency, he informed the samos, who would then attempt to collect the outstanding balance. In other cases, when the *Mahamade* wished to send a communication to someone on the island, the Samos often delivered it. Clearly, the synagogue found this job a potentially treacherous one, and thus made sure to include in its bylaws a provision protecting the samos from "insult, offen[se], or ill treat[ment]" while performing his job.[80]

The synagogue also aimed to employ a communal doctor. There was no requirement that he be Jewish; only that he attend to the congregation's sick without prejudice.

In addition to receiving voluntary contributions, the synagogue also collected funds through a system of penalties. A person elected to the position of president or treasurer who subsequently declined the post would receive a fine of twenty-five pieces of eight. Publicly disagreeing with the president during services brought a fine of four dollars, as did abusing the samos. Resisting a summons to appear at a meeting of the *Mahamade* resulted in a two dollar fine the first time, and a four dollar fine for a second offense. As with all outstanding accounts, the synagogue enforced these penalties by threatening legal action if they were not paid in a timely fashion.

The community also made certain to look after its poor. The treasurer, according to the constitution, would visit the sick and indigent at least twice a week, and provide vouchers to those who needed a doctor's care. During Passover, those who could not afford *matzah* (the traditional unleavened bread eaten on the holiday) needed only to apply to the treasurer, who would then provide the ritual food. If one of the synagogue's less fortunate needed a large amount of money for some reason, the treasurer would call a meeting of the *Mahamade* for discussion and a vote. Whatever the case, the congregation tried to maintain a basic quality of life for all its members.[81]

In its first years, the fledgling congregation still held services every Sabbath and holiday in a private home. An actual sanctuary did not yet prove financially feasible. Moreover, the synagogue membership did not yet encompass all the Jews on the island—the burial society *Gemilut Hasadim* still seemed to have several exclusive members, and other Jewish residents may not have joined *Beracha VeShalom* initially. Thus, in an audacious move, the St. Thomas Hebrew Congregation issued a challenge to all St. Thomas Jews in its constitution: should anyone outside of *Beracha VeShalom* erect a synagogue building, and allow the Hebrew Congregation to appropriate it for joint worship, the group would donate the funds necessary to obtain a *sefer* (Torah, or Five Books of Moses), and ornaments befitting a Jewish place of worship, ". . . provided this will justify naming ourselves *Beracha VeShalom,* or Blessing and Peace, and that we the present wardens and members will be equals in the new synagogue."[82] As the officially recognized Jewish body on St. Thomas, *Kahal Kadosh Beracha VeShalom* could instantly legitimize any other Jewish religious body through absorption. On top of this, the synagogue's founders also appeared to believe that the St. Thomas Jewish community could acquire the appropriate trappings for a religious congregation—namely, a dedicated building and appropriate ritual objects—only if all Jews on the island pooled their resources. This call would soon bear fruit.

When writing these ordinances, the wardens of the synagogue derived much of their inspiration from the bylaws of other Sephardic communities, including New York, Curaçao, and London. Their influences were clear: Sephardic bylaws appeared to embody a common (albeit flexible) structure, and utilized a certain set of Hebrew terms to define its leaders and operations. St. Thomas followed right in this tradition. Simultaneously, however, the new congregation personalized the bylaws to fit its own needs and reflect its priorities and biases. With no local past upon which to base the new regulations, the wardens of *Beracha VeShalom* had to approximate and guess their vision for the nascent congregation, building upon the bylaws they knew from other regions. As the congregation faced the realities of its operation, appropriate changes and modifications would come. These initial laws, however, created a place and identity from which to begin.

Thus, in presenting the government with the constitution for a new synagogue, the founders imparted a vision of faith. St. Thomas was the last island of its era to obtain permission for the creation of an official Jewish community—due in part to its status as a "secondary" Jewish community, created by Jews fleeing other, more established communities in the area. Its founding congregants brought with them the experiences of a prosperous but troubled past, in regions known for their volatility and lawlessness. Yet on this neutral Danish island at the dawn of its heyday, the Jews saw the potential for a safe haven, and a secure future. Once again, they began to lay down roots. Humble, but headstrong, *Beracha VeShalom* became an auspicious start for a body that would serve for centuries as the major voice of Judaism on St. Thomas.

CHAPTER 2

Growth
1796–1831

*T*he end of the eighteenth century produced a great boom
in the St. Thomas economy. Starting in 1792, the spare, small city of Charlotte Amalie began to fill considerably, and expanded its borders along the
island's southern shore. Merchants travelling into the protected harbor
found a concentration of wooden structures greeting them from all altitudes:
storehouses in the front, residences and houses of worship ascending on the
hills behind them. Still further back, between and beyond the hills, slaves
continued to toil on a dwindling number of plantations throughout the island. By this point, however, it was clear that agriculture had little future on
St. Thomas. St. Croix, with its larger area and expanses of flat land, was by
far the greater producer of high-profit products such as sugar and cotton. On
St. Thomas, with less land and more difficult terrain, trade began to take the
throne.

Several factors were responsible for the rise of St. Thomas's mercantile industry during this time. As illustrated in the last chapter, the complex political and colonial theater in the Caribbean caused a number of significant upheavals in the 1780s and 1790s, transforming ports in places such as
St. Eustatius and St. Domingue into difficult stations for free trade. Businesses
and mercantile firms disrupted by the unrest found the neutral haven of
St. Thomas attractive by contrast, and began to establish houses of business
there. Accordingly, ships began to visit Charlotte Amalie with some regular-
ity. Historian Isaac Dookhan mentions a stretch of mild hurricane seasons in
St. Thomas between 1793 and 1818, which allowed for undisrupted growth
and expansion of mercantile houses.[1] On top of this was a sudden burst of
slave trading activity, a direct response to the Danish government's 1792
announcement to abolish human trafficking by 1802.[2] Slaves were herded

through St. Thomas's protected harbor at record rates while importers could still bring them; their sale benefitted the local economy, and created a wider base for the exchange of other products. Through such activities, St. Thomas began to distinguish itself as a regional trading haven.

Within this environment, Jews continued to arrive from St. Eustatius, St. Croix, and Curaçao, and establish new trading houses on the island. While their levels of success were likely quite varied, some of these arrivals did a brisk trade and came to own a good deal of property within the city.[3] In 1803, a merchant by the name of Lopes came to own four large properties totalling 13,096 square feet. A. A. Lion, a Jew residing in the north German port city of Altona, owned one plot comprising 10,152 square feet.[4] Elias Sarquy's property, at 20,048 square feet, no doubt reflected the impressive success of his business; likewise with his living quarters, which bordered the town's market square.[5] Others, including synagogue warden (and former Statian) Benjamin Hoheb and French merchant Lopes Dubec, appeared to rent their property, conducting their business on a somewhat less affluent level.

As with the rest of the tropical region, life on St. Thomas was not easy: epidemics of malaria, yellow fever, and smallpox occasionally visited the island, borne, sometimes unannounced, on arriving ships. Privateering, though not nearly as widespread as in the previous two centuries, still had its place on the high seas of the Caribbean. The island was spared from hurricanes for several decades; yet St. Thomas, on the edge of a tectonic plate, still contended with numerous unexpected earthquakes. Vast swarms of mosquitos made morning and dusk hours unbearable to those who did not have the appropriate protective netting. And politically, Europe still used the Caribbean region as a remote theater for its conflicts, leading to frequent armed engagements and causing island sovereignties to change with sometimes alarming frequency. Instability and risk was thus a part of the cultural fabric on the island and throughout the Caribbean. No one was immune to sudden, inexplicable, and sometimes devastating reversals of fortune; and to many, the ability to weather such disasters effectively was an important part of their business education.

While the upheavals in St. Thomas were relatively mild at the turn of the nineteenth century, they happened nonetheless. In March 1801, the British took the island as insurance against a perceived French threat to its colonies in the region. Contrasted with the nastiness of the St. Eustatius incident, this peaceful coup did little more than unsettle trade for a while. The island's population was not fleeced or persecuted, and life for the most part continued with relatively few disruptions. Even the Jews remained secure: after the takeover, representatives of *Beracha VeShalom* presented their bylaws to the new commandant and the public notary for reconfirmation, and successfully received approbation.[6] The next year, when the island quietly returned to Danish sovereignty, the transition took place almost seamlessly.

For the Jews, it appears the brief annexation did little to prevent the community from continuing to proliferate. Since the synagogue's establishment, Jewish merchants and their families had increasingly migrated to the island from Europe and parts of the Caribbean: A conservative estimate from tax records in 1802 revealed 160 Jews, many of whom had arrived within the previous three years.[7] Several of these new settlers were well-off merchants looking for a foothold in the northeastern Caribbean. Others were ruined businessmen who intended to start anew on St. Thomas. Still others were young men sent to St. Thomas to lodge with family and seek their fortunes. The largest influx came from Curaçao—by far the most numerous and most affluent Jewish community in the Caribbean with a strong tradition and a central role in Jewish Caribbean affairs—though others arrived from St. Eustatius, London, and elsewhere. In settling on St. Thomas, these Jews immediately made their influences known, and helped to bring the young congregation into the mainstream of Jewish Caribbean society.

One of the first acts accomplished by the new Jewish population was a complete revision of the old bylaws. Finished on January 17, 1802, and read into the official record (in both English and Portuguese) on April 23, 1803, the new laws showed the speed with which Curaçaoan Jews were able to gain political leadership in the congregation. While the *parnasim* (wardens) of the 1796 congregation were mostly immigrants from St. Eustatius and St. Domingue, the 1803 wardens had a strong Curaçaoan representation (including Jacob Dineÿra, Samuel de Josias de Casseres, and probably Joshua Naar, the congregation's reader).[8] These individuals collaborated with the existing members to restructure the old laws in a manner that redefined synagogue life and organization.

Perhaps the most significant feature of the new bylaws was their remarkable resemblance to the existing bylaws of Curaçao's *Mikve Israel* congregation, including the use of the same descriptive title, "Hascamoth."[9] Of the twenty-four items mentioned in the new St. Thomas code, nineteen had analogs in *Mikve Israel*'s 1756/1786 bylaws (see Table 2–1); they were presented generally in the same order, and many of the items had almost the same wording.[10] This striking similarity may have been promoted particularly through the actions of two of the St. Thomas wardens—de Casseres and Naar—who appear to have signed the Curaçao bylaws in 1786. Regard-

TABLE 2.1 Comparison of Haskamoth

St. Thomas, 1803	Curaçao, 1756/1786
§1: Exclusivity of synagogue	Section 1, §1
§2: Composition and election of Mahamad	Section 1, §2
§3: Forbidding certain relations on Mahamad	Section 1, §11
§4: Mortgages	Section 1, §17
§5: Forbidding conversation during services	Not included
§6: Gabay remains a warden after his term	Not included
§7: Warden age limit set at 60	Section 1, §7 (age limit 70)
§8: Election of Bridegrooms of the Law	Section 2, §1
§9: Election of Parnasim and Gabay	Section 1, §5 (in much greater detail)
§10: Fines must be paid after the holiday	Section 2, §4
§11: Frequency of forced Board service	Section 2, §5
§12: Reader and Sexton must heed Mahamad	Section 3, §1
§13: Seat assignments	Section 4, §1
§14: Exclusive slaughterer	Section 3, §3
§15: Fines for disturbing religious services	Section 4, §2
§16: Births must be approved by Mahamad	Not included
§17: Marriages ditto	Not included
§18: The choice of "Misvoths"	Section 4, §7 & 8
§19: When and how many "Misvoths"	Section 4, §9 & 10
§20: ¼% poor tax on all Jewish business	Section 5, §4 & 5
§21: Forbidding interreligious dialogue	Section 5, §6
§22: Synagogue asserts power of taxation	Section 5, §14
§23: Changes to constitution resolved by majority vote and signed immediately	Section 7, §2
§24: Request to government for same civil rights as the Jewish community in Copenhagen	Not included

less of who may have been responsible for introducing Curaçao's code into St. Thomas, however, it was clear that the revised bylaws indicated a closeness between the two congregations, in both population and religious paradigm.

The first article of the bylaws carried a stern assertion of unity. "There shall Exist but one Congregation in the Island which shall be called Blessing & Peace," it trumpeted, laying to rest any doubt remaining from article twenty-three of the 1796 constitution. No other congregations, public or private, would be tolerated, and all violators would be fined. The law apparently incorporated *Gemilut Hasadim* into the synagogue, for it spoke directly to the *minyanim* held during the seven-day mourning period after burial (*shiva*): Such meetings could henceforth be held only on weekdays, when services were not in session, and only with consent of the synagogue president. Further, the law forbade "any Religious Society under any description whatsoever without being subject to the Emediate Direction of the Mahamade & Adjuntos of the Synagogue." To this they added the telling phrase, "as is Customary in all Congregations." Clearly, the new arrivals found the idea of a separate congregation and burial society impractical—on Curaçao, after all, the burial society had been developed as an *affiliate* of the synagogue—and made quick work in merging the two.

Upper administration of the synagogue was changed from a council of six adjuntos and a president to a two-tiered system. The highest echelon, called the *Mahamade,* consisted of a two-person joint presidency (with each now called a *Parnas-Presidente,* a name consistent with other New World Sephardic synagogue hierarchies), and a treasurer/*Gabay.* All served one-year terms; in order to preserve continuity, however, they were elected at different times of the year: the *Gabay* and one president during Passover, and the other president during Rosh Hashanah. The second level of leadership consisted of four wardens called *adjuntos,* which composed a separate but complementary party that assisted the *Mahamade* in its responsibilities.

The writers of the new bylaws enumerated the synagogue officers' duties in far greater detail than their 1796 predecessors, in some cases incorporating Curaçaoan norms, in other cases diverging according to their own situation. As in Curaçao, *Beracha VeShalom's* leadership was responsible for selecting a *Hazan* (reader) and *Samas* (sexton) and keeping them under control; for choosing the *Sohet* (ritual slaughterer) to supply the congregation with kosher meat; for assigning seats in the synagogue; for handing out honors (*Mitsvoth*) during services; for taxing the congregation should the need arise; and for choosing their own successors. Unique to St. Thomas, however, the bylaws dictated that all births and marriages had to be reported to the *Mahamade* and recorded before the synagogue would hold any related ceremonies. These new responsibilities gave the synagogue administration a much wider range of power, as well as a better defined role in guiding the proliferating lives of its congregants.

Rules of conduct during religious services experienced a transformation as well, modelled on (if not copied from) Curaçao's Haskamoth. Where in 1796 "Decency and Decorum" was the only criterion for maintaining proper behavior, the new bylaws included specific rules against talking in the synagogue, sitting in another person's seat, arguing, fighting, and carrying "a Stick, Sword or Dagger," into the sanctuary; violations carried a range of fines from two to sixteen dollars. Such regulations showed a new level of practical experience for the congregation, denoting and protecting against particular situations that had disturbed the synagogue service elsewhere in the past.

Two other important Curaçaoan conventions were introduced into St. Thomas with the 1803 bylaws. The first was a charity (or *Sedaca*) fund for the poor, collected through a one-quarter percent tax levied on all business commissions earned by Jews on St. Thomas, regardless of whether they were residents or visiting merchants. Second was an interesting prohibition:

> No Person or Persons shall be allowed to hold any Argument or Dispute with any of the Predominant Religion on the Island on Religious subjects, that we may not therefrom become hatefull to our Protectors & that the Freedom which We Enjoy may not be Infringed. Offenders in this Article will be severely Prosecuted.

Even in 1802, freedom and human rights were not universal. While Judaism remained a fascination to non-Jews, it did not sustain full political protection under the existing powers. The local Danish colonial government tolerated the Jews with increasing benevolence (just as the Dutch government did in Curaçao), but the process was gingerly maintained and fraught with the potential for misinterpretation. In deference to the fragile nature of this relationship, the synagogue attempted to prevent its members from inadvertently creating public religious conflicts. Any arbitrary incident, as proven so many times in the past, might reflect negatively on the Jews as a whole, endangering years of successful petitioning.

While the leaders of the Jewish community were wary of creating religious friction, however, they still took the opportunity at the end of their bylaws to assert their civil rights. In Copenhagen, the authors noted, the Jewish community enjoyed what they saw as almost complete freedom, and the synagogue *Mahamade* and *adjuntos* were recognized by the government. The wardens of *Beracha VeShalom* requested a similar form of recognition on St. Thomas. Having grown from being a small, private group into a larger, sanctioned body, the congregation believed itself to resemble less a fledgling religious fellowship than a maturing Jewish community. Consequently, it appealed for the same privileges that had been granted its counterpart in the Danish capital.[11]

Real estate tax lists of 1803 showed further evidence of the congregation's development, with the first indications that a new synagogue building had come into being on the island.[12] The new house of prayer was a small wooden structure, about two-thirds the size of its predecessor in St. Eustatius. Built with the help of contributions from the Jewish communities in Curaçao and the United States, the edifice served as a place for Sabbath services and a physical center of Jewish life on the island. A Reader, Joshua Naar, had been engaged to lead the sacred service and perhaps even to give occasional sermons, showing the Jews' further commitment to fashioning a fully functioning religious body.[13] With this bulding, the Jews thus emerged as a visible religious group on the island, taking their place alongside the much larger congregations of Lutherans, Catholics, Episcopalians, and Moravians.

Even though recent arrivals to the island had enlarged the Hebrew Congregation considerably, however, the community as a whole could not yet sustain its own numbers. Families of childbearing age were still scarce, and marriages rare. With the exception of 1801, deaths in the community continued to exceed births by a ratio of three to two. The numbers were not substantial: In 1802, for example, the congregation celebrated eight births and mourned fourteen deaths. Nonetheless, the figures portrayed a community that needed time to settle and grow roots; to move from a stage of optimistic nascency to the comfort of established residency.

CHARLOTTE AMALIE, with its closely situated wooden houses, was a virtual tinderbox. Despite the presence of a volunteer fire squad (the Brand Corps) and a special fire bell at the fort to alert the town of any emergent blazes, the island remained unprepared for most incendiary outbreaks. Water sources were usually inadequate, and firefighting equipment was heavy and hard to maneuver around the island's hilly terrain, often leaving hasty bucket brigades as the most effective measures against fires. Any significant flareup in the town thus had a strong likelihood of burning out of control, continuing unimpeded until wind changes or lack of flammable material ended the rampage. Once initial attempts to put it out failed, most residents had nothing to do but watch their possessions go to ashes.

The first of these devastating fires to be recorded took place on November 22, 1804. At about seven in the evening, a blaze broke out in the building next to the town's customs house, near the fort that stood at the east end of the town. A contemporary account attributes this blaze to a servant boy, who left a candle burning on a bale of cotton. Winds carried the fire westward, through Queens Quarter, into the center of town. Businesses and storehouses caught flame and burned to the ground, along with hundreds of thousands of rigsdalers worth of traded goods. Residences were not spared either, as the flames continued to move west and crossed over into Kronprindsens Quarter. Smoke and fire billowed all through the night, and the island's buildings fell one after the next. By the time the blaze had been extinguished, nearly two-thirds of the city of Charlotte Amalie was a smoldering ashpile; by contemporary merchant Johann Peter Nissen's estimate, 2,300 buildings on 308 lots were destroyed. Two people died. Hundreds—perhaps thousands—were homeless. Emerging from the tragic night, residents witnessed, "a horrid and pitiful sight. Nearly the whole town or at least the best and richest part of it was lying in ashes. [The people] were obliged first to clear all the streets and the heat was so excessive that no one could bear to stand still in the street. The mouths and lips of all those helping at the fire became so dry and their thirst so great that they could not endure it long." In some areas, rubble continued to burn for two weeks, as merchants salvaged what they could. All told, according to Nissen's report, the island experienced over eleven million rigsdalers in damage and lost goods.[14]

The new synagogue was a casualty of this fire, as were the Roman Catholic and Dutch Reformed churches. Yet life went on. The island lost little of its traffic, and rebuilt with considerable aid from Denmark, the neighboring islands, and insurance claims. Foundations for a new synagogue were planted, and a new reader—the Reverend Isaac Lopes, who would later serve the Spanish and Portuguese congregation of Kingston, Jamaica, for forty-seven years—was hired to bring the group spiritual depth.[15] Most houses were rebuilt from wood, as owners could not spare the exorbitant amounts of money for "fireproof" brick, stone, and rubble buildings.[16] While this method proved economical in the short run, it also left the area vulnerable to another fire.

Inevitably, disaster struck again in 1806—twice. The first fire, on October 1, began at the market square, across from the dwelling of Elias Sarquy. A woman mishandled a lantern, and within hours four to five hundred residential houses burned uncontrollably. The damage, noted Nissen, was considerable, but "thank God the loss was not so severe as it had been in the 1804 fire for only a few of the merchants houses and stores were burned."[17] Two months later, late at night on December 4, a slave woman tending a rum shop on the other side of town brought her lamp too close to a large cask of rum, and set it aflame. Fire quickly spread to the adjoining houses. In a tragic reenactment of the 1804 blaze (which, incidentally, had begun just across the street), the flames traveled west, vexing all attempts to extinguish it. Six and a half hours later, the fire met its match at the hands of one of the only fire-proof stores in town. Built by a Mr. Peneke at great personal expense, it re-sisted the flames long enough to prove the worthiness of his investment.[18] It is easy to say that the residents (and their suppliers) despaired at the frequent losses; according to Nissen, however, most just assessed the damage and started counting stock again. Their rebuilding efforts this time were much more costly: Insurance companies, stung twice in three years, refused to in-sure wooden stores on the main street anymore, and forced most merchants to incur the expense of building stone "fireproofs" to prevent future confla-grations.

The synagogue, partially reconstructed, was included once again among the property losses from these fires. Once the building had succumbed to the flames for a second time, the Jews suspended their construction efforts and reverted back to worshiping in a local home for a while. The community ap-peared to need some time to regain financial solidity before attempting to build their sanctuary again.

The start of a second British occupation in 1807 did not initially help the situation, and disruptions in trade again imposed hardship on the town's resi-dents. After adjusting to the new sovereignty, however, island affairs gener-ally seemed to return to a state of depressed normalcy, with somewhat re-duced merchant traffic and elevated prices. The occupation would last for eight years; yet even as it decimated commerce with Denmark, it improved trade relations with England, France, and the United States, allowing the is-land to maintain its status as an international port.

The initial year of British occupation proved difficult for the Jewish popu-lation as well, which lost ten members and recorded only one birth. Perhaps as a testament to the benevolence of the British, however, the subsequent years of occupation witnessed a stabilization within the community. Rather than leaving the island, young, childbearing couples seemed to take their chances with the local economy. Births exceeded deaths for the first time in 1811. In 1813, moreover, the community began a decade of consistent growth: For every two Jewish community members who died during this time, ap-proximately three would be born.

Two births during this occupation would have particular importance to American history. Dry goods merchant Moses Elias Levy, the Moroccan-born immigrant from England, had a son David in 1810.[19] David spent his early years on the island with his zealous father, his mother Hannah, and his older brother Elias. A strong activist for Jewish statehood in America, Moses Elias Levy brought up his sons as secular Jews, promoting a cultural identification with Judaism above religious practice presumably in preparation for their Zionistic roles. David would eventually shed these ideals, however, and drift fully into secular Christian life. Over the course of the following decades, he would restore his Moroccan name Yulee, become a lawyer, and serve as Florida's first senator—all to his father's great chagrin.[20]

A year later, on St. Croix, Philip and Rebecca Benjamin gave birth to their son Judah Philip.[21] The Benjamins were refugees from Barbados who stayed for only a few years in the Virgin Islands, likely in order to be near their cousins Emanuel and Esther Benjamin on St. Thomas.[22] In 1814, the family left the islands for good and moved up to the Charleston, South Carolina, area. Judah Philip Benjamin would eventually become one of the first Jewish students to enroll at Yale College.[23] His illustrious, daring, and colorful career would lead to positions as a Louisiana senator, Secretary of State for the Confederacy, and Secretary of War to Confederate President Jefferson Davis. Benjamin fled the United States after the Civil War, and settled in England, where he would end his career as a prominent professor of law.

The benevolence of the British rule could also be seen in the congregation's renewed efforts to build a house of worship. In 1810, the Jewish community pooled its resources and constructed a small, temporary synagogue building with an area of approximately six hundred square feet.[24] As many members increased their social status, gained greater financial stability, and moved to more central parts of town, a desire likely arose to construct a more ornate monument in a more visible and central location. Thus, in 1813, the congregation purchased a parcel of land just behind central Charlotte Amalie, about one hundred yards from the harbor. The street, called Skidengade ("Refuse Street"), was at the time a steep dirt road leading from the eastern border of Queens Quarter up behind the town to the West.[25] Halfway up, near the houses of several prominent Jewish merchants, were lots 16A and B, intended as the new home for *Beracha VeShalom*'s new synagogue. The transaction for the property was completed on October 14, 1813, with the synagogue wardens paying 1,325 pieces of eight to merchant Jared Shattuck for the land; the considerable sum may have been a sign of the area's gentrification, and a perhaps a portent of the street's impending name change.[26]

Along the storehouses lining the waterfront and down main street, Sephardic Jewish names appeared with increasing frequency. Louis Lopes Dubec sold textiles; Samuel J. Robles peddled liquors; Goodman & Pretto sold dry goods; Moses Elias Levy and Emanuel Benjamin had a large store that sold assorted goods; Leon Levy, across the street from Levy and Benjamin, sold Spruce-Beer, Pine Apple Cider, and other spirits; next door stood the house/store of Elias De Pinna. Other Jewish businesses included those of Elias Sarquy, Jos. M. Monsanto & Co., E[lias]. & B[enjamin]. Lindo & Co., and D'Azevedo & Robles. Many owned their own ships, which made regular circuits to Europe and ports in the Americas to bring supplies and goods; several also managed extension stores throughout the Caribbean, North America, and Europe.

Like any other group, Jews had to follow a diligent path in order to succeed in the mercantile business. Most young Jewish men began their careers as clerks, learning the various aspects of the mercantile trade at their elders' stores from about the age of fifteen. Over the course of several years, they moved to jobs of greater responsibility: keeping books, checking and loading inventory, working with clients, and even representing the firm on business trips. After the young men had attained sufficient skills and business contacts, they would apply to the Danish government for Burgher Briefs—licenses granting permission to be a business agent. The application, which consisted of a letter of intent, a small fee, and letters of sponsorship from at least two other St. Thomas burghers, underlined the importance of sustaining strong business and family connections throughout the apprenticeship process.

Reflecting a healthy business environment, mercantile firms commonly experienced changes in name and ownership. Alliances between burghers were altered under the watch of the government for such reasons as absence from the island, differences in business ideology, the coming-of-age of a young relative, the death of a partner, or simply the end of a particular venture. The firm of Jos. M. Monsanto & Co., for example, dissolved on December 31, 1812, possibly so the head partner could get married.[27] Elias Sarquy added a Mr. D'Azevedo to his business in early December 1813.[28] Levy & Benjamin added S. J. Robles to their firm in the same month, apprising the government of the new partnership in a long and involved document of incorporation.[29] These modifications provided space for new merchants to begin their careers, and gave more experienced merchants the opportunity to maintain their vibrancy through flat or difficult times.

The financial stability afforded by the Burgher Brief often paved the way for merchants to marry. In some ways, however, marriage itself was a form of business alliance. Merchants' wives often needed to have a business sense as keen if not keener than the merchants themselves, and many worked full time in their husbands' shops. Business on other islands or in Europe could require burghers to travel away from St. Thomas for months at a time.[30] Although they usually granted other merchants power of attorney during their absences, the actual responsibility of running the business frequently fell to the wife. Direct documentary evidence of this, as one might expect, is scant; however, numerous stories and circumstantial records point to women as recognized members of the business community.[31] Occasionally, women received their own listings in the tax records, or took out advertisements in the local paper. In several instances, widows continued to control their late husbands' business or real estate holdings for several years after their deaths.[32] Thus, although men were the most visible participants in the mercantile industry, mercantilism in practice often ended up as a family affair, with all members doing their part to maintain the family's financial welfare.

On April 15, 1815, Britain returned St. Thomas, St. John, and St. Croix to Denmark; the War of 1812 had been peacefully resolved with the United States, and the British apparently felt its other Caribbean interests were no longer under any immediate threat. A Danish vessel stationed at St. Bartholomew's immediately turned around and headed for St. Thomas upon hearing the news. Soon, ships from all over Europe and the United States were returning to the harbor. Merchant J. P. Nissen commented in his journal: "The joy of the inhabitants was very great. . . . Our Harbour filled again and often on Sundays we saw about 17 different colours of all nations hoisted on board the vessels. What a splendid sight this was and what hopes we all had soon to be able again to earn money."[33] Prices gradually fell back to pre-occupation levels, and St. Thomas stood poised on another period of great prosperity. The local paper—called the *St. Thomas Gazette* during the British occupation, but renamed the *Sanct Thomæ Tidende* upon the islands' return to Denmark—published a petition from seventy-seven merchants to the Danish sovereign:

> We trust that with War its calamities will cease, and that this once so highly favored Free Port, will again have its former priviledges restored, and by that means, enable us to meet your Excellency's views in every nature. . . . We are aware that an exhausted treasury and decayd state of the Public Buildings, will require great supplies for the restoration of both to their former respectability; but when the sources of Trade are reopened and cherished by your Excellency, we confidently hope they will so much augment and Increase the Public revenue, as to furnish an ample and sufficient sum for the Payment of those, as well as other public expenditures Your Excellency may consider requisite.[34]

Once again, sailors thronged the streets of Charlotte Amalie. Traders, Jewish and otherwise, likely devoted their days almost entirely to trade and commerce. It was probably little different from Nissen's 1791 description of a workday: "At 5 o'clock in the morning a gun is fired from the fort and those that then rise and indulge in a walk or a ride will argue with me that it is delightful to enjoy the morning air. . . . at 6 o[']clock in the morning the stores are opened and the tradesmen as well as the negroes that work in the stores commence their labour at this hour. At 8 o clock they go home for their break fast. At 9 they return to their work again and at 12 they take dinner[. A]t 2 pm they again return to their stores where they remain til 6 o clock when the shops are closed and every one either takes a walk or goes to play at ninepins. At 8 o clock they take supper and 10 is the hour fixed for going to bed."[35]

For the Jews, Sabbath began with a service on Friday night, followed by another service the next morning. Many took the day off as a sign of observance, closing their stores and refusing to do business. Others within the congregation, however, conducted business affairs anyway, probably opening their stores after services had ended on Saturday morning. Any religious issues this situation created appear to have been kept entirely within the community, never making it into the public sphere. For several merchants, after all, Saturday was a precious workday that could not afford to be missed.

Sunday was much more relaxed. Many Christians took off the day to attend church services, and trade appeared to slow tremendously. A number of plantation slaves, given a mandated day of rest, came into town to sell horse feed and firewood.[36] Jews who did not work on Saturday often used Sunday to settle their accounts and make personal purchases. In the afternoons and evenings, the town presented various leisure activities, including cockfighting, to help wile away the time and prepare for the next week.[37]

The Jewish community thus lived as a recognized and respected subgroup within island life, professing its religious activities and beliefs openly. Jewish merchants advertised their wares in the new *Tidende.* Jews had their domestic disputes, which at least once spilled out into the public forum.[38] As was common with all free people on the island—black *and* white—a number of Jewish households owned slaves; though as city denizens, these slaves tended to receive somewhat better treatment due to the city's higher standard of living.[39] Some Jewish men supported mistresses among the free black community.[40] And, as the 1802 bylaws illustrated, the Jews were just as prone to internal conflict as any other group on St. Thomas. Assimilated through a common mercantile culture, the Jews did not have to worry about castigation for participating in "foreign" activities—for though religiously different from the non-Jews of St. Thomas, their public lives were almost identically cosmopolitan.

By 1816, the St. Thomas Jewish community had hired a new minister—Abraham Jessurun Pinto, who hailed from Curaçao and descended from a line of Jewish scholars.[41] The synagogue was by this point a small structure on the congregation's new plot at Skidengade, possibly converted from one of the buildings already on the property. Every week and on Jewish holidays, Reverend Pinto led orderly services, administering to representatives from the De Leon, Levy, Sarquy, Lopes Dubec, Lopes, Benjamin, Hoheb, Pareira, Baiz, Cohen D'Azevedo, Lindo, Athias, Mendes Monsanto, Pomié, Wolff, and Montefiore families among others.[42] Pinto, raised and versed in the Curaçaoan Jewish *minhag* (tradition of religious ritual), no doubt satisfied the expectations of much of his transplanted flock. The young congregation's distance from Curaçao, however, also allowed it to develop a form of worship that addressed its particular spiritual needs. Pinto's leadership at *Beracha Ve-Shalom* thus effected a connection that ensured Curaçao's future support, both financial and spiritual, while probably giving Jews in both communities a feeling of empowerment and unity.

While a new preacher was bringing together the Jewish community, other members of the congregation were forging spiritual connections with non-Jewish St. Thomians through the medium of freemasonry. Particularly in England, freemasonry had proven to be a common ground for businessmen of all religions and races since the middle of the eighteenth century. Meeting "secretly" in local halls they called "temples," freemasons employed an open ideological foundation, and carved out a private space for discussion in a society where similar interaction in public was frequently discouraged.[43] Jews often participated fully in these societies when they could, and several attained high ranks in the local orders.[44] It was thus an attractive option for both the Jews and the rest of the St. Thomas mercantile community to create a similar institution on their own island.

The process of establishing a Masonic lodge on the island was not an easy one, however. Denmark, whose national masonic norms forbade Jews and free men of color admission to its orders, passed a rescript in 1780 forbidding lodges of any other nationality on its territories.[45] On an island as heterogeneously populated as St. Thomas, this restriction effectively stymied freemasonry for nearly three decades. Finally, in 1818, a group of British masons determined to establish their own temple on the island, and applied to the United Grand Lodge of England for a charter. To argue their cause, the

St. Thomas brethren employed the services of prominent London-based Jewish trader Isaac Lindo. Lindo was a Barbados-born merchant who had developed a deep and extensive association with British masonry, and served a term as Senior Warden of the United Grand Lodge—an achievement that had earned him the title of "Right Worshipful Brother." His endorsement of the St. Thomas merchants' application was likely influential, for the Lodge approved the charter on December 10, 1818. With approval in hand, the brethren then appealed to St. Thomas Commandant Casimir von Scholten for his support of the lodge; and on April 16, 1819, he granted their petition. Thus began the masonic history of St. Thomas, with a British temple established on Danish soil.[46]

Of the sixteen founding members of the Lodge, which later became known as Harmonic Lodge 356 E. C., four were Jewish: Samuel Hoheb served as First Senior Warden; Elias H. Lindo was First Junior Warden; and Elias Charles Mendes Da Costa and Moses D'Azevedo appeared as charter members.[47] The next year, Samuel Hoheb became the Worshipful Master of the Lodge, beginning a stretch that would see Jewish Masters presiding for forty-one of the Lodge's first fifty years.[48] Included among these was Isaac Lindo, the merchant who first represented the St. Thomas petition to the United Grand Lodge of England; he had moved down to St. Thomas in 1830 after his business failed in London.[49]

The importance St. Thomas Jews had in the mercantile industry could also be seen through the career of Nathan Levy. In 1818, the Baltimore-born Levy—who had by that time been a long-term resident and U.S. commercial agent on St. Thomas—was appointed United States consul of the island.[50] As American Consul, Levy zealously promoted his birth country's interests, developing in the process a tumultuous relationship with several island merchants. He further asserted an observant Jewish identity in this role, and refused to do business on the Sabbath.[51] Several times residents accused him of partaking in questionable business transactions; and other complaints filed against him pointed to social patterns considered publicly scandalous. Disgruntled merchant Joseph O'Reilly, for example, unhappy with his treatment at the hands of the consul, appealed to President John Quincy Adams in a letter that closed with a personal attack on Levy's lifestyle:

> This N Levy is a Jew and lives with a Black Woman and frequently Walks the Streets with her arm in arm to the mortification of all the Americans who are under the painfull necessity of witnessing the Same for the correctness of this

statement, I beg leave to refer your Excellency to the following most Respectable Houses on the Island . . . and in fact to anyone who knows him.[52]

It appears, however, that such accusations caused little of the political indignation O'Reilly hoped to inspire. The U.S. Government apparently found Levy valuable enough to retain until his voluntary resignation in 1832. From the synagogue, meanwhile, his purported domestic situation spurred no known reaction. Quite possibly, the wardens simply interpreted the union as a non-marriage, and therefore outside of the congregation's jurisdiction. Though it might have shocked visiting Americans on the island, the occurrence was common enough in the Caribbean to pose significantly less of a moral dilemma.

The island's more immediate concerns centered around its ability to maintain a central role within the world's communication network. St. Thomas, as a major shipping entrepôt, was a channel for international mail, thus making the island one of the richest confluences of information in the hemisphere. The local *Tidende*, published twice weekly for the St. Thomas mercantile community, commonly kept its readers up to date by reprinting stories from recently delivered international newspapers. In this manner, the island's residents could keep up expeditiously with the most important happenings in their respective countries of origin.

For the Jews, the editor's choice of stories to print proved particularly interesting. Between 1820 and 1825, for example, any resident who opened up the *Tidende* could read articles on "Mr. Rothschild, Jew Banker" (February 15, 1820), tensions within the Jewish community of Curaçao (July 11, 1820), the world Jewish population (March 1, 1822), "The Jewish New Year" (February 26, 1823), "Persecution and Tolerance" of the Jews (September 27, 1823), and a poem entitled "The Israelite's Song" (June 27, 1824). Earlier, in 1819, when American Jewish nationalist Mordecai Manuel Noah publicized his vision for creating a new Jewish colony called Ararat in upstate New York, St. Thomas residents could read all the pleas and arguments as they appeared in successive issues of the paper. The frequent references to and discussions of Jewish topics in such a public space likely served as a demystifying factor for the at-large population, and contributed to a peaceful and open co-existence between Jewish and non-Jewish islanders. The Jewish community, meanwhile, became one of the best informed in the world, regularly learning about Jewish coreligionists around the globe, and taking action appropriately.

The friendly environment the Jews experienced on St. Thomas clearly led them to expect sustained prosperity. Consequently, the Hebrew Congregation devoted a significant amount of energy in the 1820s to improving its religious infrastructure. With its current cemetery ground filling up, the Jewish community purchased a new plot of land, and began to prepare it for use. Part of a larger area of the island known as Estate Altona, the site lay on the main road at the outskirts of town, near the cemeteries of several other religious bodies. On November 15, 1822, surveyors sized the plot at 26,025 square feet, and marked off the grounds with six wooden posts.[53] The land would remain empty for fifteen more years; yet its preparation reflected the optimism with which the Jewish community viewed the future.

During the same year, newspaper advertisements selling property on Skidengade ceased. In their place were offers for lots on the more gentrified "Crystal Gade."[54] Once a backwoods receptacle for the town's filth, the steeply angled street now had a synagogue and several respectable merchants as residents. For both physical and social reasons, the vulgar label could no longer apply. Many local stories exist explaining the origins of the new name, from the chandelier of a particularly rich street resident, to the existence of a namesake of London's famous Crystal Palace that may have been built atop the hill. But whatever the source, the change reflected a rising level of respectability in the area, and its transformation from a slum into a decent and desirable place to live.[55]

With the congregation growing, the Jews decided once again to mobilize to construct a permanent house of worship. They organized a collection for the new building, and began to clear their Crystal Gade property. As each of the walls went up, the structure no doubt generated substantial interest from both visitors and residents. Sharing the Jews' expectations, all islanders looked forward to reviewing the outcome. Finally, by the middle of 1823, the workers finished, and the building was readied for presentation.[56]

The new synagogue's dedication ceremony took place on July 18. Planned with a poetic sense of contrast, the day of celebration came right on the heels of *Tisha B'Av*, a traditional day of mourning and fasting that commemorated the biblical destruction of both temples in Jerusalem. From the sorrow of the night, the readings of exile, the prayers of despair and loss, the Jews emerged the next evening with joy, hope, and celebration, joining with the entire town and island government to consecrate their new spiritual home on the island.

"A Monument to the Glory of the Supreme Being, has been erected in the spot where formerly was situated [the] Synagogue," marvelled the newspaper correspondent who later described the dedication ceremony.[57] Sharing these sentiments was a throng of people who lined the streets at five o'clock that afternoon, hoping to enter the synagogue and attend the event. With the "Ceremony Masters" (presumably the synagogue wardens) directing the seating, all the pews inside the "Monument"—both men's and women's sections— filled quickly.

The service began at six, when Reverend Pinto strode to the new reader's desk and commenced leading the congregation in prayers specialized for the occasion. Yet, as the wardens well knew, the guests were not done arriving. "Shortly after [the service began], His Excellency Commissary General of War, J. Søbøtker, Governor of this Island and its Dependencies, made his appearance, surrounded by a brilliant suite of Civil and Military Officers." The Ceremony Masters were prepared for the visit, and led the royal representatives to their "distinguished places" in the synagogue, from which they observed the remarkable proceedings.

As part of the consecration ceremony, the Israelite congregation invited all the island's clergy to the reader's table. Together in what the *Tidende* correspondent styled a "family reunion," the group of holy men graced the building with honor and pride as the islanders stood gazing in approval. In full view of all, the united ecumenical presence confirmed the synagogue as a house of prayer equal to all others on St. Thomas. The correspondent continued by describing the events on the floor of the synagogue:

> We admired above all the sublime and religious emotion, the decency and harmony which reigned in this sacred Place when the Rulers [of the congregation] brought forth from the Tabernacle the Five Books of Moses (Pentateuch) richly ornamented and surmounted with Crowns of Silver, and walked in procession seven times round the Interior of the Temple, stopping each time at the Altar [Reader's desk]; after the seventh one, the President of the Community with a distinct and audible voice and with a characteristic warmth of love for our august Sovereign FREDERICK the 6th, elevated his hands high towards the Omnipotent, addressing to Him the Prayer of the Hebrew Community for the prosperity of the King, the Royal Family, the Governor General of the Danish islands, the Governor and other magistrates of St. Thomas; the idea of reciting the same in a language (English) more generally known than Hebrew, in which it is ordinarily read . . . is worth applause.

Purifying and sanctifying the synagogue through the biblically derived ritual, the synagogue president also made sure to keep the consecration accessible to all who attended, Jew and non-Jew alike, by conducting the proceedings in a commonly understood language and acknowledging throughout the royal and political forces that made the event possible.

At the end of the service, the congregation called for contributions to their fund for the indigent. All gave diligently. "By a voluntary impulse the assistants of other congregations, among the number of whom we had the pleasure to observe his Excellency the Governor, [followed suit and] participated in this pious and charitable work." The new building, clearly visible from the harbor, became a proud part of the Charlotte Amalie skyline as the spectators recessed to their homes. That evening, the joy and happiness surrounding the occasion extended beyond the Jewish community.

Five days later, the Tidende printed an account of the service under the headline "Israelitish Temple," for "our Readers who were not present at its Inauguration." Considering the amount of time that elapsed between the event and its retelling, the detail of the analysis, taking up a full column and a half, certainly stood as an honor to the ceremony.

Times of celebration were not the only opportunities to burnish the Jewish community's image within island society. It was also up to the congregation's president—in conjunction with the Board—to deal with potentially embarrassing episodes in order to maintain the synagogue's status as a responsible Jewish authority and upstanding community organization. Such was the situation for Elias H. Lindo in 1826. Although Lindo would eventually go on to establish himself as a Jewish studies scholar and translator of some renown in England, his several decades as a merchant on St. Thomas appeared to be highlighted with an incident "[d]uring his presidentship of the congregation," at which "he felt himself called upon to interpose in preventing an illegal marriage. The matter was ultimately referred to the King of Denmark, who confirmed the decision of Mr. Lindo and his coadjutors."[58] While definitive identification of the people involved in this controversy is elusive, there is a significant possibility that it had to do with the disputed relationship between two people who would become the parents of one of St. Thomas's most famous natives.

In 1805, the island's land tax records mention Isaac Petit as the owner of one slave. A thirty-one-year-old enterprising Frenchman who came down to St. Thomas to open shop, Petit had a somewhat tragic career on the island. Land tax records and the synagogue's register show that over the next few years Petit married a woman named Esther; the two produced a daughter whose name is unknown and a son Joseph. A second son Moses was born in

1811, but died within a year. Twin girls, delivered on January 9 and 10, 1813, died so soon after being born they were not entered in the congregation's list of births. Finally, in late October of the same year, Esther bore the couple's first surviving son, David. Samuel, the only child of the union to be married on St. Thomas, followed in 1815. Soon after this, however, the family suffered two crushing blows. Isaac Petit's first-born son, Joseph, died in January 1817; memorial verses published in the *Tidende* reflected how devastating the loss must have been to the bereaved father.[59] Just three months later—twelve days after the birth of the couple's third daughter Hannah—Esther Petit died, probably from complications during childbirth.

By 1818, Isaac had remarried, this time to Rachel Monsanto Pomié, daughter of French merchant Moses Monsanto Pomié, who had fled St. Domingue for St. Thomas in the early 1790s. It is likely that financial security was an important reason for the union. Moses Pomié was a prominent merchant on the island with a good business sense—something Petit may well have needed considering his financial and familial obligations at the time. In this new arrangement, the couple seemed to subsist reasonably well, running business affairs over the next several years with little public comment. They also produced four more children: Joseph in 1819, Rebecca in 1822, Abigail in 1823, and Isaac in 1824. The last child was a sign, however, of the final tragedy in Isaac Petit's life. Six months before their last child's birth, the senior Petit died, aged fifty years old. Rachel was left alone to tend to her seven children and step-children.

Although documentary evidence is lacking, family history has it that Isaac Petit, in his will, left the family business affairs to his nephew Abraham Gabriel Frederick Pissarro of Bordeaux, France. A stipulation of this bequest was that Pissarro maintain a friendly relationship with Isaac's widow Rachel. Frederick Pissarro, accepting the charge, came down to St. Thomas around 1825 and quickly received his Burgher Brief. It seems he made an efficient and persuasive business partner, and his name began to appear in the local papers by early August, 1825 under the title "Pissaro, fils." As a companion to Rachel Pomié, moreover, he was even more successful. In February, 1826, he and Rachel gave birth to a son, Joseph Gabriel. Eight months later, the couple publicly announced through an ad in the *Tidende* that "by Licence from His Most Gracious Majesty King FREDERICK VI," they had been married "according to the Israelitish ritual."[60]

The announcement set off alarms among the wardens of the synagogue. According to the Board's response in the next issue of the paper, the ceremony had been solemnized "without the knowledge of the Rulers and Wardens of the Synagogue."[61] Rather than applying to the board for a marriage license, and organizing the wedding through the centralized powers of the island's Jewish community, Pissarro and Pomié, the synagogue alleged, had disregarded the existing legal structure and applied for their license directly from the King of Denmark. It is likely the pair had their reasons, possibly including an earlier unsuccessful attempt to obtain a congregational marriage license. Why they might have been refused is a subject of speculation, though it is possible the synagogue's president deemed the union a violation of Jewish law. Perhaps Rachel Pomié had not observed the allotted period required after the death of one husband before having a child with another man; or perhaps the couple was initially viewed as aunt and nephew—a biblically forbidden relationship, even though it had been created by marriage. Whatever the case, Pissarro and Pomié's quest for a license took them outside the accepted administrative pathways; that the King of Denmark had agreed to their appeal served as a slap in the face for the legal and spiritual authority of the Hebrew Congregation.

Thus began a yearlong campaign to validate the St. Thomas synagogue's authority, with the Pissarro wedding in the center. Letters detailing the circumstances behind the marriage and asking for responsa were apparently sent to several chief rabbis, probably including those of London, Amsterdam, and Copenhagen. Several if not all sent back answers concurring with the opinion of the synagogue leaders; and the wardens consequently sent these letters to the King of Denmark with a note of explanation. On December 26, 1827, with the King's response received, synagogue secretary Aron Wolff published the final public word on the subject. Quoting the Danish King's rescindence of his earlier permit on the grounds that the petitioners did not identify themselves as Jews, Wolff noted once and for all that the marriage was "illegal." In this manner, the congregation's integrity and place within Danish colonial society were restored.[62]

While this ruling might have been devastating in other circumstances and communities, however, it appears on St. Thomas it caused little impact either on the Pissarros' well-being or on their relationship with the synagogue. The couple's first son, though technically illegitimate, had been entered into the synagogue's protocols along with all the other births to the Jewish community in 1826. Nearly a year and a half after the controversy had ended, moreover, the couple's second son Moses was registered in the congregation's protocol of births without comment; likewise, the Pissarros' other two sons—

Jacob, born in 1830, and Aaron, born in 1833—were included in the synagogue community, written into the registers at birth. Abraham Gabriel Frederick Pissarro, meanwhile, paid dues to the synagogue in early 1831, suggesting that the family continued its commitment to the Jewish community well after the issue had been settled.[63]

In the end, then, marital status seemed to serve as little more than a sensitive political issue in the Pissarro case; to the synagogue, it served as a test case for its own religious autonomy. Once resolved, the matter did not appear to impact particularly deeply upon the island's social fabric, nor did it have much effect on the way the couple was treated. Abraham and Rachel Pissarro, meanwhile, continued to live on the island for many years, raising their children while keeping a relatively low profile in the Jewish community. Their third son Jacob, who was better known by his other name, Camille, would eventually leave St. Thomas for France, and distinguish himself as a major figure in the European art scene—becoming known by some as "the father of modern Impressionism."

December 31, known locally as Old Year's Night, was a time of celebration on St. Thomas. People of all colors and classes held balls and took to the streets to dance and drink away the final hours of the year. And Old Year's Night, 1831, was no exception. As early as four o'clock in the afternoon of December 31, large groups of slaves and "free-coloreds" paraded through the streets shouting "Old Year's Night!" in a local creole. The excitement built up from there; at nine in the evening, the town broke loose in a flurry of activity: drums, music, singing, dancing, and all sorts of frivolity. The lower classes—slaves and poor free-coloreds—celebrated in the streets, dancing to the sounds of an African-derived drum called the *gumbe*.[64] More dancers packed a tent constructed of palm leaves on the side of the town, and filled several shanty homes, as the *gumbe* pounded on all night.

To the upper classes, both black and white, such dances were not "regular," and the drums "sound[ed] very hard and [made] a great deal of noise."[65] In contrast, as the year ticked away, they spent the time pacing through traditional mazurkas and waltzes at private balls, revelling in European finery and local high culture. Although blacks and whites generally held their soirées separately, their intentions and aesthetic values were essentially the same. Several free-coloreds on St. Thomas owned businesses, received strong educations, and held positions of high financial responsibility; and such parties were part and parcel of their success.[66]

Drink—especially the cheap, locally produced rum—probably flowed freely at all the events, tinging the air with gaiety and abandon. By the time the fire bell began ringing at the fort, many were too inebriated to react properly.

Immediately, the tone of the evening turned from frivolity to alarm. Those who could shook off their drink and began to organize. The Brand Major and Vice-Brand Major hurried to their stations and took two of the island's four fire engines to the scene of the blaze, a two-story wooden building on Commandant Gade, at the eastern border of Queen's Quarter.[67] By the time they arrived, the fire was burning out of control. It quickly overcame the efforts of an army of axmen and spread along the "narrow street . . . surrounded by Lots covered with Wood as dry as timber."[68] One engine was forced to retreat. The two remaining fire engines came over Crystal Gade, attempting to prevent the fire's advance up the hill. But the persistent Christmas breezes compounded the scarcity of water in the area, making the engines no match for the flames.[69] One of those fighting the fire likened the Brand Corps to an army "unsupplied with ammunition."

One house after the next fell victim to the spreading conflagration. As a last-ditch effort, one engine found a place to fill its water tank, and the Brand Corps subsequently rolled it over to the house of Captain D'Azevedo, which was next in the path of destruction, and the only structure standing between the fire and the synagogue. The Vice Brand Major carried a hose onto the property, with hopes of halting the fire and saving the area. But as he raised the hose to wet the house down, it burst into flame, "and all hopes were lost." "Captain D'Azevedo's House having caught [fire]," a Brand Corps Man later recalled, "great exertions were made to save the Synagogue by Mr. August Schon, and some other Gentlemen,—but their endeavours proved ineffectual." The beautiful house of prayer, just eight years old, burned like all the other buildings before it.[70]

New Year's Day, 1832, was a day of mourning. Although not nearly as destuctive as the 1804 fire, the evening's blaze destroyed most of the residences in Queen's Quarter—between 800 and 1,200 structures in total—and caused over three million rigsdalers in damage.[71] Fortunately, the waterfront warehouses remained intact due to the post-1806 insurance requirements that they be built of fireproof materials, thus preserving vast fortunes of stored goods. Yet this was no salve to the substantial immediate losses of the island, which once again left many homeless.

The Jews found themselves spirtually exiled. Their eight-year-old syna-gogue building, the center of their religious world, had been destroyed for the third time in less than thirty years. Smoldering ashes were all that existed from these decades of growth and prosperity. Yet there was not much time to lament, for life inevitably continued, dragging the whole island along with it. And soon, once again, the town began to rebuild.

CHAPTER 3

Rebuilding
1831–1833

> I will praise thee; for thou hast heard me, and art become my
> salvation. The stone which the builders refused is become
> the head stone of the corner. This is the Lord's doing; it is
> marvelous in our eyes.
>
> —Psalm 118:21–23. Translation taken from *Sanct*
> *Thomæ Tidende*, September 14, 1833.

*A*fter the fire, St. Thomas experienced several weeks of
hardship. Water, depleted from several area cisterns to fight the fire, again
became a precious commodity. With so many houses burnt to the ground,
shelter was rare and came at a premium. The smell of smoke no doubt also
haunted the island's residents for weeks afterward. A few merchants, such as
Moses Elias Levy, closed up their firms and headed to other areas.[1] Most of
the exiles, however, were wives, children, and spinsters who left the island
with the expectation of returning once conditions improved. Hannah Julien,
for example, took a temporary sojourn in St. Croix, leaving her mulatto servant Reyna to tend the house and sell some of the furniture; she returned before the year ended.[2] Others followed similar paths to escape the difficulties
that would disrupt life in Charlotte Amalie.

The majority of the island's merchants stayed to rebuild their businesses.
Although their decisions showed confidence in the port's future, they also
reflected one of the great saving graces of the destruction. Thanks to the insurance companies' demands for fireproof buildings after the 1806 confla-

gration, many of the warehouses had survived the fire, and remained poised along the shoreline ready to carry on trade. The mercantile industry, as a result, rebounded from the fire with remarkable speed: by the end of 1832, a number of merchants were enjoying record sales, and several stores exceeded $100,000 in gross income for the year.[3] Business successes in turn brought more resources to the island, and presumably accelerated the pace of the city's rebuilding.

It is possible that members of the Hebrew Congregation recognized the potential for rapid reconstruction of its sanctuary. Less than two weeks after the fire, the congregation's wardens placed an ad in the paper announcing collections for the construction of a new, stone synagogue building.[4] The announcement was premature, and little came of it at first; but it disclosed the great importance a new communal structure had as a symbolic and practical necessity for Jewish life on St. Thomas.

The Old Year's Night fire proved to be the last of St. Thomas's devastating blazes. Following the success of the fireproof warehouses, the St. Thomas government revised its building codes for the burnt area, prohibiting wooden buildings on the town's main street, requiring fire-resistant roofing tiles to replace all wooden ones, and offering strong financial and legal incentives for building non-wooden houses.[5] Although adherence to such regulations remained pricey for property owners, concern for the island's safety and favorable insurance rates far outweighed the initial capital outlay.[6] Stone buildings were guaranteed to be solid investments, protecting against hurricanes as well as fires. Moreover, the large scale of destruction in Charlotte Amalie increased demand for craftsmen and building materials, which consequently came in great supply to the island and drove prices down. By 1837, according to J. P. Nissen, a fireproof store cost $3,000 to $5,000 to construct, about a third of the $10,000 to $14,000 price tag of 1805.[7]

Generally, builders had two options when erecting "fireproofs": brick or rubble masonry.[8] Brick was the more expensive option. Although St. Thomas did not produce bricks in quantity, purchasers could buy them at the wharves, where they were imported from Europe in the holds of cargo ships. The bricks served as ballast, weighing shipping vessels down in the water until they reached their destinations. Once a ship anchored, workers would extract the bricks—which came in yellow, red, and pink-hued varieties, perhaps depending upon the nation of origin—and replace them with sugar, rum, molasses, and other merchandise for export. It is likely that for many, bricks were too costly to constitute the only material for building constuction. More commonly they were used to supplement other forms of construction, filling in where smooth surfaces were important, such as wall linings and window casings and ovens.[9]

The more popular and less expensive construction technique was rubble masonry. Rubble masonry houses comprised a jumble of quarried stones, broken bricks, shells, and other rough building materials held together by a local mortar mixture. These items were placed in thick, vaguely even rows, giving the walls shape and stability through careful arrangement and liberal helpings of mortar. Once the walls themselves had been shaped, brick embellishments could be added where more even or visible work was necessary. Builders finished the job by applying a sealing coat of plaster to slow erosion and produce a more polished appearance. The result was a building that, while not as aesthetically organized as brick, was nonetheless just as strong. This was the method by which the new synagogue would be built.

Starting in late April 1832, the wardens of the Hebrew Congregation began a second, more successful campaign to raise the money for their new building. Purchasing space in the *Tidende,* they announced: "The Subscription List for raising a Fund for the rebuilding of the Synagogue of this Island, lies open at the Store of [synagogue president Aron Wolff] for Signatures."[10] The ad ran for over six weeks, and implored merchants of all faiths to assist in the effort. In the meantime, an international drive was mounted to bring in additional funds for the congregation. J. H. De Sola ran a similar collection in St. Croix. In Jamaica, the trading house of DeCordova, Esq., carried another subscription list. Appeals for help also went out to friends and relatives in London, Hamburg, Santo Domingo, Maracaibo, Caracas, Curaçao, and probably New York and Amsterdam.[11] Aid efforts of this type were common in both Jewish and non-Jewish colonial circles, due to frequent natural disasters and economic hardship. Many colonial communities faced similar situations, and recognized their obligation to help the cause, confident that aid would return in kind if they needed assistance. Because of their close connections to congregations around the world, however, the efforts of the St. Thomas Jews proved especially widespread.

The synagogue wardens set an example for the congregation, and contributed between $32.00 and $192.00 each.[12] Yet probably by design, the first signers of the list carried a far greater weight on the island: Governor-General of the Danish West Indies Peter von Scholten pledged $64.00; the St. Thomas governor gave $32.00; and four more officials in the St. Thomas government pledged $32.00, $25.60, $25.60, and $16.00 respectively. More than simply generous, the officers' contributions gave government sanction to the Jews' work, paving the way for gifts from the rest of the community.[13]

Over subsequent weeks, the list grew. Emanuel Alvares Correa contributed $50. Jacob Mendes Monsanto wrote his name down for $200. Frederick Pissarro, apparently bearing little prejudice after his run-in with the wardens in 1830, pledged $16. While most of the initial names were Jewish, many others quickly joined in: the firm of McBean, Murray and Co. signed soon after the wardens, promising $16. Two island lawyers, Stenersen and Saraw, gave $8 and $6 respectively. Free-black merchant Jacob de Castro's firm donated $20. The number of consigning names multiplied over the following months, until it resembled a who's who of island businesses and city dwellers.[14]

At 2:15 P.M. on Tuesday, December 8, 1832, the Jewish community congregated at the spot of their destroyed synagogue for the first time in almost a year. Accompanied by "His Excellency [Governor Rosenørn] and suite, and a number of the most respectable inhabitants of this island," the Jews marked the start of their new synagogue's construction with a cornerstone ceremony that had all the trimmings of a society event.[15] A large cornerstone stood on the area, awaiting "placement" by the governor. Carved into the side was an inscription that gave homage to all those involved in the building's rebirth:

> In GOD the ALMIGHTY's name. In the reigning period of the people's father, King FREDERIK the Seventh, Anno 1832, the 18th December; does His Excellency Governor von Rosenørn, Knight of Dannebrog . . . place the corner stone of this building, soon to be the SYNAGOGUE, where the previous one stood here, which was destroyed in the island fire of 31 Dec., 1831. [Accomplished t]hrough the edification of income in a general subscription whereby the island's inhabitants of all classes and of all religions had contributed most liberally.

After the governor placed the stone, the congregation sang a psalm of celebration, and then proceeded across the street to synagogue president Aron Wolff's house for "an excellent *d'jeuné.*"[16] That evening, the air of celebration continued as Judah Cappé and his wife sponsored a dinner and ball that extended into the wee hours of the morning.

Construction went into full swing by 1833. According to oral histories, the synagogue followed the blueprints of a French architect commissioned expressly for the occasion.[17] Several "Ladies of the Congregation" donated their slaves—who would otherwise be selling products in town, assisting with home responsibilities, or rented out to another person—to aid in construction.[18] Crystal Gade resident Captain Moses D'Azevedo gave the synagogue fifty tons of stones for construction. David Naar offered to transport these and all other building materials to the site. For the mortar, Meriam Ezra, Raphael De Meza, and Benjamin Levy sent over 150 hogsheads of lime; Solomon Levy donated the sand.[19] Workers combined these two ingredients with molasses—a cheap and available byproduct of rum and sugar manufacturing—to make a sticky paste that effectively kept the stones together.[20]

By March, the collection neared completion, now including $315 from London (with $100 from the German Congregation alone), $98 from Jamaica, $66 from Caracas, and $58.46 from St. Croix. Much of the island had also taken some stake in the building, and waited with interest for its reopening. The Hebrew Congregation wardens, as a token of thanks, resolved to publicize the wide base of support for their project. Thus, in an unprecedented and grand gesture of gratitude, the synagogue secured the entire front page of the local paper for three successive issues, printing the entire list of donors and their donations, "for the satisfaction of those concerned."[21] In the whole history of the Tidende, such a dramatic action would never be repeated.

A week and a half later, the paper printed an unabridged account of the dedication of a new synagogue in Barbados, noting that, "it is well worth the perusal of our Hebrew friends in this community. It is said that the building is beautiful, and will hold 300 persons."[22] Though the timing was coincidental, the *Tidende's* decision to reprint the account nonetheless helped to heighten expectations for the St. Thomas synagogue, possibly even encouraging some friendly competition between islands; no one yet saw the completed building on Crystal Gade, but many probably hoped for a building of similar description.

The Jews continued to pray in a temporary sanctuary for several months, where they stored the congregation's six Torah scrolls in wait for the day they could return them to a permanent home.[23] Finally, in September, construction on the new synagogue ended as workers placed the last touches on the building and prepared it for dedication. Merchants arriving in the harbor could see the entrance facing them, ready to open its doors in triumph. Once again, the ceremony would be cause for an entire island to celebrate along with the Jewish community.

The festivities began at the start of the final day of the Hebrew calendar, with a symbolic march from past to future. "About six o'clock on Thursday evening, [September 12, the start of the twenty-ninth of Elul,] the [Hebrew] Congregation assembled in their temporary place of worship, and shortly after proceeded to the New Synagogue in the usual ceremonial order."[24] They carried with them the centerpieces of their tradition: six Torahs, containing the basis of Jewish history, story, and wisdom. A lamp, soon to signify the ever-present vigilance of the Almighty in the building, likely was in the hands of the person leading the procession, ready to be installed into the new site.

The building that greeted the procession was a beautiful gothic-style edifice.[25] Recessed several yards from the road, it was unique on Crystal Gade as the only structure oriented along compass lines.[26] Turning from the street onto a first set of marble steps, the congregation entered into a small plaza. Across this plaza and up a second set of steps was the sanctuary entrance, a covered platform flanked by eight ionic columns.[27] Standing from this vantage point, the congregants could peer through a tall, pointed-arch doorway into the new synagogue building.

Inside, dark mahogany furniture arranged according to the European Sephardic model provided a stark contrast against the light sand-covered tile floor and white plaster walls. On the east wall, the holy ark, or *Ahal*, served as a focal point.[28] Placed so that worshipers who faced it would face the traditional direction of Jerusalem, the mahogany cabinet would soon serve as home to the congregation's Scrolls of the Law. Towering above the *Ahal*, a pair of tablets several feet high leaned toward the congregation, silently proclaiming the words of the Ten Commandments.[29] In front of the west wall, facing the *Ahal*, was an ornately carved wooden reader's desk, or *Tebah*. The beautiful desk provided steps that led to a back area, where readers could recite from the Torah while facing the congregation. A small gated vestibule in front of the reader's desk contained another small podium, to be used for speaking and sermonizing. Opposite the front entrance was a mirror image opening on the north side, that looked out onto an open patio, also meant for gathering.

Traditionally, Sephardic synagogues contained different areas for women and men to pray. Most placed the women in an elevated gallery far apart from the actual goings-on of the service. St. Thomas's sanctuary, while continuing the separation principle, contained what was perhaps the most liberal layout in the Jewish world. A line of symmetry stretched across the center of the room, from the reader's desk to the holy ark. Several sets of mahogany pews radiated outward from this line. The first few sets, resting on the synagogue floor in the center of the room, served as the men's section. Further back on both sides, a rise of about two or three feet and a waist-high mahogany screen designated the women's section. Elevated, and placed immediately next to the windows, the St. Thomas women prayed in full view of the men, with a marvelous vantage point of the service; and in the evenings, they would be the first beneficiaries of the island breezes that would circulate and cool the space.[30]

Four thick ionic columns held up a domed ceiling, which was in turn supported from above by a latticework of wooden beams and covered by a more conventional red-shingle roof. Bronze sidelamps, donated by Isaac D'Azevedo, complemented with other chandeliers, helped to bathe the synagogue in candlelight at night.[31] The effect of this new and holy building, glowing in the setting sun, could have been little short of wondrous.

At seven o'clock, the governor, his entourage, and "many respectable persons," joined the Jewish community, taking their seats in the pews. A choir of "young ladies and gentlemen" began to sing: "This is the day which the Lord hath made; we will rejoice and be glad in it."[32] With great ceremony, the consecration service began.

The reader presided. At the front entrance appeared a procession of seven congregants. The first man, the oldest member of the congregation, carried the lamp that would soon hold the "eternal flame." Then two individuals identified as an older and younger "priest" performed the initiating ritual.[33] "The Elder Priest received and lighted the lamp, pronouncing the Benediction, and . . . then handed [it] to a younger Priest, who placed it in the stand appropriated for it."[34] As the flame burned, sanctifying the building in the eyes of the congregation, attention turned back to the entrance, where the six other men held the congregation's Torahs. The reader and the five synagogue wardens approached the men, took the Torahs, and paraded them around the synagogue. The choir sang the traditional Sephardic hymn *"Baruch HaBa,"* "Blessed be he that cometh in the name of the Lord." Infused with a double meaning, their serenade addressed both the Torahs and the congregation, welcoming them to their new, and permanent, spiritual home.

The holy procession then gathered at the reader's desk, facing the ark. Together, the reader and wardens led the congregation in prayers for "Our Beloved Sovereign and the Royal Family, as also for their Excellencies the Governor-General, the Governor, and all the other Magistrates," as well as all present members of the Hebrew Congregation. As the choir sang of the glory of God, the reader and wardens traversed the sanctuary to the *Ahal*, and deposited the Torahs in their new mahogany case.

After this, Isaac Lindo rose to the podium and gave the synagogue's inaugural address. He based his speech on Kings 8:13: "I have surely built thee a house to dwell in, a settled place for thee to abide in forever." According to an account of the ceremony, Lindo knew how to affect his audience. On this emotional day, he delivered his sermon "most emphatically . . . [making] the Congregation deeply impressed with the most pathetic feelings of reverence and devotion."

As in 1823, a call for poor fund offerings followed that received a generous and liberal response. Then the choir sang a concluding hymn, and the service ended.

Most left quite impressed with the whole ceremony, with the newspaper recalling "the whole of [the Consecration] was conducted in a manner worthy of a people who were the first worshippers of the *'true and living GOD.'*" For the St. Thomas Jewish population, this service crowned a partnership with the island, the Danish government, and the world Jewish community which brought them from the depths of despair to the heights of elation. A new building, a new spirit and newfound prosperity heralded the Hebrew Congregation into a bright, exciting, and active era. Never again would the Jewish population go homeless.

CHAPTER 4

A Battle of Reforms
1833–1848

*T*he 1830s saw a dramatic divergence of fortune for the two major industries of the Danish West Indies. Sugar production, once a thriving and profitable business, became increasingly unfeasible. Although the American and European markets for sugar continued to grow quickly, competition between islands and the imposition of a free trade system drove prices down substantially.[1] Costs to planters, however—especially those who could no longer import slaves—began to rise. On top of this, Cuba's nineteenth-century emergence as a large-scale sugar power wreaked havoc on smaller producers. St. Croix was one such victim: From an estimated 23,000 tons of sugar produced at its height in 1821, St. Croix's sugar production dropped almost 70 percent by 1840, to 7,000 tons.[2] Further complicating the situation was the question of slave emancipation, which began to earn serious consideration within the Danish government in the 1830s. With no backup plan to cover the loss of revenue, the St. Croix economy began to slip into dire straits.

Plantation society on St. Thomas and St. John experienced a similar descent as the sugar trade withered. Yet within the bounds of Charlotte Amalie, an altogether different situation existed. Trade, the town's major industry, continued to strengthen, reinforcing St. Thomas's reputation as an international entrepôt. As the 1830s progressed, Charlotte Amalie took on the qualities of a major port city. A local theater provided cultural enrichment, serving as a stage to visiting musicians and acting troupes. Prosperous merchants constructed large houses on the hills facing the harbor, where they occasionally held high-society balls resounding with mazurkas and waltzes. Jobs were common and plentiful, attracting numerous whites and free-coloreds from the declining, surrounding plantations. Already by 1831, over eighty percent of St. Thomas's population—free, white, and slave—lived in the city, a proportion that would remain steady for the rest of the century.[3] Business ascended to the highest stature in the Virgin Islands, its profits often helping to offset the planters' losses.

Although the white population dominated the island's business and governmental affairs, the city's most numerous residents were free people of color.[4] They generally worked as laborers or craftsmen on the island, having attained their freedom by manumission, self-purchase, or emigration to St. Thomas. Although some, including Jacob De Castro, attained positions of respect and prominence as traders, most still suffered under strict government-imposed regulations. This continued until April 18, 1834, when the government passed a proclamation granting citizenship and full rights to all non-slaves, regardless of color. Free-coloreds could now become official burghers and open their own shops, working side by side with their white counterparts. Though it would take years for the black population to attain any semblance of true political equality, the announcement illustrated the prosperity and free enterprise that existed in the city, not to mention the liberal atmosphere that would, fourteen years later, emancipate the slaves.

In this setting, the new synagogue began its tenure as a center for Jewish life on Crystal Gade. Well chronicled in the *Tidende* during its building and rededication, the building quickly was integrated into island life as a spiritual home for the Jews, and as a beacon for Jewish congregants and travellers alike. Though obscured from view to those climbing Crystal Gade, the synagogue's façade projected clearly into the harbor, its columns, open palms, and pointed entrance appearing just above the waterfront stores to welcome incoming ships. Its congregation numbered approximately four hundred persons who together comprised more than twenty-two percent of the island's white population.[5]

On August 4, 1835, the Danish government passed a Royal ordinance allowing Jews the right to marry non-Jews upon obtaining proper governmental permission.[6] There is no direct evidence explaining why this law came into being, but societal context seems to indicate that it was more a reminder for common morality than a special request by the Jews. St. Thomas's population always had a large number of couples, but few of these pairs ever bothered to take marriage vows. Although preached day in and day out in the churches, much of the population regarded marriage as an unnecessary formality.[7] For many there were good reasons. A number of the white men on St. Thomas, including the governor, took up with free-colored women while their wives remained in Europe or the United States. The non-white population, meanwhile, never found the institution particularly useful or practical, despite several attempts by the government to provide incentives.[8] According to J. P. Nissen's estimates, fewer than 260 legally married couples lived in Charlotte Amalie out of over 12,000 inhabitants. Illegitimate children abounded, though all indications suggest that while these children did not conform to the desired moral standard on the island, they were brought up with little societal stigma.

It appears that the Jews were the only group to enforce marriage successfully as an important part of their social structure. Of the estimated 260 married couples—white and black—throughout the city, the Hebrew Congregation claimed 60, far above its overall proportion of the total population.[9] Thus, while integrated in nearly every other way with the rest of the community, the synagogue population appeared to use marriage as a method of defining and sustaining a distinct Jewish community. This value was supported by the congregation's protocols: Through the end of the nineteenth century, the synagogue only recorded (and presumably endorsed) marriages between two Jews, and recognized the births of children only if they were born to two Jewish parents. While interreligious unions between Jews and non-Jews may have existed on the island, they were not encouraged during this time as part of the Jewish lifecycle. The reasons for this are potentially complicated. Jews may have imposed a stricter standard upon themselves in line with their history of social separation in European Protestant society. By demonstrating an ability to regulate themselves successfully, they could ensure governmental protection. Conversely, the Jews could have seen this as a manner of maintaining the integrity of its small community and intimate family ties. Whatever the case, social pressure to conform to both Jewish and governmental guidelines was strong in the synagogue, and the Jews' marriage rate was thus correspondingly high.

Of course, like others on the island, some Jews defiantly followed their own paths. As mentioned earlier, for example, United States Commercial Agent Nathan Levy would openly walk the streets with his black mistress during the 1820s and 1830s. Church records from later times indicate that Jewish men usually fathered two to five births out of wedlock each year, though a significant number of these took place within monogamous, long-term relationships.[10] The new intermarriage law was probably aimed directly at such "fringe" Jews, who appeared more of an anomaly than the norm; the government, not wishing to place any stumbling block in front of their constituents' moral consciences, assured the Jews through this that at least under Danish law, the institution of marriage was more important than any religious differences. Few Jews availed themselves of the opportunity; nonetheless, this ordinance was an eerily dramatic manifestation of the enlightened, universalistic sentiments beginning to break out all over Europe.

Meanwhile, the Jews faced a local milestone surrounding a different life-cycle event. Save plots reserved for close relatives, the old Jewish cemetery filled to capacity around 1836. The congregation subsequently prepared its reserve parcel of land in Estate Altona to serve as a new burial ground.[11] Just as in the old cemetery, the congregation built a simple, octagonal burial house just inside the front entrance. Meant to store the body while the gravediggers prepared the plot for burial, it became an increasingly familiar sight as the destination of many a funeral cortège.

Deaths within the congregation almost always elicited an outpouring of sympathies from friends, neighbors, and family, especially if the deceased was well known on the island. Several received the honor of obituaries in the paper. Island merchant David Pretto Henriquez, for example, died at 10:45 P.M. on May 13, 1836, at the age of sixty-seven. On May 18, the *Tidende* mourned his passing: "With regret we have to record the loss this Community has sustained in the demise of one of its oldest and most worthy members."

As required by island law, Pretto Henriquez left an official last will and testament. Two days before his passing, as he anticipated his oncoming death, both he and his wife Rebecca signed and swore to a final draft of the will in front of a public notary and three witnesses. Reflecting a standard government-regulated format, the testament detailed the handling of the estate, named executors and heirs, and distributed funds and properties. Two other aspects of the will, however, identified it as coming specifically from a Jewish resident. The first was a traditional opening line: "In the name of God, amen!" Not nearly as common on the documents of other St. Thomians, this seemingly general phrase gave the testament a certain level of recognition as a sacred Jewish document, marking for the writer a final point in the spiritual life cycle as well as the temporal one.[12]

The other aspect of the testament that reflected Jewish authorship was a contribution to the synagogue, probably in part as a burial deposit. In a Jewish St. Thomian's will, this contribution acually came in two parts. The first was a goodwill token amount for the Danish Lutheran Church, which would be used for the island's good. This donation generally ranged from sixteen to twenty-five dollars with occasional deviances (Pretto Henriquez, for example only promised eight). Once the Jewish testator determined this, he or she seemed to face an unspoken obligation to bequeath at least the same figure to the synagogue.[13] This customary gift brought the synagogue needed revenue and helped to pay for burial services.

In addition to the will, more immediate practical concerns came to the fore once a synagogue member died. St. Thomas's constant climate of heat and humidity helped to reinforce the Jewish tradition of burying a corpse as soon as possible. Once the doctor confirmed death, members of the burial society would arrive at the house to clean and prepare the body for interment. If a person died at night, the body would have to be kept until morning, packed with ice to prevent decomposition. Members of the congregation's burial society remained to guard the corpse while the gravedigger completed his task, the solitary "drip, drip, drip" of the melting ice in the casket marking the passing time.[14] Usually the burial took place that evening or the next day: A funeral service occurred at the home of the deceased, and then a horse-drawn cart carried the coffin across the town to the Jewish cemetery. A parade of mourners followed, in a procession that frequently garnered attention from the rest of the townspeople. Once in the cemetery, the pallbearers would bring the coffin to the burial site, carrying it with rope handles. Mourners then bid their final respects and prayers, and returned home after the coffin was lowered into the ground and covered with soil. The congregation then sent away to London or New York for a gravestone, which they eventually placed atop a horizontal table of stone or brick erected over the grave. Waist-high, horizontal grave stones, although seen as non-standard or high-class in northern areas, were the rule in St. Thomas, as they were in the rest of the Caribbean region.[15]

Gravesites in the new cemetery filled in chronological order, with the first rows paralleling the right (eastern) wall and moving from the back to the front of the property. Family plots did not exist, and since many families within the St. Thomas community were large and interrelated anyway, the concept did not hold great significance. In a sense, the whole cemetery contained members of the same family.

Through this procession of events, David Pretto Henriquez, and all of his brethren, were sent to their final resting places.

In the north-eastern Caribbean, the months between May and November brought along their own kind of uneasiness. Weather generally became exceptionally hot, exacerbated by flagging trade winds. Workdays became more oppressive. The lack of wind caused ships to move more slowly to and from the harbor, causing trade to lag. But this was of comparatively little concern.

Off the west coast of Africa during this time of the year, waves of tropical disturbance formed, one after the next. They followed the trade currents westward—along the same path slave ships knew as the "Middle Passage." Most of these disturbances remained harmless, gathering a little rain and wind, but often disintegrating before reaching the Leeward islands. On occasion, however, one would develop while crossing the Atlantic, amassing strength and moisture as it approached the American continent. It would gain definition, coming to swirl clearly around a center point. Enlarging up to several hundred miles in width, packing drenching rains and containing winds near its eye upwards of one hundred miles per hour, these storms came to be known as gales or hurricanes. They were the most destructive and feared entities in the entire Caribbean region.

Even today, it is impossible to predict a hurricane's path. Although they all follow the same general route across the Atlantic, and most eventually head north parallel to the United States coast, no two hurricanes track exactly the same way. Many miss land entirely; yet even one ill-placed hurricane could easily cause untold damage and death. Two hundred years ago, preparation for such storms was impossible. Before the days of weather satellites, airplanes, and telegraphs, the only way to follow hurricanes was by word of mouth, or through the reports of packet ships chugging in from other islands. No one could know the strength or direction of a storm until it engulfed the area. To face these fearsome entities, many residents built houses with thick walls, sturdy roofs, and heavy wooden "hurricane" shutters. When the winds and the rain began to intensify, they could buckle down for the ordeal with relative ease, although security was never certain.

The onset of a hurricane is both a beautiful and a fearful thing, an experience that has no equal among meteorological phenomena. Hours before the winds pick up and the rains begin to fall, bands of darkening clouds rush across the sky, following the counterclockwise churning of the storm, and unnatural breezes interrupt the stillness of the air.[16] Slowly, over a span of several hours, the bands bring mounting winds and rain, which alternate with progressively dwindling spaces of clear weather. Soon after this, as the storm intensifies, all becomes uniform: The winds steadily pick up their pace, the rain becomes heavier, and the atmospheric pressure begins to plummet.[17] After a certain point, it is no longer safe to be outside. As the center of the storm approaches, the winds begin to send objects into flight and bend tree trunks with their force. Ships toss violently in the harbor. For most residents, this is when the time arrives to go inside to safety and wait out the rest of the storm.

The next several hours constitute a fearsome psychological battle. Even in the middle of day, the skies turn black as night. Winds scream outside, gusting across the land with enormous force. Houses shake, ready to fall apart at any moment. Metal roofs and other materials torn loose by the storm scrape down the streets with horrible sounds. Rain saturates the air and ground. Sometimes, thunder and lightning slash through the darkness, flashing with astounding rapidity. Toward the center, the storm can also spawn tornados. It is nature gone wild, unleashing everything it knows with reckless fury. For many islanders, well ensconced in their religious beliefs, the experience is tantamount to staring helplessly into the eyes of God. Once a storm is in full force, there is nothing to do except wait as it rips away at wood and rock, mind and soul.

On rare occasions, the eye of the storm moves overhead, providing a short respite of sudden calm, clear skies, and cool breezes. People occasionally go outside to observe the damage or find new shelter. Within half an hour, however, the winds are blasting away once again; and the whole process repeats itself backwards.

The damage such a storm can cause is astounding: trees defoliated, snapped off and uprooted like celery stalks; numerous houses deroofed or utterly destroyed; cargo ships either sunk in the harbor or beached several yards onto the mainland; debris strewn everywhere. Easily, life cannot return to normal for weeks or months. And rebuilding, as always, is a painful process.

Hurricanes with this magnitude of destructive force do not ravage the islands frequently—typically, they visit once every twenty to thirty years.[18] This is enough, however, to propagate stories and legends of the storms that permeate the island population. With each generation, another hurricane renews the memories and adds its own stories to the general folklore on the island. Through this the storms gain a spiritual life and significance of their own, as an accepted but feared part of Caribbean life.

For centuries in the Danish West Indies, the most active part of the hurricane season has carried a pan-religious significance. July 25 began the official storm season with an observance known as Hurricane Supplication Day.[19] Sometimes observed as a fast day, it marked a solemn time when the population gathered in its respective places of worship and prayed to the Almighty for safe and uneventful skies, calm water, and good trade.[20] Three months later, on October 25, the season ended with Hurricane Thanksgiving Day. No matter the events that took place in the ensuing months, much of the island took off from work, attending their respective divine services either to thank God for sparing their island, or to thank God for sparing their lives.[21]

The Hurricane Thanksgiving service of October 25, 1837, must have been solemn. Two and a half months earlier, on August 2, a hurricane of legendary force passed over the island, causing mass destruction. According to news reports, an earthquake hit the island that same evening, and was followed by a fire.[22] The Jewish community was particularly affected: badly injured among the numerous buildings was the synagogue, as well as the structures in both Jewish cemeteries.[23] Tending to all their personal damages, the Jews could ill-afford to handle additional repairs, and had to take up another collection to alleviate their financial onus.[24] The service ending the season thus saw several families impoverished and a synagogue in disrepair. The community, along with everyone else, searched for spiritual comfort when their material comforts were damaged. Yet the destructive year of 1837 also gave the Jews a reason to be proud: None had died in the gale, and two among the congregation, Abraham Levy and Sigismund Rothschild, put forth valiant efforts during the hurricane, and would soon be honored by the King of Denmark.[25]

The *Hazan* for the Thanksgiving service, Samuel Elias Levy Maduro, was new to the position. Born in Curaçao in 1798, Maduro took advantage of the Jewish resources there and received a good education in Jewish subjects during his youth. Coming over to St. Thomas at the age of twenty, he eventually decided to head the then leaderless congregation at the behest of several influential friends. His first year in the position, 1837, involved a great deal of adjustment, a hardship compounded by the Jewish community's inability to pay him a competitive salary.[26] Nonetheless, he remained, serving the community by leading services and officiating at Jewish rites of passage. As a non-ordained religious leader who eventually gained respect from the entire congregation, Maduro was known for "his kind and conciliatory manners, his truly religious disposition, his earnest attachment to the altar, [and] his utter disinterestedness [in political ends]."[27] He would remain in the pulpit for almost thirty years, serving as a calming voice through several of the synagogue's bitter internal conflicts.[28]

The Thanksgiving service was a time to come to terms with God's power, and to reinforce the idea of God's ultimate benevolence toward all creatures. Especially after a calamitous season, many must have found such a reconciliation necessary—and the special prayers sung by the congregation reflected this. It is possible that during this time, for example, the congregation joined to intone the hymn "O Hurricane." Attributed to Benjamin Cohen Carillon, then minister of one of the Jewish congregations in Jamaica, it remained in the St. Thomas synagogue hymnal until well into the 1960s, the only extant piece from what must have been a fascinating hurricane liturgy:

> O Hurricane! great is thy power,
> Tremendous is thy might,
> O we remember in this hour
> Thy dark and awful sight!
> But though no human care and skill
> Can e'er withdraw thy hand,
> One reigns in Zion's holy hill
> Whose fiat none withstand.
>
> Though thou canst shake both land and sea,
> Thou art a creature still;
> How measureless thy power be,
> Thou must obey His will.
> And couldst thou rage in all the sky
> Above all human thought,
> One word of Him that lives on high,
> And thou returnst to naught.
>
> We will then look on Him above,
> Whose arm alone can save
> The life, that He in endless love
> His human creatures gave.
> Nay, Hurricane, we do not fear
> Nor tremble for our lot;
> One greater yet than thee is here,
> 'Tis Israel's unit God.[29]

As a group, the Jews of the Virgin Islands comforted each other, while remaining in tune with the rest of the island. The hurricane gave everyone a common experience, a common trauma that helped to mediate what were sometimes immense and unfathomable personal losses. Simultaneously, it instilled even the most liberal and secular of Jews with a fear of God, a sense of vulnerability, and a need for some form of protection. In the end, the Jews could only look for a precarious co-existence with the hurricane, finding solace in themselves, their community, and their ever-vigilant and caring God.

———∿∿∿———

THE JEWS IN ST. THOMAS lived a cosmopolitan lifestyle. As full members of a free trading society, they spread out across town, affiliating more by socioeconomic bracket than by religious affiliation. With the exception of an occasional ceremonial winecup or Sabbath candelabrum, their possessions were little different from those of anyone else, as were their business practices. Schedules of ships and sales centered around Saturdays; while some Jews refused to open their shop doors on the Sabbath, many others had little choice, or simply did not care. The auction houses, owned by Jewish merchants Samuel Hoheb and Judah Cappé, ran their swiftest business on Saturdays, and many Jewish stores stayed open for the same reason. With full unspoken privileges as traders since the very beginning, and full citizenship from 1814, many Jews lived the lifestyles of their neighbors, identifying with Judaism only on an institutional level. Constantly balancing the Jewish and secular parts of their lives, they supported the synagogue and generally desired to propagate their faith while assimilating into the outside society.

This is well exemplified in the life and will of Emanuel Alvares Correa. Born in Curaçao in 1794, Correa moved to St. Thomas around 1816, where he set up business.[30] Two years later, he married Judith Julien, the only daughter of Abraham Julien.[31] Over the next thirteen years, the Correas had five children: Rachel, Moses (Maurice), Abraham, Gabriel, and Jacob.[32] Possibly, there were complications with Jacob's birth, because Judith passed away two months later, leaving Correa to raise his children alone. Following a custom of many St. Thomas merchants to send their children to Europe for a proper education and upbringing, Correa placed his daugher and four sons in the hands of a trustworthy friend in Altona, Denmark.[33] Correa remained in St. Thomas to cultivate his firm: Correa, Bahnsen & Company. Eventually, his business became so successful that his share alone had a value of over $66,000.[34]

Correa was affiliated with the synagogue, and likely retained some practices of Judaism. In his personal library, he owned a Holy Bible, a Hebrew Bible, at least one printed copy of the Torah, six copies of the High Holiday liturgy, the works of Roman-Jewish historian Josephus Flavius, and two books entitled *Discourses on the Jewish Religion* and *Instructions in the Mo-*

saic Religion.[35] According to custom and law, each of his children's births appeared in the synagogue register. But although Correa certainly felt a duty toward his institution, he was never particularly active in synagogue life. With the exception of a contribution to the rebuilding of the synagogue in 1833, not a single reference in the *Tidende* linked him to the Jewish community in any way.[36] Correa's attitude toward his children's religious upbringing was similarly invested: With his consent, he allowed their guardian in Altona to raise them as Christians, while asserting the children's freedom to choose a religion for themselves once they reached a mature age.[37]

In May 1837, Correa left St. Thomas for Europe, where presumably he spent some time with his children in addition to pursuing business ventures. Soon after his return on December 31, he fell mortally ill. Whether Correa's impending death gave him a change of heart, or whether he was alarmed by his observations in Altona, we shall never know. However, on January 4, the day before he died, Correa added a codicil to his will that signalled a drastic change in his religious philosophy. Facing his end, Correa desired, "That my children shall be made acquainted with the religion in which they were born and a Hebrew Master employed to teach them the custom and usage of the Jewish congregation." He appointed "Mr. David DeCastro and Mr. O. G. C. Degetau, both of Altona, to supervise the education of my Children, and to act as guardians for the same in case any thing should prevent the executors named in my will from acting."[38]

After Correa's burial, the executors of the will, business partners S. Bahnsen, John Marshall, and J. H. Osorio, sent a letter to Altona appraising Degetau of Correa's final wish. The response they received was far from conciliatory. Sixteen-year-old Rachel, the eldest child, protested upon hearing of the provision:

> Some years ago we have had a Jewish teacher for some time, but the lessons were very tedious to us and so our dear father just being here, allowed us to leave them off, and I think it would be perfectly superfluous to begin it once more, as it would expose us to great inconveniences. As we have been brought up in the Christian religion, according to the wish of our dear father, we have a predilection for it, which I think is very natural. Mr. Degetau . . . told me that whenever [he] spoke on this subject to our good father, he always said, that we could do whatever we should like, when we were old enough to reflect upon such things. Now I have attained the age and have really very often thought about it, and have always found that the Christian aggrees the most with me.
>
> As I shall be seventeen next month, and as almost all the young girls are con-

firmed with sixteen or seventeen years, I have no time to loose. I hope therefore you will have nothing against it if we get baptized.[39]

Rachel's younger brother Maurice was even more distraught with the
news, and threatened to go through a baptism against the executors' wills
should they not consent.[40]

Accompanying these letters was a badly composed note from Mr. Degctau:

> Respecting our deceased friends childeren, I have endeavoured to impress
> on their mind the will of their good father—but as disposed as I always found
> them to follow their fathers commands with veneration and obediance, they
> deffered entirely with his views of taking any more instructions in the cere-
> monials and customs of the Jewish church—Maurice and Rachel are decid-
> edly adverse to it. . . . In fact it is not surprising that these childeren after being
> brought up in the christian religion with the consent of their father and arrived
> now at the age where they distinctly can perceive all the disadvantages and
> prejudices to which the Jewish religion is still exposed in our days—should
> prefer to belong to that one which they have praticed as their own since
> infancy—
>
> As it was their fathers decided opinion to let his children have their own way
> with respect to religion as soon as they were able to judge for themselves, I am
> persuaded were he alive he would give his imidiate consent for their babtism,
> and with this consideration I am of opinion, You as their guardians ou[gh]t not
> to withold your aprobation to this act—since any delay may prove injurious to
> the future welfare of the childeren.[41]

At this point, Degetau focused on Maurice, who had decided to enter the
mercantile business; a Jewish identity, he argued, would be detrimental to
his imminent career. "I am on the look out of a good place for him either
here, Hamburg or Bremen, but I know by experience that I'l meet with
many difficulties as long as the religious obstacle is not removed," he wrote.[42]
Although such arguments appeared puzzling in the context of the Caribbean
Jewish trade, they reflected a long-standing cultural bias within Europe. Officially, Jews had the same rights in both Altona and St. Thomas. Yet whereas
Correa seemed to see such freedoms as a way for Jews to retain their religious identities while participating in a society dominated by Christians,
Degetau saw these rights as an opportunity for the Jews to join the Christian
world and eradicate all differences. Such attitudes reflected the separation

between Europe and St. Thomas, and revealed the conflicts that complicated matters for "respectable" Jews of the Caribbean.

Emanuel Correa probably took this dichotomy into account when he added his codicil, and thus did not leave anything to implication. His will, legal and binding, reflected his own views on Jewish life in European society; and though they conflicted with the views of his children and their guardian, the executors had no choice but to enforce them. Their response, dated November 3, 1838, quietly and craftily subverted Degetau's intentions with the children. "Our opinions on this subject entirely coincide with yours," they wrote back to Degetau, "and do not only join in your belief, that Mr. Correa, if alive would immediately consent, but even feel convinced, that he would cause the younger children to be baptised at the same time with Rachel and Maurice." But this was not the issue. "The consent required from us is . . . not to their baptism, but to the dispensations from such previous instruction [in Judaism]." To this extent, they charged Degetau with the responsibility of doing what he seemed least desirous to do:

> If Rachel and Maurice, as they assert, have sufficient knowledge in the Mosaic religion, it would be absurd to impede or retard the accomplishment of their intentions, by making them lose time in attending instruction in matters which they know already, and their father's provident measure might then be considered as already previously, complied with. This can however not be ascertained by us, but must be investigated by yourself, as you are near to them, and have taken the charges of their education.[43]

The fate of these children is unknown, but chances are they nominally fulfilled their father's dying wish, and subsequently converted to Christianity. This situation was not unique in Europe; at the same time, it showed the religious tensions that existed between the Sephardic merchants and their surrounding society. St. Thomas's small population, with a significant Jewish component, gave no particular advantage to Christians; thus, Jews there could wander as they wished philosophically, with little pressure to disavow their affiliation. Europe, however, represented a series of overwhelmingly Christian states, a situation that often gave Jews the choice of either facing the prejudices associated with their religion or leaving Judaism altogether. Caribbean Jews, travelling frequently from one region to another, thus faced two different standards: in the Caribbean, merchants could be nominally Jewish and remain a significant part of society. In Europe, the task was far more difficult.

One way of dealing with these religious tensions was through the institution of reforms. Sweeping across a large part of European and American Jewry during the first half of the nineteenth century, the concept was borne on a wave of new Jewish philosophy that struggled with the problem of fitting into a more accepting secular society. Nearly all of these movements emerged in the cities, where interaction between Jews and non-Jews was most intense. Committed Jewish philosophers such as Zacharias Frankel and Abraham Geiger grappled with the existing Jewish practices, calling them outdated, exclusionary, or downright embarrassing; and many suggested ways of updating Judaism to be more compatible with the "universalizing" society. These ideas caught on, though with significant controversy, and over time Reform synagogues emerged to satisfy those who wished to remain Jewish while attaining an elevated social status.

Within Europe, it was possible to split these reforming movements into two categories. The first encompassed a movement that emerged from Germany in the early nineteenth century, which spread throughout the European continent. While simutaneously posturing for their emancipation from the various national governments, these Jews began to create organized and vocal brotherhoods that sought actively to modify ritual in order to conform with modern society. The vast majority of these Jews were city dwellers from affluent families, anxious to appeal to their government by example. They denounced the Talmud and rabbinic writings, and distanced themselves from their traditional contemporaries. Their aim was a radical revision of Judaism, and their figureheads were dramatic and polarized toward the cause.[44]

Across the British Channel, the London style of Jewish reform took root under a completely different and independent philosophy. "Far more moderate and closer to Orthodoxy than reformers were elsewhere," according to Steven Singer, the Jews of both the German and Spanish-Portuguese synagogues in London had no such desires to turn traditional Judaism on its head.[45] Rather, they saw reform as a slow migration of norms that would transform Judaism over time, given the right care and patience. A large group of London Jews agreed no longer to adhere to traditional laws in their private practices, choosing instead to become more and more attuned to the practices of secular society. Instead of breaking free from their synagogue, however, they chose to remain a part of the larger community, tolerated by its more orthodox factions.[46] The British "progressives," as described by Singer, viewed the German movements with alarm, criticizing them for their rebellious spirit and their embrace of radical reforms (such as inclusion of organ music in religious worship). According to Singer, "it was not the results of such a revolution which the progressives opposed, but the revolution itself."[47] Rather than reject the Talmud outright, the London progressives simply gave the rabbinic works less consideration in their daily lives; philosophically, they justified this approach by invoking the medieval Jewish Karaite movement, which saw rabbinic law as potentially obscuring the Divine Law of the Torah. Thus, even in its dissent, the group steeped itself in tradition rather than iconoclasm. Such attitudes made the London style of reform a much more amiable, gentler process, which progressed at its own, less pressured pace.

When Reform came to St. Thomas and its city Charlotte Amalie, its inhabitants appeared to look to the London model. Although a Danish colony, a clear connection existed between the two locations: Britain's two brief occupations of the little island helped establish English as the language of preference among the trading community.[48] By the 1830s, moreover, England still had considerable influence in the St. Thomas trade. The country still used the island as a key stop in its packet shipping route, maintained thirteen trade firms in the city, and sent more vessels to the island regularly than to any other country outside of the United States.[49]

Meanwhile, St. Thomas was ready for reform. Because nearly the entire Jewish population on the island had a strong connection to secular society and the mercantile trade, change, at first, was acceptable and steady. By 1840, St. Thomas had one of the most liberal "traditional" services in the world. In addition to a seating arrangement that placed men and women in close contact, and evidence of an occasional choir that employed female voices, the congregation did away with most of its free-will offerings (*Mitzvoth*), and probably had minimal if any observances on the second days of Jewish festivals. Portuguese, once a dominant language in Sephardic prayer, likely had been reduced to serve little more than a symbolic role in the service, with most prayers chanted in either Hebrew or English. Attitudes toward Talmudic law were essentially the same as those of the English reformers. However, although the Jewish community operated with a philosophical bent nearly identical to that of the Londoners, it did not appear to derive these approaches from England exclusively.[50] Trade, ideas, and philosophies flowed in from all over the Western world, and the Jews combined these with their practical needs to forge their own unique *minhag;* the result seemed itself to serve as a model for the region. So well regarded was the St. Thomas form of the service that several congregants in Curaçao started a movement to institute St. Thomas's practices into their own religious rituals.[51]

Unfortunately, while England could remain an island of self-supporting reform, St. Thomas could not. During the next thirty-five years, the synagogue's practices would become the focal point for numerous waves of controversy among the island's Jewish community. Such disputes began to gain prominence when a minister professing a Germanic philosophy of Reform was hired to be the congregation's religious authority. Under his leadership, St. Thomas would be transformed for the first time into a battleground for Jewish identity.

On January 2, 1841, Reverend Benjamin Cohen Carillon gave his first sermon at the St. Thomas synagogue.[52] Carillon was a pragmatic and enigmatic figure, who would soon gain a reputation as one of the most colorful and controversial characters in the Jewish Caribbean scene. He was a native of Amsterdam, the son of Dutch rabbinic authority Aaron Cohen Carillon, and the product of a continental Jewish education.[53] The Caribbean, with its many small congregations, provided him with a number of open pulpits, several of which he zealously filled during his career.

Reverend Carillon was a man of learning and erudition, who appeared to see as his primary responsibility the job of providing his congregation with nimbly constructed discourses, based in scripture, that reinforced Jewish philosophy and values. In contrast to the resident *Hazan* or Reader, who led prayers during the divine service, Carillon possessed a Hebrew knowledge and learning that went far beyond a simple understanding of the liturgy. Such abilities were rare and eagerly sought after in the region; and due to this, Carillon, as virtually the only minister on the Caribbean market outside of Curaçao, became a highly desirable commodity.

St. Thomas's announcement of Carillon's visit, printed in the *Tidende* of December 30, 1840, thus signified more than just an itinerant lecture. It expressed the congregation's open desire to see how the minister would conform to their pulpit. Carillon's sermon, which he would deliver in Dutch, was thus an audition of sorts. Should he please the synagogue's wardens and members, the Jewish community would attempt to retain him for an extended period.

The Hebrew Congregation had done much to burnish its public image that year, including a campaign spearheaded by Aron Wolff, an eminent member of both the island and colonial governments. On June 21, 1840, Wolff chaired a meeting of the Hebrew Congregation that resulted in a strong statement issued against a highly publicized case of Jewish blood-libel persecution in Damascus. The statement received public acclaim on the island, appearing in the local paper accompanied by a statement from the editor calling the resolutions "manly and energetic." Emphasizing the moral imperative of this letter, the editor added:

> Weak indeed must be that religion (if any can possibly exist) whose rites and ceremonies can only be maintained by the sacrifice of human victims and the use of human blood. How such could ever be attributed to the Israelites we are at a loss to conceive; are not their Temples of worship open like every other to the admission of Strangers? Does any thing like mystery pervade their worship? Are not their form of Prayers translated into every language? And who that has ever perused them can say that they contain not the most undeniable refutation of the barbarity imputed to them at Damascus?[54]

The action seemed to energize the congregation, and perhaps encouraged the congregants to emphasize their religious particularity more freely. Later in the year, another congregant, Mr. Morris B. Simmonds, announced the opening of a public evening school. In addition to teaching English, Simmonds "purpose[d] also to devote a portion of his time, in the endeavor to promote a knowledge of the Hebrew tongue."[55] Encouraged by public approbation, these deeds indicated a move toward higher educational standards and values within the St. Thomas Jewish community, and a renewed interest in Jewish identity. Carillon's visit thus seemed in some ways to be the next logical step.

Despite his title and reputation, Carillon was a somewhat curious choice for the post. Although his learning supposedly qualified him for the position, he was not a competent English speaker.[56] His previous pulpit, at a recently reestablished congregation in Surinam, required only that he speak in his native Dutch as a vernacular language. When he gave his first sermon in the same language on St. Thomas, it presumably could be understood by only a few of the listeners. Further, his German-style educational background, with its particular currents of Reform, did not appear to conform well to the British philosophy of gradual change favored by many of the synagogue leadership. Yet when held to public scrutiny, Carillon appeared to deny any adherence to German Reform philosophies, advocating instead forms of change and updating to the service that seemed compatible to the St. Thomas synagogue's religious philosophies.[57] More practically, Carillon represented both a novelty and a status symbol to the congregants in a region where European rabbinic leaders of *any* stripe were rare. For these apparent reasons, the St. Thomas congregation decided to take the risk and hire him.

There is no doubt that Carillon's English improved over the course of the year he resided on St. Thomas.[58] As he became more comprehensible, however, his German/Dutch roots began to show more clearly, and his presence on St. Thomas became more uncomfortable. This manifested itself on January 10, 1842, when a strongly worded article by Carillon appeared in the *Tidende*. Titled "Spirit of Reform Among the Israelites," it took aim at what Carillon deemed to be traditional Judaism, criticizing strict adherence to post-Biblical canonic texts and calling those who followed such texts "blinded by superstition and false interpretations." He deemed the Talmud "that book full of beauty, but also full of nonsense"; an obscuring wall around the great "Citadel" of "the inestimable word of God." Beginning with celebrated reformer Moses Mendelssohn, however, Carillon noted, "we have had a successive history of improvement . . . 'according to the spirit of our age.'" Carillon proceeded to enumerate what he saw as the great reforms of the century: the label change from "synagogue" to "temple" to describe the Jewish place of worship; Germany's prayers sung partly in German; the recent decision in Charleston, South Carolina, to use an organ during worship; and finally, the recognition of general reforms in London, France, and Amsterdam.[59] He ended with a parting hope "that all the Congregations of America will follow the noble example, given by our Brethren of Europe."[60]

Carillon's letter set off a short-lived but intense controversy in the St. Thomas paper. A respondent using the pseudonym "VINDEX" decried Carillon's all-out attacks on the Talmud and Rabbinic Judaism, and suggested that the ancient sources of Jewish law be given more respect, even if not whole-heartedly accepted.[61] "A REFORMER" shot back his reply in the next issue, defending Carillon's position and pointing in defense to an article that appeared near VINDEX's letter, which described a Jewish religious division in Germany based on adherence to the Talmud. Through this exchange, the lines of contention were drawn: Factions professing both British "progressive" and German "reform" philosophies had come to exist on the island, and each wanted to control the spiritual direction of synagogue practice.[62]

Significantly, even as both groups advocated changes in the religious service, the conflict these two parties were to play out on St. Thomas would take on the same nomenclature as other conflicts over Jewish Reform throughout the Western world: The British-style Reformers would give themselves a label of "Orthodox," while the German-style Reformers would take on the title of "Reformers." In this way, their struggles could be broadcast to the Jewish world in a well-understood format, even as the issues themselves proved relatively unique.

Carillon's *Tidende* message seemed at first to mark the end of his tenure on the island. Within three months of its publication, the minister had left St. Thomas and moved up to New York City, where he volunteered his services and gave several sermons in English at the Spanish and Portugese synagogue *Shearith Israel*.[63] Though there is no definitive evidence to explain his departure, it seems likely that Carillon left the island to allow the heat generated by his remarks to cool—perhaps permanently.

In St. Thomas, meanwhile, attention turned back to London. During 1840, a group of London's Jews had broken off from the city's two main congregations and formed the West London Synagogue of British Jews. Part of their need was practical: London's West End, a new dwelling place for several of the city's more affluent Jewish families, had no house of worship. More importantly, though, the congregation fashioned itself as London's first Reform synagogue, filling a growing need among the Jewish population. Led by Liverpool-born Torah scholar David Woolf Marks, the group was exceedingly conservative by German standards, and differed little in philosophy or practice from "progressive" orthodox factions.[64] Their stance of questioning the Talmud remained a touchstone of their philosophy; in practice, however, the congregation's most controversial reform was the omission of the second days of festivals, which they had interpreted as a post-biblical Rabbinic construct.[65] When, under Woolf's editorship, the congregation published the first volume of their *Forms of Prayer* in 1841, the West London Jews made few major changes to accepted liturgy: They mainly cut repetitions of prayers, translated Aramaic liturgical passages into Hebrew, and omitted passages that were seen as having no direct basis in the Torah.[66] In comparison to the noisy secessions occurring in central Europe, the British appeared to conduct their campaign with relative dignity and deliberation.

Nonetheless, the Jews of the established congregations in Britain found the new synagogue intolerable and out of line, breaking the peace and going against what they saw as the natural progression of the religion. By early 1842, the London Committee of the Board of Deputies of British Jews threatened excommunication to anyone associated with the West London Synagogue or its new prayerbook, and refused to recognize any marriages performed through the congregation.[67] The Traditionalists apparently abhorred the split itself more than the ideology behind it, an attitude enforced by the numerous self-described "progressive" London Jews who joined the established synagogues in criticizing the West London group rather than joining it.

News of the new congregation moved quickly through the pages of the *Voice of Jacob*, the primary Anglo-Jewish journal of the time, where several lengthy articles detailed the philosophy and practice of the West Londoners. When such news reached the St. Thomas Jewish community, it brought great excitement. The beliefs and practices of the new congregation appealed to them as a reverent and decorous variant of their own *minhag*. Probably with some knowledge of the ban imposed on the new British congregation, St. Thomas synagogue president Aron Wolff sent off a letter to West London founding member Moses Mocatta in February 1842. In it, he congratulated Moccata on establishing the new synagogue, and then inquired about the possibility of obtaining a minister from Europe who preached according to the West London liturgy. Wolff stated that his intentions in this request were to benefit the present congregation's worship; yet he also hoped that the minister would serve as an educator for the young, "impressing upon the minds of the juvenile branches the true tenets of our blessed and sublime religion."[68] Wolff included a wish list of desired qualities for the minister that indicated the spiritual state and anticipated religious needs of his congregation. Perhaps, in addition to this, Wolff's list also revealed some of Carillon's less flattering qualities. The man they desired, he wrote, would be:

> . . . of gentlemanly deportment, possessing a thorough knowledge of the English language, a strict Mosaic believer, a liberal man, who does not place the rabbinical writings on a level with the Pentateuch; one who feels the difference between worship and heartfelt religion; a pious man of talent, of a patient and forbearing temper, always as willing to listen as to be listened to, and more ready to give instruction than to receive applause.[69]

Mocatta passed the letter on to David Woolf Marks. Though appreciative, Marks responded regretfully to Wolff's request, stating that "no provision had yet been made in England for instructing and training youth, in order to qualify them for Synagogue appointments."[70] In the absence of a decent English candidate, however, he offered to search Europe for such a man. The St. Thomas Congregation agreed to Marks's suggestion in July, and ordered fifty copies of the West London Synagogue's *Forms of Prayer* in anticipation—the first such order from a synagogue abroad. The prayer books were promptly shipped down to the Caribbean, as the Jewish community eagerly waited for

Marks to produce their new religious leader.[71] St. Thomas's Jewish renewal, meanwhile, continued unimpeded. Aron Wolff's Sunday School, which started in April, 1842, held session every week from eleven in the morning to two in the afternoon, instructing even the youngest boys and girls in their faith, and using Philadelphia preacher Isaac Leeser's "Catechism for Young Children" as its text.[72] Among the congregation's adults, subscriptions to European periodicals of Jewish interest shot up.[73] The *Tidende*, meanwhile, kept the rest of the population abreast of Jewish issues in its columns, even going to the extent of printing a Jewish calendar "for our Friends of the Hebrew Persuasion" in February 1843.[74]

In London, meanwhile, David Woolf Marks ran advertisements for a new minister for St. Thomas in the major Jewish European papers of the time: the French journal *Les Archives Israélites de France,* and the German *Orient* and *Allgemeine Zeitung des Judenthums.*[75] A number of interested candidates responded to the call, but "not one . . . was found capable of preaching with ease and fluency in the English language."[76]

In early 1843, as Marks's search fizzled out, Reverend Carillon returned to St. Thomas to reapply for his old position. After several months in the United States, his English was now sufficiently passable for the job; he also claimed to have improved "in other matters connected with his vocation."[77] Convinced by his sincerity, and again faced with little choice, the wardens of the St. Thomas Hebrew Congregation re-engaged Carillon's services, and signed him to a multi-year contract at the generous annual salary of approximately $1,200.[78] Aron Wolff wrote to David Marks informing him of the synagogue's choice, and assuring him that even though this minister was not especially attuned to the West London liturgy, the Synagogue would begin using the new books on Passover of that year.[79]

Once reinstalled as minister, however, Carillon would have none of it. When asked by the congregation in August 1843 to implement the new liturgy, the petulant Reverend turned them down on three grounds: "1st. The most beautiful hymns of the Portuguese liturgy were left out. 2d. Why should I sanction a prayer-book sanctioned by a few laymen, having no Rabbi among them? My greatest reason, however, was that the Rev. Mr. Marks had dared to deny all Talmudic authority."[80] In what seemed a complete reversal of his previous comments, he professed a newfound respect for Rabbinic law:

I would not approve a rite established by men who speak so lightly of those noble Rabbis, the pillars of the Synagogue, the spiritual fathers of Israel, and, under God, the cause of our existence as a peculiar people. I confess that we

are at liberty to alter customs, to substitute prayers; but we must not touch the
essential points of our religion.[81]

The Hebrew Congregation backed down rather than try to press the
issue. Aron Wolff, writing to the *Voice of Jacob*, reported that Carillon's unilateral decision "sets the issue at rest."[82] Passover came and went, and the
West London prayerbooks remained unused. A visitor to the St. Thomas synagogue during the eighth day of the holiday found no surprises in the service,
deeming it "the same as the Sephardim generally, except that the last hymn,
[*Adon Olam*] was sung in English [as 'Lord Over All']."[83]

In place of the West London service (and perhaps as a mollifying measure), Reverend Carillon "granted several alterations" to the existing *minhag*
that made it remarkably similar to the rejected West London form.[84] He
omitted repetitions of the liturgy in two major parts of the service, substitut-
ing instead a recitation of the Ten Commandments; he moved the weekly
reading of the prophets (the *Haftarah*) from Saturday morning to Saturday
afternoon in order make space for an English-language sermon; and he replaced several Hebrew prayers with English translations.[85] Like the West
London practice, Carillon performed no service on the second days of holidays. Instead of using Talmudic origin as the reason for his decision, however,
he claimed to institute the practice as a matter of practicality. According to
one member of the congregation, "[second days have] been so neglected for
the last five years, that very seldom ten persons were to be had to make a congregation."[86] Many of the Jews found this arrangement satisfactory, and attended services with piety and confidence.

Carillon also inherited a burgeoning Sunday School, still run by Aron Wolff,
which enrolled over seventy children. Supplementing the existing instruction, the reverend established a free Hebrew class to provide the children
further assistance in learning and understanding the liturgy.[87]

One of Carillon's first major responsibilities appeared to be the creation
and execution of a new practice desired by the island's Jewish community.
Self-imposed, it seemed to draw from the Danish sovereign's 1814 royal
proclamation requiring all Jewish children reaching the age of thirteen to
take a public examination in their faith. Upon being successfully examined,
the candidates then had to "ceremoniously take their religious vows and promise that, out of their own free will, they will not act against the fundamental
rules [of Judaism]."[88] Danish Jews who did not abide by these regulations
could not marry, obtain citizenship, engage in business, or enter university in
Denmark.[89] The rule had not been enforced in St. Thomas; yet the Jewish

community appeared actively to take it upon themselves to comply at this time. Carillon thus set to work creating a confirmation ceremony, and convened as his first candidates the Western hemisphere's first known confirmation class.[90]

For several months, indications showed that St. Thomas's minister and his congregation benefitted from each other's company. When the *Voice of Jacob* criticized the congregation's decision to omit services on the second days of holidays, several congregants approached the minister with a request to reinstate them, and he seemed to do so with little objection.[91] The congregation in general began to appear more pious and active, and the Hebrew school grew.

On August 13, 1843, joy once again filled the synagogue as the island witnessed the Sunday School's first public display of its accomplishments. Numerous island residents, both Jewish and non-Jewish, filled the pews of the sanctuary to watch the event. Once they were seated, the young students from the Sunday School filed in, and together sang an opening hymn. Aron Wolff's youngest child, nine-year-old Julius, recited an opening prayer for the occasion, and a style of catechism contest began. The students split into three classes. Reverend Carillon, the examiner, proceeded to ask each class several questions. Two high-ranking government officials, invited as judges, evaluated the responses. After hearing answers from each of the children, they named eight winners: three in the first class, and two each in the second and third classes. Nine-year-old Rachel Hoheb recited a prayer in front of the assemblage; and the winners received their prizes. A writer recounting the event in the *Tidende* gave great credit to the students. He was "pleased with the promptness and correctness [they] displayed," and noted humorously that just fifteen months ago, when the school began, "many of the scholars were unable to speak the *English* language . . ."[92]

After the examination, Mr. Benjamin Levy rose and delivered a moving speech to Aron Wolff for his efforts: "we feel our inability to convey in words the high sense we entertain of inestimable blessings conferred by you, under favor of Almighty God on the children of our faith . . . to your perseverence are our youth indebted for a knowlege of those essential truths of religion, which will constitute their surest armour against the host of trials and temptations."[93] With this, he handed Wolff a pair of silver fruit baskets, "for rich and poor alike gather the fruit of the goodly tree thy hand hath planted." Wolff, uncharacteristically overcome with emotion, delivered an acceptance address crediting the congregation for its support and underlining his belief that a good Jewish education was the key to keeping a young Jew in his or her

faith. Dr. David Pretto delivered another public address, and Reverend Carillon followed with a "discourse suitable for the occasion." Then the event
concluded with refreshments and wine, as toasts went around liberally.[94]

It soon became apparent, however, that the public view, dictated by a Synagogue Board that supported Carillon and his modifications, was not the entire picture. A faction of Jews disfavoring the Reverend's stance on *minhag*
began to send letters of complaint to the *Voice of Jacob*, appealing to the editor's sensibilities while making allegations against Carillon. Then, around
September, the group struck at the synagogue's most sacred institution: the
school. Without permission of the synagogue wardens, this self-described
"orthodox" group started its own Saturday morning religious school. Instructing the youth according to a significantly more "traditional" curriculum, the reactionary school's philosophy seemed to resemble that of the established London Jewish community that had opposed the West London
Synagogue.

The synagogue wardens, with the law on their side, acted quickly and decisively. Their 1802 bylaws, registered and approved by the Royal Danish
government, explicitly forbade "any Religious Society under any description
whatsoever without being subject to & under the Emediate Direction of the
Mahamade & Adjuntos of the Synagogue."[95] ". . . [T]he school would have
been permitted, had the formal sanction first been applied for," argued the
wardens.[96] But the seceders, they claimed, did not do this, causing the new
school to exist in clear violation of the rules. To close the subject, the synagogue board approached the police authority on the island, who promptly
shut down the seceders' effort. Although an effective stop-gap measure, this
action only increased tensions between the Jews' two factions.

On October 14, 1843, the Sabbath morning during the eight-day Feast of
Tabernacles (*Sukkot*), Reverend Carillon's confirmation class took its own
turn in the spotlight. During an "imposing" ceremony, Carillon confirmed
each of seven students, presenting each with a certificate attesting to his or
her full membership in the synagogue and in Jewish life. Of the five women
and two men who received the honor on that day, four were members of
Aron Wolff's family; the other three, Jacob Benjamin, Deborah Simha Cortissos, and Esther de Meza, belonged squarely in the pro-Carillon faction of
the congregation.[97] All were over the minimum age of thirteen—some by a
significant margin. The ceremony's symbolic import, however, was clear: it
marked what the congregation saw as an emergence into a higher, certifiable
standard of Jewish knowledge and activity.[98] The *Voice of Jacob* reported on
the event; however, by this time it was also acutely aware of differences smol-

dering between the members of the synagogue. With optimism, the editor of the paper opined that the ceremony, "must have beneficial effects."[99]

But it did not. By the time of the Confirmation account, Carillon was once again at the center of controversy. The *Voice of Jacob* a couple weeks earlier had printed a congregant's complaint against him alleging an intolerable innovation. "We are now told," the writer said, "that the *Musaph* is not only 'not repeated,' but altogether left out!"[100] The *Musaph*, an additional service that represented a rabbinical reinstatement of a certain sacrifice during the second Temple period, had been an important point of difference between the British and German reformers in Europe. While several German reform movements made attempts to abolish the service from their ritual entirely, the West London congregants consciously kept it in, aiming only to shorten the text somewhat.[101] The dissenting letter from St. Thomas, then, represented clear manifestation of these differences: "In this particular," suggested the editor of the British journal, "the St. Thomas 'reformers' would be going even beyond the London seceders [who continued to live under threat of excommunication for their actions]. . . . If this charge be true . . . we feel confident that the minister has spirit enough to do his duty in this case likewise." The protesting congregant went on to charge the minister with "public profanation of the Sabbath," though without mentioning any specifics. To both allegations, the editor of the *Voice of Jacob* withheld final opinion.[102]

The reverend fired back at the start of the next year, defending his practice and sending a complete order of services for Sabbath and all holidays as proof. The *Musaf* service appeared in its usual place; however, as the editor of the paper noted, "the charge of omission is not established: still there *is* a deviation,—the occasional reading of that important [*Musaf*] service in the English language! This is certainly no light departure . . ." Carillon, however, pressed his argument, and called as a witness Jamaican Reverend Moses Nathan Nathan. A conservative British religious leader who had come down recently to officiate at the synagogue in Kingston, Nathan had a sterling reputation among British Jews. His recent attendance at a St. Thomas service, Carillon thought, would resolve the case favorably.[103]

But this, too, backfired. Nathan responded to Carillon's request with a public letter in the same journal. His letter, however, was not what the St. Thomas minister had expected. "I regret that [Carillon] should have placed me in the position of referee in this matter," Nathan wrote to the *Voice of Jacob*. "I witnessed 'nothing contrary to our religion done in the Synagogue' [as Carillon claimed], yet I must candidly confess that *there were many deviations from the established Minhag of the Sephardim . . .*" Although the tenor of Nathan's letter was overwhelmingly positive after this, praising Carillon and the congregation for "the orderly and devotional conduct of the congregation, the impressive manner in which the prayers are said, as well as the correct and beautiful chaunting of the children," the damage had been done. Tensions continued to escalate.[104]

Even as the situation worsened, however, Aron Wolff's regular reports on the St. Thomas Jewish community continued to exhibit an eerie optimism. "The Passover holyday has been a very happy one for our congregation," began one missive. "The choir of boys and girls sang the Hallel [special psalms of praise] in Hebrew, most exquisitely. Mr. Carillon, deserves all the praise that can be bestowed upon him; for it is only nine months ago that he commenced giving them Hebrew lessons . . ."[105] Wolff acknowledged opponents, but only briefly. He then quickly continued by reporting on the school's proliferation into several divisions: a Hebrew School, Sunday School, Infant School (for children under nine), and a post-confirmation class, teaching more than 130 pupils in total.

Several weeks later, Carillon's opponents countered by sending a petition to the *Voice of Jacob* signed by seven members of the congregation. These members asserted once again the *Musaph's* "omission" from the service. Two of the members, the letter stated, refused to attend services due to the lack of a proper *minhag*.[106] Smashing the decorum of the letters written by the synagogue's leaders, the seceders intended to verify their claims in full view of the British Jewish world, where such progressive activites were now generally considered taboo. While the editor of the *Voice of Jacob* tried to explain away the discrepancies in an attempt to give credit to both sides of the story, it became clear that the situation was not improving.

The final piece to the crisis came to light around March 1844, when Samuel Elias Levy Maduro, the synagogue's reader, left St. Thomas to take an analogous job in Curaçao.[107] This proved disastrous for the St. Thomas synagogue. Maduro appeared to be the mitigating influence between the two factions that had formed; and as a member of an old Caribbean Jewish family, he commanded a respect that Carillon could not achieve. Quietly acting behind the inflammatory scenes, Maduro appeared to help keep any problems under control. His absence, whether due to opportunity, his own naïveté, pressure from Carillon, or the futility of the situation, probably opened the doors for the schism that would occur a few months later.[108]

The leaders of the dissenting party included prominent businessmen J. H. Osorio and J. Fidanque, Jr., as well as islanders Judah Sasso and Mashod

Meara. Another was a member of the Maduro family, probably a cousin of the recently absented reader. Two others, Moses and Jeudah Piza, were sons of former St. Thomas minister Joshua Piza, highly educated in Jewish ritual through their father's tutelage.[109] Over the course of time, this small group grew. Carillon, it seems, became increasingly inflexible toward the sentiments of the protesting faction. His public persona became more flamboyant and extreme, and he partook in acts that flaunted Jewish ritual even more visibly in the eyes of several congregants.[110] Possibly, a number of synagogue members blamed him for Reader Maduro's flight. By July 1844, however, the dissenters constituted a majority party in the synagogue, perhaps even including a number of the congregation's wardens. Carillon's support diminished quickly.

On July 17, the two sides reached the breaking point. The *Tidende* released the news to the island: "Schism Among the Hebrew Congregation." Noting that "a serious difference has arisen between the Reverend Minister of the Hebrew congregation and a portion of his flock," the paper nonetheless kept its distance and "decline[d] commenting on an affair which is entirely out of our province." The congregation had split into two bodies: the group who supported the embattled minister, which apparently included most of the educational leaders of the congregation, moved out and held services utilizing Carillon's modified liturgy in a private building.[111] A more "Orthodox" faction retained use of the synagogue, the Sunday School, and the old Sephardic form of prayer. Moses Piza officiated in the sanctuary as the interim reader, replacing Carillon.[112]

Non-Jewish islanders reacted with shock; one sent a letter of exhortation to the paper asking the fractured congregation to "Pause, reflect, and even weigh well the true sources of your present self-constituted task, of judging the fitness, or unfitness, of your Minister . . ."[113] The *Voice of Jacob*, once the central forum for airing the congregation's opposing arguments, fell silent. Within the St. Thomas Jewish community, the split must have produced much private controversy; but because of the stigma attached to religious disunity on the island, nothing went public. St. Thomas, and the readers of much of the Jewish media, awaited the outcome of the tragically uncomfortable situation.

About six weeks later, after litigation, arguments, and negotiations between the two sides, the congregation came to an uneasy decision. "We regret to find," stated the *Voice of Jacob* in late summer, 1844, "that the Rev. Mr. Carillon no longer officiates as minister of this congregation."[114] Raw feelings continued on the island through the next month, as the congregation observed the high holidays while Carillon and his family packed up to leave the island. With the fight ended, the victors and losers remained at loggerheads. The minister, who sincerely believed his changes were best for the congregation, felt bitterness toward his opponents, and intended to sue the synagogue wardens for breach of contract at his first chance. Jewish St. Thomians, their decision made, knew that their next course had to lead to reunion, but needed time to let the tensions dissipate somewhat.

Carillon secured a job as minister of a new congregation in Spanish Town, Jamaica, and left for the island aboard the English steamer *Forth* on October 2, 1844. The *Tidende* commemorated his departure by eulogizing: "There are many, we are convinced, who will deeply regret the Rev'd gentleman's departure from our island."[115] Another more caustic commentator, however, countered, "Mr. C. is gone, peace be with him, and all, and fortunate indeed he will be, if he succeed in obtaining another situation . . ."[116] As Carillon withdrew, the Jewish community remained knotted up by distrust and animosity. It searched for a successor who could help to heal the rift created by the adamant, misunderstood, and controversial minister.

Once established in Spanish Town, Carillon appparently closed out his dealings with St. Thomas congregation by forging a breach-of-contract suit in the territorial court; rather than airing out their embarrassing proceedings once again, the congregation settled out of court for a sum between $2,400 and $4,000.[117] Meanwhile, Carillon promptly resumed his controversial behavior with his new congregation. Breaking agreements with the synagogue's wardens almost as quickly as he made them, Carillon once again self-righteously introduced his own prayers and reforms. Again, regular letters of vehement protest against the minister appeared in the *Voice of Jacob*. Once the Spanish Town congregation fractured as well, the so-called "Jewish Luther" resigned voluntarily, and proceeded onward to a new congregation in Montego Bay.[118] He left this congregation as well, around September, 1846 and afterward seemed to appear no longer in public Jewish life.[119]

A German-oriented minister operating in a British philosophical environment, Benjamin Cohen Carillon was a preacher in constant conflict with his constituents. Concerned more with the theoretical pronouncements of empirical religion than with the realities of mercantile life, his strong stances and individualistic actions clashed with the values of community and conformity promoted in British "Orthodox" Judaism. The St. Thomas Jews constantly evaluated their religious standing by publishing their practices in the pages of the *Voice of Jacob* and the newly inaugurated *London Jewish Chronicle*; approbation by the editor of these journals was a mark of pride for the small congregation. Carillon, in contrast, disdained playing by such rules, and preferred instead to act in an iconoclastic fashion reminiscent of the German reformers. He was a passionate, eloquent minister, whose English prayers endured with the St. Thomas Jews well into the next century, and whose commitment to education brought the first Jewish confirmation to the island's shores. Yet he was in the wrong environment, leading a frustrated, self-righteous, and infamous career from St. Thomas to Jamaica, and then into obscurity.

—⁓—

TOWARD THE END OF 1844, Reader Samuel Elias Levy Maduro returned to St. Thomas after losing a hostile and embittering bid to gain the title of co-reader for the Curaçao congregation.[120] The Hebrew Congregation welcomed him back to his old position with open arms, seeing him as a prodigal son whose familial connections with the community ran deep enough to bring the island's Jewish population back together. Maduro's life experience in Caribbean Jewish liturgy and his relative distance from European Jewish politics helped him effect a smooth transition in the synagogue back to a service that all would attend. The amity he restored served as a base of comfort as the congregation searched for a replacement rabbinic leader.

The St. Thomas congregation found a perfect successor to Carillon in Kingston, Jamaica, preacher Moses Nathan Nathan. And it did not take long to find him: The same issue of the *Voice of Jacob* that announced Carillon's departure from St. Thomas also noted that "The Rev. M. N. Nathan's ministry is much desired by many influential members of the St. Thomas Synagogue."[121] Reverend Nathan could not have been a better fit for the recovering congregation. He was conservative, eloquent, intelligent, and dedicated, owning a strong knowledge of the British Jewish world and a reputation of high esteem.

Nathan had a talent for teaching and a vast intelligence that belied his age. Born in London on November 20, 1806, he was the grandson of legendary Hebrew teacher Moses Solomon, a figure whose influence colored his career.[122] Just after his Bar Mitzvah, around 1820, Nathan became one of the first teachers of the new London Jews' Free School at Petticoat Lane; there, in a prescient twist of fate, he instructed the young David Woolf Marks, future spiritual founder of the London Reform movement. By age sixteen, Nathan had received his first appointment as reader of London's Denmark Court Synagogue.[123] His career brought him to Liverpool a few years later, where he set up his own religious school and began giving English language sermons and lectures at the Liverpool Old Hebrew Congregation. Under the advisorship of the local rabbi, Nathan developed his oration and officiation skills, and became one of the first religious leaders to preach regularly in English.[124]

In 1834, at the age of twenty-seven, Nathan became minister at the German synagogue in Kingston, Jamaica. Preaching to the great satisfaction of the congregation, Nathan's powerful oratorical talents helped to bring the synagogue's status to new heights. His speeches were stirring, descriptive, and appealing directly to the hearts and minds of his constituents. In 1838, for example, on the Sabbath between the Jewish New Year (Rosh Hashanah) and the Day of Atonement (Yom Kippur) known as *Shabbat Tshuvah*, he began a commentary on the book of Jonah by picturing the prophet as the quintessential sea traveller, a position that the mostly merchant community knew all too well:

> [Jonah] is represented as traversing the ocean to fly from the pressure of the Lord when suddenly black and fearful clouds overspread the horizon, and the heavens are shrouded in gloom and darkness. The storm begins—the ship is exposed to its rage, and threatened with imminent danger. The ocean, lashed by the winds into uncontrollable fury—now ascending mountains high—and now discovering its unfathomable abyss, lifts the frail vessel to the clouds upon the crest of its boiling waves, and then dashes it down with fearful violence— vainly is human skill executed to escape the peril which appears on every side, and to gain a safe harbor and shelter under the land—the bark trembles as tho' end[owed] with feeling in the violent and forcible grasp of the raging and contending elements—destruction seems inevitable, despair siezes on the crew, and every one awaits his fate with silent honor.[125]

Such impressive rhetoric, combined with a passion for education, brought Nathan acclaim within the congregation.

In early 1844, Nathan collaborated with fellow Jamaican Dr. Lewis Ashenheim to create the second Jewish-interest periodical published in the hemisphere, known as *The First Fruits of the West*. With a published run of twelve issues over two years, the journal served primarily as a West Indian bulletin for the Jewish communities of England, sending home information on the area and keeping Londoners up to date on liturgical and philosophical currents in the British Colonies.

Nathan's stance on Reform conformed decidedly with British practices.

Commenting in 1842 on the ideas of the London seceders, Nathan placed a positive spin on their mission, but refused to acknowledge the West London liturgy as a change worthy of secession:

> . . . this word "reform" as applied to our religion, is very inappropriate, and I have always, as a minister, discouraged the use of the term. . . . That there have been deviations from the original, as for instance, in the ritual first established, no one will deny; that Synagogue worship, from various causes, has degenerated, until it has become wholly lifeless, I am prepared to admit; but the return to the former, and the amendment of the latter, will only restore both to their *original* state, without *reforming* either. . . . Reform an act of Parliament, a character, anything which has not its origin from a divine source, but to reform the institutions which man's indifference has slighted . . . is inexplicable.[126]

Later, commenting upon the Reformers' ideas to drop portions of the service, he again embraced both change and tradition as part of the same entity:

> We do not deny that many of our customs are clothed in a garb which seems unfitting to modern ideas; but they are not to be rejected on this account. It requires some little knowledge and discernment, to penetrate the artificial covering which hangs over the true nature of some of them—a covering, which the necessity of the times originally induced. . . . [I]t is not, we say, because [some] individuals raise their veto, that we throw aside, as useless, customs, which are calculated to render their followers happy.[127]

The St. Thomas wardens naturally saw Nathan as a perfect candidate, in line with their original liturgical intentions, and ideal for leading the synagogue in harmony; and the *Voice of Jacob* heartily agreed.[128] Thus, without delay, the synagogue set about trying to lure him away from his old congregation.

By early 1845, the Jews of St. Thomas succeeded in their quest to bring Reverend Nathan to the island, signing him "with a very liberal stipend, for a term of five years." As he announced his resignation to the communities of Jamaica, closing both a secular school and a religious ministry there, the congregation in St. Thomas secured a home for him, and began to make preparations for his arrival.[129]

Yet when the Jewish community presented its choice to the government, it discovered that another independent search had been taking place. Unbeknownst to the wardens, the Governor General of the Danish West Indies

Peter von Scholten also recognized the synagogue's vacancy, and attempted in his way to assist the congregation in filling the void. Von Scholten had sent a letter to Reverend Alexander Aaron Wolff, Chief Rabbi of Copenhagen, explaining the St. Thomas congregation's situation and requesting a replacement who spoke fluent English.[130] This posed an embarrassing dilemma, since any candidate proposed by Reverend Wolff was likely to obtain the King's appointment, as required by law, and supercede Nathan's recent engagement.[131] As long as the situation in Copenhagen remained unresolved, the synagogue's choice could not receive any official backing.[132]

Nathan, his affairs all but finished in Jamaica, stubbornly decided to come anyway. On March 5, the day before his departure, the Jewish community of Spanish Town presented Reverend Nathan with a lengthy and laudatory address, praising him for his valuable work and wishing blessing and peace upon his future endeavors.[133] The next day, he boarded the ship for St. Thomas, and set sail for his new congregation, official or not.

Crowds from all over town packed the synagogue and crammed into the mahogany benches on Sabbath morning, March 22, to see the highly touted minister officiate at his inaugural service. After completing the prayers, Reverend Nathan began his first sermon on St. Thomas. Speaking in his native English, "not only suitable in the highest degree for the sacred occasion, but in a strain of eloquence and genuine piety, worthy of the exalted reputation which his services in the ministry . . . have acquired for him," he enchanted the congregation with his rhetoric. In the first of a three-part address, Nathan praised the "sublime character of the Patriarch Abraham, the founder of the Hebrew people," and then proceeded to exhort the members of the Hebrew Congregation to revel in their identities as Jews. "[F]ar from its being a term of reproach . . . it was one, which every son and daughter of Israel should delight to glory in—that it bore the impress of antiquity . . ."[134] Empowering and positive, Nathan's sermon was exactly what the synagogue needed to facilitate its healing and unite once again under one roof.

After finishing his discourse and inviting the interfaith assembly to return next week for the next installment, Nathan symbolically brought the congregation into a new era. First he intoned a prayer for the royal family of Denmark. Then, with sincerity, "he fervently besought the God of Israel that peace, unanimity and love would always prevail among his congregation." Party spirit still wracked the ranks of synagogue life, and would continue to do so for quite a while to come. Nathan's service, however, showed promise for the Jewish community, ushering in a minister who aimed to return the congregation to a unified whole, once again praying without prejudice under the vaulted ceiling of the sanctuary.

For the next two weeks, overfull congregations continued to greet the Reverend, anxious to hear the continuation of his previous talks and revel in the novelty and ease of his style. Impressed to the point of concern with the sudden resurgence in synagogue worship, the Jews began an emergency collection to expand the sanctuary.[135] Although numbers dropped back down to acceptable levels after a while, it became obvious that Nathan was an ideal choice for St. Thomas. Thriving together, the new leader and his flock faced each other eye to eye, learning with each week to love and revere their common religion and its values. Although residual opposition still came occasionally from the seceders, Nathan held a course "tempered by discretion and forebearance," and slowly wore down their resistance and mistrust.[136]

Pressure mounted upon Governor General Peter von Scholten to name Nathan as the congregation's official religious leader.[137] Seeing the satisfied demeanor of the Jewish community, and the overwhelmingly positive response of other island residents to the minister, von Scholten discontinued his earlier inquiry and took steps to endow Nathan with the official Jewish religious leadership of the island. In September 1845, six months after he had arrived on St. Thomas's shores, Nathan finally received the assurances from the Danish government that allowed him to be appointed minister of the Hebrew Congregation "for life."[138] Thus established, he continued to lead his congregation with strength and zeal.

While Reverend Nathan eliminated many of Carillon's "innovations" in the St. Thomas liturgy, he retained, by necessity, the confirmation ceremony. Since the first one during *Sukkot*, 1843, two more classes had pledged to retain their faith under Carillon—on February 24 and April 13, 1844.[139] Nathan's first confirmation class, which he prepared for several months in advance of the ritual, took their oaths on the first night of *Shavuot*, May 30, 1846.[140] Toward the end of the service on that evening, the Reverend called up the nine girls and boys he had been instructing, and held an examination of their Judaic knowledge. Answering under the flickering lights of the chandeliers, the students all passed confidently. Then, the president, vice president, and treasurer of the congregation stood and walked over to the mahogany doors of the holy ark, swinging them open and bidding the whole congregation to rise. Each took out a Torah and held it before the congregation. The children surrounded the synagogue leaders in groups of three, each placing a hand on one of the scrolls. Intoning in a voice clearly heard by all present, the minister read in front of the students a promise "to fulfil all that they had been taught by their teachers and parents," and asked the class if they would adhere to this promise. "We do promise," they answered. With the confirmands confirmed and sealed in their faith, Reverend Nathan proceeded to call upon the children's parents to renew their own devotion to Judaism by blessing their respective sons and daughters. Nathan added his own benediction upon the class, and then delivered a "highly effective" address. Though the minister was new, the idea behind this ritual remained the same as it had been in Carillon's time: A new group of students educated in their faith was ready to go out and face the world, secure in their own identity.[141]

The education system for the younger children, meanwhile, proliferated. By the beginning of 1847, Jewish children not only received their religious education through the Sunday School and a new Bible class taught by Reverend Nathan, but also enjoyed *"four* schools for elementary and classical education," founded and taught by members of the congregation. So successful were these synagogue academies that a number of Christian families on the island sent their children there for education as well. Boasting of this acomplishment, a correspondent wrote to Isaac Leeser, the prominent Philadelphia rabbi: "you will find that we are ahead of you; for I hear of no elementary schools by our people in Philadelphia." And such was indeed the case. St. Thomas, aiming to establish itself as a major Jewish community in the Americas, was by now well on its way to achieving that goal.[142]

One final act was necessary to complete the Hebrew Congregation's return to harmony and erase the strife caused by Carillon's term. During the controversy and legal battles of the previous years, the body of laws governing the congregation had come under intense scrutiny. Now over forty years old, they no longer reflected the current state of the synagogue. Thus, at the end of 1845, the Danish government appointed a commission to go to St. Thomas and oversee the rewriting of the Hebrew Congregation's bylaws. Upon the commission's arrival, Governor General von Scholten selected a committee of five congregational members, led by Reverend Nathan, to accomplish this task. The Jews were given no restrictions in creating their bylaws, save that they had to adhere to the common law of Denmark, and that they prevent the kind of disunity that had so badly splintered the Jewish community under Carillon.[143] For two months, the combined committee collected suggestions from congregants while simultaneously trying to reflect on the island's current patterns of Jewish life and observance.[144] It was hoped that such actions would help clarify the areas where change was needed most in order to produce a strong and up-to-date synagogue code.

One of these areas involved the manner in which the synagogue assessed dues. By this time, the synagogue no longer received most of its income from free donations during ritual services, as customarily occurred in other western Sephardic congregations. The practice, they found, "fell [mostly] upon a few willing persons, whereas many stood aloof and permitted others to give all."[145] In its place, the institution created a universal tax—assessed on all men over eighteen years of age and on all self-supporting women—amounting to no more than $300. Privileges were granted depending upon the amout of annual dues given.[146] Those who paid at least twelve dollars per year obtained voting rights for all major synagogue decisions; all congregants over twenty-five years who paid above thirty-two dollars were eligible for election to the Board.[147] Supplementing earlier rules, the committee also added provisions for absentee membership and voting rights, taking into account the frequent business trips undertaken by many of the synagogue's members.

The ruling body of the synagogue underwent its own modifications. First was nomenclature: known initially by the Judeo-Spanish term *adjunto*, the body's title changed in new regulations to the more Anglicized "Board of Representatives." In addition to keeping order in services, this group's responsibilities were expanded to include keeping several "protocols" of records: synagogue correspondence, minutes from meetings, and government correspondence, in addition to the births, deaths, and marriages it already kept (§17). The treasurer would be elected from among the board members; his official responsibilities came to involve keeping track of the synagogue's accounts, including a few held in the island's new Savings Bank. The vice-president, meanwhile, was charged with handling all funeral arrangements in collaboration with the assistant reader (§19).

Carillon's influence could be felt in two sections of the new bylaws. Directly addressing the procedure for grievances against the "Representatives, the Minister, or any paid officer," the regulations laid out a well-defined course of action for investigating allegations of misconduct, and established a penalty system for administering punishment should these allegations be found true. Such due process would allow the congregation to put any official up to public scrutiny, and hopefully circumvent many of the the problems of the past (§24b).

The unity of the congregation remained a point of great emphasis. This could be seen through the types of financial penalties levied: While the fines relaxed somewhat for several other categories of infraction, the fine for holding unauthorized religious services stiffened to ten to fifty dollars for the host and officiator, and four to sixteen dollars for each illegal attendee (§20, 24c). Clearly, the framers of the law did not wish to repeat their unhappy schism, and decided to strike the perpetrators in the purse should conventional reasoning fail.

Probably at the behest of Reverend Nathan, the 1848 bylaws still gave the minister of the congregation full control over the content and form of the prayer service, so long as it continued to follow the Spanish and Portuguese *minhag* (§1, 33–35). Trust was the clear factor here, and the wardens simply had to hope that they could root out ministers like Carillon before they came to office. With Nathan securely in the pulpit, however, such concerns held little importance for the time being, and the motion passed.

On May 30, 1847, after a great deal of discussion and negotiation, the committee completed the new bylaws. Within about six weeks, a lawyer had finished translating a copy of the document into Danish, and sent it up to Copenhagen for approval. Meanwhile, the new code went into immediate effect in the synagogue; only the king's signature remained to make it official.[148]

The Danish government took over eight months to ratify the laws, and disappointed notices of impatience circulated in the Jewish periodicals. It is possible that other factors, most prominently the sudden emergence of slave emancipation as a priority issue in the Danish islands, helped push the review date further and further back. But the wait eventually did come to an end; on February 17, 1848, the king and his officers approved the regulations, adding only three minor clarifications to ensure conformity with Danish law. By October 1848, the entire congregation had printed copies of their new regulations, which arrived by packet ship from a printer in Philadelphia.[149] Although the process took longer than expected, the product was a worthy document that satisfactorily updated the conditions for communal Jewish coexistence on the island.

For more than twenty years, these new bylaws would remain in force, regulating synagogue life fairly and compassionately. In many ways, this was Reverend Nathan's achievement. Over the course of a year, he had helped to bring a warring synagogue community back from party lines of animosity to the negotiating table, and from there to official and pronounced unity. Ending a chapter of strife in the synagogue's history, Nathan helped the Jewish community of St. Thomas to grow together, adapting the synagogue's operations to current conditions and preparing it for the times to come.

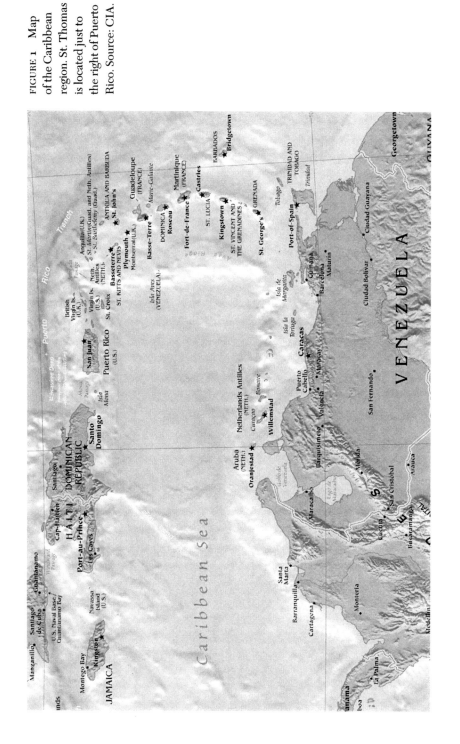

FIGURE 1 Map of the Caribbean region. St. Thomas is located just to the right of Puerto Rico. Source: CIA.

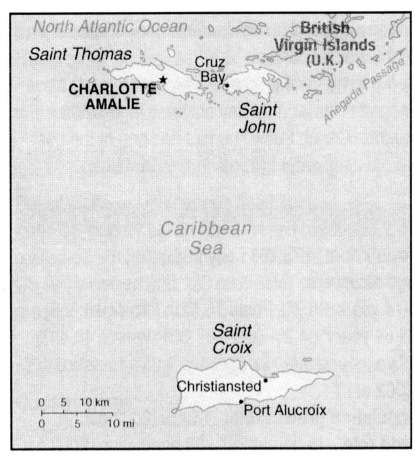

FIGURE 2   The U.S. Virgin Islands. Source: CIA.

St. Thomæ Tidende.

Vol. 17.] Löverdagen, den 6te April 1833. [No. 1685.

WEEKLY MEMORANDO.

APRIL—XXX DAYS.

7	s	EASTER DAY—5d Feb. Packet due.
8	m	Easter Monday.
	tu	

PAA Söndag, förste Paaskedag, bliver Gudstjeneste for den Danske og Missions-Menigheden.
St. Thomas d. 5te April 1833.

To the Editor of the Tidende.

Sir,—In conformity to the accompanying Resolutions, I request your insertion of them, and of the subjoined Subscription List.

Respectfully,
A. WOLFF.

28th March, 1833.

AT a Meeting of the Hebrew Congregation of this Island on the 24th instant, it was unanimously resolved,—

1st—" That for the satisfaction of those concerned, the Subscription List for the Building of the Synagogue, as it now stands, be advertised, adding to each publication, any fresh Contributions which may be made.

2d—" That the President be requested to cause the foregoing Resolutions to be put into effect at the next publication of the Tidende."

His Excellency the Governor-General	Ps. 100
His Ex. the Governor	50
Capt. Rohde, R.D.	50
His Honor Judge Berg, R.D.	40
Counsellor von Schmidten	40
Major Kiellerup	25
Messrs. A. Wolff	300
Z. L Lévy	75
A. Robles	100
J. Cappe	200
A. Hoheb	50
A. I. Levy	50
S. Rothschild	100
	Ps. 1180 $ 755 20
D A Correa	50
J H Osorio	16
Jacob M Monsanto	200
P Pizarro	16
Isaac Delvalle	16
A R Mendes	25
McBean, Murray & Co.	16
J R Mendes	25
Isaac Azevedo, Side Lamps &	32
D M Monsanto	32
A Friend	16
Samuel Baiz	16
A Baiz	16
Lawyer Stenersen	8
Lawyer Sarauw	6
Messrs Whitmore	8
J A Reed	8
H N Gage & Co.	8
P J Meinville	8
Theodore M Monsanto	8
Joseph Levi	16
B M DaCosta	32
M L Dubec	50
A Boscowitz	50
P Murdoch	8
Jacob de Castro & Wys	20
Messrs William Lamb & Co	8
J Fidanque	10
Hjardemaal & Andersen	16
Buchanan, Neish & Co.	8
E Bernard	4
A Lavalette	16
A Julien	32
Carried forward	$1597 20

Amount brought forward	$1597 20
Messrs D Deleon	4
A Friend	4
Borgeset & Co.	100
E Simmons	8
W & R Stubbe	8
A P Magens	8
Captain Wallce	10
Doctor Von Bretton	16
Miss Hart	27
Messrs H N Noetel	16
E Sarquy	16
Mrs Sarquy	16
Messrs J B Lugaro	4
S S	4
Madame Ambroise and Daughters	4
Messrs Reira & Son	8
G D Anthoni	16
John Thomson	16
J Pujals	8
M Sasso	4
H Morrison	4
M Sourdes	3
Captain Ffrench	4
Messrs Peter James	4
P v Vlierden	8
A Friend	8
S B Hoheb	10
M Benjamin	4
A Friend	8
La Monte & Co	8
John Marnan	8
J C Young	8
P Ricard	8
John Lobo	8
T McLaughlan	8
Ausin	4
Overmann & Schön	60
J Yvern	4
A J Holm	8
F D Petit	8
Cosmo Francowitz	4
P François	8
R B Wright	8
Joseph Cross	8
William Gibson	8
J B Anduze	8
M Gil	8
Doctor Stedman	4
Doctor Magens	4
Messrs B H Wetzome	4
P Boudenn	4
J B LeClerc	2
G Rüttenberg	8
R Smith	16
Cash	16
J Morel	4
R Pearce	8
J Fiza & Son	8
Jacob B Wolff	8
E Henriquez	8
T Kier	8
S B Lange	8
Miss Crastro	4
Mrs Paul	10
Messrs J A Correa	4
J H Henriques	16
Mrs Henriques	16
Messrs O Domingo	16
T O Davis	10
M Garcia	4
A N Seixas	8
A Friend	100
Major Bonnelly	16
Messrs John Wright	16
A C Stenersen	0
S Nones	8
Daniel Hart	8
George Latimer	8
E C M DaCosta	50
Master Jacob of Jn M Dacosta	5
G Nunès	8
Mr David Naar, Cartage of the materials to the spot.	
Captain D'Azevedo, 50 tons of Stones	
Mrs Ben Ezra, 100 bbls of Lime	
Mr R De Meza, 40 bbls of Lime	
Carried forward	$2488 20

Amount brought forward		$2488 20
Mr Sol Levy, a lot of Sand		
Mr B Levy, 10 bbls of Lime		
Female Labourers, supplied by several Ladies of the Congregation		
Subscriptions from Abroad.		
Messrs Aloof & Co. London		826
J M DaCosta	50	
M Mocatta	50	
M Montefiore	10	
D A Lindo	25	
Mrs G Mocatta	5	
N M Rothschild	50	
Elders of the German Congregation	100	
		315
Mr H J Levy, Hamburg	$48	
An Old St. Thomas Friend by Messrs Z & I Levy	100	148
J Abensur, Esq. Maracaibo		100
J Levy fils Esq. St. Domingo		100
E Mocatta Esq. Caraccas		16
S Mocatta Esq. Caraccas		50
Collected by J H De Sola Esq. St. Croix		
Messrs M DaGuelard	8 9	
J H De Sola	8	
A Aarons	8 20	
S L Maduro	2	
Isaac Sasso	1	
Mr Elias DeLeon	2	
Mrs R de Sola	2	
J M Monsanto	2	
Z de Sola	2	
DaGuilard	2	
Julien	2	
Messrs J Lindo	4	
S Lindo	4	
Mrs Lindo	2	
Miss Lindo	1	
Miss Levy	1	
Mr D G Fonseca	3 20	
Mrs Fonseca	1	
Miss Fonseca	50	
Master Fonseca	50	
Mrs Levy	1	
Mr Benjamin and Lady	8	
Miss Benjamin	1	
Mr A G Fonseca	1	
S Benjamin	1	48 46
Subscribed in Jamaica through DeCordova, Esq.		
Messrs A D Naar	$30	
J G DaCosta	10	
F Bolefante	4	
R Pinto	4	
J M DaCosta Sr.	2	
S Snebel	8	
A Pinto Sen'r	4	
D L Henriquez	4	
Henriquez & Alberga	4	
Rev'd J López	4	
Messrs P Bravo	4	
A N Henriquez	2	
H Samuel	8	
D M Sollas	1	
Isaac Pinto	1	
A DeCordova	4	
J R de Cordova	4	
	98	98
Received from Mr D Naar for an Amateur performance at Theatre		70 40
Messrs G M Monsanto	8	
C Dickmann	8	
R W Goodchild	8	
Jacob Julien	8	
		$3472

Subscriptions received since last publication.
Mr. James Abbott $ 4
I. Rodriquez, a lot of Sand.

WEIGHT OF BREAD.

ACCORDING to the Price of Flour, during the preceding Week, the rate of Bread, is fixed until further notice, as follows:

A FIVE STIVER LOAF SHALL WEIGH
14 OUNCES,
and all other Loaves in proportion.
Police Office, St. Thomas, 3rd April 1833. H. H. BERG.

FIGURE 3 A list of contributors to the 1833 reconstruction of the St. Thomas synagogue, printed as the front page of the *St. Thomæ Tidende.*

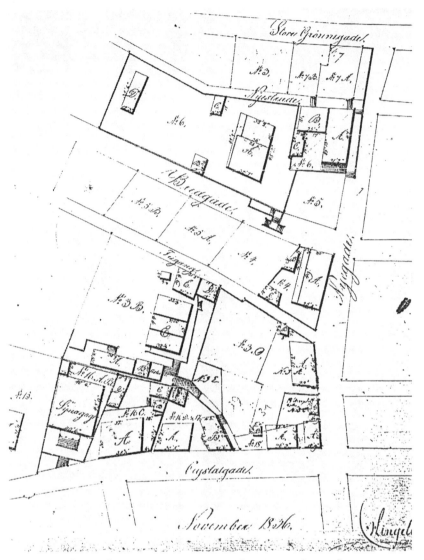

FIGURE 4   The St. Thomas synagogue in November 1836, as depicted in a government real estate survey. Synagogue is in lower left. From private collection of Katina Coulianos.

FIGURE 5   Exterior of the St. Thomas synagogue c. 1983, with the vestry on left.
Photo by George Blackhall.

FIGURE 7   Interior of the St. Thomas synagogue, c. 1983. The plaster was removed in a 1974 renovation, but replaced in the sanctuary's most recent renovation (2000 – 2002) due to erosion. Photo by George Blackhall.

FIGURE 8   Entrance and outer retaining wall of the old (Savan) cemetery. Photo by author, 1995.

FIGURE 9   Interior of the old (Savan) cemetery. Photo by author, 1995.

FIGURE 10 Entrance, outer retaining wall and preparation house of the new (Altona) cemetery. Photo by author, 1995.

FIGURE 11 Interior view of the new (Altona) cemetery. Photo by author, 1995.

FIGURE 12   The author, age 3, and Rabbi Stanley Relkin, in front of the holy ark in the St. Thomas synagogue, June 1977. Photo by Richard Cohen.

FIGURE 13   The congregation's seven-branched candelabra, popularly attributed to twelfth-century Spain. Photo by Ella Ogden, 2003.

FIGURE 14   The congregation's Chanukah lamp, dating to late eighteenth-century Amsterdam. The lamp was originally sent to the congregation in St. Eustatius, and was brought over to St. Thomas sometime later. Currently it is housed in the St. Thomas Hebrew congregation's museum. Photo by Ella Ogden, 2003.

CHAPTER 5

Development
1848–1867

It will be thus seen that there is light and intelligence even beyond the great centers of enlightenment, and the community of
St. Thomas can compare favorably with all others in this country
and Europe . . .

—Reverend Isaac Leeser, 1867

*O*n July 2 to 3, 1848, eight thousand slaves converged on
Frederiksted, a tiny but influential port city on the western end of St. Croix.
Having successfully organized a bloodless uprising, the slaves demanded immediate emancipation from the Danish government. Governor General Peter
von Scholten, recently returned to St. Croix from St. Thomas, held a meeting with his advisors to discuss the options. Just the previous year, the government had instituted a hopelessly compromised policy that intended to
free all slaves in gradual steps through 1859. Now, faced with the prospect of
an all-out battle, von Scholten saw he had little choice but to grant freedom
immediately. In a famous scene recounted in numerous Virgin Islands history books and at least one commercial movie, the Governor General
mounted his horse and rode through the streets of Frederiksted, shouting,
"Now you are free, you are hereby emancipated!"[1] With these words, the
Danish West Indian slavery system slid into the past.

While a success in the long-overdue journey to freedom for enslaved
Africans, emancipation proved an economic nightmare to the Danish West
Indies. It devastated the already-shrinking sugar trade on St. Croix, forcing

planters to pay increased wages for an ever-diminishing return. Emancipation also dealt an economic blow to the active port city of Charlotte Amalie, though the situation there was somewhat less dire. Money was plentiful and work always needed. Many slaves already received a wage (albeit minimal) for their labor, and saved it for the eventual purchase of their freedom; emancipation on its most immediate level generally meant a small pay raise. House slaves, meanwhile, ceased to be the property of their owners, and could theoretically work wherever they wished. Although the white and free black communities had to make some economic adjustments to accommodate these changes, the stable capitalistic trade system prevented drastic transitions from taking place too rapidly.[2]

A tiny Jewish community still existed on St. Croix, mostly in Christiansted. Too small and scattered to organize or employ a leader, they continued to keep up a little burial ground on a rolling hill, right across the street from the expansive Moravian cemeteries. On St. Thomas, meanwhile, Reverend Moses Nathan Nathan continued to lead services to the great satisfaction of a burgeoning congregation. Never before were the proceedings more organized and more unified on Saturday mornings, with a resuscitated choir and a demeanor that even attracted non-Jews to attend services on occasion.

While adhering to developments in the British prayer ritual, the St. Thomas congregation relied heavily on the United States for its ritual and religious items. From Isaac Leeser in Philadelphia, it ordered prayerbooks and Pentateuchs, as well as Lesser's *Catechism* for young Jewish children. From James Henry, Esq. in New York came *matzah,* the unleavened bread prepared annually for the Passover feast.[3] In the other direction, St. Thomas probably served as a supplier and distributor of locally grown citrons to North American and British Jewish communities for the celebration of *Sukkot.*[4]

The books and *matzah* came through the Main Street dry-goods store of Morris B. Simmonds, an accomplished merchant and an illustrious lay-leader in synagogue and island life. First coming to public mention in 1835 as the secretary of the island's Harmonic Lodge, Simmonds eventually held positions as secretary pro tem of the Commercial Marine Insurance Corporation and trustee of the St. Thomas Savings Bank. His Jewish activism supplemented, or even predated, that of Aron Wolff: Three years before Wolff's Sunday school opened, Simmonds was teaching evening Hebrew classes on St. Thomas.[5] An extensive Caribbean traveller, he was known to perform rituals occasionally in small Jewish communities without a minister. On February 8, 1847, for example, he circumcised David Baiz in the port town of Barcelona, Venezuela; the next year, he officiated at a Jewish wedding in

Caracas.[6] Simmonds also served as the Jewish correspondent for the island's almanac, providing annually a Jewish calendar and a list of the synagogue wardens for publication.[7] After constructing a home in 1848, he placed a marble plaque into the retaining wall that proudly displayed the Hebrew date and a Hebrew verse from the start of the 127th Psalm: "Unless God builds the house, its builders labor in vain on it."[8] Though not involved in island politics like Wolff or co-religionist Sigismund Rothschild, Simmonds repeatedly made his mark in the community. Few of his fellow congregants could imagine that a decade and a half later, his actions would also prove the prologue to the most turbulent and difficult years in the life of the St. Thomas Jews.

In 1850, the year Reverend Nathan's contract ended, the St. Thomas's Jewish population numbered 377.[9] Just before the year began, the congregation had lost the venerable Elias Sarquy and early island native Abraham Julien; several months later, Reverend Joshua Piza would also succumb.[10] Nathan, meanwhile, appeared to feel that his mission to reunify the St. Thomas synagogue had been accomplished. He began to search elsewhere for employment, and soon secured a position as minister of the Spanish and Portuguese synagogue in New Orleans. When the popular religious leader left the island in May, his impact on the congregation remained so strong that few could imagine replacing him.[11] The Jews thus found themselves once again leaderless. This time, however, they felt they had been given enough religious direction and education to sustain them for quite a while.

Services without a preacher left most of the work to the reader, Samuel Elias Levy Maduro. Every week, he faced a concentric congregation: Young boys would sit on the benches in the middle of the sanctuary, men would radiate out behind the boys, and the women surrounded the men, elevated a few feet behind them. As one visitor to the synagogue noticed, the men all wore prayer shawls (*talitot*) and covered their heads with broad-rimmed "Panama" beaver hats. Services were conducted according to a consistent ritual. The service for taking out and reading the Torah remained central to the ritual. Liturgical readings, frequently in English, were often presented responsively between reader and congregation. Merchants and sailors would make offerings and recite the *HaGomel* prayer before embarking upon or after returning from a journey.[12] Without Nathan, however, there was no one to give a religious discourse—creating a lacuna in the service that many congregants regretted sincerely.

Nathan's departure had caused the Jews of St. Thomas to face a difficult dilemma. The previous five years had been a honeymoon for the congregation. After the debacle surrounding Carillon, many had come to see Nathan as an exceptional blessing—the rare minister who could come from outside and tend their wild flock. A replacement, they thought, would be hard if not impossible to find. And although convention dictated that the synagogue advertise in Europe for its next minister, several congregants believed such a quest to be fruitless from the start. They procrastinated, opting instead to save their money; and wariness soon became inaction.

Meanwhile, a religious resurgence arose within the Christian population of the island. Already during the 1840s, open market days were changed from Sundays to Saturdays in deference to the churchgoing public.[13] By the late 1840s and early 1850s, evangelical letters to the paper brought the issue much further. "A DEPOSITOR" wrote several articles protesting the Savings Bank's policy of holding regular meetings in the vestry of the Dutch Reformed Church, reasoning that financial matters should not take place in a house of worship.[14] Other editorialists openly proposed introducing a law to prohibit all work on Sundays.[15] The Danish colonial government could do nothing about the bank meetings; but some hasty legislation soon established Sunday as an official day of rest. On March 20, 1852, the governor framed new regulations for the Christian "Sabbath Day," prohibiting business on Sundays and strictly limiting the hours of vital provisions stores.[16] The Jewish community, which might have found this proclamation a direct affront to their Saturday sabbath, put up no public protest. Quite to the contrary: several months later the editor of the *Tidende* noticed the law's remarkable compliance rate.[17]

By no means, however, did this activity dampen Jewish identity and religious affiliation on the island. Later in 1852, the Danish government, responding to public unrest, allowed the West Indian colonies to organize an elected council of local residents for the first time. Governor von Scholten, from central residence in St. Croix, announced his decision to hold the historic first vote on Saturday, August 28, 1852. Upon receiving the news in St. Thomas, however, Aron Wolff shot out a letter to the governor pointing out the election's conflict with the Jewish Sabbath and respectfully asking him to change the date. Wolff, who had been appointed one of the official vote counters for the election, added that he could not perform his function otherwise. The governor received the letter, agreed with Wolff, and quickly changed the elections to Monday, August 30. The American Jewish community reacted with admiration, and the *Occident* praised the deed as an example to Jewish communities around the world: ". . . if we respect ourselves and maintain our rights respectfully but firmly as Jews, the Christians will not be long in awarding us what they ought never to have refused."[18]

Almost a year later, the St. Thomas government appointed Aron Wolff to the islands' Burgher Council, a body governing merchant activities in the Danish West Indies. Normally, the council met on Saturdays, which again posed a problem to Wolff. He subsequently brought his complaint to the members of the council, and with little consternation they voted to change meeting times to Thursdays. Word of this action spread once again into North America, lionizing the adjustment on St. Thomas as a beacon to other communities.[19]

Yet while the community celebrated its social victories, it continued to suffer from lack of a knowledgable religious leader. Once again, jobs and mercantile dealings rose in prominence, and service attendance returned to compulsory status. Many sat in the pews, helping Reader Maduro to perform the ritual with great order and solemnity. But the Hebrew words slowly drifted into empty sounds, the English prayers into parroted chants. Without a person to bring the words to life, to implore the congregation weekly to take these words into their hearts, the service lost much of its meaning. The synagogue's education system, established under Carillon and expanded under Nathan, diminished, no longer earning the glowing reports that the *Tidende* once proclaimed. Confirmations ceased. Stories circulated of congregants attending other churches simply "for the gratification of hearing a sermon."[20] Life went on, however, as St. Thomas provided many pursuits that could fill the religious hole left in the wake of Nathan's departure.

A number of congregants felt the vacuum of religious leadership acutely and feared that a continued vacancy would spell disaster for the Jewish community. Their exhortations no doubt convinced the synagogue's board to publish advertisements in the international Jewish press in 1853. Appearing in the *Occident, Archives Israélites*, and *Jewish Chronicle*, among others, the ads requested a minister who was a talented instructor with a good demeanor, had expertise in English, and fluency in the Spanish and Portuguese *minhag*. A minister who met these qualities would receive a salary of $1,200 annually, which could be supplemented through other instruction.[21]

At least two eager responses came across the Atlantic applying for the position. To each, however, the synagogue board, led by island merchant J. H. Osorio, sent a lukewarm answer, "that at a future day, they (the representatives) will decide on making the election. But that day has not yet come . . ."[22] In fact, as the ads quickly disappeared from the papers, not a single minister received an invitation to preach in front of the congregation.[23]

A number of people were disturbed by what seemed to them an ingenuous search process, and they challenged the board's sincerity. In response, the wardens argued that the congregation did not have enough money to pay the $1,200 salary. Behind this lay a strong ambivalence over engaging a minister in the first place, and possibly incurring the same litany of problems as had plagued them before. Nothing the small pro-minister faction said could affect the staid board.

In 1856, another chance opened up with the changing of the synagogue leadership. In elections at the beginning of the year, the congregation appointed J. H. Osorio to his third three-year term as president. Exercising his rights under the 1848 bylaws, however, Osorio declined to take the position, preferring instead to remove himself from the public eye.[24] Chances are, Osorio was an advocate of hiring a minister and became frustrated with the rest of the board's inaction.[25] Some members recognized this move as a major blow to the ministerial selection process, for within a few months, several letters appeared in the *Tidende* and *Occident* pleading with the congregation's board for a minister.

Penned under pseudonyms by at least four individuals, the letters portrayed a devoted and frustrated faction who feared for their religious lives and those of their children. In grandiose, powerful prose, they rendered their argument time and time again. All appealed directly to the synagogue members to "unite . . . in relieving ourselves of the charge of apathy or neglect in regard to the matters of education."[26] A minister, they said, was essential to Jewish identity, for his teaching kept scripture fresh in the mind, and his lessons provided everyone with the appropriate armor to resist proselytizing. "Education, you are aware, is power," wrote one appellant. "[I]t is therefore the *lever of mankind.*"[27]

Moreover, the letters spoke of the guiding power of Jewish education to the religious lives of children. "Religion must be the basis of education, or else it is valueless. Israel has been educated by God himself to be a people of religion, and how can our children know this fact without the aid of religious knowledge?"[28] More ominously, another added: "Do we not frequently witness faith sacrificed at the shrine of [youthful] passion? grief and sorrow and estrangement introduced into the bosom of families, where before peace and affection dwelt? And all mainly attributable to communities who failed to perceive the want of a Minister to communicate whilst youth is just building the first lessons of their religion . . ."[29] A third aimed straight for the throat: "Parents. . . . Do you remember your wedding-day, and the promise you then made before God and men, that should your union be blessed with offspring, you would educate them in the religion of your forefathers? Alas! I do not wish to think that the other promises made on that solemn occasion have been alike violated!"[30] The object of a minister and teacher, the writers insisted, was crucial to the welfare of the Jewish community; a requirement for the health of the Jewish adult, and the mind of the Jewish child.

The heartfelt appeals, from all angles and attitudes, fell on deaf ears. Even a public call to mobilize families by name was ineffective.[31] While these active members campaigned, a majority of the congregants remembered back to the cocky Reverend Carillon, who inculcated the congregation with a deep-seeded distrust through his intellectual exercises; or Reverend Nathan, who could hardly achieve unity without the most strenuous of efforts, and who then left after only five years with the congregation. To invest in another outside minister, and possibly destroy the public peace, would be too much of a risk.[32] Further, Reader Maduro was seen to perform an adequate job, and served as an adequate figurehead for the time being. The congregation thus remained complacent; and after a while, the voices of protest died away.

In August, 1856, J. H. Osorio re-emerged as the co-founder of a new Hebrew Benevolent Association on the island. St. Thomas, as a prosperous port, was also a beacon for the poor and destitute from other Caribbean areas. This was especially the case in the 1850s, when a rapid series of revolutions caused havoc throughout Venezuela and Central America. Many well-established residents in these areas lost their property and personal rights during the conflicts, and felt compelled to relocate to places with more stable governments.[33] A number of Jews—relatives and business associates of residents in St. Thomas and Curaçao—were included among the victims of the uprisings. With their other options poor to nil, they travelled to these islands with hopes of an amiable reception and some financial assistance. The Hebrew Benevolent Assocation served these needs, trying to provide the immigrants with a smooth transition into a new environment.

Subitled "Refuge of the Poor," Osorio's organization appeared to have been inspired by an analagous association created three years earlier in Curaçao. That group administered funds to its poor through a central bank account supported by subscriptions from the community, a setup that initially had proven effective in absorbing the Jewish community of Coro, Venezuela, when it was hastily expelled in 1855.[34] Although conditions in Coro had improved a few months after the crisis, most of the 160 Jews who fled to Curaçao never returned to their offices and homes. It is possible that some of the Coro community decided to move north and settle in St. Thomas over the next year, thus necessitating the establishment of a similar institution there.[35]

Whatever the case, the Hebrew Benevolent Association's establishment on St. Thomas proved that at least some active Jewish presence still existed on the island—culturally if not religiously. The organization was entirely separate from the synagogue board, electing its own officers, holding meetings in private homes, and relying heavily on female congregants to collect (and give) donations. Over the next several years, the Benevolent Association operated in full view of the local society, and its fundraising functions became some of the most popular social events on the island.

It also appears that this organization may have been responsible for a new emphasis on Jewish religious life in St. Thomas. In late 1857, the Curaçao congregation's chief religious leader, Dutch Reverend Aaron Mendes Chumaceiro, made his first trip to St. Thomas at the congregation's request. An esteemed intellect and a renowned scholar, Reverend Chumaceiro's visit aimed to wake the St. Thomas Jews into observance. By occupying their pulpit, though only temporarily, he hoped to remind the Jews of the importance of education and learned religious leadership to their faith.

Chumaceiro arrived on the Dutch packet-steamer *Essex* in the middle of November to a pleasing reception and great anticipation. His imposing, bearded figure and halting English must have impressed the community. However, when Reverend Chumaceiro delivered his initial sermon on November 21, it fell flat. The content was not to blame, as several came out attesting to the fluid, eloquent style of the discourse. Rather, the difficulty was an unanticipated language barrier reminiscent of Reverend Carillon. Insecure with English, Chumaceiro gave his sermon in Dutch. Few understood his message; but, thirsting for a sermon of any sort, most of the congregation appreciated the Reverend's passionate delivery nonetheless.[36]

The next Wednesday, Chumaceiro gave another sermon—this time in the more commonly understood second language of Portuguese. Speaking from the reader's desk for an hour that evening, his long discourse touched upon religious understanding of the commandments, transitioned into a polemic against reformers who tried to change rabbinic law, and concluded by enumerating his refutations to the reformers' arguments. Members of the congregation who were by then "Israelites only by name," according to one observer, attended the service and listened raptly as "every word the Reverend uttered [had] its counterpart among the Israelites of Saint Thomas."[37] Even in a foreign language, the minister found his way to the hearts of the congregation, teaching once again a compelling argument for direction and professional leadership. A final service the following Sabbath ended Chumaceiro's stay; but by this point the community had been galvanized. Again, the minister delivered his sermon in Portuguese; and again the audience listened with great appreciation. The overwhelming public response to Chumaceiro's sermons would soon make it clear that hiring a minister was an inevitable next step.

In the meantime, however, Chumaceiro brought honor and legitimacy to Reader Samuel Elias Levy Maduro. During his visit, the Curaçao reverend presented Maduro with a certificate of recognition, attesting to his "qualifications and piety" as leader of the St. Thomas congregation. In addition to the written tribute, Chumaceiro conferred the honorary title of "*Negnim Zemirot Yisrael,*" or "Sweet Singer of Israel," upon the man. Although purely symbolic, the title accomplished a spiritual revolution on the island.[38] Curaçao's Jewish community recognized and endorsed a religious figure on St. Thomas. Maduro's distinction as an international "official" gave him a status above that of lay-leader; and it also served to smooth over his relations with the Curaçao congregation after the bitter disputes surrounding him there in 1844 to 1845. Moreover, Maduro's honor reflected positively upon the congregation, giving the members an elevated self-image and an increased desire to fulfil their religious obligations in partnership with Curaçao.

As Chumaceiro left the island, the empowered synagogue presented him with a statement of gratitude signed by eighty-one congregants, and made preparations for a tribute of thanks to be sent to Curaçao in the near future. Chumaceiro thanked the community for its hospitality in response, and suggested that he would return the next autumn with one of his sons, presenting him to the congregation as its next religious leader.[39]

This anticipated young minister never arrived, however. For the next two years, Reader Maduro remained alone in the St. Thomas pulpit, singing sweet songs of hope to his impatient flock.

—◦◦◦—

WHEN THE ST. THOMAS JEWS least expected it, their next minister appeared—and it was not who they expected. In the middle of 1860, a packet steamer from Barbados made a routine stop at St. Thomas, docking for a while to drop off and pick up mail before continuing on to Jamaica. One of the passengers on this ship, a twenty-four-year-old bachelor named Meyer H. Myers, was unwell, suffering from a fever that had ailed him for the previous six months. Rather than continue on to Jamaica, he decided to disembark on St. Thomas and remain there until his condition improved.[40]

Myers's family boasted a known and respected lineage of British rabbinical leaders, represented especially well among his immediate relatives. His uncle, the Reverend J. H. Myers, served as a chaplain to the prominent financier and philanthropist Sir Moses Montefiore. Reverend Moses Henry Myers, his father, served the congregation of the Great Synagogue in London.[41] On the other side of the globe, Myers's brother, Reverend E. M. Myers, served in the pulpit of the Melbourne Hebrew congregation.[42] Although uncredentialled himself, Myers knew all about the role and skills of ministering, and had a good deal of practice in the art of English sermon intonation. His abilities did not go unnoticed for long on the island.

On Myers's first Sabbath in St. Thomas, a number of congregants approached him and requested that he give a discourse on that week's reading from the Torah. Myers conceded.[43] That Sabbath morning, as he climbed into the pulpit and delivered his religious lesson, a new dawn seemed to shine on the old congregation. Ten years without a teacher, many found Myers's words to be electrifying; they saw before them a prospective instructor for their children and a sage mind for the island. With little hesitation, the congregation resolved to extend the young man's stay as long as possible.

The next day, Sunday, the congregation held a meeting to discuss hiring Myers as their full-time minister. Although the Jews overwhelmingly agreed to employ his services—only one voting member opposed the action—they faced a dilemma in his lack of credentials.[44] Myers was not an ordained minister, and thus could not perform marriages or funerals for the congregation until he received authorization from the Danish government. After some debate, the Jews settled on a solution that would satisfy all sides. Myers's salary for the first year would be raised through private subscription, which the synagogue would supplement through a two hundred dollar donation.[45] During this time, the members stipulated, Myers needed to solicit recommendations from other rabbinic figures in order to apply for rabbinic ordination through the Chief Rabbi of Copenhagen.[46] Myers agreed to the plan, scrapping his intentions for Jamaica and directing his full attention to the St. Thomas community.

Miraculously, the spontaneous partnership worked well for the first few months. Myers gave lectures every Sabbath and Holy Day, eventually supplementing them with a series of children's lectures on Saturday afternoons. During the high holidays that year, the synagogue once again filled past capacity as the new scholar delivered a "soul-stirring" discourse, attempting to spur at least some of the congregation to pursue stricter observance.[47] The Hebrew School, rejuvenated under the auspices of one Mrs. Mesquita, a Curaçaoan lady who arrived in the island around the same time as Myers, supplemented the preacher's lessons with Saturday morning classes. Reader Maduro, meanwhile, continued at his post, guiding the congregation through the liturgy at each service.

Contributing to this renaissance of Jewish life were several refugee families from Barcelona, Venezuela. Once a prosperous port city about 550 miles due south of the Danish West Indies, Barcelona bowed to the revolutions ravaging the rest of the country in the early 1860s. Its outpost Jewish community—generally small, unorganized, and secularized—realized the dangers of remaining there, and many left their shops and businesses for safer shores. Most headed to St. Thomas due to its close familial, mercantile, and spiritual ties to the area. Arriving on the island, destitute and with little Jewish knowledge, the immigrant families strapped the St. Thomas Jews with a substantial demand for aid and education.[48] The Hebrew Benevolent Society sprang into action, planning a large benefit ball to meet the increased strain on its funds.[49] Preacher Myers and co-religionist J. L. Penha applied successfully for governmental permission to form new schools that addressed the needs of the new immigrants. Penha's school, for example, taught students in English, Spanish, and Hebrew, and provided extra English lessons for those who needed them.[50] Myers and Penha also took joint control of the St. Thomas Commercial Academy, inviting the new arrivals to train for a mercantile career as they acculturated to the island's language and customs. Meanwhile, Jewish pride continued to flourish. By March 1861, the town bookstore, owned by synagogue member Gabriel Correa, proudly distributed free copies of Myers's sermons; and auctioneer Judah Cappé caught the fever started by Aron Wolff, countering anti-Semitic remarks in the paper and protesting events scheduled for Saturdays.[51]

Myers, meanwhile, sent requests for references out to England. A number of testimonials returned, praising Mr. Myers's abilities and recommending him for the ministerial post. Along with these, however, came one other note, seemingly originating in the Caribbean, which cast a shadow over the entire proceeding. Sent by Myers's uncle, it came into the hands of Mr. Abraham Elias Pretto, who then presented it to the Board of Representatives. The missive was surprising and damning, accusing the aspiring minister of scandalous conduct during his younger life that "would have made him perfectly unfit for his calling and position in life."[52] It reflected badly on Myers's character, and, claimed Pretto, jeopardized Myers's future with the synagogue. At first the board took no notice. But Pretto pressed his case, threatening to suspend his synagogue membership if the board did not proceed with an investigation. Reluctantly, the officers agreed to look into the charges.

On November 18, 1860, the group presented its findings at a select meeting of the voting members, and claimed that the letter's accusations were baseless. Above the protests of Mr. Pretto, who by this point had been joined in his objection by Dr. Daniel Pretto Henriquez and merchants Jacob and Mordecai Maduro, the Board passed a motion to drop the case.[53]

Several months later, however, the issue reared up again. Early in 1861, the uncle whose accusations had created the first controversy embarked on a trip from Europe to the Caribbean. The journey brought him to St. Thomas, where he and a travel companion remained for several days while preparing to transfer to another ship. The board saw this as an opportunity to prove Myers's innocence beyond a doubt, and consequently called the uncle in to a meeting. In the presence of the younger Myers, they asked him to retract his statements. But the scheme backfired: Myers's uncle was obstinate and refused to change his story. To make matters worse, the travel companion stepped forward a few days later and, in the presence of Myers, his uncle, and the board, "stated the same accusations that were contained in the letters of the uncle, and added other accusations."

After the second meeting, young Myers flew into a rage. For the uncle who, he claimed, "persecuted him, with a bitter, but unmerited hatred," Myers delivered a string of loud and abusive epithets in the middle of the street. After this, the aspiring preacher dragged his uncle's travel companion into a store and horsewhipped him for his complicity. To many on the island, this stunning show displayed by the minister was a justified, if not excessive, reaction to alleged slander; but the incident also fed his critics with new and dangerous fodder. The Maduro brothers, who opposed Myers from the start of the allegations, used the outburst to label him "unfit to fill the Station that he temporarily . . . excercised."[54] Others as well began to question their minister's once unblemished reputation.

Damage to Myers's career was minimal at first. The offending uncle and his friend departed on their trip across the Atlantic, and memories faded. Sometime later, on May 3, 1861, Myers's good references came through and he was granted a certificate from Copenhagen's Chief Rabbi Alexander A. Wolff. Conferring the title *Moreinu Rab* ["Our Teacher"] upon the preacher, the document granted him the power to perform official synagogue functions.[55] Soon after, the congregation held a special installation ceremony in celebration. The young ladies of the congregation presented themselves before their newly confirmed religious leader, and gave him "an elegant clerical robe, as a memento of their regard."[56] This gesture, and the service that surrounded it, signalled the congregation's enthusiastic and expectant acknowledgement of Myers's fitness for the post.

Months passed. High holiday services, where the Jewish community was most exposed to God, the public, and themselves, appeared to go smoothly.[57] Nonetheless, a small group continued to harrass the minister through small but telling events. On the Day of Atonement that fall, for example, Reverend Myers sent the synagogue's sexton on an errand to another part of the synagogue. Jacob Maduro noticed this and stopped the sexton en route. According to the Myers's own testimony, Maduro then turned to preacher "and winked at him with a triumphant smile," an act Myers saw as threatening to his authority.[58] Such indications enforced the growing rift between the preacher and a part of his congregation.

The situation eventually became so tense that the congregation needed but a minor mistranslation to set the fires loose. During the first days of January 1862, Myers set off on a visit to Curaçao in order to introduce himself to St. Thomas's sister congregation. Staying in the port capital of Willemstad, Myers gave a successful sermon to a synagogue packed with Jews and interested islanders, and earning the admiration of the island's governor in addition to the Jewish population. On February 1, a few weeks after his return, the *Tidende* reprinted a short article from Curaçao's newspaper that gave an outline of the trip. As a local Dutch scholar translated it, the article began: "The Israelitish congregation of this island were lately favored with a visit from Rev. Dr. M. H. Myers, preacher of the Israelitish congregation of the island of St. Thomas."[59] And with this, a great controversy arose.

Dr. Daniel Pretto Henriquez, a native son and one of a handful of authorized physicians on the island, was the primary complainant. Already unhappy about the turn of events surrounding the minister's character the previous year, he bristled at Myers's new title of "Reverend Doctor." Writing under the pseudonym of "ISRAELITE," he criticized what he saw as outright deception. "This honorable title [Rev. Dr.] would point out a man of distinction, of great talent, deep research, &c. &c. . . . but when a man has never received a diploma from any part of the world, but merely the character of 'Morenu,' which signifies 'Instructor,' he should be ashamed to try to impose himself, under false colors, to a congregation of his co-religionists in any colony."[60] To Dr. Pretto, Myers was a devious miscreant, who masked his previous wrongs in order to reap a false respectability. Knowledgable in the pains required to attain the true title of "doctor," Pretto wished to defend the honor from corruption.

Other congregants did not see the situation in the same light. The synagogue board was first to respond, stating simply that *Moreinu Rab* did indeed translate into "Reverend Doctor"; case closed. But this was far from the last word. In the same issue of the paper, board member Benjamin Cohen D'Azevedo led the charge against "Israelite," by "briefly call[ing] attention to a few facts regarding the villany and falsehood contained in [his] communication." D'Azevedo abhorred Pretto's attempt to discredit Myers in the public eye, and responded in a brash and forceful manner, calling the doctor a "dastard," and refuting every one of his points at length.[61]

The ensuing debate comprised a heated, eloquent, and lengthy exchange of letters in the *Tidende*. Pretto remained the primary voice for his faction, holding steadfastly that Myers was a rogue who would never deserve "Doctor" status. The title of "Morenu" was "but honorary and require[d] further confirmation," in his eyes; and the translator of the original Curaçao article was a "fool" who added the title unnecessarily.[62] D'Azevedo held strongly to the other side, attacking Pretto's character and intelligence and maintaining unwavering support for Myers. For a month the battle raged, causing several other island residents—including the translator of the original Curaçao article—to add their thoughts and rhetoric to the melée. Personal threats passed publicly between Pretto and D'Azevedo, even including what appeared to be a veiled challenge to a duel.[63] Throughout all of this, Meyer Myers wisely kept his peace, allowing others to speak for him; he had more important plans in mind.

Curaçao Reverend Aaron Mendes Chumaceiro's visit to the island that March carried a double purpose.[64] One part of his mission was pastoral: He attempted to play the "messenger of peace" and patch up the differences bringing so much friction to the members of the congregation. But his main purpose was far more personal. The sage rabbi, who had befriended Myers earlier that year, was to officiate at the young reverend's wedding ceremony. Gratifying the hopes of many, Myers's rapport with the young women of the congregation proved fruitful, and he soon became engaged to twenty-four-year-old Rachel D'Oliveyra, daughter of the deceased St. Lucian–born merchant Jacob D'Oliveyra. Chumaceiro sailed into St. Thomas's harbor on a hot and sunny Purim day, Sunday, March 16, 1862.[65] The Hebrew Congregation, excited to host the great man once again, took him into the community.

That Wednesday, the synagogue filled with "persons of all denominations" as they observed a rare event—the only wedding in the history of the St. Thomas synagogue conducted by a Curaçaoan minister. Following the conventions expected of visiting scholars, Chumaceiro first gave an "eloquent and appropriate address," presumably speaking to some of the issues in the St. Thomas Jewish community while praising the awaiting groom. Then, showing public approbation for Myers in front of the entire island, he joined the minister in holy matrimony with his bride. Reader Samuel Elias Levy Maduro took an active part in the program, assisting Chumaceiro with his duties and signing the marriage contract.[66]

Reverend Chumaceiro's actions worked wonders for the congregation, which reaffirmed its unity under his supervision. Remaining for two weeks after the wedding, he preached in the synagogue several times, always earning the profound respect of his audience. Chumaceiro's topics dealt directly with the synagogue's conflicts, and encouraged the eradication of strife and discord. His sermon on Sabbath morning, March 22, was a perfect example. The gifted speaker chose as his basic text Ezekiel 36:25–26:

> And I will sprinkle upon you clean water, and ye shall be clean; from all your impurities, and from all your idols will I cleanse you. And I will give you a new heart, and a new spirit will I put within you; and I will remove the heart of stone out of your body and give you a heart of flesh."[67]

The powerful meaning of this passage in light of recent events extended beyond a literal and mystical foundation. To the congregation, the opening allusion to ablution from sin linked their spiritual and residential lives: The libellous insults and mistrust that had threatened to rip the synagogue apart over the past year, notably, had been accompanied in St. Thomas by a severe drought. Ezekiel's promise of cleansing was thus not just symbolic, but also a desperately real allusion to the need for rainfall. When Chumaceiro ended his sermon with a prayer for the welfare of the congregation, his audience consequently felt the weight and enormity of his exhortations.[68]

Nine days later, at Chumaceiro's final sermon before returning to Curaçao, the minister finished his presentation with a direct prayer for "'refreshing showers' of rain," hoping that with the communal dispute on the mend, the water crisis would soon end as well. The congregation gave him a solemn farewell, presenting him with a statement of gratitude signed by one hundred and seventeen synagogue members and thanking him for promoting peace among the local populace, "an object so dear to your heart, [and] so dear to the heart of every Israelite." On Wednesday, April 2, the Dutch Reverend boarded the packet schooner *Sarah* and left his adoring coreligionists, never to return.[69]

All remained quiet and content for about three months as Chumaceiro's magical spell was sustained. Life returned to normal, and harmony appeared to reign among the Jews. Then, in July, Reverend Myers approached the board with two strange requests: He wanted an advance on his salary for the quarter, as well as a month's leave. The first of these solicitations went against accepted practice, and both inspired suspicion; but the board appeared to be worried more about continuing a good rapport with the minister, and so voted to give him what he desired. At least one congregant, upon hearing of the situation, criticized the board for being far too naïve. He noted, "[it is] well known to them and to the whol[e congregation] of Israelites, that [Myers] proceeds to [Jama]ica . . . [in] search of more lucrative employment, in which if successful, will be paying him for what he cannot render here . . ."[70]

Myers took his money and left on a late-July steamship for Jamaica. By the time he returned, the worst of the congregation's fears had been realized. While away from St. Thomas, Myers had indeed taken the opportunity to seek ministerial positions with better financial offerings and more supportive congregations. His search did not take long: An opening was confirmed at the German congregation in Kingston, and Myers applied for the job. Once the synagogue's committee had confirmed the preacher's abilities and qualifications, they extended to him an attractive offer. Soon after, Myers announced his resignation to the St. Thomas Board.

Within a month, the preacher and his wife had sold their St. Thomas real estate (a large property with a house down the street from the synagogue), auctioned off the goods that could not be easily shipped (including a piano and a "Porto Rico racing PONY"), collected all their debts, and left for Kingston.[71] For all the rumor and speculation that had come before Myers's defection, his loss still shook the Jewish community, depriving it of an educator, a teacher, and a charismatic leader.

IN SHORT ORDER, ads for a new minister appeared in the *Occident* and elsewhere. Identical to the ads placed in 1854, they appeared almost compulsory.[72] Isaac Leeser, editor of the *Occident*, attempted to make the vacant pulpit look more attractive by extolling St. Thomas's virtues in his journal:

> St. Thomas is favorably situated for a man of talent and piety to obtain an enviable reputation. It is a stopping place for the various steam packets navigating the West India seas, and therefore many Israelites must continually stay there, if it be but a few days or hours even; a person therefore residing there is

not so shut out from the outside world as others though in larger islands. Educating a number of children from St. Thomas and other islands would add considerably to the minister's salary. All these considerations will, we trust, induce a truly worthy man to apply for the position.[73]

Additionally, the St. Thomas Jews took two expensive risks that they expected would both improve the congregation and attract a new minister. Soon after Myers left, the congregation reconsidered its policy on the minister's salary. Embarrassed by its compromised "unofficial" arrangement with Myers, and tired of the constant ambivalence of its congregants to donate to a minister's salary, the synagogue board applied to the colonial government for help. The government responded on November 22, authorizing the board to raise the minister's salary through taxation of the congregants, even if doing so doubled the synagogue's annual budget. Should any collection difficulties arise, the directive noted, the government would step in to assist.[74] Ample funds for a new minister thus were theoretically assured.

The board also turned its attention to expanding the congregation's physical space. The synagogue building, comprising solely a one-room sanctuary, was deemed too small for the congregation's needs: the Board of Representatives, for example, had to hold its meetings in the office of a local store, while religious schools needed to assemble in private homes. Experiencing a burgeoning population, the wardens thus decided in early December to transform a small plaza space on the southwest corner of the property into a fireproof vestry room. The proposed structure would centralize the congregation's nonritual functions, acting as a classroom, a meeting chamber, and a space for the anticipated minister to prepare for services. Protests arose among the congregants, with some arguing that the additional structure would be an aesthetic aberration that would obscure the synagogue's façade. But the perceived need for the additional space caused such arguments to fall by the wayside. The congregation took out a $1,400 loan and began construction.[75]

It is possible to suggest that the St. Thomas Jews made these preparations blindly, preparing for a new minister to come from afar and take root. But more likely, the congregation enhanced the synagogue with a candidate already in mind. Their intended preacher was intelligent, delivered eloquent English sermons, performed the Spanish and Portuguese rite ably, and carried an agreeable disposition. He was also an old friend.

In early 1863, Reverend Moses Nathan Nathan found himself once again standing at a synagogue pulpit in Jamaica. After several years preaching in

New Orleans, Nathan turned down a $2,000 salary offer in order to live a quieter, less politically charged life at a pulpit in Galveston, Texas.[76] A few years later, Nathan retired, his own investments assisted by a 15,000 franc bequest left by his friend, the famous Jewish philanthropist Judah Touro.[77]

By this time, however, Nathan had garnered an international reputation, and his attempts to disappear from public life were futile. Nathan and his wife moved back to Kingston, Jamaica, with the intention of living out their final years in comfort and warmth. Instead, they found a somewhat reduced Jewish community who welcomed the minister back and clamored for his leadership. Nathan, bound through a sense of duty to his co-religionists, could not refuse. In 1859, he dashed his ideas of retirement and recommenced his ministry on the island, to the joy of the Jewish residents.[78]

Four years later, with Myer Myers now preaching at the neighboring German congregation, the St. Thomas Jewish community approached Nathan. They presented their suit, offering him several strong incentives to return to St. Thomas's empty pulpit. Nathan carried positive memories from his tenure in the 1840s, and the generous terms proposed for his return were too lucrative to pass up; the minister accepted. He closed his school, announced his resignation from the Kingston pulpit, and began to gather his belongings for transport east.

But while Nathan made his preparations, more trouble began to brew. The St. Thomas board's recent actions had shown strength and direction for the synagogue; the same decisions, however, had resulted in increased taxation, which angered a number of the congregants.[79] In particular, the synagogue's decision to assess voting and non-voting congregants equally proved hotly controversial. Several of the non-voting members, most of them young men who found such taxation a hardship, joined with several voting members in September 1863 to petition the government to reassess the board's judgments.[80] The board, receiving a copy of the letter, seems to have dismissed the missive and subsequently introduced a punitive act barring non-voting members from attending meetings of the voting community.[81] Only three of the five wardens signed the proposal, but the majority was enough to send the motion to the voting population. For the next three weeks, the text of the proposition appeared on the synagogue wall, and was announced at Sabbath services. Protests calling the measure "illegal, unwarranted, and tyrannical," came and went, reflecting the sentiments of a young and increasingly powerful portion of the congregation.[82] In the end, the protests seem to have succeeded in killing the referendum. Tensions between synagogue factions, however, did not dissipate so easily.

By the time Nathan had left Jamaica on September 9, 1863, the Jews of St. Thomas were beginning a silent standoff. The reverend, who likely sensed this upon his arrival, appeared to view the scene as a less explosive variant of the conditions surrounding his previous tenure. Accordingly he took a positivist's approach and dove straight into his work. Nathan moved to the island on the day before *Rosh Hashanah*, led services through the holidays with little incident, and subsequently resumed his trustee position at the St. Thomas Savings Bank. On October 25, Hurricane Thanksgiving Day services took place at a new time, enhanced by one of Nathan's sermons; soon after this the minister opened a boarding school on the island and restarted the long-neglected synagogue confirmation class.[83]

A month and a half later, the well-regarded Danish King Frederick VII passed away after a fifteen-year reign. All the religious buildings draped their edifices in black, but the synagogue was granted the honor of holding the island's memorial service. Surrounded by the governor, numerous officials, clergymen of all denominations, and much of the Jewish population, Reverend Nathan declaimed a sermon entitled "The Citizen King" as a poignant reminder of the sovereign's benevolent rule. The event received a great deal of attention: The *Tidende* printed an account of the service, and Nathan's sermon soon appeared in published form from the *Tidende*'s office.[84]

Yet dissent still coursed through the congregation's ranks, especially from those who loathed the synagogue's new high taxes. Whether voting members or not, everyone had to contribute according to his or her income. Others who were in a more comfortable financial position simply disagreed with the opinions and acts expressed by the board. Probably the most ironic and tragic of these stories centered around Mr. Morris B. Simmonds, former Hebrew teacher, *Mohel*, and synagogue emissary. Mysteriously, when taxes became due in late 1863, Simmonds did not respond. The board sent Simmonds several letters insisting that he pay his share, but received only the response that Simmonds no longer regarded himself as a member of the synagogue. Although he offered to give a forty dollar annual donation over the next five years as a form of severance pay, he claimed to profess Judaism no longer.

The board, confounded, refused to accept this arrangement. Simmonds then responded by sending a communication to both island and synagogue governments, further detailing his split from Judaism and reiterating his claim of exemption from synagogue taxes. The board appealed to the island government, denouncing Simmonds's argument as a paltry excuse to avoid taxation. The government, however, thought otherwise; it considered arguments about this case for three years, and finally sided with Simmonds. For the board, which hoped to receive full cooperation from the government for tax collection, this was a stunning setback.[85]

Although there is no direct evidence that Simmonds left the synagogue out of differences with the ruling board, his secession note gave some interesting details to his ideological journey. Writing to the government on December 16, 1863, he claimed "that his religious convictions are such as to render him no more a believer according to the Jewish faith." Instead, he considered himself a Unitarian—a free thinker who valued his own approaches to religious belief.[86] Simmonds's new identity did not rest on pressures from other religious groups: While other denominations boasted several hundred, or even several thousand members on St. Thomas, an 1850 census revealed only two Unitarians; and there is no reason to believe their numbers were significantly higher in 1863.[87] Instead, Simmonds's apostasy from Judaism seemed to signify a personal dissatisfaction with religious lifestyle. Considering the restrictive and financially strapping policies implemented by the board over the past year, Reverend Nathan's known conservative stance, and Simmonds's strong religious activism in the past, political motives for his "conversion" are attractive—albeit speculative—motivations as well.

Simmonds's case legally established membership in the Jewish community as a voluntary activity based on religious beliefs. A sincere claim to observe another religion became all that was necessary for a congregant to leave the fold, and effectively become exempt from paying synagogue taxes.[88] While most discontented congregants would not take a step as drastic as converting out of their faith, the precedent set was nonetheless significant. Simmonds remained on the island professing dignified independence for several more years, while taking on prominent roles in the island's Savings Bank, Gas Company, and Marine Insurance business.[89] His successful legal defense, meanwhile, would soon be reinvoked on a wider and much more devastating scale.

Throughout this time, the board, in conjunction with Reverend Nathan, appeared to take a more conservative tack, reflecting the needs of the older, wealthier, more established members of the congregation who provided the synagogue with much of its income. Younger congregants struggling to set up their businesses and start their families, in contrast, began to feel disenfranchised and overlooked. Contemporary trends in Judaism—such as instrumental music in the synagogue, new prayerbooks, or new approaches to integrating religious and secular life—were gaining acceptance in America and England; but although they had their adherents on St. Thomas as well, there was little representation in the leadership to help implement them. The strongest advocate for innovation on the board, twenty-eight-year-old Moses De Sola, had to face a majority of older men on every issue.[90]

The next year, news of a religious struggle began to filter north from Curaçao. *Kahal Kadosh Mikveh Israel,* thought to be the impregnable stronghold of Caribbean Jewry, was crumbling. A militant faction of reform-minded Jews had emerged from within the congregation and started to cause enormous upheavals. Calling themselves *El Porvenir* ("the Future"), the group began publishing a scandalous newspaper called *Shemah Yisrael* ("Hear, O Israel!"), which made cruel accusations against the synagogue and nearly caused an anti-Jewish riot to break out on the island.[91] Although the uprising fell short of causing physical violence, its ideological and political aims met with resounding success. Not only did *El Porvenir* establish its own synagogue, which adopted the Reform liturgy of New York's Temple *Emanu-El;* it also forced *Mikveh Israel* to make liturgical changes of its own, and add an organ and choir to its worship service.[92] Jews in St. Thomas observed these events with interest. While they hoped to avoid such a confrontation on their little island, they also realized that the "Orthodox" moniker no longer reigned as the standard in Jewish life—even among approval-conscious Caribbean Jews.

By 1865, the younger faction of the St. Thomas congregation had mustered enough confidence to make its first move. Several members approached the board on August 28 with a petition recommending "changes or alterations" to the Divine Service. Their board ally, Moses De Sola (now thirty years old), had become president of the synagogue. Although he had no greater vote than he had as a regular board member, De Sola's mere presence in the high post ensured a voice for younger concerns. This was confirmed with the board's communication the next day, requesting the petitioners to submit a description of the changes they wished to implement.[93] In response, the congregants drafted a series of proposed reforms to the Divine Service in a pamphlet, and carefully circulated it to anticipated supporters, both young and old. Although a couple of the more established members would not support the proposal, it still gained strong minority support as forty-five congregants affixed their signatures to the cover letter.[94] "We do not claim perfection for our labor," the document read, "being aware that even learned men differ in their opinion whenever called upon to perform similar tasks, & convinced therefore of this well-known fact, we claim due indulgence . . ."[95] Though only congregants, they nonetheless felt their mission to be important and worth consideration. President De Sola received the papers on Septem-ber

14, 1865, and subsequently called a meeting of the board and minister to deliberate on the issue.

As the board reiterated the purpose of their meeting that evening, a surprised Reverend Nathan interrupted. Previously unaware of the petition's progress, he felt his power and authority breached. "I objected to take part in its deliberations," he later stated, "assigning as my reason, that it was out of the power of the Representatives to decide whether these modifications and changes could be affected, since they related altogether to the regulation of the Divine Service and its ceremonies 'which,' by law, 'was under the control of the minister.'"[96] Nathan proposed instead that the pamphlet of proposed changes be submitted to himself alone for consideration. Of the four board members present at the meeting, three agreed, voting by majority to place the issue in the minister's hands. But as the one dissenting vote, Moses De Sola went on the record denying Nathan's absolute control over the contents of the Divine Service. "[I]t would be strange & quite against common sense," he reasoned, "that the Board of Representatives should be set aside altogether in the decision of a matter of such importance as the one now under our notice, and all the power vested in the Minister, who is a paid officer of the Congregation, and under the supervision of the representatives."[97]

Reverend Nathan, with the board's majority approval, did not need to acknowledge De Sola's objections. In the interests of peace, however, the minister and synagogue president agreed to present their case to the local government before dealing with the petition—with each confident he was in the right.[98] Nathan and De Sola sent in their arguments, and waited for a reply. Nothing was immediately forthcoming.

In the meantime, the controversy began to spread, and the division between synagogue factions deepened. With their position publicly revealed, the reformers began to campaign in prominent Jewish periodicals. Under the title "ST. THOMAS — RELIGIOUS AGITATION," the *Jewish Chronicle of London* printed the first letter. "One Who Signed the Petition," presented the proposed reforms to the editor as a matter of natural development for St. Thomas's Jewish life, and accused the "profound orthodoxies" who objected to the petition as "non-cultivators of civilization."[99] The newspaper's editor refrained from comment.

Two months later, the *Jewish Chronicle* published a pair of civil but strong-handed responses to this first letter. Sent by opponents of the petition, the missives viewed Reform less as a series of changes to the service than as a specter of protest and party spirit. "Orthodoxy is our doctrine," wrote one:

We wish to preserve [it] intact. . . . we do not want to change the substance for the shallow; we do not object to gradual changes; but what we do object to is to allow those who profess extreme views, half Jewish and half rational, from introducing the thin edge of what they call reform into our worship, and drive in the wedge up to the head afterwards, splitting the community into fragments.[100]

With both sides presented and no resolution in sight, the paper decided to terminate any further coverage of the issue. But the St. Thomas reformers, passionate about their cause, would not go quietly. Early in 1866, a long and eloquent discourse from "Reformer" appeared in the *Jewish Chronicle* as a paid advertisement. Picking apart the letters from the last round, the author continued to argue for modifications while "lament[ing] that our purest intentions should be so grossly misrepresented." The synagogue's current practices, refuted "Reformer," were far from "Orthodox": dietary laws went unheeded, the congregation rarely celebrated the second days of holidays, and the ritual seemed old and forced. "'J'appele un chat, un chat,'" he contended. "We do not want that the non-Orthodox congregation of St. Thomas should carry the name of Orthodox."[101]

As these rhetorical jabs were exchanged through the London paper, both sides of the controversy waited for the government's response in St. Thomas. Tempers simmered, but the year came to an end without action; Moses De Sola left his office with the issue unresolved. In his place, David Cardoze, Jr., came to the helm. A successful St. Thomas merchant and bank clerk, Cardoze was the son of a Curaçao *Hazan* and had received a thorough education in Jewish prayer and ritual.[102] As the most knowledgable Jewish layman on the island, he garnered a nearly universal respect within the congregation, from young and old alike. Once he assumed the presidency in January 1866, Cardoze continued what had by that time become a string of fruitless reminders and notes to the government requesting some form of decision.[103]

The year that followed was quiet and uncertain. With no definitive response from the government, the issue of modifications froze the congregation in a spiritual rut. A frail and aging Reader Maduro performed services each week without variation. Reverend Nathan preached sermons of peace and harmony from the pulpit, while campaigning subtlely for the overhanging dispute to resolve in his favor. Several of the petitioners allowed their differences to slide with time; others, hurt by the minister's refusal to recognize their liturgical integrity, grew colder toward Nathan and adhered more steadfastly toward instituting their reforms.

Holidays and special occasions took place with little disturbance during the year, but reports showed obvious stress within the community. In October, on *Simchat Torah,* Reverend Nathan held the island's first confirmation ceremony in twenty years, welcoming a class of three girls and two boys into Jewish adulthood. Yet contrary to previous confirmations, this one received no special attention in the *Tidende,* and only a sentence's reference in the *Occident.*[104] A month later, when Reverend Nathan marked his sixtieth birthday, only a portion of the congregation attended. The board presented the minister with a testimonial promising support from the congregation, and wishing that "under your Spiritual Guidance this congregation advance every day more in the path of moral enlightment, and in the promotion of that most Blessed of Heavenly Gifts, Peace." Choosing his words judiciously, Nathan reflected the board's concerns and hardline ambitions: "I value highly your 'esteem and regard,' because I must consider them to be also those of the Congregation, whose mouthpieces you are by virtue of your Offices."[105] In reality, the officers could make this claim only nominally; but it helped paint a rosy picture in the hope that ignoring the situation would prevent it from deteriorating further.

The end of the year brought with it a raging cholera plague, which decimated the lower classes of St. Thomas society. Twenty-five to thirty people died each day at the height of the epidemic, and the island came under a strict quarantine. While the disease affected the Jewish community only minimally, the Hebrew congregation joined the island in its appeal for divine intervention, saying special prayers every week and holding a supplementary service to appeal to God for mercy.[106] Finally, as the year broke, so did the epidemic. From a population of about fourteen thousand, over eight hundred were dead. Out from the ordeal, the island recorded its losses and began to rebuild.[107]

For the Hebrew Congregation, however, a natural death would prove the most devastating. Between the hours of three and four in the morning of January 22, 1867, old age took the life of the synagogue's beloved reader, Samuel Elias Levy Maduro. As the one constant and trusted presence in the synagogue's pulpit over the last thirty years, Maduro was a monolith. Through several ministers and crippling controversies, the reader performed his job week in and week out, satisfying the community at every service. As a teacher, he worked in the minister's shadow to instruct many of the congregation's children in their faith. A long-time resident, he was a fixture in Charlotte Amalie, an unsung and venerable figure whose loss could be felt across society. Four days after his death, a lengthy and laudatory "Tribute of Respect" appeared in the paper. Introduced by two biblical quotes, the article mirrored the sentiments of the mourning congregation through simple and sincere wording:

> It is becoming, that when a man of strict piety, honesty of purpose and integrity departs this life, a statement, beyond the limits of a mere obituary note, should be given of his life and the manner in which it was spent. It is not alone to the hero of many a battlefield, nor the successful statesman to whose memory the columns of the journalist should be dedicated, but also to the man whose long life was one of truth and sincerity. Such was the noble career of the lamented object of this note: true! it was not given to him to command the applause of a listening audience, but it was his high privelege to live and die among a people who honored and respected him, and to whom his death, though at an advanced age, is a cause of deep regret.[108]

Maduro's funeral, on the same day as his death, ended an era. As his body descended into the ground, accompanied by the voice of Reverend Nathan, a number of congregants lost their final connection to the synagogue's spiritual center. Familial ties no longer crossed at the pulpit, as the final piece holding the congregation together disappeared. Now, feeling ruled-over by an old, rigid, outside minister, these congregants no longer had any reason to remain a unified body. In the face of Nathan's calls for submission, the voice of Reform could now break free to turn Jewish life on the island upside-down.

CHAPTER 6

The Hebrew Reformed Congregation
1867–1875

$\mathcal{T}$he fourteen men who defected from the St. Thomas Hebrew Congregation on March 14, 1867, averaged just over thirty-one years of age.[1] Emanuel Correa Osorio was the youngest at age twenty-five, a soon-to-be store proprietor who was less than a year away from marriage. Jacob Jessurun Lindo, at forty-six the oldest member of the breakaway congregation, served as its first spiritual leader. Several had spent time in Venezuela before unrest sent them fleeing back to St. Thomas in the 1850s and 1860s. All but one of the members dedicated their lives to the island's mercantile trade, and most had young families. Their efforts to found and sustain a second Jewish body on St. Thomas would both energize and destroy Jewish life on the island, sending two ministers fleeing for greener pastures, and leaving the St. Thomas congregation in a peaceful dark age that would go untouched for half a century.

The final barriers to secession began to crumble four weeks after Reader Samuel Elias Levy Maduro's funeral. On Monday, February 18, 1867, the widow Rachel Cohen D'Azevedo received a letter from one of the packet steamers bringing news of her sister's death. Following Jewish tradition, she began a seven-day mourning period, receiving comforters and holding services nightly at her house five lots down from the synagogue. On the first evening, Reverend Nathan did not appear at the house. Instead, when it came time for the evening prayers, D'Azevedo's friend Jacob Jessurun Lindo stepped forward to lead the ritual. By most accounts, he performed his position ably, and likely thought little of it.

Not everyone was content, however. Elias Wolff, a son of prominent resident Aron Wolff, was also at the gathering that evening and reacted indignantly to Lindo's actions. In his view, Lindo had usurped Nathan's position by reading the service in the minister's absence. The letter of the bylaws dictated that anyone leading a service outside the synagogue grounds needed first to seek permission from the synagogue president, a charge that Wolff knew Lindo had not fulfilled. Dutifully, the whistleblower approached Reverend Nathan the next day and reported the infraction in the presence of a witness. Nathan reacted decisively to the information, already feeling threatened by the liturgical demands placed against him by the reformers. On February 20, 1867, he sent a letter to the board explaining the situation and warning that: "Such deliberate violations of the Law, and defiance of the constituted authorities, should at once be repressed, or else further irregularities will be the consequence."[2] The board, whose own problems with the reformers made Nathan a stronger ally, took up the case against the unsuspecting Lindo.

On Thursday, February 21, four notes shuttled back and forth between the synagogue board and Jacob Lindo. The first surprised and angered Lindo by accusing him of violating the bylaws and levelling the threat of a fine. Lindo immediately retorted that he had violated no laws, and righteously declared that "I shall continue to act in the same manner . . . whenever requested to do so, in defiance of the threats held out . . ."[3] The board snapped back, calling Lindo's remarks "discourteous" and assuring him that such actions would incur additional penalty.[4] Not to be outdone, Lindo sent off a final, taunting letter:

> I merely acknowledge the receipt of your communication, to acquaint you that I intend to continue reading the Evening Prayers at the residence of the Widow R. E. D'Azevedo, + will do so this evening, as such, you are at full liberty to enforce the penalty for my so doing, if in your power, + without making use of your out of the way expression "discourteous."[5]

The act of assistance Lindo performed at Rachel D'Azevedo's house was indeed a technical violation of the synagogue bylaws. But by this point the issue seemed less a question of well-intentioned misjudgement than a litmus test of the board's power. When treated as an all-out offense by both minister and board, what had begun as a difficult but resolvable situation turned into an unnecessary exercise of authority—and another reason for those who felt disenfranchised to secede.

Whiplash politics reigned as Jacob Lindo joined twelve members of the congregation five days later to present a letter to the board assassinating Reverend Nathan's character. Citing technicalities in the 1848 bylaws, they accused him of failing to preach on every Sabbath and holiday, of abolishing the Saturday afternoon service, and of "attending to the collection of deposits at the Savings Bank during the hours of Divine Service."[6] Then they waited to see how the board would react. When, one week later, the board exhonerated Nathan from the charges based solely on the minister's own testimony, the group decided that enough was enough. Facing a system that taxed them heavily and refused to give them a fair hearing to air their grievances, they took a historic and daring step.

On March 14, fourteen congregants, including nine of those who had signed the previous accusation, sent a simple note to the board: "We beg to notify you that . . . we cease to be members of the . . . Congregation."[7] The move was unprecedented. Even during the 1840s, when religious differences had compelled the congregation to break into two conflicting houses of worship, the sanctity of the body politic had remained relatively untouched. Common knowledge deemed the congregation to be too small for a prolonged division; it was widely understood that the government would tolerate only one synagogue on the island anyway. Now, for the first time, a Jewish community existed that did not want to belong to the synagogue, did not abide by the directives of the board or minister, and refused to pay the taxes the congregation attempted to collect. In a more detailed letter to the presidency of St. Thomas, the seceders explained their separation as a rational, preventative measure intended to circumvent the scene caused in the 1840s. Unhappy with the minister, board and bylaws, and "considering that if they allow these dissatisfactions to continue it would only create party-spirit and lead to contention and strife in the Congregation," they decided "to preserve peace and harmony" by breaking away.[8] For some, however, the action was also important on religious grounds, a valiant attempt to restore a feeling of personal investment in their religious observance. "[I]t became necessary to those who are earnest and resolute," said one member, "to secede from the old congregation and establish a new one, and by this means save Judaism in St. Thomas from the painful indifference which was creeping over it."[9]

The secessionists assailed the synagogue bylaws, which had remained unchanged through almost two decades and two major revisions of the island's Colonial Law.[10] Such laws "can no longer be adapted for this age," they declared, referring in particular to the minister's absolute control of the liturgy and the board's recent unilateral actions.[11] To them, Reverend Nathan and his inflated ego represented an abuse of power and an insult to the congregants. His training in rabbinical law appeared obscure and unnecessary, skewing and obstructing the "simple" paths to peace sought by the reformers.

Their new congregation, in contrast, would follow the reformed liturgy of the West London Synagogue—the same order that failed to take root on the island a generation before. It would eliminate the supposed greater competence of a hired minister in favor of a grassroots leadership style typified by the late Samuel Elias Levy Maduro. The Torah, accessible to all, would be regarded as the only holy text. Music would gain a new life in prayer, and laypeople would take a more active role in religious life. According to the seceders, it was precisely what the bylaws—and the minister and board—had failed to implement.

A recent revision of the Colonial Law, introduced in November 1863 and put into effect a year and a half later, gave the seceders a strong argument for their new institution. Section seventy-one of the code provided the islanders with the Danish government's most explicit freedom-of-religion clause to date: "allow[ing] all subjects to assemble in Congregations to worship God in accordance with their convictions."[12] Without mentioning any specific denominations, the law unwittingly ensured all religious movements, present and future, small and large, a right to survival. The secessionists, by asserting a contrasting form of prayer, thus felt entitled to their own religious body; and they began to speak openly against the provision for only one synagogue in the congregation's old bylaws. "The Jews have," reported one member, "by a strange step taken about twenty years ago [i.e., the 1848 bylaws], deprived themselves of the rights which Denmark has always granted its subjects without distinction of creed."[13] Now, the new Reform congregation determined to have its rights ratified by betraying the old congregation's obsolescence.

Official correspondence aside, the new congregation made a concerted effort to separate from the synagogue as quietly and amicably as possible, so as not to cause a public stir. Though probably empowered by the loud Curaçao reformers, the St. Thomas seceders took pains to avoid resembling them and maintained no public contacts with them.[14] Rather, the group framed itself as a collection of progressive thinkers within the Jewish community who could not wait for Nathan's gradual changes. Most of its members were St. Thomas natives, but others hailed from France, Jamaica, Barbados, and Curaçao. They were a young, dynamic, and energetic collection of people who took pride in their own interpretation of Judaism and wished only to impart it to their children in privacy.

No response came from the Hebrew Congregation. Self-assured that members could resign from the synagogue only by renouncing Judaism, the board ignored the communication. In the meantime, the seceders obtained a place of worship two blocks away, at the property of German-Jewish merchant Joseph Levien on 19 and 20 Commandant Gade. On March 23, 1867, the group met for an official meeting, drew up a quick set of bylaws, and held officer elections. Moses De Sola, former president of the Hebrew Congregation, was appointed president of the new synagogue. Jacob Lindo, the vice-president, also gained the honorary title of religious leader and took initial responsibility for performing all ritual functions and duties. They also decided on a name for themselves: Paying homage to the first Reform synagogue in the hemisphere in Charleston, South Carolina, during the 1840s, they adopted the title "The Hebrew Reformed Congregation, *Beth Elohim.*"[15] The St. Thomas synagogue board remained silent.

A week later, on Sabbath morning, March 30, Beth Elohim's members met for the new congregation's first service. Squeezing into the largest room on the second floor of their rented building, the founders, their families, and several interested non-Jews listened to an introductory meditation read by Jacob Lindo. "We form, at present, a small assembly," he said, "but we are well aware that many others are anxiously awaiting our successful establishment as a congregation, in order to enroll themselves among its members." Lindo emphasized exhibiting exemplary behavior, both in and out of services. "As we fly from tyranny and oppression, we wish to . . . practice . . . charity, forbearance and good-will." Quoting from Psalms, he exhorted his audience to "'Seek peace and pursue it.' Let such be your aim, and not only shall we be the promoters of our own happiness, but we shall also be fulfilling the will of our Heavenly Father, who has promised us a blessing that he would establish peace on the earth."[16]

A radical departure from the "traditional" synagogue service followed. After twenty years of planning and deferment, David Woolf Marks's West London liturgy finally saw light on St. Thomas. Jacob Lindo led all spoken prayers. For the first time in island history, an organ accompanied the hymns, played by Paris *Conservatoire*-trained pianist Sylvain Levy.[17] President Moses De Sola reflected the atmosphere among the congregants with a discourse on Joshua 1:9, "Be strong and of good courage, be not afraid, neither be thou dismayed; for the Lord thy God is with thee withersoever thou goest." Inspiring the seceders to stay on course, De Sola impressed upon them the importance of the Reformed Congregation's mission and added his voice to the religious and solemn tone of the service.[18] All knew that challenges would lie ahead, but that morning helped to solidify the congregation's desire to unite and face these challenges with defiance, righteousness, and respect.

The next day, both congregations sent letters to the island government. *Beth Elohim*, the Hebrew Reformed Congregation, informed the presidency of its newly elected officers, place of worship, and appointed religious leader.[19] *Beracha v'Shalom v'Gemiluth Hasadim* sent its first communication on the matter since March 14; it refused to acknowledge the new congregation, enumerating several of its infractions in the bylaws, and requested that the government "put an end, at once, to this deliberate violation of our rights."[20] The next Sabbath, two Jewish services once again took place on St. Thomas, with each assemblage asserting its own political rights. Both congregations observed the start of the Hebrew month of *Nisan*, marking a two-week countdown to Passover, the holiday of freedom. Reader Lindo took the opportunity to exploit the connection between his congregation's struggle and the upcoming holiday: "May we truly observe the Passover commemorating our deliverance from thraldom and entering upon freedom and light."[21] Reverend Nathan, meanwhile, likely preached on a similar subject, though advocating the opposite end.

After two successful weeks of separate officiation, the Hebrew Reformed Congregation began to spread news of its existence to the rest of the world. Abraham De Jongh sent letters to the *Occident, Jewish Chronicle of London*, and a more recently founded American Reform movement organ called the *American Israelite*. Another letter from the Hebrew Reformed Congregation's board of directors, dated April 11, 1867, went to Dr. David Woolf Marks of the West London Synagogue.[22] All of them discussed the difficulties the new congregation faced against the island's "Orthodox" minister and congregation. The *Jewish Chronicle* apparently declined to print the letter.[23] Isaac Leeser, of the *Occident*, allowed De Jongh's letter space in his journal, but reacted with sadness and disgust. He criticized "the flippant arrogance of a handful of people . . . not very learned in the law, setting themselves up as a competent tribunal to select a new form of prayer, composed by a man of yesterday . . . [and] rejecting that manual of devotion and life which their ancestors have used and followed from time immemorial."[24] Leeser, near the end of his life, would print no more communications from the St. Thomas reformers.

In contrast, Isaac Mayer Wise, editor of the *Israelite*, enthusiastically supported the "spirit of progress" that "has also reached our brethren in St. Thomas." The perennial advocate of Jewish reform in the United States, Wise predicted, "If they in St. Thomas succeed as fast as we do here, they will soon be a blessing to the cause of Israel on that happy island."[25] For a short tme afterward, the *Israelite* served as the primary voice for De Jongh and the new congregation, even printing a rebuttal letter to Isaac Leeser that had been refused space in the *Occident*.[26]

In London, Dr. David W. Marks responded positively as well, congratulating the seceders on their new synagogue and "trust[ing] that the Blessing of God will rest upon it and that it may conduce, like my own synagogue, to the advantage and the edification of public worship and to the interests of our common Judaism."[27] To help the congregation's travails, he sent along a copy of the West London Synagogue's *Ketubah* (marriage contract) with translation. Accurately hinting at the next issue to face the fledgling congregation, he noted that the *Ketubah* helped the West London Synagogue prove its respectability in the face of opposition—"lest it might be said that our [wedding] ceremonial was incomplete, or, in other words, did not constitute a Jewish Marriage."[28] Accordingly, Marks passed the information on to the Hebrew Reformed Congregation.

K. K. Beracha v'Shalom v'Gemiluth Hasadim, powerless to force the seceders back into their fold, still held one major advantage. Employing the only state-accepted Jewish minister on the island (and the only Jewish religious figure the government thought necessary), the congregation still held the coveted and exclusive right to perform and record the Jewish community's lifecycle events. Though the seceders could remain separated from the Hebrew Congregation through their own invocation of local law, the government refused to recognize their group as an official religious body. When the Reformed Congregation thus requested permission to give Jacob Lindo temporary power to solemnize births, deaths, and marriages, their appeal failed, denying the new congregation the right to keep its own records.[29] Two different forms of Jewish lifecycle ritual, ruled the island's presidency, were unnecessary. Rather, the government upheld Reverend Nathan's position as religious leader for the *entire* Jewish community, and thus required his presence at any Jewish official activity. The decision left the Reformed Congregation little more than an organizational shell, falling far short of its religious ambitions. The members of the young synagogue were determined to gain autonomy, however; so it was only a matter of time before tensions mounted once again.

By the middle of the year, the Hebrew Reformed Congregation had named a new reader, the old and respected merchant Jacob Haim Osorio. Osorio, sixty-eight, was the father of two of *Beth Elohim's* founding members and a strong strategic choice to replace Lindo.[30] In addition to his long tenure on St. Thomas, Osorio was the only other person on the island who had legally solemnized a Jewish wedding. As an unofficial backup to Reader

Maduro, Osorio's signature had validated four of the population's Jewish unions, the most recent only four years earlier when he had signed "in consequence of the Hazan's disposition."[31] His appointment thus reinforced the new congregation's determination to establish itself as an independent institution, setting up a challenge to the government's decision to give Nathan exclusive Jewish ministerial rights.

The test case for this challenge came soon after, and could not have been better planned: Osorio's daughter Betsy Bertha and Reformed Congregation founding member A. D. De Jongh expressed their public intentions to marry, and in doing so set the legal mechanism in gear. The Reformed Congregation first showed its inability to function according to the government's decree on religious leadership. The couple approached Reverend Nathan (who was the only person legally authorized to conduct the wedding) and requested that he perform the ceremony. Nathan, following protocol, went to his synagogue board; and predictably, the wardens refused to consent.[32] *Beth Elohim's* formal campaign began from there.

On June 20, 1867, the Hebrew Reformed Congregation sent a letter to the government. "[W]e would most respectfully solicit the Honorable Presidency's permission, to appoint Mr. J. H. Osorio to perform the marriage ceremony, said Gentleman, having on other occasions, performed the same ceremony for the Old Congregation."[33] But though submitted with high expectations, the communication flew into a vacuum. The government stalled, still uncertain about the reformers' political status in relation to their old congregation. Undaunted, the reformers held fast to their intentions, finding other fronts for asserting legal independence. When the first new child came into the congregation, the seceders refused to register it with the old congregation. Claiming they found the synagogue's circumcision ceremony unacceptable, they consequently opened up a second battle against Nathan's lifecycle officiation monopoly.[34]

Meanwhile, the overspent *Beracha VeShalom* drifted deeper and deeper into arrears, and turned increasingly to its bylaws for protection. Facing a substantial and unexpected loss of revenue from the secession, the congregation called for the government's assistance in collecting taxes from the separated members. No official communication had stated that the old congregation's bylaws were obsolete; by this reason, they claimed, there should be no impediment to assessing the appropriate funds. "[T]his Board does not suppose that the Government will now withdraw its assistance to collect these taxes forming the principal item of the Budget by allowing members to separate, while the contract made with the Minister when they were un-

doubtedly Members of the Congregation is in force."[35] In the board's opinion, all Jews on St. Thomas, seceders or not, were obligated to contribute to
the welfare of the synagogue. To these requests as well, the government
stalled.

Throughout the initial stages of conflict, the island's general population
had remained optimistically oblivious to the situation. Both original and seceding members took precautions to prevent a public embarrassment of the
Jewish community: Nathan's congregation did not wish to jeopardize its solid
reputation, and declined to bring up the matter in a territory court; the reformers, establishing their connections and gaining grassroots support, did
not want to garner undue publicity too early. Only when Adolphe Nones
reprinted the *Israelite*'s short article on the Reformed Congregation in the
Tidende—on September 28, more than six months after the fact—did the
public receive any official apprisal of the split.[36]

On Hurricane Thanksgiving Day 1867, the new and disputed synagogue
conducted a separate service expressing gratitude for a safe and relatively
prosperous hurricane season, holding its own among the island's houses of
worship. St. Thomas's prayers of thanksgiving that year, however, would prove
premature. Trouble was brewing across the ocean, and its consequences
would send the island spiralling into a serious decline.

The year preceding October 1867 was an interesting one in the St. Thomas
mercantile business. Larger and more powerful steamships had begun to
proliferate along major international trade routes, and the most expansive of
these ships had begun to find St. Thomas's natural harbor too shallow for their
needs. Improving steam-engine efficiency, meanwhile, affected St. Thomas ad-
versely as well, allowing some ships to avoid a once-mandatory refueling stop
on the island. Nonetheless, many important merchant houses remained on
the shores of Charlotte Amalie, and vessels continued to exchange their
goods by virtue of the strong financial relationships they had previously
established.

In order to help its businesses remain active participants in international
trade, the Danish government implemented several initiatives. One of the
most important had been the creation of a floating dock, a huge metal con-
traption in the middle of the harbor that could service ships larger than on-land
docks would allow. Opened in 1866 after years of planning and construction,
it accompanied a dredging of the harbor and new gas lighting in town as a way
to update the island's infrastructure and resources. Unfortunately, mechanical problems plagued the dock, causing it to see painfully little action—and

rather than representing St. Thomas's bright new future, it helped to signal the island's downfall.

After enduring a cholera epidemic that closed down the island in late 1866, the floating dock successfully accomplished its intended use through the first half of 1867. Once July rolled around, however, a comedy of errors began. Late that month, the great mechanical hulk malfunctioned and sank into the harbor, becoming not only useless in itself, but also introducing an underwater hazard for smaller ships needing to dock on shore.[37] Numerous attempts to raise the dock over the next several months were unsuccessful, and the *Tidende* provided frequent updates with increasingly concerned amusement. Then, in the middle of the fall, the paper went dumb.

October 29, 1867, marks a day that remains forever infamous on St. Thomas. In a turn of irony in the greatest degree, St. Thomians watched as the skies went black, the winds began to gust, and the sea started to churn. Merchants escaped to their homes and closed their hurricane shutters, while poorer classes huddled in their shanty huts. Ships began to rise and fall on huge ocean swells. Four days after the end of the "official" hurricane season, the most violent storm in the recorded history of the island slammed on-shore. Its fury deroofed and destroyed hundreds of houses, sank numerous moored ships, and killed over one hundred and ten people. The *Tidende* stopped printing for two weeks.[38] *Harper's Weekly* would dedicate a large illustration to the aftermath of the disaster, depicting broken vessels floating in a devastated harbor.[39] Many probably recounted their prayers to the Almighty on Hurricane Thanksgiving Day just a few days before, wondering what could have gone wrong as their businesses, property, and fortunes toppled with the storm.

Bands of heavy winds and drenching rain passed over the island intermittently for several days afterward. As the members of the Hebrew Reformed Congregation emerged from their homes and climbed over the the mess of fallen trees, roofs and rubble, they rejoiced to find their building unscathed— without a single window broken. Immediately, they offered refuge space to three families rendered homeless by the gale.[40] The members of *Beracha VeShalom*, however, were not so lucky. Their beautiful synagogue, once proudly overlooking the harbor, now looked a shambles with a badly damaged roof. That Sabbath, a large number of Jews gathered in the broken building for services and spiritual renewal. The scheduled scriptural reading for that week—ironically, the story of Noah—provided ample opportunity for congregants to relate to the experience of the Great Deluge and ponder how close God could come before breaking His promise that week. Together, the group chanted the prayer *HaGomel*, expressing sincere gratitude to the Almighty for sustaining their lives through the terrors of the storm.[41] Though many in the congregation had sustained substantial losses, none had perished.

Then Reverend Nathan ascended the dais and delivered one of the most beautiful, sincere prayers of pathos and despair ever to grace the ears of the demoralized congregation. "O Lord our God!" he pleaded:

> . . . if Thou dost not save us, who should? . . . Conscious of our utter helpless-ness, trembling mid the wreck and havoc which meet our gaze on every side,— in the depth of our misery . . . we implore Thee 'Save us from more calamity, more distress, more affliction.'. . . undeserving as we are, be not angry with us, if we enumerate the many and successive visitations we have experienced over the last twelve months. Cholera, small-pox, yellow fever, the utter pros-tration and suspension of trade and commerce, by which our population gains its bread, had barely departed, the first three after fitting the grave with many, many hundreds of dead, and the last after making credit stagger and reel: then this terrific hurricane immediately appears . . . darkening the little gleam of comforting sunshine which began to brighten our hearts. Our houses are roof-less or in ruins, our shipping lies engulfed before our eyes; here the tops of masts only are seen above the waters, there hulls lie floating, wharves and ware-houses are partly or wholly destroyed, merchandise of great value has sunk be-neath the waves or been spoiled, hundreds of brave mariners have met a wa-tery grave, while the air reeks with the effluvia from the bodies of those not yet recovered. Wilt Thou, O mighty God, punish us still more? . . . if our trans-gressions demand further chastisement, we implore Thee, spare the guilty for the sake of the innocent. . . .[42]

Once the congregation left the building that day, it would not return for the rest of the year. Damage to the roof had made the sanctuary an unstable structure, and extensive repairs were necessary.[43]

But the volatile Caribbean had not finished with St. Thomas. Just as the island began to clean up, buoyed by a rumor that the United States was about to purchase the Danish West Indies, another disaster added to the mythic di-mensions of the season. On November 18, at 2:45 P.M., as merchants counted their losses in the stores, the ground began to shake violently. Everyone rushed into the streets to avoid injury, only to "see the houses tottering, and the bricks and mortar falling from them . . ."[44] According to one account, the initial tremors lasted for almost two minutes, damaging nearly every building in town.

Just south of the island, the earthquake caused another massive and dangerous disturbance. "No sooner had the shocks ceased," wrote a correspondent to the *Israelite*, "than an ocean of water (calculated 50 feet high) of snowy whiteness, and forming one wave, was seen at the south-west beyond our harbor, majestically and steadily rolling on toward us, foretelling, in its every movement, that it must engulf all things encountered by it."[45] The giant wave broke at the entrance to St. Thomas's protected harbor, sparing the island its worst. Nonetheless, a six-foot tide of water came storming through the main street, flooding the one-story warehouses and causing significant additional damage to the surviving inventory.

Aftershocks continued for three weeks, as many people fled the town and camped out "on the hills under tents."[46] Ten people had died in these secondary disturbances, and the rest were clearly traumatized. "[T]here was not one single person in the island, who did not believe, that they would soon be ushered in the presence of the Awful Judge," claimed the *Israelite* correspondent. Though neither synagogue building appeared to suffer substantial additional damage, the houses and stores of many congregants did, and thus both groups held special services to temper the shock. Reverend Nathan called for a special day of fasting and atonement to take place on Wednesday, November 27. Weighing necessity over politics, the congregation met in the home of Hebrew Reformed Congregation Reader Jacob Haim Osorio, where Nathan led a full and solemn service using the *Yom Kippur* liturgy to express the feelings of awe and insignificance reinforced by the disasters.[47] The Hebrew Reformed Congregation held a palpably similar service the following Sunday, probably attracting a decent overlap of the Jewish population. "[I]t was . . . a remarkable Kippur day, offenses were forgiven, hands which have for years been refused were outstretched in solemn and sincere shaking, enemies embraced each other, friend and foe all met and implored God to receive the soul and to have pity and mercy on us."[48] Differences between the two congregations seemed to lessen as their common experiences brought them together. Terrified by the recent events, they gained strength in each other's company.

Although two Jewish congregations continued to exist on the island, the impassioned rhetoric that had passed between them toned down. Neither sent any more accusatory letters to the local government. Members of both congregations began to work together to run meetings of the Hebrew Benevolent Society.[49] Perhaps the most dramatic illustration of the reduced tensions between the two congregations occurred on December 4, when Reverend Nathan performed the long-debated marriage ceremony between A. D.

De Jongh and Bertha Osorio.[50] Although Nathan would not perform another ceremony for the Hebrew Reformed Congregation, he ceased to make public complaints about the reformers' policies. Conversely, the reformers made no further complaints against the minister.

The next year, 1868, began with promise. The repaired St. Thomas synagogue reopened its gates to prayer. Three blocks away, the reformers continued to hold services, and were making significant strides toward convincing the St. Thomas authorities to allow the group recognition as a religious body.

Trying to build an overwhelming case, the secessionists began to acquire and create all the accoutrements they felt a bona fide congregation needed. As disaster survival became less of a priority, the new congregation set to work creating its own set of permanent bylaws. Much of the content would mirror that of the old congregation. Paralleling the board of representatives, the reformers established a council of administration containing a president, vice-president, secretary, and treasurer, as well as a deputy who would fill in if one of the other four had to vacate their position. Member privileges and election procedures were little changed from the old congregation's 1848 bylaws. On other key issues, however, significant differences appeared. Members of the Hebrew Reformed Congregation paid their dues through voluntary contributions and bequests only, eschewing a tax system altogether. The minister had no power to dictate the contents of the service: He was required mainly to appear on time, officiate at weddings and funerals, and keep the congregation satisfied. In the event of the minister's absence, the president of the synagogue had the power to appoint a lay-reader to fill in. Descriptions of other positions in the synagogue included the new categories of "choir and organist." Women received explicit permission to vote in elections. And, most importantly, a new tribunal system was established to interpret and modify the bylaws.[51] The regulations were ratified at a meeting of the members of the congregation on March 4, 1868. The council of administration sent them up to New York for publication, and then proudly sent a copy to the governor-general for consideration and safe-keeping, just as *Beracha Ve-Shalom* did in 1848.[52]

The Hebrew Reformed Congregation also put a great deal of energy into acquiring its own physical space. Around the same time as the framing of the bylaws, the reformers sent a public plea out to the readers of the *Israelite* for contributions toward a new synagogue building.[53] While few steps toward realizing this structure actually took place, the Jews were able to gather enough money to purchase their own burial ground by the end of the year. Bought for eight hundred dollars in gold, it stood adjacent to the Altona Jewish cemetery, spreading off to the west as a second "House of Life."[54] The congregation mapped the land into rectangular plots, and gave the synagogue deputy the responsibility of parcelling it out fairly. This turned out to be easier than anticipated, for the young congregation never had occasion to use the grounds.[55]

Births to the congregation continued to give the reformers reason to press their case with the government. Continuing their arguments from before the hurricane, the reformers claimed to reject the "traditional" Spanish and Portuguese ritual surrounding circumcision, opting instead for their own circumcision liturgy. Reverend Nathan, however, was the only competent *Mohel* on the island; and he refused to follow the reformers' rite.[56] Because of this, several of the Hebrew Reformed Congregation's newborn boys went uncircumcised, causing a sore spot of contention to fester between the two congregations. The dispute was illustrated once again by the new congregation's claims to keep its own records: Instead of registering newborn children with the old congregation, as required by royal decision, the reformers sent announcements directly to the government under a handwritten letterhead—"Hebrew Reformed Congregation 'Beth Elohim' Council of Administration"—and embossed with its own seal.[57] This comparatively quiet campaign persisted for years, further indicating the reformers' desires to attain autonomy.[58]

The Hebrew Reformed Congregation's strong trend toward organization after the hurricane helped it expand. Ambivalent supporters of the seceders who would not break off in April began to see the new synagogue gaining depth and integrity. By August 1868, the reformers counted eighty-seven members in their ranks, split almost evenly in thirds between men, women, and children.[59] Even the government took a temporary interest, which the congregants interpreted as a gleam of hope for recognition. But a hopeful letter to the colonial rulers for official sanction received no response, and the ambitions of the congregation returned to dormancy.[60]

Up the street, *Beracha VeShalom* entered into financial crisis. The loss of revenue caused by the additional seceding members, in addition to costs for repairing the synagogue and personal damages sustained by the congregants themselves, finally drained the synagogue's resources to the point where they could no longer support the minister's salary. Reverend Nathan learned of this, but having experienced the previous year's disasters with his flock, he knew he could not abandon his congregation. In early February 1868, Nathan issued a communication to the synagogue board, proposing "for the sole motive of promoting peace and quietness, . . . that the whole annual amount assessed on the seceders, present or future and thus lost to the synagogue treasury, should be deducted" from his salary.[61] The minister's sacrifice eased the synagogue's financial strain significantly, while ensuring that the congregation would retain Nathan at a time when his services were most desperately needed.

Reverend Nathan's school, which taught many of *Beracha VeShalom*'s children, also fought financial straits. The seceding families, once subscribers to the school, likely had their own educational system by this time: J. L. Penha, the schoolteacher who had worked with Reverend Myers at the start of the decade, had after all been one of the original seceders. After the hurricane, moreover, a number of Jewish families remaining with the synagogue began to rely heavily on charity, and could ill afford to pay tuition. Naturally, when the Danish government announced an annual gift of $2,500 to the island to assist the poor of the island's church schools, Reverend Nathan applied for a share. The government considered the request, but decided that the school was private, and not an official organ of the synagogue. The Virgin Islands Colonial Council reasoned that the school could not be "a congregational one, as children of other persuasions also visited it." Moreover, the council picked on a technicality of the synagogue's constitution to show it did not qualify for the funds: "according to the bye-laws of the congregation, the said congregation is obliged to support its own poor."[62] Nathan's school went unaided. While a great cry arose from the synagogue members, the Colonial Council took no further action.

Despite the setbacks and devastation of the previous year, Jews retained their respectable place in St. Thomas society. Aron Wolff, by this time, had left for London due to ill health, and many of his generation were either dead or retired. His cousin Judah Cappé, however, had been appointed the island's consul to the Netherlands, and became responsible for leading a public celebration and flying the Dutch flag every year on the Danish King's birthday.[63] Alfred Nones, St. Thomas consul to Belgium, became an inductee into the prestigious order of the Knights of Leopold in 1869.[64] Isaac H. Moron, once a trader in Barcelona, Venezuela, received the title of consul to that country in 1870. Benjamin D'Azevedo served as the island's postmaster. Jews generally held three or four of the nineteen trustee positions at the St. Thomas Savings Bank, occasionally occupied posts on the Colonial Council, and attained advanced positions in the local Masonic brotherhoods. Local firms owned by members of the Jewish community continued to suffer along with the rest of the island's mercantile trade, but they did their best to revive business. Although new mercantile arrivals were fewer and further between, optimism still held its place within the town, and the Jewish community joined the island in its attempts to rebuild.

Throughout this time, the island's Jews publicly professed their religious doctrines and rights with little fear of reprisal. They protested a local election scheduled for a Saturday in April 1869, asking the government through the paper, "Have you forgotten ISRAEL?"[65] Later that year, local pressure increased to provide Jews appropriate accommodations within the island's court system. Though the process took nearly three years to accomplish, this movement succeeded by 1869 in extending an 1864 Danish law to St. Thomas and St. John, effectively creating an oath for swearing in Jews that did not include references to the Christian Bible, and exempting Jews from being forcibly sworn in on Sabbaths or other holy days "except when it is urgently necessary."[66] These actions underlined the extent to which Jews were respected as esteemed members of the Danish colony.

Reverend Nathan's activities, meanwhile, still seemed to focus on the rift within the Jewish community. Fortunately for Nathan, the question of how Reformed and Orthodox communities could coexist successfully was also being asked on a far larger scale in Germany. In August of the previous year, twenty-four rabbis from Germany and Switzerland had convened to discuss the issues brought up by the strengthening *Haskalah* ["Enlightenment"] movement in the area, and decided as a result to hold a synod in Leipzig during June of the following year. Announcements for this synod, which aimed to create a common ground for Reform and Orthodox Jews, appeared in Jewish papers all over the world with the warning that Judaism, "[a] religion of the minority, a religion of scattered small divisions, can be exposed to no greater danger than to become internally divided, conflicting, hesitating, and agitated by violent party strife."[67] These were sentiments to which Nathan could relate all too well, and probably served as a major influence in his decision to travel to the 1869 gathering. Appearing among the international assemblage as the only one of the eighty-three delegates to hail from the Caribbean, and one of two from the Western Hemisphere, Nathan also had the opportunity to see the first rank of European Jewish scholars debate and discuss on a large scale what he had seen in microcosm on St. Thomas.[68]

Covering as acting reader on St. Thomas during Nathan's absence was respected island merchant David Cardoze, Jr. The pious congregant and several-time synagogue president had assisted the minister in ecclesiactical matters as early as 1864, and regularly took over when Nathan was away. Through this experience, Cardoze gained a more intimate working knowledge of ritual and ministerial duties, supplementing a respectable Jewish background from his youth in Curaçao.

Cardoze performed his first recorded religious function at a funeral service on June 24, soon after Nathan's departure for the 1869 Synod. Co-performing the final rites for Elias Wolff, son of Aron Wolff, Cardoze began his emergence as a respected religious leader to his congregation.[69] During the same week, however, another officiation provided more fuel for contention between the two Jewish congregations. One day before the funeral, and the same day that the secretary of the old synagogue reprinted an official letter from the island presidency in the *Tidende* reminding the island's residents that "[no] Ecclesiastical acts performed by [the reformers] will have any public authority," Moses Osorio officiated at the Hebrew Reformed Congregation's first marriage ceremony.[70] Performed in the presence of a "numerous and highly respectable party," the event flew blatantly in the face of the government's communication.[71] There is no evidence as to why the reformers chose this time to go ahead with such a ceremony. However, with the reverend away, it is possible the reformers could have argued that the sanctioned Jewish religious leader was not on the island and thus could not officiate, leaving the Reformed Congregation to fend for itself. The marriage did not become legal by popular consent, however. For three years following the ceremony, the Hebrew Reformed Congregation continued to campaign the colonial government for the union's official recognition, with little progress.[72]

Opposing parties within the Jewish population continued to needle each other, even after Nathan returned from the synod. The island's population as a whole, however, was doing what it could to rebuild its self-confidence. It did this in part by organizing humanitarian efforts to aid various world crises. Located at a center of trans-Atlantic communication lines, many of the residents considered themselves international citizens, who had the resources and progressive philosophies to assist any place in need. Over the years, the population had rallied as a whole against human suffering in St. Thomas, the Caribbean, Denmark, and wherever else the need arose. After enduring the hurricane and earthquake, and receiving much charity relief from off-island sources, the island looked for another cause to show its self-sufficiency. What would emerge, whether intentionally or through pure chance, was a concerted drive to aid Jewish orphans in Poland and Russia. The visible campaign would bring pride back to the island, which once again wanted to show the world its resources, liberal spirit, and sense of responsibiity.

Between 1868 and 1870, the western provinces of Russia suffered a severe famine. The region, known popularly as the "Pale of Settlement," was the center of Russian Jewry, containing a Jewish population of millions in hundreds of villages known as *shtetlach*.[73] The famine affected many of these towns, killing hundreds of adults and leaving their children to fend for themselves. Paris-based Jewish philanthropic organization L'Alliance Israélite Universelle publicized the tragic circumstances and issued an international appeal for money to transport the orphans to France. They requested that collectives of donors "adopt" orphans by sending a sum for each, to cover their transportation to France, their food, and expenses for education. The message crossed the Atlantic, and arrived in St. Thomas around June 1870. Reverend Nathan consequently called an urgent meeting at one of the local hotels, "to which all members of the Jewish Community in this Island, and all *irrespective of creed*, whose hearts respond to the plaintive cry of charity and mercy, are respectfully and earnestly invited to attend . . ."[74]

A large and respectable assembly of all denominations converged on the hotel the next week, and unanimously expressed its desire to help with the efforts of the Alliance. Reverend Nathan explained the situation in detail to the crowd, and several attendees, Jewish and otherwise, added their votes of affirmation. W. O. Allan, religious leader of the Dutch Reformed Church, became one of the strongest advocates for the cause, relating admiring stories about Russian Jewish refugees during his missionary work in Turkey, and emphasizing the tragedy of the drought. Together, the assemblage resolved to appoint a committee to create a fund for the orphans demonstrably entitled "Joint Subscriptions of the Jews and Christians of St. Thomas in aid of the Jewish Orphans of Russia and Poland."[75] With the help of the Masonic Lodge, the committee raised eleven thousand francs (around $2,200), which Reverend Nathan sent off to a surprised and delighted Alliance.[76] "We do not know how to explain to you our regards for the wonderful subscription that you organized in St. Thomas," the Alliance replied in a note sent to Nathan, which he subsequently submitted to the *Tidende*. "The Central committee is pleased that Jewish subscribers joined Christian subscribers and it is profoundly touched by beautiful sentiments of fraternity which unified, for this wonderful work, all the inhabitants of St. Thomas without distinction of creed."[77] For years afterward, the island kept up with its adopted orphans through the pages of the paper, which printed periodic updates on their condition.[78] The campaign had shown St. Thomas's need to cohere as a community at this time; though squabbling might occur, the island's population found their greatest strengths to lay in common action.

Reverend Nathan, however, was entertaining serious doubts about remaining on the island. After enduring a frustrating and fatiguing second pulpit term with the congregation, he no longer believed that his presence would be beneficial either for the Jewish community or for his personal well-being. Consequently, Nathan began to look for a new position outside of St. Thomas.[79] Even as the minister raised funds for the Alliance, a committee of synagogue wardens in Charleston, South Carolina, was reviewing his application to serve as their religious leader.[80] Soon after this, Nathan announced his retirement from the synagogue. The recent events on the island were too much for him, helping to turn an anticipated retirement pulpit into a difficult, embarrassing, and overtaxing job.

The congregation accepted Nathan's resignation with regret, and applied to London for another minister. But as Nathan prepared to leave, the synagogue wardens humbly requested that he continue to officiate at the pulpit until the new minister's arrival.[81] Nathan could not refuse: He knew that until another ordained minister took his place, the synagogue would be in limbo. Without his official signature, the island government would not recognize his congregation's marriages; without his teaching, his Jewish community would slowly slip back into ignorance. Further, Nathan's job-hunting campaign in the United States had been fruitless.[82] The aging minister, now well over sixty, no longer found a place for himself in America, and had no impetus to rush off the island. He thus took the time to honor his congregation's request and ensure the line of continuity.

During this period, the minister finished grooming David Cardoze, Jr., as a congregational lay-reader. On occasion, Cardoze would co-lead services with Reverend Nathan. Serving in a role reminiscent of the late Samuel Elias Levy Maduro, the successful merchant helped to bring religious empowerment back to the island's Jewish community. On October 24, 1869, a few months after he had officiated at his first funeral while Reverend Nathan was away in Leipzig, Cardoze co-officiated at his daughter's wedding ceremony, conducting the ceremony with Nathan and reading the seven benedictions (*sheva brachot*) required for a legal Jewish union.[83] In this way, Cardoze continued his initiation as the synagogue's folk leader.

Aside from Cardoze's accession, however, the outlook became bleaker for *Beracha VeShalom*. As of March 8, 1871, the government finally gave in to the constant requests of the Hebrew Reformed Congregation and provisionally recognized the group as a separate and autonomous religious body. The stipulations were particularly stringent in regard to marriages: each required a special grant from the colonial government, at a cost of twenty-five dollars, to legalize and officially register the union.[84] Nonetheless, the governmental acknowledgement proved a large step for the reformers, who continued to send quarterly birth registers in increased confidence.

On March 31, 1871, *Beracha VeShalom* sent a communication to the colonial government announcing its new religious figurehead. Reverend Elias Nunes Martinez, a talented teacher known for his good disposition and "commendable" orthodoxy, had come down from England to take Nathan's place.[85] A graduate of and teacher in the Shaaré Tikvah Schools of London, who could speak intelligently on Shakespeare as well as scripture, the twenty-nine-year-old Martinez faced an interested but skeptical group of Jews in St. Thomas.[86] After a succession of ministers who had strapped the synagogue with strife and dissension, and the imminent departure of the one minister once considered worthy at the pulpit, the congregation showed no desire to jump directly into another potential personality conflict. Desperate for help, but reluctant to grant Martinez complete ministerial powers—and a salary to match—the wardens instead signed him to a three-year contract as "Reader and Religious Teacher," effective May 1, 1871.[87]

As Martinez prepared to assume his job, Nathan, his health declining, made his final plans for departure.[88] On May 13, 1871, the old minister gave his "valedictory address" at the synagogue, where he likely thanked the congregation for its support and expressed regret at having to leave the island.[89] As a matter of formality, the congregants presented Nathan with a testimonial "referr[ing] in grateful terms to Mr. Nathan's services, not only as minister but as teacher." The testimonial itself, however, showed true emotion, and requested that "notwithstanding his resignation, he would, so long as he might remain in the island, retain his canonicals, and take his place on the reading desk."[90] Although excited about a new minister in Reverend Martinez, the congregation clearly did not want to see Nathan leave.

Yet Nathan's departure for Europe was unavoidable. Severing his final ties to the island, the reverend transferred his position as St. Thomas representative for the Alliance Israélite Universelle to Alfred Nones in late April 1871.[91] The week after his final speech, Judah Cappé auctioned off Nathan's non-portable possessions, which by then had come to include such finery as a Chickering piano, two sets of china dishes, numerous mahogany chairs, tables, and sofas.[92] Nathan's house, #32 Queen's Street, went up for sale a few days later.[93] Soon after this, the minister and his wife boarded a steamer for

Europe, bidding a final farewell to their supporters. Nathan attended a synod for Jews of the newly unified German Republic later that year, before moving back to London for good.[94]

———∿∿———

REVEREND MARTINEZ OPENED HIS NEW SCHOOL, the St. Thomas Academy, on Monday, June 12, 1871. A secular institution, it taught both boys and girls "the subjects usually taught at public schools," and emphasized English as an important part of the curriculum. The minister also taught Hebrew, "but only as a language," in order to follow rules of church-state separation laid out by the colonial government. Religious instruction would be relegated to a separate Sunday School, which Martinez also planned to maintain.[95] Having logged thirteen years' teaching experience in England, the new religious leader seemed adept at finding ways to gain his constituents' confidence, and to this effect he made clear overtures to involve his pupils' parents in the educational process. Each child, he made sure to note, would keep a daily register, "showing the progress, attention and conduct of each pupil, and which will be sent home to be signed by the parents."[96] Through such approaches, Martinez probably gained the confidence of most of Nathan's former students.

The new minister's mere presence on the island, meanwhile, caused a dramatic change in the chemistry of the Jewish population. Nathan, a twelve-year veteran of the island, had all but defined *Beracha VeShalom*'s system of organization and worship in 1848, and fought valiantly (perhaps overzealously) to maintain it throughout his second run in the pulpit. Keeping an inflexible standard, Nathan's leadership revolved around keeping a tight grip on the Jewish community. Although this had helped the synagogue regain its footing in 1845, Nathan's unswerving approach had also served as a primary cause for secession twenty years later. Martinez, by contrast, began with a clean slate. Entering into a split Jewish community, his approaches and aims were fresh and unknown, his political affiliations untested. And because nobody knew his next move, Martinez's short tenure at St. Thomas became highly effective.

From his first actions, Martinez showed unprecedented compassion toward the Reformers. As a newly arrived minister, he heard wind that "a child of two and a half years old had been refused the rite of circumcision, because the father was a member of the Reform Congregation."[97] Martinez deemed this to be embarrassing, "mak[ing] known his views that it was not right to permit the child to grow up without receiving the sign of the Jewish Covenant," and expressed his willingness to perform the Reform ritual "if the parents were agreeable thereto." The surprised parents, "who had often regretted that they were not able to see their child admitted into the Bond of Israel," gladly took Martinez up on his offer. Shortly thereafter, the minister brought the child successfully into the covenant, to the satisfaction of all. The Hebrew Reformed Congregation commended Martinez on his actions—sentiments that were later echoed in the *London Jewish Chronicle*. A new hope for unity came to light on St. Thomas. "In so far as the Reform Congegation is concerned," wrote the *Jewish Chronicle*, "it is certainly not in Mr. M[artinez]'s power to unite them into the old fold, but his tolerance is an ample guarantee that he will not widen the breach."[98]

Martinez began to inspire others in the Jewish community to work toward reconciliation as well. By the next April, several members of *Beracha Ve-Shalom* began to emerge in favor of revising the old synagogue's bylaws. Their presence became so conspicuous that hard-line supporters of the bylaws began to protest: "It is the opinion of Some Members of the Congregation," wrote Benjamin Delvalle to the island's governor, "that the Congregation is in the full right of laying aside the present laws [and] of framing new ones of their own accord without the necessity of obtaining the Sanction of His Majesty . . . which the Undersigned in his humble opinion considers illegal. . . ."[99] Issues of legality, however, were secondary to perceptions that the synagogue needed a new start, freed from the restrictions of a document that had often been cited as an originating source of the previous decade's strife.

Further contributing to the tide for revision was the island's economy, which no longer favored two separate congregations. After another pair of hurricanes hit the island in 1871, resources became scarce, and once flowering mercantilism began a long descent into economic depression.[100] Although the number of ships calling at St. Thomas continued to grow marginally from year to year, the island's reputation as an international port declined.[101] A failed attempt to sell the Virgin Islands to the United States in 1867 had a negative effect on the population's morale, bringing feelings of worthlessness to the recently stormswept area. St. Thomas's profits, which had for decades provided Denmark with income to cover St. Croix's losses, would soon become deficits.[102] And as prosperity disappeared, dissatisfaction started to spread among the people. The Jews who faced this new environment saw their homeland become a shadow of what it was in 1848, and began to realize that the luxury of disunity would not last for long. Their time required a rethinking of the Jewish community's organization, emphasizing co-operation and fiscal consolidation. With Nathan gone, pride became less of an issue, and survival the order of the day.

Already, motions toward a common Jewish ground were apparent. Alfred Nones, a co-founder of the reform congregation once derided as a "business-man who keeps no Shabbat," had become a leader in this regard.[103] Speaking at *Beracha VeShalom* as early as 1869, Nones subsequently rejoined the congregation and rose from board representative in 1871 to vice-president by 1872 to president in 1873; he had even forged a relationship with Reverend Nathan to the point of becoming his chosen successor as representative to the Alliance Israelite Universelle.[104] Emmanuel Correa Osorio, the youngest reformer, also returned to the old congregation, becoming a member around 1870.[105] But the act that appeared to begin the reconciliation in earnest occurred in late August 1872, when the voting members of *Beracha VeShalom* elected Reverend Martinez as official minister of their congregation "for the unexpired term of his contract, say to the 30th April, 1874."[106] A popular figure among the entire Jewish community, Martinez's inclusive style seemed to provide broad satisfaction. Soon after his official accession, the Hebrew Reformed Congregation stopped reporting its own records to the government. Less than a year into its new-found official independence, the reformers' insistent quarterly reports gave way to regular notes, written in gothic Danish by a disinterested government clerk, which compulsorily noted no new additions.[107] By the next year, one of the couples married by the Reformed rite re-applied to join *Beracha VeShalom* and have their son entered into the congregation's records. Taking a comfortingly sympathetic stance, the board agreed to both requests, and informed the government of its decision.[108] Through such actions, the Jewish community showed its readiness to reconcile, and the Reformed synagogue began to melt back into the fold.

For those who remained discontented with *Beracha VeShalom*, the disintegrating Reformed Congregation served as an effective excuse to begin looking elsewhere for business. As St. Thomas descended, a new region— the isthmus of Panama—began to increase in prominence. The brilliant rhetoric of French entrepreneur Ferdinand de Lesseps, who expressed grand intentions to connect east and west with a huge canal, caught the imagination of the world. On St. Thomas, which was increasingly relying on steamship coaling for its livelihood, many merchants realized the enormous potential markets that could open up through the Panamanian venture. Older merchants began to send emissaries to the isthmus in order to estab-

lish branch offices. In most cases, these emissaries were young men beginning their careers as clerks; their enthusiasm, it was hoped, would provide
the necessary energy to make the new offices successful. At the same time,
however, the flight of these fortune-seekers reinforced St. Thomas's failing
status as a place for new business.

Perhaps perceiving the darkening conditions on St. Thomas, Reverend
Martinez resigned suddenly from his position as reader of *Beracha VeShalom*
in December 1873, a full year before his contract was to expire.[109] The reasons for his departure were unclear, but there were no indications in either
the local press or in Jewish periodicals that he had been facing adverse circumstances. Nonetheless, the congregation appeared to take the resignation
in stride. They marked the occasion with appropriate notes and dedications,
though apparently with an evident dispassion.

Immediately filling Martinez's place was David Cardoze, Jr., who took
over the congregation's clerical tasks as an unpaid lay-reader. By October
1874, when the Jewish community celebrated its next wedding, Cardoze had
attained sufficient credentials with the government to conduct the service
alone, and he validated the marriage contract with his own signature.[110] Upstanding and dedicated to the community, he would commence a run of forty
years of sincere and tireless service as the congregation's acting reader, becoming one of the only bright spots of the declining Jewish life on the island.

The sweeping changes to the island's Jewish community, as well as the
lack of a formal resolution between the two congregations, enhanced the need
for a regrouping and recasting of the population into a single entity once
again. Thus, in August 1875, the Hebrew Congregation successfully completed the revision of its bylaws with the intention of ending the synagogal
rivalry once and for all. Although the committee appointed to rewrite the
laws was notably lacking in known members of the Reformed Congregation,
the changes it implemented clearly showed a strong influence by the latter's
1868 regulations. Moreover, after years of debate, the new code finally and
openly acknowledged the reformers' original assertions that the previous bylaws had become obsolete, "dependent on presuppositions now lapsed, in
consequence of the tenor of [the 1865] Colonial Law §71."[111] Clearly, this revision aimed to bring the entire community back together, under one roof,
and with one form of religious practice.

Using the 1848 bylaws as their model, the framers of the new regulations
essentially reproduced much of the text verbatim. In this context, however,
the differences from the 1848 laws illuminated themselves clearly, and
helped to reflect a rhetorical resolution of the decade's issues.

One of the most drastic changes in the code applied to the issue of membership. In 1848, the synagogue had a compulsory membership policy, which incorporated "all Israelites who may, now or hereafter, reside in the Island."[112] By the 1870s, however, this law had been battered by numerous defections from the synagogue and several failed congregational appeals to the government to enforce it. Realizing that the congregation no longer could assume its membership, the statute was changed to take a far more democratic approach: "The members of the Congregation shall consist of the present ones who are willing to abide by these laws, and of such other Israelites as may hereafter apply, and be admitted by the Board of Representatives."[113] As the Reformed Congregation had shown, religious worship and affiliation had become a choice of the individual, dictated by conscience as much as by birth. *Beracha VeShalom* learned from this, and as a result made acceptance of the bylaws the primary criterion for gaining entry to the synagogue's collective religious identity.

Other areas of congregational life also changed through this new individualism, particularly when it came to discipline. The 1848 bylaws had noted several occasions where the synagogue board could appeal to the governor or the presidency in order to collect fines or deal with difficult congregants. Yet when put into practice in the debate against the reformers, the government's response was unsatisfactory, often exacerbating the situation rather than helping it. Possibly because of this, the congregation removed all references to the island government in the bylaws, taking its discipline issues entirely in-house. Enforcement, especially with the new voluntary membership policy, would almost certainly be dealt with more efficiently under this revision.

In general, the fine infractions and amounts themselves remained the same. However, one of the more sensitive of the synagogue fines quietly disappeared. The bylaws still forbade "meeting for the divine service out of the Synagogue," though this time no financial assessment was imposed on such an infraction.[114] Probably by no coincidence this was the same infraction that had created the Reformers' initial conflict with the synagogue in the first place. Its subtle softening was likely a method of defraying future contentions and defusing bad memories. The concept of ritual unity, though properly acknowledged, thus received careful treatment in a manner sensitive to the conflicts of the past.

The new laws also redefined the positions of the paid personnel at the synagogue. Most notably, the minister's previous control of all ritual dissolved. Now referred to as the "Minister or Reader," the religious leader became subservient to the wishes and practices of the people. Once unquestioned in *minhag*—as envisioned and enacted by Reverend Nathan—the minister under the new bylaws would be under constant scrutiny of the synagogue board. His style of prayer-leading, and his additions to and deletions from the traditional Spanish and Portuguese liturgy, could be rejected by a sixty per-cent vote of the membership. Moreover, should the membership independ-ently vote additional changes to the liturgy by the same percentage, the min-ister would be obligated to introduce them.[115] His responsibilities to the synagogue were delineated in more careful detail, including the devotion of two hours per weekday to children's religious instruction and a required re-hearsal before reading from the Torah.[116] The now-voluntary synagogue membership clearly felt it could not afford the effects of another strong-willed minister; thus, it attempted to keep all subsequent religious leaders in check, more evenly balanced between their own wills and the will of the congregation.

Finally, the synagogue added items to its bylaws that clarified its ritual practices. For the first time, the bylaws included provisions (and incentives) to form a volunteer choir "to assist in divine service."[117] Organized and pro-moted under the auspices of both the board of representatives and the minister, it seemed to come directly out of the Hebrew Reformed Congre-gation's bylaws.[118] Also, the reframers took the opportunity to insert starting times for services throughout the liturgical year, taking into account seasonal sunset differences and including the commencement and conclusion days of the hurricane season.[119]

These bylaws helped update the synagogue and the Jewish community to its new socio-political environment. Submitted to the Danish colonial gov-ernment in the fall of 1875 and officially accepted a few months later, they were the remnants of a code that had itself been remade through crisis. Through the immense natural and technological upheavals of the previous few years, the fortunes of the island—and the Jewish community—were facing shrinking resources and a departing population. Having experienced the ravages of partition, and embroiled in an internationally publicized con-troversy for nearly ten years, the Jewish community now sloughed off its old and toughened skin—the outside ministers and contrasting ideologies, the defections and violent disagreements—and began to come together. Under their new bylaws, the congregation gathered at the times posted in the syn-agogue to pray, led by a fellow merchant most had known personally for decades. They used the Spanish and Portuguese rite, placing the London Reformed Liturgy to rest on St. Thomas once and for all. And they united in their original sanctuary, organized under its original name "Beracha V'Shalom V'Gemilut Hasadim." For the next forty years, this situation would remain: The congregation insular and detached from the Jewish world, the commerce of Judaic ideas to and from St. Thomas reduced to a trickle, and the general population, with a few notable exceptions, remaining stagnant. Reform on St. Thomas was over; the era of survival had begun.

In July 1876, Panama's new Jewish society *Kol Shearith Israel* ("The Voice of the Remnant of Israel") conducted its first funeral, utilizing a cemetery ground it had consecrated just days earlier. The deceased was Emil Rothschild, son of St. Thomas banker Sigismund Rothschild, who had left his father's St. Thomas business a few years earlier to embark on a promising career with the Panamanian firm of Aepli, Salmon & Co. Officiating at the ceremony, in his new propensity as president and acting reader of the Panama congregation, was Elias Nunes Martinez.[120]

WHAT HAPPENED TO THE MAJOR CHARACTERS who left St. Thomas during this period? The stories of their lives after St. Thomas are necessary for placing the island's activities in perspective.

Upon retiring to England, Aron and Rachel Wolff lived in Manchester for a short time. Aron's health remained fragile, however, and the couple moved in with their son-in-law, Jacob M. DaCosta, in Warrington Crescent, Maida Hill, London. On January 15, 1872, Aron Wolff ended his illustrious life at age seventy-six. Interestingly, his sterling reputation did not seem to follow him across the Atlantic. An abbreviated obituary appeared in the Jewish Chronicle of London, which did little more than mark his passing; and his grave, at the Ball's Pond cemetery in London, was indistinguishable from any other.[121] Even on St. Thomas, the response was surprisingly quiet: although the synagogue sent a letter of sympathy and tribute to the widow Rachel, the *Tidende* devoted only a short paragraph to his passing, which spoke of him in equivocal, albeit regretful, terms.[122] There is a partial belief that Wolff left the island after experiencing some kind of financial downfall, and departed to finish his life in peace.[123] Whatever the case, however, his death did not seem to befit a Lieutenant Colonel in the Danish colonial militia and a Knight of the Dannebrog with family spread out all across the world.

After Aron Wolff's death, his wife Rachel moved to Paris for a few years to live with her daughter and son-in-law before moving to New York City at the invitation of another one of her sons. She died on January 22, 1879, aged eighty-seven. "[W]hen called from this world to join him with whom she most cared to be with, the majority of her family were present to receive her parting blessing. The genial and kind hearted old lady drew always around her a large circle of admiring friends, and her charitable disposition made her beloved by the poor."[124]

Reverend Moses Nathan Nathan left St. Thomas with an international reputation tarnished little by his dealings with the reformers on the island. Jewish-interest periodicals continually praised Nathan throughout his second tenure on St. Thomas, attesting to his knowledge, his abilities of oration, and the solemn manner in which he performed the sacred service.[125] He received no blame for the strife that had blossomed there; instead, the public understood through publications that "[t]he secession in the [St. Thomas] congregation occurred from causes beyond Nathan's control."[126] Such testimonies exhonerated him from a sticky situation, and framed his migration from St. Thomas as a simple career move from a successful pulpit with difficult constituents.

The final stage of Nathan's life revealed his relationship with Reform Judaism to have a greater complexity than his actions on St. Thomas suggested. Nathan returned to London, where, according to a correspondent in the *Jewish Chronicle*, "before determining to which synagogue he should attach himself, he visited every synagogue in the metropolis."[127] After this search, notably, "[h]e at length fixed on the West London Synagogue of British Jews," the same institution whose liturgy he had opposed so bitterly on St. Thomas. A "constant attendant," Nathan would come to listen to sermons delivered by his former student, now Reverend Professor David Woolf Marks, while praying according to Reform rite that Marks himself had compiled. He became a deeply respected member of the congregation and of the London Jewish community in general, taking "an active and earnest part in the founding of the Anglo-Jewish Association, and for several years act[ing] as Honorary Secretary of the Educational Committee of that society. . . . He was also a member of the Roumanian Committee [presumably a committee for the improvement of conditions of Rumanian Jews] and of the Committee of the Society of Hebrew Literature."[128] No longer an opponent of Reform, Nathan came out as a strong advocate and a representative of London's Jewish life. Nathan found his place and thrived, ensconced within a society that accepted Reform as part of its intellectual continuum.

Reverend Nathan's declining health finally forced him to leave London in the early 1880s for the more pastoral climes of Bath, where he stayed until his death on May 13, 1883. After the congregation in nearby Bristol performed Nathan's final rites, his body was brought back to London; and on May 16, a final funeral service accompanied Nathan's interment in the West London Synagogue's cemetery at Ball's Pond. Reverend Marks himself performed the burial service, paying homage to "his earliest teacher, who through his earnestness had induced [Marks] to qualify himself for the sacred calling of a Minister."[129] Among the many individuals present were Nathan's widow and three high-ranking representatives of the Anglo-Jewish Association.[130]

The pallbearers lowered Nathan's body into the grave, and Marks "delivered a brief address," recounting Nathan's life "from his youth to his death, and prais[ing] the good work he had performed in England, the West Indies, America, and finally again in his native country." Marks concluded with a line of tribute: "This is a bald but true sketch of the life of a good man, whose every action was prompted by a desire to glorify his religion and his people. *Moshe, avad Hashem, met.* 'Moses, the servant of God, is dead,' and, having confidence in the truth of the Scriptures, we may rest assured that his spirit is now with the Almighty receiving its true reward. May his memory be for a blessing. Amen!"[131] With this, the ceremony ended, and Reverend Moses Nathan Nathan reached his final resting place.

Nathan's eroded, New Orleans–style gravestone still stands in the Ball's Pond cemetery, the only one of its type in that section. A small weathered inscription in the grave's side identifies the reverend, accompanied by a quotation from the Book of Daniel, 12:3: "All men who have been wise shall shine forth with the brightness of [the heavens; and they that turn many to righteousness shall shine as the stars for ever and ever]."[132] Less than ten feet away, the shining cylindrical grave of David Woolf Marks keeps vigil over his teacher, his ideological adversary, and, finally, his respected constituent.[133]

After almost fourteen years at the helm of Panamanian congregation *Kol Shearith Israel*, Reverend Martinez was forced to leave in 1890 due to debts incurred through failed business ventures.[134] He moved to Tangier for a time (where he was a schoolmaster) before finally settling in London. When a new synagogue began on Lauderdale Road around Maida Hill, Martinez served as an assistant to the *Hazan*, tutoring members' children and orphans during his free time. A respected and devoted servant of the new congregation, it was said of him that "at no time was he happier than when reading the service, indeed it was a labour of love for him."[135] Martinez continued his work with the Lauderdale Road Synagogue until his death on March 27, 1911.[136] A large crowd attended the preacher's funeral, and witnessed his body lowered into the earth with the rites of a Levantador at the Golders Green cemetery.[137] Today, his marble gravestone remains clean and legible, distinguished from those around it by a corroded copper rail.

Of the fourteen original seceders, not a single one is buried in the St. Thomas Jewish cemetery. There are many possible reasons for this, the most plausible of which is that the young members were the most likely socio-economic group to move from the island in search of better conditions. Aside from speculation, however, it is difficult to come to any conclusion about their whereabouts and later lives, for they were not prominent residents on the island, and left little to no trace of their subsequent activities. Thus, the chronicle of those who most vehemently supported Reform on nineteenth-century St. Thomas must end here, scattered and awaiting further discovery.[138]

CHAPTER 7

Changing of the Guard
1875–1914

SATURDAY LAST was observed by those of the Israelitish persuasion, as a close holy-day, it being Kipur, or Fast-day. The Congregation in this place attended at the Synagogue the usual services; there were many present, but the recent departure of many
families has reduced it greatly, and their vacant places produced
a feeling of sorrow. We trust that the fasting and the prayers of
the Congregation may be received, and their day of expiation be
answered with Providential Blessings.

—*St. Thomas Herald*, September 27, 1882

$\mathcal{W}$ith its days of booming trade and relentless growth
over, the island of St. Thomas began to lose its gleam as a colonial jewel of
the Danish crown. Throttled by the catastrophes of 1867, theatened by new
shipping and communications technologies, and troubled by labor issues left
unresolved since the emancipation of slavery, the island found itself receding
into the background of the Caribbean theater. Once a source of cultural and
economic pride for Denmark, the Virgin Islands began to run at increasing
deficits starting in the 1870s, causing a taxing strain on the Danish treasury.[1]
The once-ideal protected harbor of Charlotte Amalie began to show its
obsolescence, now too shallow for the new, larger cargo ships that raised
the stakes in international trade. The floating dock constructed earlier to
temper the situation had been resurrected, but could serve only one large
vessel at a time, and its frequent and embarrasing mechanical problems

often brought it more ridicule than respect. Smaller ships, meanwhile, became increasingly rare in the St. Thomas port as well. Powered by more efficient steam engines, they could travel all the way from Europe to the American continent in one trip, without having to refuel at St. Thomas. The island could only watch as its once burgeoning business withered, helpless in the face of such developments.

Overlooking the less-crowded St. Thomas harbor, the synagogue continued to open its doors for Jewish worship every week without fail. Lay-reader David Cardoze, Jr., alternated between his store duties at the waterfront and his ecclesiastical duties on Synagogue Hill. An emerging fixture on the island, Cardoze developed into a patient and passionate acting minister. In many ways, he had a difficult job providing spiritual comfort to the population: The generations of Jews who moved to the island for a better life in the eighteenth and early nineteenth centuries no longer found St. Thomas the inviting, bright trade center it once was. Older and more prominent merchants remained dedicated to their businesses, but new enterprise was difficult to sustain. Younger members of the community hoping to start businesses departed in step with their non-Jewish compatriots for more lucrative markets such as Panama and Costa Rica. Although these younger merchants retained ties with their older relatives, they rarely returned for any appreciable period of time. David Cardoze, Jr., could only watch from the pulpit as he administered to what seemed the last generation on a fading island.

A census taken in 1870 had revealed a population of 375 Jews in Charlotte Amalie. Though substantially fewer than the estimated high of over six hundred during the mid-1860s, the number still represented a relatively vibrant portrait of the community. The vast majority were native to St. Thomas, though the significant migrations of the past century still showed clearly. Nearly ten percent came from Curaçao, close to five percent were emigrants born in Venezuela, and just under two percent came from parts of France. Even historically distant St. Eustatius still had a five-person representation, four of whom were over the age of sixty. Large, young families abounded, keeping the average age of the community under twenty-six and providing the synagogue some reason to take stock in the future.[2] Applications to the government for business permits from the Jewish community were at lower levels than before, though they still saw steady approval at around three per year.[3] The community, though shrinking, still had some semblance of health.

But the next decade saw much change. On the final day of 1874, David M. Piza closed up his storefront for the last time, and likely left the island soon afterward with his wife and three young children.[4] Sylvain Levy, the former organist of the Hebrew Reformed Congregation and a conservatory-trained pianist, gave his final public concert at the end of March, 1875 before moving out to Buenos Aires with his Catholic wife Clothilde and their young family.[5] Several senior members of the congregation passed away: Joseph Levi, a "worthy and respected citizen" and a member of the Knights of the Dannebrog, died of Bright's disease on July 10, 1875, at age seventy-one.[6] Judith Levy Maduro, widow of long-time reader Samuel Elias Levy Maduro, died on January 15, 1876, aged sixty-six.[7] Two months later, financier and high-standing citizen Sigismund Rothschild died at age seventy-seven after a long illness.[8] And on June 1 of the same year, Eleanora Jacobs, one of the last remaining St. Eustatius natives, passed away at age ninety.[9] In other circumstances, their deaths would have been part of the natural order, opening spaces of prominence for others to fill. Combined with the flight of many young and promising members of the congregation, however, these losses were a great blow to the congregation's self-image and outlook.

Even under heavy clouds of mourning, the synagogue still showed sparks of life. The financial crises hitting the islands appeared to pull attention away from religious and administrative activities, and caused the congregation to enjoy a quiet respite from internal turmoil. Waning trade caused the synagogue wardens to be more concerned with the welfare of their financially troubled congregants than with the collection of a new preacher's salary. Although fiscal woes effectively eliminated the congregation's chances of engaging a knowledgable religious authority, they also prevented new, controversial ideas and customs from the outside world from invading and ripping the congregation apart. The simple retention of the existing *minhag*, conducted each week by a local lay-minister, began to contribute to a quiet renaissance. Even though bad times had descended upon the island, the situation had yet to reach its nadir: Between 1875 and 1880, the synagogue's on-island births still outnumbered deaths, albeit barely.

The remaining families continued to support congregational activities in an attempt to revitalize their communal life. Primary among these was reestablishing a Jewish education system for the congregation's children. Cardoze made this one of his responsibilities at the start of 1877, reinstituting the congregation's Sunday School to the delight of parents. Becoming a vital organ of the synagogue, the school was a lightning rod for Jewish expression on the island, and a popular success among the Jewish population. At the first year-end examination, the students publicly demonstrated their progress, and all who attended reportedly expressed a feeling of pride in their congregation, not to mention some comfort during the recession.[10]

Meanwhile, Cardoze's confidence and ability grew as he spent more time in the pulpit, as could be seen by the manner in which he signed marriage certificates. Like many other synagogues, the St. Thomas Hebrew Congregation had its own pre-printed marriage forms: A banner displaying the synagogue's name lay centered at the top. Underneath was a formulaic paragraph in English describing the essentials of the union, including dotted lines for the names and signatures of bride and groom, the date, the witnesses to the ceremony, and the signature of the officiating minister. This latter was a dotted line to the lower right of the paragraph subscribed by the italic printed phrase "Minister and Registrar." Upon completion of each ceremony, the minister would likely fill out the form in duplicate, presenting one copy to the married couple, and keeping the other for the synagogue's records.[11] When David Cardoze signed his first marriage certificates, he seemed uncomfortable with the position of responsibility granted him under the dotted line; he crossed out the "Minister and Registrar" designation and replaced it with the more modest appellation "Acting Reader." By the 1878 wedding of Isaac Levy Maduro and Clara Jessurun Lindo, however, a change had taken place. Whether through new appreciation by the congregation, a feeling of personal growth, or an actual alteration in legal status, Cardoze for the first time left the title printed under his signature untouched. The "Acting Reader," it seems, had come into his own as the island's Jewish minister.[12]

The synagogue protocols continued to add births, deaths, and marriages to its register, though by the 1880s it did so at a much slower pace. Where once dozens of these life-cycle events graced the community, now only a handful of births and deaths and perhaps one marriage took place annually. The records, however, were becoming more than a gauge for St. Thomas's attrition rates: They also served, ironically, to clarify emigration patterns among the congregation's members. Off-island births, deaths, and marriages had been entered into the register throughout the congregation's history as a way of keeping up with St. Thomas congregants who were in transit, on leave, newly arrived, or being married in a foreign territory. At the end of the nineteenth century they began to appear more frequently. Non–St. Thomas birth records, for example, would eventually account for almost eighty percent of the total births reported to the congregation, and similar statistics would apply to marriages. Deaths, however, remained almost exclusive to St. Thomas, as if to emphasize the erosion of the population.

The St. Thomas congregation thus became a hollow center of sorts for Sephardic Jewish life in the northeast Caribbean. Just as Curaçao had served as the "parent" congregation to St. Thomas throughout much of the nineteenth century, so St. Thomas had become a place of origination for new congregations taking root in Panama and Costa Rica. Former St. Thomas resident Emil Rothschild's untimely death in Colon, Panama, in 1876 led to the first funeral performed by the new *Kol Shearith Israel* ("The Voice of the Remnant of Israel") congregation there. Rothschild's death record was also entered in the St. Thomas synagogue's protocol book, and one of the local St. Thomas papers printed an account of the ceremony.[13] In Alajuela, Costa Rica, on February 20, 1878, longtime St. Thomas resident Samuel Levy Maduro presided over the marriage of Abraham Alfred Jessurun Lindo and St. Thomas native Judith Levy Maduro; the St. Thomas synagogue officially recorded the union on April 1 of the same year. Such acts show that the St. Thomas Jews took an active role in supporting and promoting Jewish life among their descendants, even as these descendants dispersed to other lands.

A perusal of the local paper during this time would reveal the same Jewish family names as before, only in smaller quantity. Sassos, Maduros, Monsantos, Prettos, Lindos, Pizas, Delvalles, De Castros and Da Costas continued to make their presence known on the island. As always, they would gather weekly in the synagogue, attend board meetings, and close (or not close) their shops on the Sabbath. Further perusal of the paper, however, revealed a second, non-Jewish population holding the same last names. Individuals such as highly successful free-black trader Alexander DeCastro existed and operated on St. Thomas throughout the nineteenth century; their numbers, however, began to proliferate by the 1870s. No longer in sole possession of the Jewish community, the names were becoming an entrenched part of the greater island culture.

They migrated into the outside community through several processes: illicit liaisons, young "indiscretions," interreligious marriages, "common-law" marriages and, occasionally, straightforward conversion. In doing so, they portrayed the Jewish community from a different perspective: as a porous segment of a larger population. As with the other religious groups, the Hebrew Congregation kept its own tenets of purity. While other churches would indicate whether these tenets were met by simply checking off "legitimate" or "illegitimate" in their protocols, the synagogue would make them criteria for inclusion. Both members of a couple wishing to marry had to be Jewish to receive the synagogue's sanction; and children had to be born of two married, Jewish parents to be penned legitimately into the congregation's record books. The synagogue's official entries thus provided an incomplete picture of the Jewish population, leaving the messiness of relationships that did not conform to such criteria to the registers of other churches. Understanding what these other relationships were like in the second half of the nineteenth century should provide a more textured concept of the Jewish community both as an integrated part of an island culture, and as a heterogeneous body in itself.[14]

During the eighteenth and nineteenth centuries, liaisons between white men and non-white women were thought to be common practice in the Virgin Islands. Even Governor Peter von Scholten, during his tenure in the 1830s and 1840s, kept a well-known non-white mistress with little popular dissent. This practice seems to have existed among some members of the Jewish population as well. By the second half of the nineteenth century, for example, large families of non-Jewish Monsantos already lived on St. Thomas. Their origins are unknown, but it is likely that the families arose through liaisons several generations back (and not necessarily on St.Thomas) between Monsanto men and non-Jewish women (legal or otherwise).[15]

Yet an analysis of church records between 1867 and 1880 shows a portrait of relatively responsible, if slightly wayward, interreligious affairs. During this time, the island saw only one birth from confirmed extra-marital relations between a Jewish merchant and a non-Jewish woman.[16] This one birth was to David Delvalle and Henrietta Lucas (the latter an Episcopalian) on March 14, 1875. Two years earlier, the twenty-eight-year-old Delvalle had married sixteen-year-old Grace Cardoze, the young daughter of the synagogue's reader. Apparently, during the first year of their marriage, Delvalle formed a liaison with Lucas, impregnating her. The child of this affair, Henry H. Delvalle, received a Catholic baptism on April 28, 1875, in a ceremony that included sponsoring godparents. There was apparently little public issue with this display, and the Cardoze family in particular seemed to take the incident in stride. The next year, Delvalle's proper wife Grace gave birth to Benjamin, the first of what would be nine children (six of whom survived past infancy); her marriage with David would last until his death in April 1909. This single illicit extra-marital affair was apparently dispatched smoothly, becoming an isolated incident within the records.

Slightly more common were the liaisons between single Jewish merchants (usually young men) and non-Jewish women. These as well did not occur with any great frequency, and in most cases, the long-term outcomes of such couplings were unknown. In the case of Moses Halman, who fathered a daughter Nanette with a Protestant woman named M. Ratclif in 1874, the daughter was baptized Catholic and then taken in to live with Halman's extended family.[17] On July 29, 1882, Halman married Rebecca Rosabelle De-

Meza, joining the ranks of the respectably wed.[18] In a second case, sixty-four-year-old Samuel B. Halman was a widower when he fathered Maria with Jeanette Ross in 1872. "Illegitimate" as these births were, they did not seem to inspire strong social stigma.

The dominant form of Jewish parentage in a Jewish/non-Jewish couple, however, appears to have been within the context of a committed relationship—whether officially recognized or not. Substantially outnumbering the both previous categories combined, monogamous long-term relationships accounted for over fifteen baptisms on the island beween 1867 and 1880. Sometimes, these relationships resulted in a marriage solemnized by a religious body other than the synagogue; in other cases, a kind of common-law marriage was invoked; and in still other cases, the relationship had the appearance of a long-term monogamous liaison.

The records indicate five official intermarriages on the island, denoted in the church protocols by the legitimate births of their children. By far, the most fruitful of these marriages was the union between Rachel and William Charles Lamb. Rachel, possibly born to the Moron family on the island in 1841, appears to have retained her religious identification after wedding Lamb, an Episcopalian. All of her five children, however—Albert, Alexander, Adele, James and Regina—grew up as members of the English Church. Another couple, Elias (Jewish) and Ellen (Moravian) Sasso, had a similar situation in the Moravian Church; their two daughters, Leah and Julianna (the latter of whom died when only two days old), were recognized as legitimate births in that church's registers. In the Dutch Reformed church down the street from the synagogue, Mr. M. Leon and Ms. R. E. Delvalle (the father Jewish, the mother not), baptised Esther Anita Leon in a telling mix of names in 1870. And, as mentioned earlier, Sylvain Levy, before leaving the island, baptized his daughter Mannette Azelia at the All Saints Church with his Catholic wife Clotilde.[19] Notably, these births were exclusive from the synagogue: None of the parents made an effort to bring their children into Judaism. Even the Lambs, where the mother's Jewish status technically made the children Jews themselves, made no apparent efforts to gain the synagogue's approbation. It thus appears that intermarriage was enough of a reason on St. Thomas for parents to raise their newborn children outside of Judaism.

The argument also extended to the children of long-term unmarried Jewish/non-Jewish couples. Several of these couples nested on the island during the late nineteenth century; and while church records indicated their children's illegitimacy, the couples' own personal views of their relationship sometimes differed considerably. Salomon J. Delvalle, for example, fathered two children with Ludorisca Lange, a Catholic woman.[20] In the 1870 census, Delvalle and Lange listed themselves as a married couple; the Catholic Church, apparently, did not agree and labelled both births as illegitimate. For others, legitimacy did not seem to matter: Herman Levi had two children with Episcopalian Esther Monsanto between 1867 and 1880, accepting their illegitimate status with little issue.[21] As with the intermarried couples, there seemed to be a tacit understanding that these births would not gain acceptance in the synagogue records. Perhaps, without any proper authority on conversion, affiliation with the Hebrew congregation was simply not an option for these children. Perhaps the reason was even simpler: The other churches were the paths of least resistance, and the parents were content to place their child's official record on any church baptism list. Whatever the case, only one known child born out of wedlock ever became Jewish during the nineteenth century; this child—Victoria Elizabeth Levien—would become an important part of the coming years of the congregation. Her story, intertwined with the rest of the narrative, will be discussed in the next section.

Two "fatherless" births also occurred during this time, to the same person, and both children were baptized in the Catholic church. Leah D'Oliveyra, identified in the records as a Jewish woman, gave birth to Ludvic B. in 1874, and Alexandrine in 1875. No father's name appeared on either record; and notably, D'Oliveyra gave her own family name to at least one of the children (suggesting the absence of a father). Yet D'Oliveyra's name was also elusive: It did not appear in the synagogue protocols, nor did it show up as Jewish in any of the existing census records.

In addition to births, the church records from this time reveal one other important situation on the island. As opposed to the strict bounding of religious communities maintained throughout the eighteenth and early to mid-nineteenth centuries, there was a hint that such required adherence to a particular religious identity was relaxing by the end of the nineteenth century. This was certainly the case for Morris B. Simmonds, whose self-declared Unitarianism eventually freed him from his synagogue responsibilities in 1866. Perhaps empowered by Simmonds's example, a few others seemed to leave and enter Judaism on their own accord. Though this can so far be determined only through their own accounts, they appeared to leave no evidence of dissent among or discordant relations with their co-religionists.

On two occasions, for example, church record keepers attributed Jewish status to people who did not consider themselves Jewish. Lucien A. Nunes, who fathered Julius Nunes in 1874, with Catholic woman Dolorita Ochoa, listed himself as a non-Jew next to his Jewish brother in the 1870 census. Aaron Cappé, father of a son August with Catholic woman Luisa Van Scrack in 1871, died and was buried on St. Thomas but has no synagogue death record (or birth record, for that matter), and no gravestone in the Jewish cemetery, making a Jewish identity unlikely. On the children's baptismal records, however, Nunes and Cappé were identified as Jews. This seems to suggest that personal choice had by this time come to take at least some stake in determining spiritual identity.

Two other stories of conversion out of Judaism also emerged from these records. The first involved the conversion of two sisters, Clara and Esther Benlisa, to the English Church. Born on St. Thomas, they were two of the four daughters of widow Rachel Benlisa, who kept a shop in town in the 1840s, 1850s and 1860s. Over the course of two years—1865 through 1867—Clara and Esther experienced the deaths of their sister Zipporah, their newly married sister Julia, and their mother. Three years later, on July 25, 1870, Clara converted to Anglicanism; and on March 15, 1871, Esther followed. Unwed and in or approaching their thirties, chances are they turned to the new religion for some sort of security.

These instances show the level of integration the island population had achieved by this time. While the religious institutions—especially the synagogue—kept a tight rein on defining legitimate and illegitimate births, the people themselves seemed to withdraw from these ideals to concentrate first and foremost on living and existing in a multi-faceted, complex community.

—◦◦◦—

WHEN THE COLONIAL COUNCIL attempted to ameliorate its financial crisis by levying a new tax on the merchants in 1881, the mercantile faction responded with exasperation:

> Let the Hon. members compare the number of Wholesale Merchants of 1876 with those now existing, and see what a great falling off there has been. . . . On what customers can the St. Thomas Merchants rely today? St. Croix; St. Johns, Tortola; and the local consumption of this barren Island. If anyone could introduce some new Market as a customer for St. Thomas he would confer a boon on the Community at large.[22]

Those at the bottom of the labor pyramid seemed most vulnerable to the new tax. Three decades after abolishing slavery, the Danish West Indies still suffered under the weight of thousands of farm workers and house servants still waiting for living wage legislation. Foundering under a system hardly modified since emancipation in 1848, the islands' workers saw their jobs as little more than enlightened indentured servitude. Private contracts forged with house and landowners provided them with a scant income, but gave them no leverage or bargaining rights. The goverment spoke of its intentions to improve the situation, but all motivation to do so disintegrated as the economy eventually lost its ability to support the anticipated laws. Expectant workers, as a result, experienced one crushing disappointment after another. On October 1, 1878, labor difficulties in the territory came to a head as riots broke out in and around Frederiksted, St. Croix. The unrest finally ended more than two weeks later, after the destruction of well over half a million dollars in property and crops, and a suppression effort that called on the assistance of military ships from England, France, and the United States.[23] Charlotte Amalie, with its higher-paying dock jobs, experienced less tension than agriculturally based St. Croix, but discontent continued to simmer everywhere.[24]

Looking desperately for a new source of income, the islanders gained some solace by glancing westward to the Central American peninsula. A massive project was underway to connect the Atlantic and Pacific oceans by constructing an enormous canal across the isthmus of Panama. When completed, it was expected to renew maritime traffic through the Caribbean and serve as a shining example of mankind's technological prowess and ingenuity. St. Thomas saw itself as a major port en route to the proposed canal, and the local papers highlighted the project's potential for bringing strong economic growth back to the region. Promises of better times buoyed the island's hopes, as residents were presented with frequent updates on the canal's progress.[25] In the meantime, as the present looked bleaker and bleaker, the island had to make do with its own self-assurances that it would not fall into irrelevance.[26]

By 1880, the Jewish community on St. Thomas had aged. The average congregant was now over twenty-nine—more than three years older than in 1870.[27] Deaths on the island in 1880 outnumbered births, twenty-three to seventeen. And for the first time, the synagogue's protocols recorded more births off-island than on-island.[28] These statistics were reflections of the current island situation, and portended worsening conditions in the future.

Under the failing economy, the Jewish community remained a visible part of daily island life. Along the waterfront, storefronts and mercantile firms continued to bear the names of synagogue members. Local papers through the end of the century commemorated major Jewish holidays, sometimes accompanied by explanations for the uninformed.[29] Articles of Jewish interest culled from international journals continued to appear occasionally: following the travels of British philanthropist Sir Moses Montefiore, deploring the hard conditions of the Russian Jews, and describing general trends within world Jewish life.[30] And although the world had begun to lose touch with St. Thomas, the Jewish community of St. Thomas had not lost touch with the world. In 1880, the *St. Thomas Times* printed a speech from radical New York Reform Minister Gustav Gottheil at the behest of "An Israelite," which protested recent anti-Jewish actions taken by German Chancellor Otto von Bismark. "The Jewish race, as Dr. Gottheil says," reported the letter, "will outlive Prince Bismarck's persecution as it has outlived all other ones. . . ."[31] At other times during this period, the newspapers printed short biographies of famous Jewish leaders to come out of the Virgin Islands, most notably Judah Benjamin, David Levy Yulee, and Judge David Naar.[32] These articles helped to imbue the islands' readers with a feeling of significance, showing them their proud legacy in the face of encroaching adversity.

Each year, the High Holidays gave the Jewish community an opportunity to regroup and bond as a congregation. Every Jewish business on the island closed for Rosh Hashanah and Yom Kippur, as the synagogue constituents entered into intense introspection about their situation, often with a solemnity that eerily matched the spiritual solemnity of the occasion. Strikingly well-informed wishes of good faith appeared toward the Jews in the local papers, showing that the Jewish community's concerns were well known in town. In 1882, for example, an account from one of the papers' correspondents—cited in the epigraph to this chapter—seemed to report from inside the synagogue, illustrating the pathos of the congregation during Yom Kippur services.[33] The next year, the editor of the *St. Thomas Herald* noted of the Jewish community: "We trust that 5644 will be a better year to them than the past, and that the persecution abroad will give place to peace, prosperity and happiness assuaging in some degree the bitterness of the past."[34] Each time, the Jewish community hearkened to the words of David Cardoze, Jr., who yearly looked out from his pulpit and saw his flock shrinking.

By the 1890s, most of the child-bearing families associated with the St. Thomas synagogue no longer lived on the island: of the thirty-eight births registered in the synagogue's protocols between 1891 and 1895, only six of them occurred to on-island families. Of the community's nineteen deaths during the same time period, meanwhile, nearly all were St. Thomas residents.[35] The only comforts afforded by the synagogue came in the form of personal anniversaries. On July 1, 1879, for example, Jacob Fidanque's "Dry Goods and Crockery ware business" celebrated its sixtieth year of operation, receiving mention and honor in the local paper.[36] Seventeen years later, Mr. and Mrs. Jacob B. Delvalle marked their twenty-fifth wedding anniversary.[37] Serving as a focal point for the community's optimism, these events came to be relative high points in a time where positive occurrences were becoming increasingly rare.

Among the most prominent of these personal milestones was the fiftieth wedding anniversary of Reader David Cardoze and his wife Rachel, which brought together elements from all over the island to give tribute and honor to the aged but active couple. Preparations for the celebration began well in advance of the occasion. Children and grandchildren were invited from Panama and other islands. Music was composed and learned, and logistics arranged among the several parties organizing the fete. At eight o'clock Saturday morning, May 19, 1900, a crowd that included the governor, the acting Dutch consul, the policemaster and the entire Jewish community began to enter the synagogue sanctuary and take seats in anticipation. The building was transformed, enhanced with displays of flowers cut for the event. At nine o'clock, all attention turned toward the entrance: A parade of the Cardozes' grandchildren led the way across the sand floor as if they had never left the island. Behind them strolled David and Rachel Cardoze, the septuagenarian pair still in good health. Members of the synagogue board met the honored couple, and led them to seats of honor in front of the congregation. Once all were in place, a special service commenced, led by the reader's son Moses Cardoze. "The service throughout was very touching, particularly when the son invoked divine blessing upon his parents and when subsequently the father responded. [Cardoze's] response was short and appropriate, though [he] showed signs of emotion."[38] A second tribute came from the aged Abraham Sasso, who fondly recalled the celebrated couple's original wedding ceremony fifty years earlier. After this, the Cardoze children and grand-children sang a hymn composed for the occasion by the couple's daughter.[39] To close the ceremony, the congregation sang a traditional rendition of "Lord Over All," but added an extra verse specifically created as a salutation to the Cardozes:

> With mingled voices and joyous feelings
> We now will wish the happy, happy pair
> Bless them with years of health and save their children unto them
> Long may they live to adorn this edifice.[40]

The celebration had a strong ring of nostalgia to it, commemorating events long past with an energy that seemed lacking in the current days' affairs.

After the service, a military band in the town's public garden played the Danish and Dutch national anthems, and the members of the Cardoze family reunited on the island of their births, with the renewed fanfare of a lavish and long-missed community celebration. But in fifty years, the synagogue had changed dramatically. In 1850, the congregation easily filled the sanctuary. As the century closed, a census of Charlotte Amalie showed a Jewish population of ninety-two. Where many children had graced the Jewish community in 1850, the start of the twentieth century saw the average age leap to thirty-five.[41] The frivolity and happiness of the day, which included a three-hour reception at David Cardoze's home the same afternoon, could only be temporary. Joyful as it was, the moment had to end, the visiting family moving back across the sea to their new homes.

Significantly, however, one of the most obvious anniversaries fell neglected. In 1896, the one hundredth anniversary of the Hebrew Congregation came and went in silence. With attrition as severe as it was among the Jewish community, there were probably not enough people present to organize the commemoration. Many had moved or passed on, and the remaining community likely had enough trouble merely planning its own survival. A shrinking—and struggling—congregation apparently had more pressing things to do than create a Pyrrhic celebration.

Such concerns were not helped by the ever-worsening island conditions. In 1885, St. Thomas lost its position as the relay point for the Royal Mail Steam Packet Company to rising competitor Barbados, effectively ending the island's information monopoly in the region.[42] Population figures continued their steady decline, falling from nearly 40,000 in 1850 to just over 30,000 by 1901.[43] Increasing pressure and mounting losses from the tiny islands placed Denmark in a bind, and the country's several attempts to institute reforms in its colonies met with little success. Meanwhile, over on the isthmus of Panama, the St. Thomians' hopes were eroding. Under Ferdinand de Lessep's hyperbolic and overblown leadership, the panacean canal project was amounting to little more than an expensive, overhyped, dangerous, disease-ridden, and embarrassing hole in the ground.[44] Denmark, convinced it could no longer pull a profit from its colonies, once again began looking for a buyer.

—⁓—

GERMAN-JEWISH MERCHANT JOSEPH LEVIEN and his illegitimate daughter Victoria Elizabeth would unwittingly help to usher in the next stage of life in the St. Thomas Jewish community. While the Sephardic synagogue population was aging, dissipating, and moving away, the recently arrived Levien and his daughter heralded a new wave of Jews, many of whom came from Eastern Europe. Travelling across the Atlantic in tandem with many hopeful others, the new infusion of immigrants appeared in St. Thomas just in time to add new religious energy to the synagogue and new mercantile life to the island. Compared to the millions of Eastern European Jews who entered the New York harbor during this era, the numbers for St. Thomas were miniscule: only two extended families, comprising a handful of people. However, in the island's deteriorating state, these two families were able to make a difference that would affect the course of local history for over a century.

A Hamburg native, Levien came from a mercantile family that had expanded its business offices to the Caribbean. His brother, Leo Levien, had spent a great deal of time as a merchant in Arecibo, Puerto Rico, presumably establishing a field office in the city.[45] Joseph, perhaps with the intention of expanding the business network, arrived on neighboring St. Thomas in 1850; and his dealings and business relations over the next four years afforded him enough status to obtain a burgher brief and commence his own business.[46] A sixteen-year-old relative, Joshua Levien, joined Joseph on St. Thomas in 1857, presumably to serve as his apprentice. Joshua's stay, however, was short and tragic: After less than a year on the island, during which he also appeared to become a rising star within the synagogue, he died of yellow fever. He was buried in the island's Jewish cemetery, likely representing a crushing blow to the family.[47]

Joseph continued to advertise his store regularly in the papers, selling products such as Meerschaum pipes and cigar tubes.[48] On the side, he came to own and lease several properties in town, including the building on Commandant Gade that he eventually leased to the Hebrew Reformed Congregation.[49] A responsible member of society, Levien managed to keep a good public image and reputation throughout his tenure on St. Thomas.[50]

By the beginning of the 1860s, Levien had formed a relationship with a woman named Eliza Flax, a non-Jew who hailed from the neighboring island of Tortola. On April 7, 1861, Flax gave birth to their daughter, Victoria Elizabeth. This, however, seemed to be the summit of their relationship. Two years later, Levien had left Flax for a more "respectable" union within the Jewish community, marrying Emilie Leffmann—daughter of the late German-Jewish merchant Moses Leffmann—on February 15, 1863. Though there is no evidence that Levien and Flax kept up their liaison after this point, the newly-wed merchant took pains to keep up and care for his illegitimate daughter. On May 31, 1867, Levien performed the ultimate act of retribution for his actions, and redeemed his daughter from illegitimacy in front of a Danish Colonial Court. Through this act, Victoria was able to reclaim her own status, with Joseph Levien as her official guardian. Days later, Leo Levien, in Puerto Rico, deeded property he owned in St. Thomas to his brother; and Joseph promptly placed it in trust for his newly legitimized daughter.[51] This transfer apparently provided the young lady with a respectable dowry as she took up residence with her father and step-mother.

A few years later, probably around 1870, a Lithunanian-born man in his early twenties disembarked onto St. Thomas's quieting shores.[52] His last name is uncertain, but his first name was Israel. As the first Eastern-European immigrant to come to St. Thomas, he was a stranger within the Jewish community. Israel had been brought up in a different religious setting and was unrelated to any of the synagogue families, sporting a round face with small features. He likely had few connections to the shipping industry, and little experience in mercantile matters upon his arrival. Nonetheless, he was apparently willing to work hard to achieve success and acceptance.

Accounts of Israel's early life on the island are sketchy. It is worth suggesting, however, that he spent a long time accommodating to the new island culture. The Lithunanian town from which he came was likely poor and predominantly Jewish, separating itself from secular society through both common practice and governmental decree. Interactions with non-Jews were tentative at best, and life progressed almost entirely under the jurisdiction of Jewish law. In St. Thomas, however, Israel found himself part of a society that was almost diametrically the opposite of his originating city. The Jewish community was a small minority of the island population, treated as equals under law. It had thrived through a tradition of free interactions with outside society, and worshiped in congregations with liberal laws and a progressive *minhag*. This, combined with an inevitable language barrier, probably led Israel to experience significant culture adaptation issues before coming into his own.

Exercising his new-found freedoms during his first years on the island, Israel entered into a relationship with a Methodist woman named Catherine Busby. Busby became pregnant from this union, and gave birth to their daughter on December 16, 1878. The girl was baptised Alice Eugenie in All Saints church four months later and recorded as the illegitimate daughter of a father named "Israel Leon"—one of the first recorded incidences of the recent immigrant's last name. Although "Leon" was probably inaccurate, it nonetheless might have been an indicator of the young man's other activities during this time. For a church scribe likely prone to hasty error and more familiar with existing names on the island, the name "Leon" was probably a misrendering of the name "Levin."

During his first few years on St. Thomas, it appears that Israel had gained the acquaintence and trust of Joseph Levien. Possibly through Levien's kindness and support, Israel took on a variant of his benefactor's name: spelled without Joseph's second "e," yet pronounced the same way, with emphasis on the second syllable. This name association was a likely indicator of the relationship fostered between the two men. By 1875, Israel had solidified this name and began his business life under the title "I. Levin." He probably worked closely with Joseph, perhaps even managing a section of his store.[53] Within a few years, however, their business association would become a familial one.

Although legitimized in the eyes of the Danish colonial authority, Joseph Levien's daughter Victoria had been born to a non-Jewish mother, and therefore was not recognized as a member of the Jewish community. Consequently, the synagogue was unlikely to give official sanction to any marriage into which she might enter. When she and Israel Levin were engaged, then, it became imperative that she undergo a formal conversion. The groom-to-be was a young, foreign, unestablished newcomer without family on the island, who probably carried little influence among the older members of the mercantile community. For the elder Joseph, an unendorsed marriage to Victoria would do little to help anyone's status or future. Complicating the situation further, St. Thomas had no religious authority qualified to perform a conversion to Judaism. Thus, Levien took an unprecedented measure.

In early 1879, the aging Levien brought Israel and Victoria to Copenhagen, where they met with Reverend Abraham Alexander Wolff, chief rabbi of Denmark.[54] Wolff likely oversaw Victoria's conversion, and presided as she took on the Hebrew name "Sarah," joining the Jewish people in heart, mind, and soul.[55] With this major step now accomplished, she was ready to join Israel Levin in holy matrimony. Reverend Wolff performed the ceremony on August 19, 1879, assuring the couple's Jewish identity beyond any doubt. Six weeks later, an announcement of the wedding appeared in the pages of the *St. Thomas Times*.[56] It effectively informed the island community of the event, giving the marriage the legitimacy it needed to garner respect for all involved.

Israel Levin worked hard, slowly rising through the ranks of St. Thomas mercantile life from itinerant peddlar to dry-goods shop owner. He learned from his mentor, gaining a strong business sense and building good relations with other merchants. Before long, his own store, "I. Levin," stood proudly on the main street in town. Joseph Levien died in early 1896, but by this time his family legacy was secure—so secure, in fact, that Levien's name was erroneously printed as "Levin" in one widely distributed death announcement.[57]

Israel Levin was one of several pioneers from Eastern Europe who made their fortunes in the Caribbean and South America. Upon achieving financial security, this first wave of immigrants would send money back to their hometowns, informing friends and family of new life and employment opportunities in the New World. By inviting them down to join their ventures, this first wave of immigrants triggered a steady westward movement from Eastern Europe to the tropics by young men wishing to make new lives for themselves. Their most common route involved taking a train to Hamburg, followed by a westward-headed boat, a trip that would often take several weeks.[58] When their ships arrived in the new ports, established relatives or townsmen would pick up the disoriented passengers and help them begin their lives anew. For many, such a trip felt like a gamble, a leap into the unknown. Unsure of themselves and their surroundings, they occasionally took a wrong turn, or had trouble negotiating the system in the outside world, and needed additional help and guidance. When this situation took place on St. Thomas, Israel Levin, who had successfully negotiated this journey, often stepped forward to provide such assistance.

One clear example of this took place in 1905. On March 17, the R.M.S. *Severn* docked in St. Thomas's harbor. Among its disembarking passengers were "four Russians, the Chodominsky brothers, Lipschitz, and Adnoproff."[59] They were young—only seventeen or eighteen years old—and out of money. Israel Levin came to their aid. In response to an erroneous article written after their arrival, Levin explained the situation: "They were advised by a friend who is an uncle to one of them and is Venezuelan Consul in Aux Cayes to come to Haiti where he promises them lucrative employment, and instead of going to Hamburg and thence per German steamer direct, they were misdirected by ignorant Steam-Ship-ticket traffickers to go via Libau, London and St. Thomas. This roundabout route exhausted their funds . . ."[60] Presumably, with the help of private contributions, the merchant helped send the young men off to their final destination. Other Eastern Europeans arrived on St. Thomas, intentionally or not, and decided to stay. Levin welcomed them and helped acclimate them to the new environment. Although the total number probably amounted to fewer than a dozen, the influx was nonetheless significant. St. Thomas, with a tiny population and a quiet economy, could be easily affected by the actions of a few people.

The Jewish Eastern European migration, so prodigious in the United States, yielded six long-term residents in St. Thomas after Levin: four men and two women. Representing a kind of extended family, the members relied on each other for support and assistance. All came over young and penniless, with little to no experience in the English language or in trade management. After a few years of hard work, however, these immigrants would develop into some of the brightest lights of commercial and Jewish energy on the island.

The first two immigrants Levin welcomed to the island were Max Eleazar Trepuk and Jacob Paiewonsky. Trepuk, who probably arrived in the early 1880s, became popularly known as Israel Levin's younger brother; though their eighteen year age difference may have made some islanders privately suspect this relationship, the issue never became a subject of public debate. A young man in his mid-teens, Max earned his mercantile experience in Levin's store, eventually rising in status to become his assistant manager. In April 1907, ready to hold his own, Trepuk opened his own fine clothing shop on the town's main street. His experience and commitment earned him high respect in the community—including, eventually, an island consulship.[61]

Jacob Paiewonsky arrived on St. Thomas in 1885. He was fifteen years old, the oldest of six brothers who would all eventually seek their fortunes in the region.[62] Born in Wilkowishek, Lithuania, Paiewonsky's descendants would also claim family connections to Israel Levin. Regardless of how easy this was to verify, Paiewonsky and Levin soon became close associates on St. Thomas. Young Jacob found himself working as a clerk in Levin's store as well, gaining knowledge of English and learning the various aspects of the mercantile business: how to keep inventory, how deal with suppliers, and how to balance financial books, among other things. Over the course of ten years, he attained proficiency in the dry-goods trade and prepared to start his own business. Paiewonsky returned to Lithuania around 1895 to see his family and report on his progress. The visit had another agenda as well, however, for when Paiewonsky returned to St. Thomas, he had a bride: Esther Rachel, or Ethel as she would be familiarly known.[63] On October 7, 1896, the newlywed merchant received his license to open a general store in Charlotte Amalie.[64] Well prepared for the endeavor, he left his clerkship with Israel Levin and began to serve as his own boss.

Eighteen-year-old Abraham Frankel, another cousin of Israel Levin's who had come over to St. Thomas in 1897, replaced Paiewonsky as clerk in Levin's store.[65] Frankel lived with the Levins during his apprenticeship, eventually working in partnership with Israel's own son Zorach to keep the business in order. On March 21, 1906, Frankel integrated into the Sephardic merchant community by marrying Rebecca Sasso, daughter of islander Abraham Sasso.[66] His tenure on the island, however, did not last long. Following the financial concerns and migration patterns of the other Sephardic families on the island, the couple soon moved, probably to Colon, Panama, to join Rebecca's relatives.[67]

About the same time as Frankel's arrival, four other members of the Paiewonsky family were also making their way through St. Thomas society. Moses Paiewonsky arrived with his wife Isabella sometime before 1898, and moved out to Santo Domingo within a year.[68] Fourteen-year-old Isaac Paiewonsky landed on on St. Thomas's shores on September 15, 1898; he came to live with his brother Jacob and began his apprenticeship with Israel Levin.[69] On November 4, 1904, Isaac married Rebecca Kirchner, a nineteen-year-old girl from his hometown.[70] Zorach Paiewonsky, another brother, married Rebecca's sister Anna on St. Thomas on June 25, 1908, before moving out to Samana, Haiti. Wolf Paiewonsky spent little if any time in St. Thomas, more likely immigrating directly to Santo Domingo to meet his older brother Moses. There, he would father two sons and two daughters with his wife Rachel. A sixth brother, David, also came down.[71]

Isaac Paiewonsky remained on the island after his marriage, opening a dry-goods store that specialized in clothing and furniture. According to his son Ralph, the shop "was really more of a haberdashery, which sold mostly men's and women's clothing. . . . An interesting example of Isaac's ingenuity was his practice of collecting the discarded wooden crates that brought merchandise from Europe to St. Thomas and then hiring carpenters to convert them into household furniture that he sold in his store and also used at home."[72] Ever in need of ideas to sell a product, Paiewonsky, according to his son, created a living by selling these items inexpensively to seasonal workers stopping off on St. Thomas before returning to their own island homes.

The new Eastern European Jewish immigrants helped fill the St. Thomas congregation's need for young families, which in turn helped to rejuvenate the island's Jewish community. Between 1880 and 1912, the Levin, Paiewonsky, and Frankel families were responsible for twenty-nine on-island births—more than the rest of the Jewish community combined. More importantly, they had found little reason to leave, having started successful or developing businesses. In contrast with the Sephardic population, which had seen better times, this group of people seemed to see St. Thomas as a land of promise. With complete freedom, full rights, and a great potential for success, they continued to thrive.

These new families served as a reviving balm for the synagogue. Attending services regularly, even as the reader performed a liturgy that was foreign to them, the Levins, Paiewonskys, and Frankels would help keep the congregation alive for decades to come. The eighty-year-old sanctuary continued in use. Joining the Sassos, Morons, De Castros, Halmans, and others, the Lithuanian newcomers would constitute a financially and religiously secure force in the Jewish community, ensuring its uninterrupted worship of God on the shrinking island.

Reverend David Cardoze celebrated his ninetieth birthday on the last day of 1913.[73] By this point an old and highly respected merchant, he seemed to be a persistent symbol of the island's once-golden age. A brass band "serenaded" him in the early morning to commence the occasion; and for the rest of the day, visitors came bearing gifts and notes of congratulations.[74] Cardoze had become the patriarch of a large family, including five surviving daughters, thirty grandchildren, and nineteen great-grandchildren; but he also accorded the respect of many others as an elder who spent much of his life working tirelessly for the island's welfare. Newspaper accounts of the celebration emphasized the reverend's remarkable health and energy. "[T]he grand old man was equal to the occasion, receiving his visitors with a cheerfulness that in no way betokened a weariness of body. . . . Hale and hearty, in the full possession of his faculties, more erect than many at sixty is our venerable friend," wrote *Lightbourne's Mail Notes*. *The Bulletin* boasted: "To reach such a great age, still physically and mentally active, and able to read and write without the aid of glasses, is an event not of common occurrence even in large communities, therefore well worthy of commemoration." Visitors echoed these sentiments. The government secretary joked in his remarks that "he was glad to find Rev. Cardoze looking the same as when he arrived here many years ago [in 1840]"; and the head of one of the local Harmonic Lodges hoped that "Almighty God . . . may continue to preserve you in health and mental power as in the past. . . ." Cardoze's continued life seemed to be an inspiration to others: an excuse to escape the mounting difficulties of the age for a moment to celebrate a resident whose resilience seemed to come from his family and communal ties rather than his financial ones.

The Jewish community presented a tribute to Cardoze as well. One part, presented by consuls Max E. Trepuk and David M. De Castro, was a purse of money intended as a token of thanks to Cardoze for his services to the congregation. In an accompanying note, the consuls called him *Shomer Israel*—the "Guardian of Israel"—and on the part of the congregation sent their best wishes for him "to continue as the 'mouthpiece' of our congregation at the

Achal [Holy Ark], on days, when our congregation is open for public worship." The sum presented was not substantial, "bearing in mind the small number we muster," but it was heartfelt and represented high esteem for a reader whose synagogue activities had been voluntary for half a century.

The second part of the congregation's gift, also mentioned in the consuls' letter, was a note from Panama. Though shorter and less flowery than the first message, the note nonetheless showed a great deal of forethought. Dated three weeks earlier, it bore the signatures of "many co-religionists" who identified themselves as "members at large of your Synagogue." These individuals recalled with affection their roots and families in St. Thomas. Simultaneously lauding the community's role as founder of several new congregations abroad, the letter at the same time promoted the less-pleasing concept that few from the former St. Thomas Jewish population now lived on St. Thomas. All hoped for a bright future; but no one knew where that future would be. Perhaps this was one reason why the Jews—and the whole island—prayed for Cardoze's continued health. When the "astonishing vigour" of Cardoze's voice, "as powerful as one half his years," ceased echoing through the synagogue's sanctuary, the silence remaining would be stifling.

The congregation's fears, however, became reality all too soon. Less than six months later, on Saturday morning, May 30, 1914, the congregants heard Cardoze's voice echo through the synagogue for the last time. While leading Sabbath morning services on that day, the beloved reader became stricken with illness, and could not continue. He lay bedridden for two weeks as doctors and relatives tried in vain to improve his failing health; yet even as he saw himself dying, Cardoze "spoke of and viewed his approaching end with the greatest assurance," reminding one attendant of the famous line from Psalm 23: "Yea, though I walk through the valley of the shadow of death I shall fear no evil for thou art with me."[75] On June 14, the old reader's daughter, Grace Delvalle, died after her own three-week illness. Two days later, Cardoze succumbed as well.

The funeral took place the next day at four o'clock in the afternoon.[76] A large crowd of mournful friends and relatives, many of whom had just congratulated the minister on his ninetieth birthday, gathered at Cardoze's residence. Slowly, they travelled with the minister's body to the entrance of the synagogue. Isaac Paiewonsky's son, Isidor, would later recall the image of Cardoze's plain wood coffin laid at the entrance to the sanctuary as one of his earliest memories. The "Sweet Singer of Israel" was silent in the portal as the congregation held the funeral service—ironically, the first service in decades not performed by the minister. After the appropriate rites, the mourners placed Cardoze's coffin onto a horse-drawn hearse and traced the familiar route down Synagogue Hill and across town to the Altona Jewish cemetery. There, the members of the congregation and the island paid the deceased spiritual leader their last respects as they laid him to rest with "full Masonic honors." Once the body had been interred, the crowd placed wreaths and flowers on the reverend's grave "as a last tribute," and then left the cemetery. "Of the departed we can say nothing but good," wrote the editor of *Lightbourn's Mail Notes* earlier that day. "[H]e spoke ill of none and was charitable to the extent of his means; he was a friend to all; he will be missed, for although of such advanced years infirmity had taken no hold of him; erect in body and clear in mind he was able to attend to his duties to the last[. A]nd now friend, R. I. P."

Within two weeks, the wardens of the synagogue had appointed Reverend Cardoze's brother-in-law, Elias Athias Robles, to serve as acting reader. To assist him, the board chose Moses De Castro Sasso, a twenty-year-old merchant recently returned to the island.[77] Neither of the new leaders had lived on St. Thomas for very long: Robles and his family had just moved from Costa Rica; and Sasso, though born in St. Thomas, had lived most of his life in Panama. Both identified themselves as expatriate members of the island's Jewish community, however—part of the closely woven web of Sephardic families that had moved from St. Thomas in the previous decades. Most importantly, they both had at least some knowledge of Hebrew, as well as experience (or interest, in Sasso's case) in leading services. While Robles and Sasso probably exhibited little of Cardoze's erudition and leadership style, they could be counted upon to maintain at least some measure of regular Jewish observance for the families that remained on the island.

The death of Reverend David Cardoze marked the start of an age of uncertainty for the St. Thomas Jewish community. The Sephardic community gradually grew smaller and poorer; the new German and Eastern European communities began to lay down roots; and the island itself, once a center of world trade, was by 1914 a small piece of land in search of significance. Trade in St. Thomas slowed significantly: Resources became rarer, and the cosmopolitanism that once provided the mercantile community with cultural life dissipated in favor of a small-town atmosphere. After Cardoze—perhaps one of the last figures on the island to embody the international, intellectual spirit of the earlier age—the Jewish community was left without a guiding light. They faced the realities of the changing world and the island's changing population, doing what they could to continue their traditions even as memory and population began to fade.

CHAPTER 8

Struggle
1914–1946

I wish I could see some future for the congregation. But
trade is dead here. And as you know, nearly all the old families
have moved away.

I am afraid it is the same story on other islands.

They need a regular Hazan, Teacher and Mohel but they
really cannot afford to pay anything like enough to support a
man. They pay a nominal amount to Mr. Sasso, but he is in business. He is an amateur Hazan, quite untrained, cannot read
sefer, but a more sincere man I never met. He loves his religion.
He is also rather deaf.

What can be done under the circumstances?

It is a problem.

I wish I could see a solution. Can you?. . .

—Rev. Dr. Henry Pereira Mendes to Rev. David
de Sola Pool, April 19, 1925.

On August 15, 1914, the completed Panama Canal finally
opened its locks to the world. For St. Thomas, this opening ended forty-four
years of anticipation and breath-holding. From Ferdinand de Lesseps's announcement to build the canal in 1870, the St. Thomas shipping community
had seen a panacea for its flagging trade. Articles had appeared in local papers hailing the project, and predicting vast increases in business within sev-

eral years; all took heart. And then the island, as well as the rest of the world, had waited for decades.

When the great opening finally came—at the hands of the Americans, far later and at far greater expense than anyone had expected—the world was not there to celebrate. A month and a half earlier, on June 28, a young, radical student named Gavrilo Princip had jumped onto the running board of a convoy in Sarajevo and assassinated Austro-Hungarian Archduke Francis Ferdinand. By August 3, Europe was at war. Mercantile concerns in the Americas immediately lost their urgency, and the mighty passage between the oceans garnered comparatively little notice.

For all practical purposes, St. Thomas was not there to celebrate either. Although its strategic location en route to the canal was no less important than in 1870, the island's economic base had imploded. As the "Great Ditch" awaited completion, increasingly efficient generations of steam ships took to the oceans, causing St. Thomas's coal refueling industry to fade. Many of the younger merchants, searching for greener pastures, moved stateside or decided to try their luck in Panama. Those who remained faced greater financial dependence on the Danish government; and Denmark, seeing these islands more as a remnant of the past than as a viable investment, actively sought to pawn them off to the highest bidder. When World War I began, St. Thomas's reputation as a "Little Paris" was but a memory, its industry in shambles, and its future uncertain. The island's patient wait for prosperity had proven a bitter disappointment.[1]

On Crystal Gade, the synagogue still stood prominently, looking out over a quiet and often empty harbor. Its walls echoed with the sounds of prayer each Sabbath, but to an aging and dwindling population. Elias Robles, the new reader, and his young assistant Moses De Castro Sasso were not learned men; rather, they were leaders by necessity whose desire to keep the congregation alive brought them to the pulpit. During the week, both worked at stores in the town; Robles also served on the board of trustees of the St. Thomas Savings Bank, following in the tradition of previous religious leaders. On weekends, they made sure services proceeded smoothly and with decorum, reciting the traditional prayers and chanting the traditional hymns. Yet conditions did not bode well for the island's community. To those individuals not yet established in the island's mercantile fabric, there was little practical reason to stay; and many of the women, who lacked the same mobility as the men, resigned themselves to spinsterhood for lack of available husbands. Some fostered hope that the United States would finally purchase the Danish Colonies and return St. Thomas to better times. As conditions stood, however, the congregation could at best maintain its numbers for a few years. In April, 1916, Reader Robles apparently recognized this, and, at age fifty, announced his plans to leave the island as well.

Perhaps the congregation found the twenty-two-year-old Sasso too young and inexperienced to ascend the pulpit. Perhaps they wanted a more revered figurehead for their congregation. Whatever the case, the members of the synagogue voted to retain Sasso as the assistant reader, and elected David M. De Castro, St. Thomas resident and consul for Nicaragua, Costa Rica, Guatemala, and Panama, as reader.[2] A prominent and well-liked island citizen, De Castro accepted the opportunity to be the Jews' spiritual leader, and once again gave the congregants a feeling of security even as their society and surroundings became quieter and more sparsely populated.

Yet the island was again in for change—and on two different fronts. On August 4, 1916, the United States signed a treaty with Denmark for the purchase of the Danish West Indies. Little more than a month later, in a remarkable parallel with the aborted 1867 agreement, a monstrous hurricane roared across the island and caused widespread damage to houses, harbor, and storage facilities. Then-seven-year-old Isidor Paiewonsky, the third son of Isaac Paiewonsky, was huddling from the storm in his home near the synagogue when fierce winds lifted the roof off its supports, whipped it around, and replaced it upside-down.[3] A neighbor soon moved Isidor and his sister, Paulina, next door to safety. Paiewonsky would later recall of the aftermath, "There wasn't a roof left on St. Thomas. You [could look] down into everybody's bedrooms, parlors, everything . . ."[4] Many families experienced massive property loss: One local paper sent a correspondent around to survey the area, house by house; his report included several Jewish names: "Da Costa Gomez's house, also wrecked. Levi's and Moron's properties much damaged," and the next day, "Mr. M[ax] Trepuk['s house], High Road, fared badly."[5] On top of personal losses, however, the Jewish community also found that the hurricane had damaged the synagogue's roof.[6] Despite a generous grant from the Danish government to assist personal losses, the Jews' dwindling resources could not shoulder the cost of synagogue repairs. For many years afterward, the community made do with rough patches to the roof and other stop-gap measures, in order to prevent water from seeping into the sanctuary and causing further problems.[7]

Despite the hurricane's toll on the island, the United States maintained its commitment to the purchase. Five months later, on March 31, 1917, the people of the Virgin Islands started anew under a new sovereignty. In a symbolic ceremony, the Danish flag descended over Fort Christian as a brass band played the Danish national anthem for the last time on the island. With a twenty-one-gun salute, the 245-year history of Danish mercantilism came to an end. The United States reenacted the ceremony, now on its own ground, to signify the territory's transfer.[8] What had once been a thriving center of trade was to be transformed into a naval base, intended to protect the Panama Canal and rid the Caribbean Sea of suspected German U-boats. All remaining hopes to bring St. Thomas back to its classy entrepôt days had evaporated; the island's strategic position had become its greatest asset. Nonetheless, some looked to the changes as a new chance at prosperity, even as others shed tears at the prospect of leaving Danish sovereignty. All knew that a new age was dawning, for better or for worse.

For the sixty-five or so Jews remaining on St. Thomas, the years following the transfer would be ones of devotion and perseverance, dedicated to preserving the Jewish community and its synagogue. At the same time, the change in sovereignty marked unequivocally the low point of the St. Thomas Hebrew Congregation. By 1920, the congregation had become so small that a United States Congressional Report on the Virgin Islands neglected to mention Judaism among the religions practiced in its new territory.[9]

On July 15, 1920, at seven o'clock in the morning, the synagogue's reader, David M. De Castro passed away at age fifty-eight from kidney, heart, and liver failure. The next day, in the late afternoon, a cortège of mourners gathered at his residence on the west side of town and began a slow procession east toward the synagogue. Following a horse-drawn hearse that held the coffin, the procession went past the Main Street stores and residences in the hot afternoon sun. A final left turn brought the procession round to Crystal Gade, where the group then progressed up the hill until the familiar marble steps of the synagogue appeared. Pallbearers walked up onto the tile plaza and laid the coffin at the building's entrance. Here, the congregation paid its final, sad respects to the deceased reader and esteemed citizen. At the conclusion of the ceremony, the coffin was lifted back onto the cart. The driver, followed by the crowd, returned down Main Street and across town toward De Castro's final resting place in the Jewish cemetery.[10]

The community now had no choice but to turn to its remaining spiritual leader. Moses Sasso, now twenty-six, was a short, homely man with large ears and piercing eyes. Born in St. Thomas on February 2, 1894, Sasso and his family were among those who had emigrated to Panama in search of new business. As a young man, he learned the ins and outs of the mercantile business; he also developed and exhibited a strong passion toward Judaism, which rarely went unnoticed by observers. Yet true to his family's roots, "Molito," as he was familiarly called, kept in close touch with his relatives on St. Thomas. During a 1914 visit to the island, Molito witnessed the tragic death of the revered Reverend Cardoze, and recognized what he saw as his calling to fulfil the spiritual needs of his birth congregation. Finally, after six years of apprenticeship to older and more knowledgeable leaders, he became the religious figurehead of the community. Less than three weeks after De Castro's death, on August 6, 1920, Government Secretary C. C. Timmons issued Sasso the power to perform religious functions on the islands of St. Thomas and St. John. The congregation did not elect an assistant reader to take his place, probably because there was none available to fill the role.

In the early 1920s, the synagogue relied almost entirely on Sasso's spirit. With only rudimentary Hebrew knowledge, no training in Rabbinic literature, and notoriously dull oration skills, he led weekly services and officiated at synagogue life-cycle functions (mostly funerals by this time). The ponderous length of the Saturday morning ritual became the talk of legend as Reader Sasso trudged through each prayer with profound awe and seriousness. That he often did not know what he said was a moot point, for the congregation was no more knowledgeable in Hebrew than he. As a religious leader, his main function was to preserve tradition by going through the motions of ritual; and although he lacked the scholarly knowledge to perform this office with much agility, Sasso's sincerity, devotion, and family pedigree helped him gain the respect of his congregation.

Services and gatherings at the synagogue brought out all the character and color of the island's Jewish community. Each family had its own self-assigned place to sit, and the twenty people or so who turned out on a given week scattered to their approriate areas. Israel Levin would arrive even in the hottest weather in "a heavy vest and a heavy coat, and [carrying] a big watch and a big gold chain. . . . [A]t a designated hour, he used to pull out the watch, look at it, and wind it," loudly, in services. The children watched the bearded, heavy-faced man and waited for this moment, exclaiming "Levin's haulin' anchor!" when he began the action.[11]

Another part of the sanctuary contained the seats for Esther Consuelo Cardoze Robles, a daughter of the late minister David Cardoze, and her four teen-aged daughters. Though born in St. Thomas, Robles spent over twenty years in Costa Rica with her husband, Joseph Athias Robles, before returning to the island in June 1914 in an unsuccessful attempt to improve her husband's health. Having also experienced the deaths of her sister and father just a short span earlier, Esther decided to remain on St. Thomas with her other relatives. Her appearance in the synagogue likely brought back memories of the venerable reader from times past.

Elsewhere in the women's section sat three sisters from the Maduro family. The young Isidor Paiewonsky thought they looked like "three little blackbirds" in their dark dresses, and remembered the nicknames quietly given them: Faith, Hope, and Charity. Maidens all, their titles described their chances at marriage on the male-depleted island. "The first one they called Faith because she had faith that she was going to get a husband. They called the [second] one Hope because the other one said that if Faith got a husband then she had hope too. The last one was Charity. They called her that because she was always ready to give it away but nobody wanted it."[12]

The children present found the service to be excruciatingly boring and always searched for something to do that would not disrupt the decorum. Paiewonsky recalled that sometimes all they had to do was look down at the sand floor of the synagogue. The sand was brought in from a local beach, and apparently contained sandworm eggs. While waiting for the service to end, the children would find these eggs, hatch them, and then race them along the mahogany benches. In this and other ways, the younger set survived the morning.[13]

Chances are, the single women kept an eye on the bachelor reader during the service, since he was one of the only eligible Jewish men on the island. Molito, however, appeared to have made up his mind quickly and decided to court Rosa Athias Robles, sister-in-law to the late Reverend Cardoze and nearly twice the reader's age. One contemporary's account of their courtship stated that their fondness for each other did not stop at the synagogue door. From time to time, Sasso would pause while conducting services just long enough to make eyes at Robles from the pulpit.[14] Apparently, this technique worked, for Sasso and Robles recited their wedding vows in 1923, at ages 29 and 55 respectively. The ceremony had an ironic twist, however, which again emphasized the dire predicament of the Jewish community. As the only person on St. Thomas who could solemnize Jewish weddings, Sasso could not himself be the beneficiary of a Jewish ceremony. Consequently, the reader and his bride had to participate in a civil marriage. In order to make the union official, Isaac Paiewonsky took the honor of blessing the union and recording it in the synagogue protocols.[15]

The congregation followed what it continued to call the traditional Sephardic rite, even though by then it had become mostly rote recitation. Where prayer books were once common property in Jewish homes, now few if any remained; and to most of the congregation, unable to read Hebrew, the books would have proven useless anyway.[16] Instead, the community learned and sang prayers from memory. Their melodies were often the traditional ones used in the Sephardic synagogues of New York and London, though one observer in visiting St. Thomas noted that they were ornamented with "vocal flourishes [and] vocal fire-workish turns."[17] Sasso, who was not musically inclined, lent whatever voice he could to each hymn, and led the congregation through the liturgy each week.

Others present at each service included Max E. Trepuk, brother to Israel Levin, with his round, clean-shaven face and barbell moustache; Samuel Halman, a tall man frequently dressed in a white suit who was known for appearing discretely and constantly inebriated; the Paiewonsky brothers, Jacob and Isaac, whose strong features and clean looks portrayed an aura of sophistication; and their children Benjamin, Ralph (a future governor of the islands), Isidor, and Paulina. After services ended, the attendees left the synagogue to open their stores, prepare meals, and continue with their work. For most, the Sabbath had become a day of social gathering, which ended once the last prayers were intoned and the heavy wooden doors of the synagogue were closed shut.

Unmodified, untouched, there is every possibility that the synagogue could have died out, giving in to assimilation, ignorance, and entropy. St. Thomas's Jews may easily have followed those of Barbados, Jamaica, Nevis, and so many others into extinction. Yet precisely when they needed it most, the congregants found themselves serendipitously graced by a remarkable personality whose formidable talent as a teacher, rabbi, and leader rejuvenated Jewish life on the island for years to come.

In November 1922, Reverend Doctor Henry Pereira Mendes, rabbi emeritus of the Spanish and Portugese Synagogue *Shearith Israel* in New York, sent a letter from travels abroad to his friend and colleague Reverend David de Sola Pool. In the communication, Mendes expressed a strong concern for the Jewish communities of the Caribbean and Latin America, as well as his desire to take action:

> I want to make our congregation, possibly with Bevis Marks [the Spanish and Portugese Synagogue in London], the guardians and helpers of young or decadent communities [in the Caribbean and Latin America]. Young communities were in e.g. Caracas, Panama, Colon, etc. Decadent communities in e.g. Barbados, St. Thomas, Montego Bay etc. Bevis Marks took charge of Barbados [a

British colony]. But with me, it is not a question whether you are British or American or Danish etc. It is enough that you are Sephardi-Jewish. My idea is that [the major Sephardic congregations] ought to combine to supply religious pabulum to the said congregations. . . . It could be done by a pastoral visit to organize, [an] 'Education by correspondence' with leading people there. . . . Lately, being now free, I expressed my willingness to go myself, feeling that just because Coz. Rosalie and I have so many personal friends, besides relatives, in all those places, we might succeed.[18]

Reverend Mendes by this time was a revered force in the Sephardic Jewish world, and one of the most brilliant Jewish minds of his generation. Born in Birmingham, England, in 1852, he came from a long line of celebrated ministers, doctors, and intellectuals, dating back thirteen generations and hailing from all over Europe; this lineage included his father, who spent several years in Jamaica as minister of the Sephardic synagogue at Montego Bay.[19] Mendes, as a student, attended Northwick College and University College in London. He studied Hebrew and rabbinic subjects privately with his father, who was by then the minister of Birmingham's Sephardic congregation. Mendes no doubt showed promise, for in 1875, three years after leaving University College, Sephardi Chief Rabbi of England Dr. Benjamin Artom found him ready to assume a pulpit. Artom gave the prospective leader two choices. One was a position as minister of a small but dedicated group of Jews in the Danish West Indian island of St. Thomas. The other was a ministerial position at a new Sephardic synagogue in Manchester, England. For whatever reason, Mendes chose the Manchester position, which he served ably for two years.[20]

In 1877, the New York congregation *Shearith Israel* invited Mendes to give a series of four lectures at their synagogue. His visit was a resounding success, and soon afterward the congregation installed him as both their rabbi and assistant *Hazan*. After officiating at the *Hazan's* funeral later that year, Mendes was also elected to fill that vacancy, thus completing the last step in his rapid rise to prominence. In his multiple roles, Mendes proved a success, and consequently cleared up a conflict in the synagogue over whether there was a need for a separate rabbi and *Hazan*. By age twenty-five, the young man had become the head of the largest Sephardic Jewish community in America.[21]

Mendes was a brilliant yet humble scholar who excelled in just about everything. With his beautiful voice he easily intoned the prayers on Mondays, Thursdays, and Sabbaths, and his musical knowledge allowed him to compose several original settings for religious texts, some of which became standards in the synagogue repertoire. Soon after settling into his job, Mendes also decided to pursue a side interest in medicine, enrolling in New York University's medical school, and receiving his degree in 1884. A prolific author, Mendes penned numerous books, sermons, plays, and essays on topics ranging from history and theology to humor and children's literature. Socially aware and adept, the young man constantly championed charitable causes. He helped to organize several major New York institutions—including the Jewish Theological Seminary, Montefiore Hospital, and the New York Board of Jewish Ministers—and interacted constructively with state and religious leaders of all denominations. Such activities brought him renown in both the Jewish and secular world, causing New York Governor Herbert H. Lehman to recall after his death: "his spiritual and beautiful life was a constant inspiration to those of our faith, and his example a potent influence in good citizenship."[22]

In the late 1880s, Rev. Dr. Mendes's first ministerial choice came back to haunt him. While teaching a religion class as part of his duties at *Shearith Israel,* Mendes became acquainted with a young woman named Rosalie Rebecca Piza.[23] Though born in Hamburg and raised in Panama, Piza associated deeply with her parents, who were St. Thomas natives, and kept in close contact with her remaining St. Thomas family.[24] Mendes came to care deeply for the young and charming Rosalie, and the two married on October 15, 1890. The union suddenly gave Mendes numerous friends and relatives in the Caribbean Jewish community, and, combined with his father's ministerial turn in Jamaica, probably caused him to develop an increased awareness of the region. Likely stemming from this association, Mendes began to expedite efforts to assist and preserve Caribbean Jewish communities, many of which were in financial straits at the end of the nineteenth century. In his eyes, these early communities held great historical, personal, and sentimental value to both the old Caribbean families who lived there and to American Sephardic Jewry in general.

In 1920, after forty-three years of service to *Shearith Israel,* Rev. Dr. Mendes left his pulpit due to fragile health. Although his official ministerial duties ceased, however, his activity with the Jewish community did not. Reverend and Mrs. Mendes travelled the world extensively over the next few years, visiting and aiding Jewish communities around the globe. They would regularly send holiday greetings to their congregation from abroad, as well as detailed letters describing their adventures and activities; it was likely they also made several appeals to the congregation for aid in order to help the communities they visited. The synagogue's new minister, Mendes's cousin David de Sola Pool, served as prime correspondent in these matters, receiving his predecessor's letters and periodically returning updates on the New York congregation's condition. Mendes was in Buenos Aires, Argentina, in late 1923 when he declared to Pool his intentions to "visit Central America and some West Indies this summer, to see what I can do first for the Sephardim of the set to which we belong."[25] His prospects soon settled on St. Thomas, the place of origin for his wife's family.

When, in early 1924, Reader Moses Sasso presented the board of the St. Thomas Hebrew Congregation with a letter from Reverend Mendes stating his intentions to spend the winter on the island, the representatives were naturally overjoyed. "In the name of our Congregation," they responded on August 6, "we want to assure you that you will have a most hearty welcome at our hands, and we will feel honored if you will be good enough to occupy the pulpit of our Synagogue whenever you wish to do so during your stay here." With humility, they added, "Our congregation is, unfortunately, very small. . . ." But hope and excitement were the order of the day, as the members of the board affixed flourishing signatures to the letter, impressed the synagogue's official seal at the bottom, and sent it off.[26]

Mendes's decision to come to St. Thomas seemed to derive from an incident that had occurred the previous November in Buenos Aires. At that time, he and his wife had sustained a conversation with a local woman:

> It turned out she was born in St. Thomas. You can imagine the 'Did you knows' and 'I remembers' when she was introduced to Cousin Rosalie!! But we found out that that lady and all her sisters had married Christians! Why? Because her generation (she is next generation after Cousin Rosalie) never had spiritual guidance, for they never had a minister after Mr. Martinez.[27]

This meeting both disturbed and inspired Reverend Mendes, giving him a concrete mission and a clear direction for his next travels. After much abstract discussion about helping the Caribbean Jewish communities, he summarized in the same letter his new intentions: "Our duty is this—to try and regain some of those [Jews from Caribbean communities] who are straying."[28] St. Thomas, where he and his wife would enjoy a number of familial connections, appeared the best place to begin.[29]

In choosing St. Thomas, Mendes also sought a quiet place where he could resume his literary career. His tenure as minister in New York had placed him under enormous psychological and physical stress (including a gunshot wound in 1892), and though his health had improved considerably since his resignation, Mendes expressed no desire to return to pressures of the city.[30] "When therefore I say I am ready for work," he wrote in the fall before coming to St. Thomas, "I mean work quite outside Synagogue precincts, for if God has mercifully given me back health and energy, it is only His due that I should dedicate both to His service, somehow, somewhere and somewhen."[31] Taking into account his age and abilities, he saw the new American territory as a place where he could also relax, administer his services to the congregation, and concentrate on his studies.

On Tuesday, December 9, 1924, Reverend and Mrs. Mendes disembarked from the S. S. *Guiana* onto the quiet shores of Charlotte Amalie. During his first day on the island, Reverend Mendes went to inspect the synagogue. Probably hosted by Moses Sasso, the minister walked across the sand floor of the old sanctuary, opened up the holy ark, and inspected the seven Torah scrolls inside. One account of the day noted: "By a curious coincidence . . . [Mendes] found inscribed on the silver handles of one of the scrolls of the law, the name ISAAC H. ABENDANA MENDES, dated 151 years ago."[32] Though the family relationship was likely only tangential, this discovery nonetheless served symbolically as an auspicious beginning. That evening the minister and his wife checked into the island's Grand Hotel, and began to make inquiries into a permanent place to stay, "[o]n or near the Synagogue hill if possible."[33] Four days later, a local paper publicly introduced the couple to the island population with a detailed biographical article.[34]

Mendes found only a remnant of Israel on the island: forty to fifty Jews, a synagogue building damaged and worn with age, no form whatever of organized Jewish education, and an inexperienced and uneducated minister. But for all of this, Mendes could see a clear spiritual center, a group of Jews clinging to their religion through memories and traditions. Some had *mezuzahs* on their doorposts; some still lit candles on the Sabbath; some still held a Passover *seder*. During services, the congregation intoned the old Sephardic tunes with fervor. In addition, excepting the parts of the synagogue that required heavy repair, the congregants saw to it that the building remained clean and presentable.[35] Welcoming Mendes as the long-awaited answer to their professed ignorance, many of the island's Jews expressed their willingness to benefit from his font of knowledge. Mendes, who had arrived to ameliorate their condition in the first place, was more than happy to oblige.

The reverend and his wife rented a dwelling near the synagogue, and over the next few weeks sent the Jewish community into a flurry of activity. For the six children on the island under the age of fifteen—all girls—Mendes organized a Sunday School, the first on the island since Rev. Martinez's departure fifty years earlier.[36] Over twenty older members coalesced into a Thursday evening "circle," meeting to study Jewish ritual, philosophy, and thought. Of these twenty, eight (including Reader Sasso) expressed a desire for additional instruction; so Mendes established a Monday evening "Consecration Class," meant to "enable [its members] to promise intelligently that they will consecrate their lives [and] homes to preserve Judaism on the island."[37] Through such provisions, Mendes began to transform the old synagogue from a sedentary structure to an active place of worship and learning.

The minister also climbed back into the pulpit, directing synagogue activities on several levels. Temporarily replacing Sasso, Mendes led services on Friday nights and Saturday mornings; he gave public lectures whenever possible; and he started the young men and women of the congregation rehearsing a Purim play of his own composition.[38] He was determined to improve the community's literacy in the Jewish sacred tongue, and as such Mendes took it upon himself to begin one-on-one Hebrew instruction with as many in the congregation as he could handle.[39] Such was the flurry of his activities that he had very little time to write over the first weeks. One of his first letters to Reverend Pool from the island, dated December 28, 1924, stated in its entirety: "Your welcome, but all too short letter, arrived yesterday. Today has been more than busy—school—rehearsal for tonight—correspondence to catch mail that closes 3 P.M. (now 2.30!)" Healthy, enthusiastic, and dynamic, he threw himself into the project of resurrecting Jewish religious life on the island.

The reverend further recognized the importance of restoring the synagogue building itself, and subsequently set up a repair fund to address the situation. Placing the fund under the direction of the synagogue's treasurer, Mendes then sent out letters of appeal to congregations and Jewish publications across the hemisphere. On St. Thomas, he issued "Repair Fund" boxes to all Jewish families, with instructions to give liberally whenever possible, particularly around Jewish holidays, personal milestones, and Yahrtzeits. He then organized a committee of women to make fortnightly collection rounds of these boxes and deposit the money into the central fund.[40] Over the course of time, the repair fund would close in on its goal (which Mendes estimated as at least $1,000 for a new roof), with significant contributions coming from the community itself.[41]

Soon after the start of 1925, the minister and his wife received another honor. On Sunday morning, January 4, the congregation held a symbolic meeting to elect their eminent guests to full membership. The vote, taken by standing count, was an impressive and meaningful sight to the minister. Mendes commented on the event to Reverend Pool in New York, complimenting the congregants' dedication by their "very attentative and passionate" responses to his initiatives.[42] A healthy relationship continued to flower, with both reverend and congregation appreciative of each other's presence and touched by each other's devotion.

Reverend Mendes quickly bonded with his Jewish constituents; yet his influence did not stop there. Many in the island's non-Jewish population found him a fascinating curiosity, and began to attend his lectures as well. During one address, he estimated that out of the fifty to sixty who attended, about half were non-Jews.[43] Many were attracted by his intellect and charisma; others simply found him to be the most interesting person to visit the island in quite a while. Over time, the retired preacher became a popular and revered religious figure in general St. Thomas life.

Hebrew lessons within the synagogue progressed smoothly, and soon Mendes decided to take the next step. On February 8, 1925, he sent his first order for prayer books and Bibles to his old congregation in New York. To Mendes, such materials were crucial to the St. Thomas community for two reasons. The first was practical: In this environment, the main purpose for learning Hebrew was to understand and read the liturgy. Mendes wanted everyone to accomplish this with utmost speed, and eventually regularize use of the prayer book during services. The congregation, meanwhile, was gaining morale through his instruction, and anticipated the new books with excitement.

His second reason, however, was far more interesting, and revealed a deeply hidden agenda. In addition to ordering prayerbooks for individual congregants, Reverend Mendes appealed to his New York congregation to supply additional books for visitors, which would be kept at the synagogue. When he received a discouraging reply from the *Shearith Israel* board, he confided to Reverend de Sola Pool: "I wish our trustees had presented the books for synagogue use, because a suitable inscription in each would have kept the name of our congregation in the minds of the people here with an *aroma of gratitude*. Then, when they close up the synagogue, as they must do when this generation dies out, they would give the seven sefarim [Torahs], the beautiful silver crown, the silver bells, the pointer, Kisé shel Berith [Briss Chair], Shofar, etc.: etc. into our keeping in New York. True we must say, 'may the day be far away when St. Thomas shall be as Barbadoes is today!' [that is, extinct]."[44] With all he did for the synagogue, Mendes held little hope that the population could sustain itself for more than a few more years. The next best thing, then, was to make sure that the holy artifacts of the synagogue found their way to a secure and appropriate final resting place—and for Mendes, there was no better place than New York's *Shearith Israel,* the symbol of Sephardic life and history in America. A strong connection between the St. Thomas and New York Sephardic communities, he believed, would ensure this transfer. While his sentiment seemed sincere, it is troubling to suggest that Mendes saw his mission with the St. Thomas congregation as ultimately futile. To his credit, however, he did not allow such reasoning to affect his efforts to educate the island's Jewish community. Ironically, the Reverend's tireless efforts would ultimately help to subvert his own pessimistic predictions.

As February began, rehearsals for the Purim presentation intensified. Reverend Mendes attacked the project with the same zeal as his numerous other undertakings. Secretly, however, he felt his ill health returning. "I am not well—have not had many, if any, days free from lassitude," he revealed to Reverend Pool in a confidential letter. "[N]ow after four years, the same pains are reappearing. Yet it is my constant physical depression, tiredness that most makes me think something else is wrong."[46] The tropical climate and direct sunlight, while beneficial to his wife, did not aid his own condition, and Mendes began to realize that his days on St. Thomas were numbered. This knowledge added urgency to his mission, and left him with an unhappy conclusion: "The people here will not hear of my leaving them; but I must."[46]

A month passed, and the prayer books did not arrive. Mendes grew more anxious with each week, writing Reverend Pool time and again to send them post haste, and expressing deepening alarm as each mail steamer came and went without the delivery. Mendes's order had grown from thirteen to twenty-seven prayerbooks, including one for just about every family in the congregation, and their receipt became imperative. When Purim came, Mendes found himself with a dozen Bibles and no prayer books. He was adamant:

> . . . not to receive the long expected books!
> Believe me, it is quite a damper.
> They feel it.
> So please attend to it at once, and earn their gratitude.

> Or what is of greater importance in your eyes, take part in the Mitzvah I am
> doing, to promote Jewish loyalty in this distant and *neglected* flock.[47]

Apart from this, however, St. Thomas's first Purim celebration in decades
was a success. The congregation filed in to hear Mendes chant the Book of
Esther while they followed along in their old bibles. After the reading ended,
the reverend continued the festivities, taking advantage of the occasion to
hold an examination of the Sunday School. The six girls Mendes had instructed
delighted their parents and relatives with a show of ritual singing, Hebrew
reading, and Jewish history and philosophy. To conclude the evening, the congregation joined in singing several concluding hymns; then everyone headed
homeward.

The next night, at the close of the holiday, the minister held a gathering at
his house, where more than a dozen younger members performed the Purim
pageant they had been rehearsing. While Mendes narrated, the youths acted
out the Purim story, complete with songs, choruses, and *Bakashot* (Hebrew
exhortations). At the close of the play, Reader Sasso rose and thanked Mendes
on behalf of the congregation. So extraordinary was this series of events to
the local population that the next day one paper devoted nearly a whole page
to the celebration.[48] Mendes later recalled, "the spirit was wonderful."

The first shipment of prayer books, held up by debates among *Shearith
Israel*'s board of representatives, finally arrived on March 28.[49] Mendes was
grateful despite the delay, and immediately began distributing them for
use. By this time, attendance was beginning to improve at Saturday morning
services; as per the island's work schedule, however, the congregants would
often appear in two shifts. A few young men with government jobs entered
the synagogue at 7:00 A.M., and stayed for the early part of the service before
departing for Government Hill two blocks away. The rest of the congregation, which sat through the entirety of the rital, numbered about twenty-
five, including several women and children. Mendes hoped the new prayer
books would help maintain or improve this attendance. Not only would the
congregants receive a unified text from which to pray, but they could also
view the new possessions as an opportunity to practice and internalize
Mendes's liturgical Hebrew lessons each week. The volumes thus completed
the minister's educational schema, becoming the ultimate goal for his instruc-
tional plan.

In the years before Mendes's arrival, Passover's festival meals would be
celebrated in private homes. The most well-known of these *seders* took place
within the expansive homes of the Levin, Paiewonsky, and Petit families;

little was said of the commemorative meals eaten in other Jewish homes that evening, if they were held at all. With Mendes on the island, however, the celebration became extension of congregational life. The minister and his wife took pains to organize a "congregational *seder*," creating a communal religious meal for those without the means or desire to observe it. Well over half of the Jewish population attended the ritual feast, which featured a special kosher shankbone imported from New York and a galvanizing recitation of the traditional Four Questions by three young congregants; Mendes even reported that some members of the families who held regular *seders* stopped by to take part in the event.[50] Again, the congregation congratulated Dr. and Mrs. Mendes on bringing it together to revitalize its religious practices.

A few days later, on April 13, the Jewish community returned the favor with a grand celebration of the minister's seventy-third birthday. At 8:00 A.M., a group of young congregants gathered outside of the Mendes' house and proudly sang three hymns in honor of the minister, who had just returned from morning prayers at the synagogue. More people arrived, and a public, formal ceremony began as Reader Moses De Castro Sasso presented Mendes with an engraved ice pitcher bearing his name, the date, and the name of the Hebrew Congregation. Young synagogue president Morris De Castro followed, reading a speech of heartfelt appreciation to the minister: "May he who guided you to little St. Thomas, to be a source of inspiration and religious assistance to us all, see fit to cause your stay here to be so extended that this privilege may again be ours next year." The speech was signed: "ALL THE JEWS IN ST. THOMAS." After Mendes responded in thanks, as was requisite, Max E. Trepuk rose and presented yet another tribute to the minister. The local Masonic temple, Harmonic Lodge 356 E. C., then conferred upon the reverend a letter of thanks and recognition for his contributions to their society. Outside, in the garden, bandleader Alton Augustus Adams conducted the island's Naval Band as it punctuated the ceremony with musical interludes.[51] Once all the tributes had been given, everyone present sang a final hymn to conclude the celebration, and returned home in high spirits.[52]

Recognizing themselves as hosts to one of the leading Jewish intellectuals of his day, other islanders joined the Jews in admiration and reverence, requesting Reverend Mendes's services at their own gatherings and events. It was like having a celebrity in their midst; the minister's mere existence on the island gave many residents confidence and self-esteem during the difficult early years of U. S. Naval rule. Mendes agreed to many of these invitations; and through this, his intellectual contributions to island life crossed denominations and disciplines. He lectured at the Masonic Lodge, gave the keynote address at the island's combined school commencement exercises, and spoke during the territory's first National Music Week, all to great warmth and enthusiasm. Mendes apparently found these engagements personally enriching, adding them to his complement of synagogue-related obligations even as he felt his own health deteriorating from the workload.

On Sunday, May 31, 1925, just after the close of the Shavuot holiday, Mendes completed one of the focal points of his mission to St. Thomas. On that evening, in the synagogue, four men and four women celebrated the completion of their course of study with the minister, and expressed their willingness to be consecrated "to maintain, promote, and champion their religion."[53] The eight congregants, ranging in age from fifteen to thirty-five, constituted the reverend's most promising students, and included synagogue Reader Moses Sasso. In performing the ceremony, Reverend Mendes installed what he hoped would be a new generation of knowledgeable Jews on the island—educated in their faith and ready to take on leadership responsibilities in the newly resuscitated synagogue.

Mendes spoke to those gathered in the gaily decorated sanctuary, and gave a lesson based on Jewish teachings, but carrying a universalistic message. He impressed upon his audience that Judaism taught love: of neighbor, Jew and non-Jew alike; of friend, but also of enemy; and of life. Those being consecrated, he said, had chosen to do so as mature and thinking adults, pursuing Judaism as an important part of their lives, and promising to demonstrate its love and devotion throughout the rest of their days. With this, he took out one of the synagogue's Torahs, placed his hand on it, and proclaimed in a loud and resonant voice: "HEAR O ISRAEL, THE LORD IS OUR GOD, THERE IS ONLY ONE GOD!"[54] All present heard and heeded this cry; and, by all accounts, everyone was deeply impressed. Earnestly, and with feeling, the consecrants responded with their own statements of devotion. Each was received and appreciated by those in attendance. For Moses Sasso, however, the ceremony was an especially transformative experience, publicly marking his improvement as the local religious authority. The approbation he garnered at the hands of a learned and respected teacher bestowed him with a new legitimacy as the island community's present and future spiritual leader. "No one present," wrote one reporter, recounting the ceremony, "will ever forget the impression created by the scene and the responses."[55]

Other indications showed both how successfully Mendes had energized the synagogue community, and how the synagogue community started to recognize Mendes's frailty. In a board meeting held around the same time as the consecration service, the congregation began taking steps to transfer several of the minister's projects into its own hands. From the Sunday School to the burial society, from "Box-Collection" to "Synagogue fitness," the board formed committees consisting of "one member of the 'confirmation class,' one of the [congregation's] older members and a warden, or trustee."[56] Although such an arrangement may also have been a condition of the confirmation class, it nonetheless showed the congregation's determination to internalize the changes Reverend Mendes had instituted. Perhaps the meeting was also meant to lighten the minister's workload, or even anticipate his imminent departure from the island.

Mendes's health continued to worsen. By the middle of June, both he and his wife were bedridden. Mendes tried to lead services on June 20, but found it impossible, and had to step down from the pulpit in the middle of the ritual. Two weeks later, on doctor's orders, he and Rosalie began to pack up their belongings, deciding tentatively to take advantage of the next ship leaving for California. The couple secured spaces on the Danish ship *Chile*, which was to leave in late July, and made their final preparations to depart from the island. Mendes gave his farewell speech on Sunday, July 12, and with this, conducted the closing exercises for the Sunday School. Friends and well-wishers gathered at his house that evening, remaining to show their gratitude until near midnight.[57]

On July 18, after the Sabbath had ended, Reverend Mendes and his wife were treated to a final farewell party. With songs, gifts, and dedications, the congregation fêted him, expressing their thanks for all he accomplished on the island. Together, they sang Harry Kennedy's 1893 sentimental ballad "Say *Au Revoir*, But Not Goodbye," modifying the lyrics to address the reverend: "You'll soon be gone, but memory gives // One clinging thought: the future lives."[58] Indeed, with reconstruction of the roof underway, an established system for Jewish education on the island, a reader better prepared to perform his station, and an enthusiastic congregation, the future looked bright. Mendes had been the force behind all of this and more.

Soon after, "[i]n a shower of tears [and] lamentations," the Mendeses boarded a small boat that made its way out of the protected harbor to the awaiting ship *Chile*, leaving St. Thomas forever.[59] Nearly three weeks later, and after crossing through the Panama Canal, they arrived at Los Angeles.

On the day of their departure from the island, Rosalie Piza Mendes made an incisive and fateful observation that cut through much of the prevailing optimism: "For [the Jews of this island], the sun [and] moon have left them to their Egyptian darkness once more.—Such darkness as this is appalling. It is intellectual [and] spiritual starvation–[and] death—"[60] Reverend Mendes had served as a light to his nation, a prevailing force that singlehandedly spurred the Jewish renewal on St. Thomas. Without him, the Jews were back to where they had been before: lacking a revered Jewish authority, and with little opportunity to advance their knowledge. The past seven months had helped the congregation immensely by restoring organization and self-esteem, and providing the congregation with a limited Hebrew literacy. But afterward, the Jews were once again on their own, hoping to outlast the forces of entropy.

Sasso continued his work, opening the synagogue's heavy wooden doors for services every Sabbath, leading prayers with an ardent passion, and supplementing services with occasional sermons sent down by Reverend Mendes. His ministerial skills were presumably much improved; nonetheless, Sasso's attempts to lead his people in prayer never carried the same learned spark as those of the great Reverend Mendes. Most found the services simply boring, though they continued to attend week after week. Versed with Mendes's teachings, Sasso did his part, and the attendees did theirs. Yet once again, with no one to continue the lessons needed to maintain a strong and knowledgable Jewish life, the ritual slowly slid into an eroding routine.

—⁓—

THE 1930S BROUGHT A PERIOD of social unrest in the Virgin Islands. Lorded over by a monarchic U.S. military government ever since the transfer, islanders began to express their discontent with increasing vigor.[61] The new United States regime had invaded the area with a harsh, American-style racism and an attitude toward the islanders that cared little for the cosmopolitan civilization that had existed in St. Thomas for the previous century and a half. More concerned with establishing a military presence on the island, the U.S. government took ten years to decide whether or not (and how) to make the Virgin Islands residents American citizens, a delay that angered and disillusioned many.[62] Local residents, seeing themselves as powerless and overlooked in the eyes of the American administration, took little role in official governmental activities. Rather, they ran their own separate colonial council and attended to their own internal affairs, continuing the practice from Danish times.[63]

Adding insult to injury was a visit by United States president Herbert Hoover in 1931. After a five-hour tour of St. Thomas, Hoover shocked the people of St. Thomas by lamenting "we acquired an effective poorhouse." He added: "Viewed from every point, except remote naval contingencies, it was unfortunate that we ever acquired these islands. Nonetheless, having assumed the responsibility we must do our best to help the inhabitants."[64] A once-hopeful populace felt let down and misrepresented by the president's remarks, and rallied in its own favor as best they could under the circumstances. Respect was not easy in coming, however: While the American government acknowledged a need for civilian rule on St. Thomas, attempts to create a constitution in 1924, 1927, and 1931 fell flat. Finally, after the third attempt, Washington appointed American Paul M. Pearson as the territory's first non-military governor. Upon his installation, Pearson found a frustrated people who held great contempt for what they saw as a transplanted and imperialistic administration. Pearson took many steps to improve the island community by introducing scholarships, civic projects, and the like; yet his attempts to address his critics came to no avail. Instead, his sincere though controversial politicking led to sometimes violent demonstrations.

The island stood together in protest. Joining in its unhappiness against the new governor, the Jewish community voiced its own grievances. Moses Sasso vented to Reverend Mendes in a letter dated October 10, 1934, giving a clear idea of the indignities he saw:

> Am sure you read of the awful conditions prevailing here under Pearson's tyrannical rule! We 15,000 inhabitants of the V. I. are praying our Great President Roosevelt will soon dismiss him [and] send a new Gov.—he unjustly had a young Jewish attorney (our District attorney) summarily dismissed because the fellow did his duty to the letter.—But now <u>his own executive assistant</u>, one Jakes has now "<u>Spilled the milk</u>," [and] we are awaiting the outcome at Washington.[65]

Sasso, and the rest of the island, soon had their prayers answered. Six days after he wrote the letter, violence again erupted in the streets during a demonstration, resulting in injury to the police commissioner. The U.S. government moved into action, investigating these and other grievances. Pearson, as a result, was removed from his position. Simultaneously, the U.S. Department of the Interior and representatives from Virgin Islands began work on what would become the Organic Act of 1936, the first successfully implemented constitution of the U.S. Virgin Islands.[66]

In addition to the eventual bestowal of civil rights to island residents, the Jewish community also had other reasons to celebrate. In 1934, their preacher reached a milestone, marking twenty years at the pulpit of the little synagogue. Having started with little background and only cursory experience, Moses Sasso's energy and enthusiasm had helped to power the Jews through increasingly difficult years. Even after Mendes's tutelage, Sasso's knowledge and ability remained limited, with only modest opportunities for growth. Nonetheless, he continued to lead the synagogue ritual each week, retained contacts with religious authorities and organizations in America, gave the children regular religious instruction, and effectively acted as the island representative for the Jewish community.[67] Synagogue life continued uninterrupted due to his verve, and at the end of 1934, the whole congregation gathered to honor his devotion.

By this time, Sasso's flock had experienced some significant demographic changes. Several of the congregation's young women, without a pool of single Jewish men to choose from, had chosen members of the non-Jewish population for lifetime partners. Due to the small size and social cohesiveness of the Jewish community, however, the women remained active in congregational life; consequently, a new population of non-Jewish men became integrated by association into the Jewish populace. Olga Rachel Henriques Moron married U.S. Marine John Frank White during the first years of American rule. Three of Jacob and Esther Paiewonsky's six daughters married Danish ship captains; another married a Norwegian merchant. Leah Else Levin, daughter of Israel Levin, fell in love with German ship engineer Eugene August Franz Siggelkow and eventually married him in Hamburg. Max Trepuk's daughter Mariette married Alfred Evelyn, a local Christian clerk.[68] As seen by those outside of St. Thomas (such as Reverend Mendes), these inter-religious unions were a harbinger of dark times, threatening the integrity Jewish life on the island. In hindsight, however, these marriages had precisely the opposite effect on the St. Thomas Jewish community. Capitalizing on a characteristic openness toward other religions, and retaining a strong family orientation, the intermarried couples became esteemed synagogue attendees who would ensure the continuation of the congregation's traditions. Non-Jewish husbands frequented the Jewish community's events, attending services and assisting with matters within the synagogue. The children of these unions, moreover, became the next generation of Rabbi Sasso's students.[69]

Though these couples could not by definition be recorded in the synagogue's marriage registers (since one member of the couple was not Jewish), they necessarily served as the key for religious self-perpetuation on the island. As such, it was within the synagogue's best interests to welcome the children of these unions into the congregation. The board of representatives thus devised a method that retained the historic exclusivity of Jewish identity while simultaneously accommodating to the situation at hand.[70] In order to register a child in the synagogue protocols, the non-Jewish parent of each pair had to submit to the synagogue board a notarized statement expressing intent and desire for the child to grow up in the Jewish faith. Only after the board approved the letter could the new child become a full member of the congregation, with his or her name entered in the register.[71] Significantly, this practice rarely met with opposition from any of the parties involved. Seeing a strong and meaningful community in the synagogue (or with the knowledge that such consent was a condition of their marriage) the non-Jewish parent seemed to have few misgivings about their children's religious upbringing. For the synagogue, meanwhile, these children were crucial to ensuring the congregation's survival. Through such a process, the sounds of young voices continued to reverberate through the synagogue, giving hope to the old members and faith to the new.

In light of the elevated intermarriage rate, the rare wedding between two Jews was prime reason for celebration within the Jewish community. On November 30, 1930, Jacob Paiewonsky's daughter Lena and Rebecca Paiewonsky's youngest brother Moses Kushner fulfilled this charge, marrying in the sanctuary under the aegis of Reader Sasso. It was the first Jewish wedding in the community in over a year, and the last until 1935. *The Daily News* recounted the celebration as a high society event on the island, referring to the service as "one of the most colorful ceremonies at the Synagogue." Proceeding as if detailing an exclusive function, the reporter's account began with a comment on the "illuminated" sanctuary "filled with guests and spectators until it resembled a scene from some opera of joy."[72] The wedding procession began to the "grandiose music" of the St. Thomas Community Band. Isaac Paiewonsky, the bride's uncle, entered as the best man, accompanied by Henry Holst, the "page of honor drest in blue velvet." Next to enter were the bride's sisters: Ethel "in pink chiffon . . . with picture hat and cream roses," Alice, in "blue chiffon and carr[ying] assorted roses," and Amalia, who "carried assorted bouquets of tea roses and pinks." Elaine Holst, a friend, rounded out the four maids of honor. Mrs. Sadie Puritz, whose son Alfred had married Isaac Paiewonsky's youngest daughter Paulina the previous year, came next, wearing "an outfit of apple green, and carr[ying] a large spray of pink tea roses." The flower girls, Gladys Watson and Laura Evelyn, "in blue and pink ruffled dresses," entered behind them, dropping blooms on the sand floor. Both were children of Jewish mothers and non-Jewish fathers, the first a future step-daughter of Moses Sasso, and the second the granddaughter of Max Trepuk. Behind them, the focus of the ceremony, came a radiant Lena Paiewonsky, "arrayed with meticulous taste in a satin and tulle gown which trailed in a royal manner. Her bouquet was white and no rose in it lovelier than herself, her face framed in dark hair and her delicate color like opalescent pink now and then flushing her slightly pale face." Covering her visage, in traditional Jewish fashion, was a hand-embroidered veil, making "a spun magic covering for her head and shoulders . . . [T]he wreath surrounding it was of rare design." Lena's father Jacob Paiewonsky walked by her side as she made her way to the center of the sanctuary and came to stand next to the awaiting groom.

Reader Sasso performed the ceremony, after which "the principles withdrew to the outer court where the necessary documents," such as a marriage license, and probably the *Ketubah* as well, "were signed." Sasso confirmed the validity of the Jewish wedding, and the island's governor notarized the documents for the territory and the U.S. Government. With this, the crowd went off for a reception and dance at Isaac Paiewonsky's house further up the street. The Virgin Islands Orchestra accompanied the revelers as they danced for the happiness of the couple. Most, however, danced with the knowledge that such an event would probably not happen again for long time to come.

Whether intermarried or in-married, there seemed to be a great deal of encouragement for young couples to raise their children within the Jewish community. On the rare occasion when this did not happen, troubles ensued. In the mid-1910s, for example, Esther Athias Robles married a non-Jewish clerk on St. Thomas named Walter I. Watson. The couple produced six children—three boys and three girls—between 1918 and 1926. There is evidence that unlike other intermarried families in this period, the Watsons had little if any affiliation with the Jewish community during this time.[73] Perhaps this constituted a significant problem in the relationship; for the two divorced in 1933, with Esther Robles receiving full custody of the children in the settlement. On Thursday, November 30, 1933, Esther wrote a letter to the board of representatives informing them of this result and immediately requesting that her children be entered into the synagogue register. A quorum presumably approved this letter's request with great speed, for Reader Sasso circumcised Robles's three boys that same morning in the Municipal Hospital, with the synagogue's president and vice-president as witnesses. At least one of these children, ten-year-old John Douglas Watson, soon joined Reader Sasso's confirmation class.[74]

Two years later, on November 24, 1935, Moses Sasso's first wife died after a long illness at age sixty-seven.[75] Sasso, apparently having developed close relations with the Watson family, spent little time unattached. On April 5, 1936, he married Esther Watson (again through a police court license) in a ceremony that completed her return to the synagogue and gave the reader a new responsibility as stepfather of six children.

Even in the synagogue's depleted state, the Hebrew congregation observed much of the full liturgical year. Moses Sasso continued his career as merchant (his position in the synagogue was essentially unpaid), and often went on business trips during the week; but he always made sure to be on the island in time for services. On Saturday mornings, he opened up the synagogue's doors to accommodate sometimes as few as four people for a long, slow, and highly regimented service. At eight o'clock in the morning sharp, Sasso would commence the service with the morning prayers—a combination of psalms, readings, and blessings, some spoken, some chanted. These continued until about 9:30, at which point Sasso walked across the sanctuary floor to the *Ahal*, or holy ark, in order to take out the *Sepher* (Five Books of Moses, or *Torah*). He processed around the congregation with the scroll, set it on the reader's table, and then proceeded to read a portion to the congregation. At about 10:30, Sasso would pick up the *Sepher* and cross back to the *Ahal*, often singing an English hymn such as Reverend Henry Pereira Mendes's "O God to Thee."[76] At the *Ahal*, congregants would come up and pledge monetary offerings to the synagogue, receiving formulaic blessings for health in return. The *Sepher* went back into the *Ahal*, and at 10:45 the reader would continue with the hymn "Ein Keloheinu" ("There is none like our God"); this marked the start of the service's final stretch. At 11:20, according to the reader's godson David Sasso, there would be "a twinkling in [Reader Sasso's] eye." Then he would cock his head up and begin to sing the final hymn, "Adon Olam" ("Lord Over All"). At the conclusion of this hymn, Sasso raised his hands and, in a high-pitched nasal voice, intoned the priestly blessing in English and Hebrew: "May the Lord bless and preserve thee! May the Lord lift His face to shine upon thee! May the Lord lift up His countenance upon thee and grant thee peace!" The service ended at 11:30 A.M.[77]

Above all, the High Holidays still served as a magical time to the Jews. The community by the 1930s numbered about sixty, and the local paper lamented the lack of numbers and the change in times: "[T]he high holy-days used to be a season of much ceremony and feasting. Especially with the Osorios, the Morons, Sassos and De Castros, there was no Gentile friend unremembered. . . . [O]utdoor meals and visits to the temple . . . were so typical of the lavish hospitality of the times and Jewish good cheer meant the best there was."[78] Most of the old synagogue families were now represented by a handful of elderly islanders, subsisting on a quiet trade and unable to supply the energy or funds for the "lavish" entertaining of the past. Even with the public openness reduced, however, the congregation and its reader continued to spare no formality in the sanctuary. On the Sunday morning before Rosh Hashanah, the reader opened up the synagogue at four in the morning, enacting a version of the *Selichot* (forgiveness) service traditionally held on the occasion.[79] The new year, Rosh Hashanah, remained a holiday of gathering usually marked by good wishes in the island's newspapers. Everyone in the community attended services in the morning before adjourning to social gatherings and receptions held by the most prominent families.

Yom Kippur, ten days later, remained an intense experience in the synagogue, prepared and followed as if the pews were brimming over:

Yom Kippur 1937—the afternoon in itself often was dreary looking, dark, it had been a rainy eve; Yes, Yom Kippur would start at sundown tonight: St. Thomas Jews had long closed their business places, and were at home, some reading prayers in the house, and others dressing to attend "Kippur Eve" services as they called the Holy Day's eve:

At the St. Thomas Synagogue now at 5 PM Willie Levi the Shamis [building curator] was huffing and puffing on and off of tall ladders lighting the wicks of the beautiful candelabra in the center of the ceiling and those with candles on the side; the Center Candelabra had small tapers tucked in oil cans under the shade; Willie Levi, the son of a Jew himself, was a man of color, but the children teased him calling him "Vigilant and Dryland" when he walked, since he walked bowlegged with each leg wide apart; He more often rode a bicycle. The more tapers Willie lit the more he perspired, and the sweat could be seen trickling down his face, and his hair was wet as though he had been sea bathing:

Six o'clock, sharp, the service would begin with Rabbi (Reader) Sasso walking into the edifice from the vestry; Rabbi Sasso would be wearing his long Black gown over his usual black suit, shirt and tie; His three-cornered black hat gave him the look of "A man of God": By this time the congregation had gathered, some walking somberly, some briskly, most all men and women dressed in somber colors; Even the BIG businessmen had an humble look on their faces at this time; the Eahal [Holy Ark] doors would stand wide open—each Torah would be colorfully dressed in its best satin gowns; Since there was no air condition[ing] the windows were all open wide—one could smell the night air infiltrating. Rabbi Sasso seemed to drag his feet as he ascended the BEAMER (Pulpit) his hands clasped all the way as though in solemn prayer;

Not a sound was heard: A hairpin could drop and you would hear it: for

those few moments at the beginning of the service, even the children seemed
to be quiet, and stopped kicking the sand on the floor; YOM KIPPUR was indeed
a very solemn Day . . .[80]

Services the next morning began around eight o'clock and continued
throughout the day. At around two in the afternoon, Max Trepuk ascended
the reader's desk and intoned the Book of Jonah, sniffling all the way through.
At three, the memorial service (*Yizkor*) took place. At 4:30, the reader's
brother Ernest came up and blew the Shofar, ushering in *Neilah*, the final
service of the day. After sunset, services ended and the community emerged,
ready to begin the year anew.[81]

By the 1930s, the first wave of Eastern European immigrants had begun
to pass on. Esther Rachel Paiewonsky died in 1927. Israel Levin died in 1934.
Max Trepuk passed away in October 1938. Their departures, sadly noted by
the town as well as the Jewish community, left gaping holes in the synagogue,
mercantile life, and (for the men) the local Harmonic Lodge. Their Ashkenazic practices, meanwhile, had made some inroads into synagogue ritual:
most prominent among these, it seemed, was the Bar Mitzvah, which had
begun to supplant confirmations as the most visible coming-of-age ceremony
in the community. Such changes were a harbinger of the years to come, as
the next generation of Levins and Paiewonskys rose to prominence.

By the late 1930s, as Reader Moses Sasso struggled to keep the doors of
the synagogue open on St. Thomas, the dark cloud of Nazism began closing
synagogue doors throughout Europe. The Jews of St. Thomas knew about
this menace as it began to threaten large communities in and around Germany, and found themselves affected by it in several ways. Else Siggelkow
and her daughters Gertrude and Franzi had been on St. Thomas since 1921,
about a year after the death of her German husband Franz. In early 1939, the
widow went to visit her aunts-in-law in Hamburg. Yet upon her arrival, Else
received a rude awakening:

[The aunts] were very serious and they were very nice, but they made a pact
among themselves that they would cut off of each other because we were Jewish
and they were not Jewish, and Hitler was *just* startin' up. . . . They [had] cor-
responded and everything [for] years and years and years but when [Else] got
there and she saw the situation she says "You know, you are older people" (and
it's mostly aunts and cousins who were in their 70s and 80s). "Stop writing. We
don't need to exchange any conversation or anything because this man [Hitler]

is not good. So don't mix up yourself with us Jews over there." . . . [T]hey were old people, they didn't need somebody knocking on their doors . . . and throwing them out, because they were cousins of a Jew in St. Thomas.[82]

Upon her return to St. Thomas, Else Siggelkow excommunicated herself from her husband's family. By the time her son-in-law went to find them after the war, all but two had died from old age.[83]

Amalia (Paiewonsky) Mylner, conversely, found herself an unexpected champion of her religion during a business trip to Germany with her Danish husband Svend during the early years of the Third Reich:

When the Germans were makin' trouble, my father didn't want me to go to Germany, because I had to travel even where Svend went. [I went nonetheless.] And we stayed in a hotel in Berlin. And I saw the little [Jewish children], 8 or 9 years [old], buildin' ditches. Yes. And one night we went to a dance hall. And when we saw all the Nazis come up with their armbands in the hotel, Svend left. Because we had many German friends. [His shipping company worked with] German ships, and it's funny what happened, [at] the time. When Svend was going to work he asked me to take a captain to go out to the beach to a beach party with the others. And [Svend] said, "If I can come, I will come". . . . [The captain I accompanied] was a Nazi. . . . And I listened [during the trip down] and he was calling down the Jews; and we went to the beach and when we came back, he thanked me for [taking] him, and I said "Captain. I want to tell you one thing. You must be careful what you say. Because you are sittin' next to a Jewess!" . . . [H]e was so sorry! This was a German warship that was in and we were invited to a cocktail party that day, and [also a party on] a French [ship]. And we went on the French [ship]. But we didn't go on [the German ship], and he [the captain] couldn't send gifts for me [to convince me to go on board] and he was so sorry![84]

In the unique position as a Jewish woman protected by both her nationality and the status of her husband, Mylner could take a rare safe jab at what would soon be the deadliest regime in Jewish history.

The year 1939 also marked the twenty-fifth anniversary of Moses Sasso's tenure in the St. Thomas pulpit. During the interdenominational "thanksgiving" service held for the occasion, the tone remained tense and filled with anti-Nazi rhetoric. Both speakers placed the St. Thomas Jewish community in the theater of the hour. Reverend Howard E. Thomas spoke from the perspective of the Christian community. In the face of the Nazis, he said, the enmity classically held between Jew and Christian must desist. "This Central European program is not a Christian persecution, for it violates the most elementary laws of the Christian Faith. It is the battle of irreligion against Religion. Today the Jews, tomorrow the Christians." Moreover, he added, this was as important a time as ever to maintain a strong religious identity: "My Jewish friends! I plead with all the strength at my command. Be true to your own faith. . . . The outlook is dark, but it is dark only because the faith of both Jew and Gentile is so frail."[85] Morris De Castro, who by then had become acting governor of the Virgin Islands, spoke of the historical endurance of the Jewish community. In setting the scene, he stated: "Even today in the enlightened twentieth century unspeakable horrors are being committed against the Jews in certain foreign countries, horrors equal to if not worse than those suffered by the Jews in other days, horrors which have shocked and bewildered the civilized world." In the face of this environment he praised Reader Sasso, "whose watchword has been that this Holy Place of Worship shall not be closed so long as there remains one Jew in St. Thomas who can join in our religious services."[86] Joyful in St. Thomas, and unified with the rest of the island community, the Jews nonetheless kept a wary eye to Europe, already scared and outraged at the atrocities being perpetrated in the spreading German empire.

The increasing inhumanities taking place in Central Europe were common knowledge on the island at this time. Thus, even as individuals such as Else Siggelkow and Amalia Mylner had personal experiences with the regime in Germany proper, the rest of St. Thomas participated from afar by taking bold political action. In late 1938, the recently created Virgin Islands legislature passed a resolution to declare its islands "a place of safety" to "Refugee peoples of the world."[87] Following in their pattern of extending help to peoples in trouble across the world, the Virgin Islands opened its gates in principle to the thousands of desperate refugees who were no longer being treated as people under Hitler's regime. Two years later, facing significant opposition from the American government, the islands' civilian governor moved the resolution forward by signing a proclamation accepting two thousand refugee families for entry into the territory. Yet the American government, under the guise of fearing German espionage, summarily frustrated and dismissed these attempts, forcing closed the doors of the historically open and welcoming port to those who needed it most. The Navy declared the territory a restricted area over the protests of the people and pleading letters from German refugees, leaving the island with little recourse but to watch as millions met a terrible fate.[88]

By 1940, the St. Thomas Jewish community had reached its nadir. Where Jewish periodicals had once praised the community as substantial, respectable, and forward-looking, with strong religious convictions and nail-biting controversies, they now saw the island as a curiosity if anything at all. No longer newsworthy by itself, the Jewish population had to make do with being "discovered" by safari-ing travellers in search of "exotic" Jewish communities. One of the first of these came through the pen of photographer Alexander Alland in a four-part series published in the *American Hebrew* in 1940. "We have commissioned Mr. Alland to prepare for us a series of articles, illustrated with photographs, which because of their unique subject, should be of great interest to our readers," explained the editor before the first instalment. The articles that followed, under the general title "The Jews of the Virgin Islands: A History of the Islands and Candid Biographies of Outstanding Jews Born There," were combinations of travelogue, historical overview, ethnographic observation and biography, intermingled with photographs of the area and its population. Judah Benjamin and Camille Pissarro received ample mention; but Alland also focused on contemporary figures such as political servant Morris De Castro, former telegraph operator and Botanical Gardens founder Eugene Petit, and transplanted New York lawyer Jacques Schiffer. Services and religious rituals received only passing notice, taking a back seat to the tourist appeal of the island. Controversies from the synagogue's history no longer existed in the account: rather, Alland portrayed an idyllic, storybook setting on a quaint, unspoiled island just waiting to be documented.[89]

In the early 1940s, psychologist Albert Angus Campbell went down to St. Thomas to study the island's Afro-Caribbean population, but also found time to take a short look at the existing Jewish population.[90] His resulting article, "Note on the Jewish Community of St. Thomas, U.S. Virgin Islands," appeared in the nascent periodical *Jewish Social Studies*. Its publication seemed to be more of a lark than anything else, and the editor of the journal accompanied the six-page entry with a line of justification: "Despite the limited importance of this community its history is interesting as typifying the experiences of the several Jewish groups which migrated to the West Indies."[91] The drastically small size of the congregation caused St. Thomas's Jewish population to be seen as a curious relic, "the remnants of a once prosperous and considerable community."[92] No longer contributing to contemporary religious issues, the Jews were now a mere subject, a fleeting glimpse of the Sephardic Jewish world that had flourished before the enormous Eastern European influx at the turn of the century.

Campbell's description of the 1940s Jewish community still evidenced international experience and business savvy:

> They are all native-born, although many of them have lived for varying periods in America or Europe. For the most part they constitute an economically privileged group, composed of merchants, government officials, or salaried employees of local or American companies. In the administration of the island the present incumbent in the highest office held by a native, namely, the commissioner of finance, is a Jew. Two of the seven members of the municipal council of St. Thomas are white and one of these is a Jewish merchant. The Jews are not included among the island's wealthiest men but even the poorest of them has not fallen into the island's large dispossessed class.[93]

The Jewish community, which by this point numbered about fifty, was versed in world affairs according to Campbell; but at the same time, it experienced unique conditions relative to the rest of the recognized Jewish world. Antisemitism, an issue of much concern in the United States, hardly deserved mention St. Thomas, "and there is no indication whatever that any change in that direction is now taking place."[94] Marriage among a group of people so small, Campbell noticed, was impossible, and resulted in a number of interfaith, or, on occasion, interracial weddings. And for every Jewish family with a "traditional" last name, there was sure to be a black family with the same name.[95] The article exuded a tone similar to that of Reverend Mendes almost a generation earlier, concluding with an ominous final prediction:

> If present trends continue it seems inevitable that the Jewish colony in St. Thomas will eventually disappear. With no prospect of a rebirth of commerce or agriculture the island seems destined to remain indefinitely in its present depressed state. There is an almost complete absence of economic opportunities with which to attract new residents or to prevent ambitious native youths from migrating to the United States. The Jews of St. Thomas, traditionally engaged in business and trade, cannot resist these overwhelming economic forces. Their once thriving community is in the process of gradual extinction.[96]

Campbell's conclusion had an air of authority. The St. Thomas Synagogue, he implied, had enjoyed its day in the sun. Now, however, it was time for the 150-year-old outpost congregation to close its doors. Caribbean Jewry, a phenomenon of a past era, was no longer viable.

If the war in Europe had dragged on much longer than it did, or if

St. Thomas had been a colony of a more distant nation with a smaller Jewish population, these gloomy predictions might have seen light. Yet the two commentators underestimated several factors, including the devotion of Reader Sasso and the determination of the United States government to make the Virgin Islands look like a useful purchase. After the Axis forces fell in defeat to the Allies, a new era would dawn on St. Thomas, replete with yet another change in population.

CHAPTER 9

A Revival from America
1946–1967

> The synagogue of St. Thomas . . . is today one of the most
> charming sights of the Island, and an important architectural
> monument of the Jewish people in the New World. Visitors of
> all faiths experience a moment of awe at the sight of the austere
> Sephardic interior, the heavy hurricane-proof walls, the vaulted
> windows, and the sand-covered floor.
>
> —Herman Wouk, in his preface to the pamphlet
> "Jewish Historical Developments in the Virgin Islands,
> 1665–1959" (1959)

*I*n 1946, Pan American World Airways flew its first direct flights between New York and San Juan, Puerto Rico. The new route, in the wake of celebratory victories in World War II the previous year, marked a dawning era of prosperity and leisure time in the United States. Thanks to new labor contracts and early retirement benefits introduced to much of the American workforce after the war, personal income rose and vacation days increased substantially.[1] With the hopes of fulfilling an "American Dream," Americans took advantage of cheaper, more efficient transportation technologies to explore regions that were further and further away from their homes. Puerto Rico was an early and obvious recipient of this newly mobile population: As an American territory in a tropical climate, it provided a promise of relief for those suffering cold and snowy Northeast winters. In addition, it was an exotic locale that combined the ease of domestic travel with the pleasures of an "international" setting.

Pan American's flights also opened up new opportunities for St. Thomas. Just a short, fifty-mile jaunt east from San Juan, the island suddenly became accessible to the mainland United States. What was a "three and a half to four and a half days' journey from New York," just six years earlier warped into a speedy eight hours.[2] For travellers venturing from Miami, the twelve-hour clipper plane flight to St. Thomas was shortened to six hours by turboprop.[3] Adventurous tourists disembarking in St. Thomas's small airport discovered the lush, rolling mountains, the undeveloped resources, the poor, mostly black population, the breathtaking views, and the ideal climate—all without leaving American soil. To many, it was the perfect place for a vacation, and an "obvious" occupation for the otherwise "unusable" island.

The idea of turning St. Thomas into a tourist destination was not new: films about the islands produced by the Department of the Interior in the 1930s portrayed the islands as a place where "even the landing of a ship was cause for a holiday," and included scenes of outdoor verandas populated with white continentals who beamed angelically while white-shirted black waiters mixed drinks for them with "swizel" sticks.[4] Indeed, the occasional cruise ship or naval vessel would turn the island into a port of call, allowing well-off visitors and sailors a few hours at a time to explore the island and its pleasures. From San Juan, a shuttle boat brought passengers back and forth, providing options for an extended stay at the few hotels and inns that dotted the island.[5] Successful only on a modest level, St. Thomas tourism in the 1930s catered primarily to a few affluent travellers who had the means to find sun, peace, and quiet in a secluded area outside the continental United States. With the advent of near-direct air travel to the island, however, a sojourn on St. Thomas became a reality for a much larger part of the American population. Many millions would soon desire to take advantage of the new tourist mecca; and many developers and entrepreneurs would come down to satisfy the new demand.

The tiny Jewish population was also in for a jolt. After several decades of quiet subsistence, the sparse congregation sustained so stubbornly by Reader Sasso was about to start a period of augmentation. Suddenly situated eight hours away from the largest Jewish population in the world, the old families promptly found themselves hosts to a new cohort. Several Jewish families from the New York area would come down with the rest of the tourists and developers. The newcomers knew little of the island's history or of the Sephardic culture that had dominated the Jewish communities of the Americas through the early nineteenth century. They were unfamiliar with Sephardic Jewish ritual—and often, their secular lifestyles had also distanced them from Eastern European "Old World" Jewish practice. American Reform Judaism served as their major organization of religious affiliation; and to this effect, the new arrivals practiced different religious traditions and norms, and expected different music and prayer books during worship. Most significantly, however, they were Americans, who saw the Virgin Islands as a new, exciting part of the United States, blushing with promise and much room for growth. In a little over two decades, they would give the synagogue a new form and a new life, reviving the old edifice, yet in doing so retooling the congregation into an American suburban-style religious institution.

To some degree, the path from New York to St. Thomas built upon the well-established trade routes of the Caribbean rum industry. Reinforced particularly during the time of American Prohibition, these routes would connect the rum manufacturing plants that had become famous in the northeast Caribbean region with desirous clientele in and around the city. After Prohibition ended in 1933, the St. Thomas/San Juan/New York rum trade route became a lucrative above-ground operation, channelling several of the most popular brands of rum to the States in significant quantities.

Among the many men to partake of this industry was Sidney Kessler. Born and raised on the Lower East Side of New York and educated at Columbia College, Kessler amassed a small fortune during the 1920s and early 1930s. How he did this remains unknown, and is, to date, undocumented. What is certain is that Kessler must have obtained some knowledge of the rum industry by the mid-1930s, and perhaps had some contacts in trade and distribution routes; for in 1938 he moved down to Puerto Rico and started a distillery that made, among other brands, Carioca Rum. He and his wife, Frances, visited nearby St. Thomas with some frequency while in Puerto Rico, and both grew to love the place. Kessler decided to expand his financial interests to St. Thomas in 1940, and founded the V.I. Distillers with Boston-area investor Benjamin Bayne. Five years later, he sold his Puerto Rico interests and moved to St. Thomas with his wife, where he maintained a temporary residence at a converted Danish tower called the Bluebeard's Castle hotel. At the time, this inn was the largest and most "modern" of St. Thomas's few guest houses.[6] According to a story told by his grandson, one day while living at the hotel Kessler complained about the temperature of his bathwater. In response, the hotel manager snapped: "Why don't you build your own hotel if you want hot water?"[7] Whether this episode motivated him, no one can be sure; however, Kessler's distillery business seemed to be in both financial and legal trouble at the time as well.[8] A change in career might have been an appropriate course of action.

Whatever the case, this event became an allegory for Kessler's next venture: teaming together with Bayne and his two sons-in-law Henry Kimelman and Elliot Fishman to build a new, modern, one-million-dollar, one-hundred-room, luxury hotel on St. Thomas. Kessler purchased land for the new building on a hill overlooking the harbor from one of the old island families and broke ground for the structure in August 1948. The gesture was dramatic and well-publicized, making headlines both in St. Thomas and New York. An early account of the hotel from the *New York Times* stated that the plans included such amenities as "private baths. . . . a salt water swimming pool and outdoor dining terraces . . . modern cabanas and a private yacht basin."[9] Never had St. Thomas seen such a private construction project of this magnitude, as excitement and controversy swirled around the prospective site. With an investment greater than the island's annual operating budget, the prospective power of the hotel's presence gripped the island with anticipation.

As Jewish families, the Kesslers, Baynes, Kimelmans, and Fishmans also visited the synagogue from time to time, and became active in some of the congregation's affairs. Along with several new families who came down from the United States for various reasons, they presented the synagogue with both a blessing and an enigma: their numbers and energy once again helped fill the sanctuary's seats, and swell the membership. At the same time, the new families presented a clash of cultures. For the most part, the Americans were Reform Jews, who emphasized Friday night services over Saturday morning services, pronounced Hebrew prayers with a peculiar accent, and expected organ music to accompany their worship. Just as in other facets of island life, the meeting of old and new island residents was sometimes awkward, leading to a style of factionalization. Some older synagogue members argued for separating the two forms of ritual, even, as one congregant later recalled, at the expense of the synagogue's future:

> . . . [the Americans] walked into the synagogue and they were dissatisfied with [the content and performance of services]—which of course I thought was very presumptuous of them, 'cause they came *here* and they found us with *our* synagogue. And truthfully if I had been Rabbi Sasso, I would have closed that synagogue for a museum and they would have had to build their own synagogue. . . . I would have closed it. Because some of them came and were downright insulting to the man. And he never accepted any salary. He worked here

for twenty five years for fifteen dollars a month! . . . And they're going to come here and tell him what to do . . .? And I would say . . . "Look, gentlemen, you're welcome to come to services; but if you don't want to come to services here, build your own synagogue!"[10]

Others were more amenable to the cultural influx; all, however, noticed a new but strange energy passing into the congregation.

As a mediator between the established families and the incoming residents, Reader Moses Sasso vehemently resisted implementing sweeping changes. At the same time, however, it appears he tried to accommodate the new American Jews as well as he could. Slow, constant pressure and the changing population caused Sasso to introduce several modifications—some of them quite noticeable—to the synagogue's ritual. One of the most drastic of the early changes took place around 1950: The congregation abandoned the Sephardic service and introduced in its place *The Union Prayer Book*, the official prayerbook of American Reform Judaism. According to Reader Sasso's nephew, the new prayerbook and prayer aesthetic made services shorter, and privileged English over Hebrew as the primary language for readings. The new book also had other repercussions. Friday night services, a staple of the Reform movement at the time, began to gain prominence at the synagogue.[11] Moreover, the liberal tenets of Reform Judaism also eliminated the need for the mahogany *mehitza* separating the men and the women; while the separator remained in place, seating arrangements began changing to accommodate mixed attendance.[12] The *Union Prayer Book* did not replace all of St. Thomas's Jewish prayer traditions, however. As part of a seeming compromise between old and new, the synagogue continued to publish a supplementary book with transliterations of its most popular congregational hymns.[13] In the end, the supplement may have made the new prayer book an acceptable addition to the older families. Since none knew Hebrew particularly well, the English readings may have brought relevance to the prayers—for the first time in a long time many of the old congregants could follow a service's text in their hands. Many congregants also seemed to see the substantial length of Sasso's Sephardic rite as an unnecessary formality in the first place. For the Americans, the addition of *The Union Prayer Book* not only made them comfortable praying on the island: It also gave the synagogue a modern, progressive atmosphere that would be both familiar to them and attractive to other American Jews visiting St. Thomas. Such adaptations resulted in a transitional, hybrid form of observance the congregants called "Reform Sephardic," forged around a prayer ritual that incorporated the interests of two contrasting groups without greatly disrupting either one's traditions. In this way, all parts of the Jewish community managed to live in a kind of contrapuntal harmony that would continue for many years.

Around the same time, and perhaps related to the introduction of the new prayerbook, the more successful older families and the new American families began to pool contributions in order to provide Sasso with a regular salary for the first time.[14] The amount was small—probably not enough for a living—but it turned Sasso from a devoted volunteer into a professional. The salary also re-established an employment relationship between the synagogue and its chosen religious leader, and thus likely served to give the congregation a greater degree of control over its own activities.

While the new members began to effect change in the synagogue, the old members found themselves growing into social positions of honor. The German and East European families who had maintained successful businesses since the turn of the century became experienced colleagues to the new arrivals, gaining respect among those in the burgeoning St. Thomas commercial industry. Sephardic families, not as well-off financially overall, nonetheless held on to an air of society and integrity representative of the "old" island spirit; due in part to this, a few Sephardic Jews gained prominence in the island's government. Together, they took on important roles in serving the island during its transition to a center for American tourism.

One of the most beloved of these figures was a native islander who helped St. Thomas take its first cautious steps toward determining its own commercialization. In late 1949, when appointed continental Governor William Hastie left his office for a U.S. Circuit Court appointment, the Virgin Islands Legislative Assembly urged President Truman to appoint a native Virgin Islander to the position. The assembly had in mind a forty-eight-year-old "native son" and career government employee named Morris De Castro, who had assumed the acting governorship after Hastie's departure.[15] President Truman approved the assembly's suggestion on February 28, 1950, unleashing a wave of celebration and victory on the island. For the first time under the Americans, the Virgin Islands had one of their own citizens at the political helm.[16]

Morris De Castro was a sincere, dynamic, tall, and gaunt man. Though not a Virgin Islander in the most literal sense, he had numerous reasons to claim his nativity. Morris's parents, David Maduro De Castro and Hannah Nannette "Ada" (Sasso) De Castro, were born, raised, and married on St. Thomas as members of well-established families with long histories in the island. Soon after their wedding in 1895, the young couple decided to try their luck in

Panama. Their only child, Morris, was born there on February 5, 1902. The family's fortunes took a drastic turn for the worse a few years later, however: Ada contracted fever (possibly yellow fever, which was gripping the area at the time) and died on June 21, 1906. Stung by the loss, David De Castro returned to St. Thomas to live with his family. On October 1, 1907, he sent a letter to the wardens of the synagogue, requesting Morris De Castro's name to be entered into the institution's birth records.[17] This they duly noted and performed, and the young child became a bona fide member of the congregation.

Young Morris grew up on the island attending the Catholic School of the Convent of Les Sacre Coeurs, joining with Jewish and non-Jewish children in what was considered the best education on the island. Along with a liberal arts education, De Castro also developed his clerical skills during his school years, having "studied stenography and typewriting after school hours" and taken some time to focus on accounting as well.[18] At age fifteen, he graduated from the convent school, and the next year began work as a junior clerk for the sanitation department in the naval government.

A competent, confident, and intelligent worker, De Castro quickly rose in rank from junior clerk to secretary for the naval station in 1920, to chief clerk to the governor and governor's secretary in 1921, to assistant government secretary and assistant commissioner of finance in 1931, to commissioner of finance in 1934.[19] In the ten years that followed, De Castro spent several stretches as acting governor, filling in the holes between a rapid succession of administrations. In 1944, he continued his political rise with a promotion to administrative assistant to the governor, and, the next year, to government secretary of the Virgin Islands.[20] When governor Hastie vacated his office in October 1949, Morris De Castro became acting governor once again, causing *Time Magazine* to quip: "he has already served more actual time in the Islands' top executive job than anyone officially appointed to the post."[21] Experienced, active, and popular among Virgin Islanders, De Castro was thus already in power when President Truman made his appointment official. The native son nonetheless took his final promotion with humility and gravity. According to the same *Time Magazine* report, when De Castro first heard of his nomination, he immediately went to the synagogue to pray.[22]

De Castro's nomination served to galvanize and empower the inhabitants of the islands. The older residents, who owned little more than real estate, maintained their primary influence through the local government. Until De Castro, however, appointed Americans filled the highest government positions. With a "native" now in the top spot, Virgin Islanders hoped they could soon address their own needs and destiny in a time of great change and activity. On March 10, 1950, the Virgin Islands Legislative Assembly confirmed De Castro's appointment unanimously.[23] A week later, during an island-wide weekend of prayer preceding the inauguration festivities, the governor-elect spoke at the synagogue's Friday night service offering a vision of unity consistent with what he saw as the societal values of his island. "He stated that he looked forward to the sincere cooperation of all the people, not alone those of his own faith, and that while he was proud of being of the Jewish faith he wanted the congregation to follow through with him, not alone as good Jews, but as good, spirited progressive citizens who would whole heartedly join in all endeavors toward community affairs."[24] In his statement, De Castro beseeched the populace to overcome its recent factioning—attributed to American influence—in order to partake of a common mission and future. Echoing sentiments from his youth, he equated religious devotion with civic service, and ethnic identification with local pride. At 10 A.M. the following Monday, with six thousand people, numerous news agencies, and several U.S. dignitaries in attendance, the gubernatorial inauguration began as "Rabbi" Moses D. Sasso gave an invocation.[25] Capping the ensuing activities, Morris Fidanque De Castro took the oath of office and promised to fill the position of Governor of the Virgin Islands. From the very beginning, De Castro saw his mission to improve and develop the territory as a personal one. "These islands are my home and have been the home of my family for generations," he announced. "I have shared your problems, your joys and your sorrows. I am one of you. If I fail, you fail. If I succeed, you succeed. My administration, then, must be a community undertaking, and I plan to make it so."[26] No longer would the islands be subject to the policies of colonial leaders: They now had the power to rule themsleves, make their own decisions and chart their own destinies.

―◦∿∿◦―

THE VIRGIN ISLE HOTEL OPENED ITS DOORS for business on December 15, 1950. Billing itself as the "Most Magnificent Hotel in the Americas," it had far exceeded its original plans in every way. Cost had ballooned from $1 million to $3 million; construction took a year and a half longer than expected. The two-story structure originally designed by architect Harold Sterner had doubled to four stories, and the number of rooms increased from one hundred to one hundred forty. According to *New York Times* travel reporter Aline B. Louchheim, the new hotel touted all the most modern amenities, including a "kidney shaped swimming pool and French cuisine. . . . a lobby with a terrazzo floor and marble columns, a writing room, a breakfast patio with lush planting, and stores." She continued by focusing on one of the communal areas: "The main air-conditioned bar, coyly titled 'The Foolish Virgin,' preserves the [harbor] view through one glass wall and has aquariums set into one of its other, mahogany walls."[27] Enjoying tax breaks created by the De Castro administration, and benefitting from a revived Virgin Islands Tourist Development Board, the Virgin Isle Hotel served a brisk business from the very start.[28]

In many ways, Sidney Kessler's venture offered one of the first completely manufactured portrayals of St. Thomas, based on a conception of the island as a carefree "tropical paradise." Steel bands, sea turtle races, and other forms of entertainment occupied the guests in the evenings.[29] During the day, vacationers could enjoy the the lush scenery and views of the island either outside on the patio or from the comfort of air-conditioned guest rooms. Promising "the utmost in Old World Luxury without sacrifice of New World Comfort," the Virgin Isle Hotel's furnishings and amenities came almost entirely from the United States.[30] New York, specifically, seemed as much a focal point for the hotel's creation as St. Thomas: New York–based companies comprised over half the building's contractors, and the hotel's owners maintained a New York office for reservations and information at 730 Fifth Avenue.[31] Such provisions invariably led tourists to expect—and receive—a well-choreographed taste of "Caribbean" life, replete with all its pleasures, yet protected from its hardships.

The effects of the Virgin Isle upon the tourist industry were dramatic.[32] Tourist expenditures on hotels and guest houses on St. Thomas more than doubled from $535,000 to $1,218,000 between fiscal years 1950 and 1951, and trebled by fiscal year 1952 to $1,624,000. In the island's shops and restaurants during the same time period, visitor expenditures nearly doubled from $1.1 million to $2.03 million.[33] The Virgin Isle Hotel further capitalized on creative vacation packages and positive word of mouth to enjoy continued success, even during the off-season.[34] Once a daring venture, the hotel soon became merely a precedent on the increasingly alluring island. Dreams of similar success and a friendly development environment attracted more investors to the island, spawning construction of roads, transit systems, and additional modern buildings.

In addition to its economic impact, the Virgin Isle Hotel also contributed to an interesting social phenomenon taking place on the island. Americans began to see St. Thomas as a place of opportunity, envisioning the territory as the ideal place to start a new life. Those who vacationed at the hotel some-times became so enamored of the environment, the weather, and the people they met, or became so inspired by the optimistic economic opportunities on the island, that they decided to move to St. Thomas for the long term.[35] Oth-ers simply came down to open new local businesses, often abandoning com-pletely their careers in the United States. Renting and/or building their own homes, these "resident tourists" dwelt in St. Thomas for a few months, years, winters, or the rest of their lives, and contributed to the island community in significant ways.[36] Their numbers were not great, but their percentages were notable: From 1950 to 1960, the total white population in the Virgin Islands rose over eighty percent (from 2,975 to 5,373), comprising approximately fif-teen percent of the overall population by the end of the decade.[37]

Several of those relocating to the island during this time were Jewish, in-cluding Springfield, Massachusetts, resident Kate Shpetner. Shpetner first came to the Virgin Isle Hotel during a winter season in the early 1950s. One day in the early part of her stay, Sidney and Frances Kessler noticed the "very handsome, very striking" fiftyish woman, and engaged her in conversation; she mentioned she was Jewish, and the Kesslers asked her to join them for Friday evening services at the synagogue. After sitting through the ritual, Shpetner met several of the congregants, including Governor Morris De Cas-tro, and received an invitation to attend a community reception for a dock-ing naval vessel the following evening. By the end of her stay, she had come to know many of the island's more prominent residents, even discovering a college connection with one of St. Thomas's old families. Between the people and the climate, Shpetner found a return to the island inevitable.

Arriving back home in the middle of a New England January, Shpetner quickly weighed her options, and made the decision to return to St. Thomas for another four to six weeks. This pattern continued for the next few win-ters: Shpetner would rent a room at a house on Government Hill, staying sometimes at the more pricey Virgin Isle Hotel when space was not available. To supplement her stateside income, she worked for one of the local mer-chants whom she knew through the synagogue; in the evenings, after the workday ended, she would occasionally visit a social club to dance and/or commune with friends. By the mid-1950s, Shpetner had decided to buy land on St. Thomas; she had a house built, and moved in permanently.[38]

The founders of the Virgin Isle Hotel built permanent homes for them-selves on St. Thomas at this time as well. In 1955, the Kessler, Bayne, Kimel-man, and Fishman families purchased a plot of land on the hill behind their hotel and constructed a small group of spacious houses. Their residence on the island, however, did not sit well with some. Islanders knew the religious identities of these families very well, and in time, they began calling this group of houses "The Gaza Strip."[39] The name, strongly disliked by the families, reflected a level of wariness among the significant elements of the populace with the new, major changes happening in the island's landscape and economy. Identified with an infamous region of the Israeli political scene, it expressed some islanders' discontent with the newcomers, viewing them as an intrusion from abroad whose efforts at business came more at St. Thomas's expense than its benefit. For new residents, the question of "belonging" was a serious one, and the debate over who was (or deserved to be) a "true Virgin Islander" continued to roil for decades.

Shpetner joined the Kesslers, Baynes, Kimelmans, Fishmans, and others in services at the synagogue on Friday nights. Reader Sasso, who turned sixty in 1954, continued to lead the prayers and other synagogue functions; and he enlisted his new *Union Prayer Book* Rabbi's Manual to aid with unfamiliar readings and practices. While the newcomers respected him as a figure, they often criticized his skills as a spiritual leader. The opposite of the imposing, erudite religious leader seen as an ideal in the United States, Sasso was a small, simple man with little education, whose protruding belly and drooping jowls caused one congregant to compare him to a walrus when he spoke.[40] To supplement his income, Sasso took on a part-time job selling liquor at the Paiewonskys' Main Street store.[41] This was entirely consistent with his mercantile training and his role in St. Thomas's Jewish community, but the Americans found such behavior to be scandalous.[42] His devotion to the pulpit impressed everyone, however, and his small salary placed little financial burden on the synagogue. Thus, the congregation decided simply to wait until he retired before looking for a replacement.

While Sasso was an object of ridicule for some, he still inspired reverence in the boys he trained for their Bar Mitzvahs. Paul Hoffman, son of a lawyer who came down to the island with his family in 1948, viewed the aging reader as a man who seemed to connect "all the way back to Moses and Abraham." During their lessons after school, Hoffman would join a small group of boys in Sasso's house at the bottom of Crystal Gade. The reader would serve them cake and "specials" (shaved ice topped with a sweet syrup) as he taught them the service and the biblical readings for their respective Bar Mitzvah days. Sasso's technique was purely phonetic: The boys learned to read by ear, never understanding the Hebrew letters over which their fingers passed. Nonetheless, they studied diligently: after all, when Sasso was not pleased, it seemed that "the patriarchs were not far behind."[43] At their respective Bar Mitzvah days, the young men would present their progress to the congregation. The Jewish community, which came out to support each individual, would listen to the words of the reading (which probably sounded equally cryptic to them), and then congratulate the boy on his passage into adulthood.[44] Sometimes the day continued with a reception and celebration at the Virgin Isle Hotel. In the process, Sasso would gain credit for his role in the boy's Jewish education.[45]

As the community developed, the new members began to increase their involvement with the synagogue by founding subsidiary social groups modeled after those that existed in American suburban congregations. By far the most successful of these groups was the women's club. Started by Kate Shpetner in the mid-1950s, the group enfranchised the female members of the congregation for the first time in decades, and created an outlet for social action and fundraising on the synagogue's behalf. Women from all walks of congregational life became active in the group in some way or other: Frances Kessler and Irene Bayne (wife of Benjamin Bayne) joined with Franzi Coulianos (Israel Levin's granddaughter), Marilyn Kreke (a member of the Moron family) and others to discuss local issues and bring up worthy projects for consideration. Once per month, the group would meet for a social function; at other times, the organization planned and ran island-wide activities such as rummage sales and benefit film showings. Its financial and cultural contributions to the synagogue soon became considerable, causing the group to wield a great deal of power within the workings of the congregation.

One of the most successful undertakings the women spearheaded was the institution of an annual community Passover *seder.* Started around the same time as the women's group itself, the *seder* took place each spring at the Virgin Isle Hotel and proved to be one of the most attended-to events in St. Thomas's Jewish liturgical year. A large majority of the Jewish community came to the meal: Even members of the Paiewonsky and Levin families, once hosts to elaborate *seders* themselves, showed their support by purchasing tickets and attending the celebration. Importantly, however, community attendance was not exclusive: the *seder* also billed itself as a public event. Advertisements and stories in the local paper implied that anyone who purchased a ticket was welcome to join the Jewish community in the affair.[46]

The local press also served a role in publicizing and popularizing the *seder.* In 1958, for example, the event became the subject of a front page story in the *Daily News.* Mentioning that year's *seder* would be in honor of "Rabbi and Mrs. Moses D. Sasso," the paper continued with a description of the upcoming evening, presumably provided by the *seder*'s planning committee: "The Passover Seder will begin with the Traditional Service recalling the events leading to the exodus of the Jews from the land of Egypt and out of bondage. Then there will be served the Passover feast, complete in every memorable detail. . . . The Committee members of this affair are making certain that this Feast of Passover will be the most elaborate event in St. Thomas in our time."[47] Phrased in hyperbolic fashion, the article fit right in with the promotional tone gaining strength on the island.

The Passover feast itself was also a point of vigorous debate in *seder* preparations. The organizing committee's ambitious aim, according to the news story, was to "recall the festive Seder in the homes of Jewish parents and grandparents all over the world."[48] Such an accomplishment was no mean feat: To some Jewish residents, the Passover Seder was a family event often recalled by the smell and taste of the food prepared "just so." Organizers of the St. Thomas *seder* argued vehemently over numerous details in the menu, from the foods themselves to the size and texture of the traditional matzo balls (or *knaydloch*).[49] After all the disagreements took place, however, the affair came off as a success. A program for a *seder* in the mid-1960s presented a choice of food consistent with the dietary restrictions of Passover: "Gefilte fish [with] red horse radish, Chicken soup with knaydloch, Roast Chicken [with vegetables], matzos, Passover wine, club soda, fresh fruit cup with sherbet, sponge cake, macaroons, demi-tasse."[50] Notably, the meal was consistent with Eastern European Passover cuisine traditions, indicating the backgrounds of its major organizers and further hinting at the changes taking place in the synagogue.

As the *seder* commenced, guests in semi-formal attire sat around tables while Moses Sasso, sitting at the head table, led the retelling of the Passover story. Each table had its own *seder* plate, displaying symbolic items specific to the Passover celebration; and each guest received a program listing the synagogue officers and *seder* organizing committee as well as the evening's menu.[51] By all accounts, those attending enjoyed the *seders* thoroughly. The event, meanwhile, caught on famously, eventually providing an annual forum in which the Jewish community could share its old and new traditions with both islanders and tourists.[52]

The synagogue's proximity to the American Reform movement became more pronounced as time went on, as evidenced through the congregation's expanding range of activities. In 1955, for example, the congregation brought in guest lecturer Rabbi Dr. Bernard Heller for a weekend of lectures on religion, including the sermon at the synagogue's Friday evening service.[53] Heller, a visiting professor of Philosophy of Religion and Ethics at Hebrew Union College at the time, was a prominent and colorful member of the Reform movement: the author of two Ph.D. theses and several books, Heller counted among his pulpits the University of Michigan and Bombay, India.[54] He had, additionally, a distant connection to the St. Thomas Jewish community: twenty-five years earlier, he had officiated at the marriage of his cousin Ethel to Ralph Paiewonsky.[55] The visit to the island appeared to go successfully; and Heller himself became so overtaken with the beauty of the islands that he commented during a speech to a group of island ministers:

> A poetic individual was so overwhelmed by the transcending view of Naples . . . that he coined the adage, "See Naples and Die" by which he meant when you see Naples you have seen all there is to see. I should like to apply this adage in a rephrased form to these Isles. "See the Virgin Isles and Live," for they afford not merely an inkling of Paradise on Earth but its very exemplification.

By 1958, Rabbi Heller, too, had become a "resident tourist," in St. Thomas; he would live on the island either full- or part-time for nearly a decade.[56] His continued relationship with the synagogue, however, would be minimal if it existed at all.[57]

As the annual number of tourists to St. Thomas skyrocketed through the late 1950s—breaking the hundred-thousand mark in 1958—the synagogue found itself becoming a popular historic landmark. Intellectual interest in the congregation had already hinted at its significance within American Jewish history: In July 1952, representatives from the recently established American Jewish Archives in Cincinnati swept through St. Thomas as part of a whirlwind expedition of the West Indies and South America, recording and photocopying the congregation's archival materials for deposit in its own facilities.[58] Around the same time, the St. Thomas public library's head librarian Enid M. Baa began compiling a card file of the synagogue's births, deaths, and marriages as part of a larger project involving the island's churches. In 1958, however, the synagogue received its first public honor: It became one of twelve Virgin Islands buildings "of outstanding historical and architectural significance" selected by the national Historical American Buildings Survey Program.[59] Moreover, since it was situated just north of the rejuvenated town center, the old sanctuary also began to attract the interest of tourists. Romantic imaginations became active at the sight of the building's exotic Sephardic interior, sand floor, and mahogany furniture, not to mention its very existence on St. Thomas.

When interested tourists began to ask about the synagogue's past, the congregation realized that its own history was also a matter of public interest. A written account of the congregation's past, in addition to providing the amateur historian with information, could serve as a lucrative fundraiser for the financially needy congregation. Synagogue president and local lawyer Harry Dreis was the first to address this need in 1958 with a small, typed fold-out pamphlet entitled "Jewish Historical Development in the Virgin Islands." Dreis's intended audience was clear from the beginning: "The visitor to the Virgin Islands finds the oldest synagogue of the Americas. . . ."[60] After a short introduction, Dreis entertained the reader with a survey of significant dates and events in Virgin Islands Jewish history. While a sincere start, the pamphlet was itself in part a product of an overactive imagination and sophomoric research, and contained some woeful inaccuracies, beginning with his assertion that the synagogue was the oldest in the New World. Dreis's cardinal error, however, was confusing the history of St. Thomas with that of Sao Tomé, a small Portuguese island off the West Coast of Africa. This produced impressive but ridiculous results. According to the pamphlet, Jews first came to the island as exiles from Portugal in 1493, but died at the hands of the Carib Indians; in 1643, St. Thomas had "Sixty flourishing sugar mills operated by Jewish inhabitants"; eight years later, the first Jews from Holland arrived on St. Thomas; the current synagogue, meanwhile, had become "a memorial to the first synagogue built in St. Thomas in 1688."[61] Dreis's work indeed answered popular questions; rather than clarifying myths, however, the history created new ones. Congregants who saw the pamphlet had other concerns as well: Although they criticized the history for its spotty factual accuracy, they also deplored its amateurish presentation and writing. An account of the synagogue's past needed to be correct; but it also needed to be a desirable and handsome souvenir, equivalent to the other amenities on the island.[62]

Isidor Paiewonsky addressed this need the following year. Although "by day a prosperous merchant," the forty-nine-year-old Paiewonsky also enjoyed collecting information about the history of his island, in the process becoming a "skilled and passionate antiquarian."[63] With research associates in Denmark and elsewhere, Paiewonsky conducted a much more thorough search of sources, and compiled a well-written, well-documented text. While the format of the history remained essentially the same as Dreis's work—an introduction followed by a chronology of major events—it was substantially longer and more detailed, with footnotes citing sources for many entries. To add to the account's appeal, Paiewonsky added a black-and-white photograph of the synagogue's interior and convinced renowned author Herman Wouk—who himself became a "resident tourist" with his wife and two sons in 1958—to write an introduction.[64] Published in 1959, the twenty-two-page "Historical Developments in the Virgin Islands, 1665–1959" was a welcome replacement for Dreis's work. The overall product was attractive and readable, providing the interested tourist with a colorful yet more or less accurate story of the Virgin Islands' Jewish community. Though updated and expanded somewhat over the years to accommodate new eras and new printing technologies, Paiewonsky's text remained the standard reference for the St. Thomas synagogue's history for over four decades.

As part of his entry for 1959, Paiewonsky recognized an important change in the status of the women's group. He commented: "A Sisterhood was formed recently that is making its weight felt in the community." Indeed, through Kate Shpetner's determination, the women's group assumed the title of "Sisterhood" in the late 1950s. The self-designation was significant, for it showed the group's identification with synagogue-based women's social service organizations throughout the United States. By early 1959, the Sisterhood numbered twenty-three members, and held meetings in the synagogue vestry on the first Monday of each month.

The Sisterhood also became the first synagogue group to seek affiliation with the American Reform movement, a sign that Reform Judaism had made significant headway as the observance style of choice for the congregation. In a historic move, the group applied on March 27, 1959, to the National Federation of Temple Sisterhoods to sponsor a chapter in St. Thomas. Marilyn Kreke, corresponding secretary of the St. Thomas Synagogue Sisterhood, sent in the appropriate papers. At the time, Kate Shpetner was president; "Mrs. Sidney Kessler" was vice-president; "Mrs. Jerome Solomon" took on the responsibilities of treasurer, and Elaine Robles served as recording secretary.

Based on its membership application, the St. Thomas Sisterhood had aims completely different from those considered "standard" among Reform synagogue Sisterhoods. When faced with the task of filling in "chairmen" for committees representing such organizations as "Youth, Education and Sisterhood (YES) Fund" and "World Union for Progressive Judaism Activities," Kate

Shpetner responded with a handwritten note. "None of these have been organized," she wrote, adding: "There has *never* been a Sisterhood in St. Thomas.
With a possible 30 members & *no more* to draw on, our chief aims at the moment are—*possible*—school[,] restoration of ancient, historic synagogue
and cemetery and establishment of a library."[65] With a basic mission for the
congregation's welfare, the Sisterhood could barely afford to take on responsibilities that it saw as secondary. The National Federation of Temple Sisterhoods, apparently recognizing the congregation's unique needs, approved the
application on June 30, bringing a part of the synagogue under the umbrella
of the American Reform movement for the first time.[66]

On St. Thomas the following evening, Kate Shpetner joined Morris De
Castro, the St. Thomas Choral Society, the members of the Hebrew Congregation, and many well-wishers from around the island to honor Rabbi
Moses D. Sasso on his forty-fifth year leading the congregation. Sasso had
enjoyed an honorary commemoration every five years since his twenty-fifth
anniversary in 1939. This time, however, he received a local honor that he
likely considered his most prestigious: By virtue of his long and dedicated
service to the synagogue, the congregation conferred upon him the high distinction of "Negnim Zemiroth Israel," the "Sweet Singer of Israel." In one
way, this title placed Sasso on a level with his predecessor, David Cardoze,
and served as a heartfelt token of the congregation's gratitude. More than
that, however, the ceremony seemed a symbolic end to the Jewish community's struggle for survival, and a mark of triumph for the once-foundering
synagogue.

After an opening prayer, Rabbi Sasso entered the portal of the sanctuary
and walked along the sand-covered floor as former Governor Morris De Castro sang the hymn "Baruch Aba" ("Blessed be [he] who comes"); once a familiar Sephardic prayer, the song's new designation in the evening's program
as "Ancient Hebrew Hymn" subtly indicated the synagogue's new orientation. In between selections sung by the St. Thomas Choral society, dedications by Shpetner and two members of the synagogue's board, and a sermon
by the pastor of the island's Evangelical Lutheran Church, Sasso received his
new designation along with a gift of tribute from the congregation. Sasso's
title bore little significance within the American Jewish organizational structure: None of the United States Jewish movements, least of all the Reform
movement, recognized a "Sweet Singer of Israel." Nonetheless, the congregation showed great respect by keeping the old tradition alive, even retaining
the Sephardic spelling of the title in the evening's program.[67] Sasso, who fin-

ished the program with remarks and a closing benediction, probably appreciated this gesture, especially as American Jewish influences continued to transform his world, his work, and his traditions.

—*w*—

By the start of the 1960s, St. Thomas had come a long way toward fulfilling its potential as an American tourist paradise. Over half of the 165,000 tourists who came to St. Thomas and St. John in the fiscal year 1960 arrived via airplane; and cruise ships docked at St. Thomas with ever-increasing frequency.[68] Once on the island, tourists had the option of staying in one of forty hotels, offering a wide spectrum of luxury and price.[69] They could shop for jewelry, fabrics, and other items at steep discounts in the town's "duty free" stores; spend time basking and bathing at the beaches; and wile away the evenings at a growing number of restaurants and night clubs throughout the territory. Increased diplomatic difficulties between the United States and Fidel Castro–controlled Cuba diverted many prospective Havana vacationers to the Virgin Islands, accelerating growth further. Tourism became so central to the islands' economy that the government turned the once-experimental Virgin Islands Tourist Development Board into an official Department of Tourism and Trade in 1955, and eventually moved its office into the governor's house. The department's annual budget, which was at first negligible, would grow to nearly half a million dollars by the middle of the decade.[70]

Once a "backwater town" where "you couldn't pass on the street without saying good morning or good afternoon," according to one resident, St. Thomas began regaining its cosmopolitan atmosphere and reputation.[71] The island attracted numerous celebrities and politicians, whose vacation visits would receive ample coverage in the local and national press. According to Paul Hoffman, it was not surprising to meet such personalities as Isaac Stern, Jan Peerce, or Coleman Hawkins while walking down the street. On one occasion Hoffman's father disappeared for three hours, only to come back reporting that he had just eaten lunch with Winston Churchill.[72]

In addition to its famous vacationers, the island and its promising future also attracted the interests of large corporations. In 1959, the Chase Manhattan Bank bought out the local West Indies Bank and Trust Company; and in early July 1960 the Hilton Corporation brokered a fifty-year lease with Sidney Kessler's lawyers, transforming the Virgin Isle Hotel into the Virgin Isle Hilton.[73] Such moves showed the confidence with which development took place, as nationalized industry began to recognize the desirability of maintaining properties in the newly rising region.

In 1961, a new, dynamic, savvy, and business-minded politician took office as governor of the island. Raphael Moses "Ralph" Paiewonsky—the son of Isaac Paiewonsky and brother to Isidor—was a native to the island as well. Like Morris De Castro, he was a member in good standing of the synagogue. His background and rise to leadership of the island, however, was substantially different. Ralph Paiewonsky's primary education in the island's Convent School had been curtailed: When he was in eighth grade, the institution closed down, and he took on a job as a messenger-clerk at the island's Navy Supply Office. Two years later, in 1923, Paiewonsky moved with his mother, brother, aunt, uncle, and cousins to Bensonhurst, Brooklyn. While maintaining contact with his St. Thomas family and taking occasional trips to the island, he continued his education in New York at Boys' Commercial High School and New York University. Graduating with a bachelors degree in chemistry in 1930, Ralph promptly went back to St. Thomas at his father's request to help run and expand the family's small empire of businesses.[74]

Paiewonsky wrote that deplorable local conditions and strained relations with the United States authorities brought him into politics. Starting in 1936, he served five consecutive two-year terms on the Municipal Council of St. Thomas and St. John. After leaving the council, he helped found the territory's Democratic Club; this eventually led him to represent the Virgin Islands at the 1952 Democratic National Convention in Chicago. Further activities on the island kept him continually in the heat of the spotlight. In 1953, Paiewonsky helped establish the West Indies Bank and Trust Co. The next year he had a role in drafting the islands' Revised Organic Act, and lobbied the United States Senate for the document's approval.

In 1958, Paiewonsky hosted Senator John F. Kennedy during his trip to the Virgin Islands to speak to the local Democratic Committee. Three years later, the newly elected President Kennedy nominated Paiewonsky for governor of the territory. The U.S. Senate confirmed the nomination on March 27, 1961, and the inauguration took place on St. Thomas the following week.[75] "Lord and Master of all men," began Rabbi Sasso, as he presented the opening prayer. "May Thy Spirit rest upon our Governor, Ralph Paiewonsky, and may Thy grace come in ever flowing measure upon him. . . ."[76] Professing a strong American orientation, a great deal of business experience both in St. Thomas and stateside, and ample connections in Washington, D.C., Paiewonsky saw himself as a local success story, a "Man for the People" with a deep concern for improving the lives of the Virgin Islanders. As he took the oath of office, he ushered the islands into a period of dramatic, though sometimes controversial expansion.

Although he did not appear to be a particularly observant man, Paiewonsky maintained involvement with the synagogue during his years as governor. He seemed to identify with Judaism as a system of moral convictions (particularly in business dealings and personal relations), and viewed the synagogue as a place for social gathering and interaction. There was reason to this approach: As a child, Paiewonsky learned little in the areas of Hebrew and prayer. However, he grew up with the camaraderie of a close Jewish community, associated his father's business ethic with his religious tenets, and appeared to associate with the Jewish holidays through the social gatherings they precipitated.[77] Maintaining these approaches to Judaism throughout his life, his visits to the synagogue appeared to be mainly social ones. Services would be an indicator of who was on-island that week, and who was away. It was also a time to share new ideas, and discuss progress on old ones.

The renewed business mentality of the island caused many of the recent resident tourists to take up a similar approach to their religion. Newer arrivals tended to see synagogue gatherings as opportunities to find others with similar backgrounds and pursuits. "It was where we went to meet people. . . . it wasn't until we came down [to St. Thomas] that we joined the synagogue," recalled Carol Weinberger, who moved to the island from the Bronx with her husband in 1959 to start a nightclub. Though the island population was growing, it was still hard for Jewish continentals (and continentals in general) to find a "neighborhood." Many therefore looked to the synagogue as a community.

With each passing year the percentage of continentals in the synagogue grew, while the veteran members from the first half of the century passed away. Isaac and Rebecca Paiewonsky died in July and November of 1963 respectively, leaving their legendary "Big House" to the care of their sons Ralph and Isidor and their daughter Paulina Puritz.[78] Else Siggelkow, daughter of Israel Levin, died in November 1964. Meanwhile, according to the congregation's records, the German and East European families appeared to take two different trajectories. The children of the East European families (such as the Paiewonskys) established social and familial ties with New York, and many married the descendents of other East European Jews; the majority maintained connection with their businesses in St. Thomas, and affiliated with the synagogue. The descendants of the Sephardic families, however, were more likely to intermarry. At least two of these couples stayed on the island as members of the congregation; nonetheless, the Sephardic culture held by the synagogue's founders was declining to a low ebb. Rabbi Sasso's union to Esther Watson in 1936 turned out to be the last marriage of indigenous Sephardic Jews on the island, and the birth of their daughter Emmeline Joy three years later was the last birth in the synagogue's register attributed to Sephardic parents. The congregation's Sephardic religious background, though cherished, was receding from practice into exoticism.[79]

Perhaps the last celebration of the congregation's active Sephardic tradition came on July 1, 1964, on the occasion of Rabbi Moses Sasso's "Golden Jubilee"—his fiftieth anniversary with the synagogue.[80] Entering the twilight of his career, Sasso was both the only remaining minister on the island to remember serving under the Danish administration, and the last person in the Jewish community who could conduct a service according to the Sephardic rite. Beginning as a young, inexperienced lay-leader, Sasso had become a seasoned old veteran, serving nearly three generations of congregants through one of the most difficult times in the synagogue's history. On a night soaked by "heavy rains," about two hundred people packed the synagogue to celebrate the minister's achievement.[81] Former congregants and well-wishers arrived from all over the Caribbean region: A delegation of more than fifteen friends and relatives came from Panama for the event; other visitors hailed from Puerto Rico, New York, and Washingon, D.C.[82]

At 8 P.M., aging former governor and Master of Ceremonies Morris De Castro chanted "Baruch Aba," just as he had done five years previously. Sasso processed into the sanctuary, across the sand floor, and up to his place on the pulpit. Rabbi Nathan Witkin, representing the Jewish Welfare Board of Canal Zone, Panama, led an opening prayer. Ernest Sasso, the Rabbi's brother, recited the "Prayer for the Rabbi, Congregation, Government and Country." Then Svend Mylner, Danish sea captain and husband of Amalia Paiewonsky, read the 1914 letter confirming Sasso's appointment as assistant reader in its original Danish; Governor Ralph Paiewonsky followed by reading an English translation of the same document. The president of the island legislature rose and delivered his remarks of admiration, and then four ministers from other island churches added their congratulations. Sasso received a gift and more greetings from his congregation; and Walter Clarence Watson, Sasso's step-son returned from Panama, presented his father with a tribute from the Sasso family. Finally, after the president of the congregation gave his address, Rabbi Sasso rose to the reader's desk to speak.

Sasso was grateful for the honor, for his health, for reaching this milestone, and for his wife and family. However, instead of dwelling upon past

memories, Sasso preferred instead to look forward. "While it is good to celebrate the achievements of the past," he intoned, "the accent tonight must be
on the FUTURE. . . . We must dedicate ourselves anew to the great tasks that
lie before us. Let us re-consecrate ourselves, in the spirit of consecration that
filled the hearts of the founders and the builders of our Institution, so many
centuries ago, so that the future of our Synagogue, our Religion may be even
greater and more glorious than was its past. Let us resolve tonight to strive to
bring closer that glorious 'and it shall be' . . ." Sasso's comments expressed
hope for the synagogue, and optimism for island harmony. Americanization
had taken its toll on the island over the past fifty years through the outside
imposition of racism, cultural differences, and indifference—toward the
Jewish community, as well as the island community—but Sasso felt he now
had reason to see a bright future. The economy was improving, island residents were enjoying their own rights and obtaining better educations, and
constructive dialogue between the continentals and the islanders seemed to
be the focus of the day. Sasso rued the loss of so many of his relatives and ancestors; but at the same time, he invoked their spirits to bless the congregation as it moved onward. As the Rabbi delivered his speech, he looked out
over a living, resurging congregation. Many new people inhabited the mahogany benches his ancestors had occupied over a century ago. Now these
people watched and listened as an old man from a bygone time pushed them
forward.

After the service, the celebration adjourned to dinner at the Virgin Isle
Hilton. A crowd numbering about five hundred applauded Rabbi Sasso as
George W. Westerman, the International Secretary of the American International Academy, presented the minister with the Star and Cross of Academic Honor. Westerman conferred the award with a wish that "the significant
ceremonies of this anniversary, now culminating in this brilliant reception,
inspire all of us to play a more positive role in creating a world order dedicated to human solidarity and international goodwill."[83] The presentation
honored Sasso as a model of conduct for the entire Virgin Islands; an island
"native" whose honorable activities symbolized the territory's integrity, and
justified its calls to the United States for increased self-determination.

For over a year after the celebration, Moses Sasso continued to serve as
Rabbi in St. Thomas. His pulpit tenure, however, was in its final phase. Sasso
saw the synagogue's future ensured; but for him, the time was fast arriving to
step down and let momentum take the congregation in new directions. Over
seventy years old, he ministered to a community composed primarily of
Americans, and led a "Reform Sephardic" service on Friday nights and Sat-

urday mornings. His congregation's newfound activity came through recently formed groups, including the Sasso-Cardoze Lodge of B'nai B'rith (#2488) and the Sisterhood. In his own eyes, Sasso had done his duty to the congregation; he soon announced his plans to retire, citing both his long run in the St. Thomas pulpit and his declining health. At first, the synagogue's board resisted Sasso's efforts. The minister continued to press his request, however, and by the end of 1965, the synagogue's board of representatives reluctantly accepted the rabbi's resignation, effective once another replacement had been secured. By the overwhelming support of the congregation, he was granted the honorary title of "Rabbi Emeritus" and given a monthly pension equal to his current income of three hundred dollars per month.[84]

The synagogue immediately began to search for their next religious leader. One of the greatest issues the congregation faced was the matter of a salary for the new minister. Sasso had performed his office for a pittance: Even when the synagogue started paying a more substantial wage for his services, it was far below a standard stateside rate. In order to attract worthy rabbinical candidates to fill the position, the synagogue's members thus realized that they had to assemble a good financial package. An American rabbi, after all, required an American salary—whether or not it was a substantial economic burden on the congregation.

Meanwhile, the St. Thomas synagogue president contacted the Rabbinic Placement Commission of the Union of American Hebrew Congregations in New York for suitable candidates. In late January 1966, the congregation invited its first applicant, Rabbi Sol H. Oster of Baldwin, Long Island, down to the island to meet the congregation and interview with the board. The invitation met with some excitement throughout the island community; even the *Daily News* reported on the impending visit, under the expectant title: "New Rabbi May Serve Synagogue."[85] Yet the anticipation was premature. Oster and the Hebrew Congregation apparently did not see eye to eye, and his name quickly disappeared from St. Thomas.

In the meantime, the older generation continued to pass on. On January 31, synagogue member Enrique Moron died at the age of sixty-five; Morris De Castro gave the eulogy at his funeral.[86] Two days later, Isaac Paiewonsky's sister-in-law Anna Paiewonsky passed away at age seventy-seven. Though buried in the Jewish cemetery, "Aunt Anna's" funeral took place in a local funeral parlor.[87] These people no longer played a part in active synagogue life. Their presence and achievements on the island, however, still warranted recognition and respect from the island's business community, as the local news recorded each name with sadness.

The rabbinic search continued. At a May B'nai B'rith meeting, the male synagogue leaders reaffirmed their hopes of hiring a rabbi before the High holidays that fall, and announced a $50,000 fundraising effort both to renovate the synagogue's physical plant and to provide the prospective religious leader with a competitive salary. Sasso, meanwhile, complained that he could not continue at the pulpit due to his ill health, forcing a series of lay-leaders to conduct most services in his place. Although the congregants tried to fill Sasso's shoes, their efforts apparently only emphasized the congregation's needs. At the synagogue's annual meeting for the election of officers that July, "the Board was given a mandate by the Congregation to secure a Rabbi at once."[88]

Former governor Morris De Castro returned to the synagogue presidency after this meeting, and helped redouble the congregation's rabbinic search. It soon bore fruit: Within a month, the congregation had agreed to a temporary, unpaid three-month trial period with retired Reform rabbi Samuel H. Markowitz (then living in San Diego). At seventy-five, Markowitz was older than the outgoing minister, a fact that initially distressed a number of congregants who had been looking for a younger minister to renew the congregation's energy. His authority and erudition, however, in addition to his remarkable health, quickly swayed the synagogue to hire him through the end of the fiscal year.[89] The new rabbi's rigorous style of leadership occasionally led to friction with congregants, particularly when they expressed a lack of basic Judaic knowledge.[90] At the same time, however, Markowitz's regimented approach gave the synagogue a new model for organization consistent with the American Reform movement. He organized services meticulously, and included controlled participation by congregants whenever possible.[91] Renewing the imperative for Jewish education, Markowitz and De Castro dealt personally with the parents of children who had missed religious lessons. Musical accompaniment was also a great concern to Markowitz, who was able to secure funds to install an organ little more than two months after his arrival.[92] Such actions, in addition to numerous smaller suggestions and demands regarding all aspects of synagogue life, gave the congregation a more contemporary and active face, and eased the way for its full transition into the Reform movement.

On December 9, 1966, the congregation suffered the loss of another pillar of the community: Morris Fidanque De Castro, St. Thomas's first "Native Son" governor, died of a heart attack at the age of sixty-four. Since leaving the governorship in 1954, De Castro's career had remained active and prominent: At his death, in addition to being the active synagogue president, he was also serving as director of the budget of the government of the Virgin Islands. True to his homeland and his congregation to the very end, De Castro was missed and mourned by much of the island. Those who attended his memorial service two weeks later recited Psalm 23, "The Lord is my shepherd," and concluded with a central statement of Jewish faith: "Hear O Israel: The Lord is our God, the Lord is One. Praised be His name whose glorious kingdom is forever and ever."[93] Following this the long cortège accompanied De Castro's body to the Jewish cemetery, where he joined his island family for eternity.

March 31, 1967 marked the fiftieth anniversary of the Virgin Islands as an American territory. Celebrations took place throughout the year, the most prominent of which included the hosting of the national governor's conference that October. Symbolically, though not intentionally, the St. Thomas Hebrew Congregation observed this anniversary as well by consummating its relationship with the United States Reform movement. In part to improve their chances of attracting a rabbi, and in part to continue their momentum and growth, the synagogue members applied to the Union of American Hebrew Congregations, the central organization of the American Reform movement, for membership. On May 27, 1967, at the headquarters of the Reform movement in Cincinnati, Ohio, the "Hebrew Congregation, Blessing and Peace and Acts of Piety" acquired a new identity as an official member synagogue of American Reform Judaism; true to its patterns of migration, the congregation became a member of the New York region, retaining its ties to the area that many of the congregants identified as their other home.

By the time Markowitz left, the St. Thomas Hebrew Congregation was making preparations for the arrival of their "permanent" minister. On Friday night, July 14, the congregation installed Rabbi Murray Blackman as its new spiritual leader. Five men in the congregation—presumably members of the search committee—led the service from the *Union Prayer Book.* Rabbi Daniel L. Davis, Director of the New York Federation of Reform Synagogues, spoke to the congregation about Blackman's qualities, and officially named him to the post. Governor Ralph Paiewonsky, Bishop Edward Harper, and Reverend Raymond Abbitt greeted Rabbi Blackman at his pulpit, reminding him of his responsibilities both to the synagogue and to the island community. Following this, Rabbi Moses Sasso, the congregation's first Rabbi Emeritus, looked over his transformed congregation as he raised the ceremonial cup of wine and proclaimed the *kiddish.* Blackman, at the end of the ceremony, introduced himself by intoning the closing benediction. The sound resounded against the age-old walls, and echoed through the peaked portals of the synagogue. In one sense, nothing changed: the sand remained on the floor, the mahogany benches continued to provide a place for congregants to sit during services, the cool evening winds continued to waft through the sanctuary's windows; the doors of the synagogue would remain open on the small island. Yet the prayers inside the sanctuary would be different, the activities changed; the people who were mere visitors to the island in the 1950s were now its permanent residents—and its future old families.

Sifting through the Sands of Time

$\mathcal{I}$n the summer of 1975, my parents decided to go on an adventure. My father, after years of teaching in the Boston area, wanted to join the National Forestry Service; but the agency had placed a freeze on hiring, requiring him to look elsewhere for employment. It was in this spirit that he came across a classified ad for a teaching position in Charlotte Amalie, USVI. My father applied for the job, and was granted an interview; while he was in the area, he also interviewed for a second opening at a private school in Frenchman's Bay. Eventually he was offered this second job. At the time, my parents found little difficulty in uprooting their lives in Boston for what they saw as an attractive lifestyle on a beautiful tropical island that, surprisingly enough, also sustained an old synagogue and active Jewish community. My mother soon procured a position at the same private school as the special education instructor for the primary grades. Fully set up, they moved down to the island with their two-year-old son, tentatively expecting to spend an exceptional year or two there.

They encountered a synagogue that, just the year before, had undergone a large-scale renovation and rededication: the back foyer became an enclosed space, storage was added above; and, presumably in deference to contemporary aesthetic norms, the plaster was stripped off the sanctuary's interior. A new rabbi, Stanley Relkin, had just been hired, beginning what would become a fifteen-year tenure on the island. Few older Sephardic members remained. The newest congregants, meanwhile, generally came from the United States. Lured by business prospects, sheer interest, or, like my parents, an adventurous spirit, they came to experience the weather and fabled atmosphere, chronicled in travel brochures across the United States.

The congregation was blossoming into a full-fledged member of the American Jewish Reform movement. Programs, committees, organizational styles, prayer books, and youth activities had been instituted by a succession of Reform rabbis and active lay-leaders, serving to link the congregation's culture and practices to that of American Reform Judaism.[1] Yet even in the midst of this transformation, the St. Thomas synagogue and its congregants took on the unique task of embodying, preserving, and displaying a Sephardic heritage and legacy that had given the synagogue its historic significance. The sanctuary—a beautiful gem of Caribbean architecture visited daily by tourists of all faiths and nationalities—complemented two historic cemeteries housing generations of the congregation's past members. Consequently, the congregation took on the role of curator. As it privately forged ahead with its day-to-day operations, the synagogue took pains to present publicly its own collective past.

From 1975 to 1977, much of my family's social life revolved around the Hebrew Congregation. We would go to services almost every Friday night, where I would play in the sand floor; and whenever the historic ark was opened, I would run up to the Torahs and stand there as the rabbi took my hand. On Saturday mornings, my parents took responsibility for two of the congregation's Hebrew School classes, walking the students from lessons at our house downhill to a short service in the sanctuary. We celebrated the holidays together: I was dressed up in costume for Purim, for example, and competed for prizes at the synagogue's communal reading of the Book of Esther. My father, moreover, became a member of the board in his second year, and entertained with the rest of the officers ways of inducing more on-island Jews to join the congregation. After two years of island life, replete with its droughts, hurricanes, overblown government, security issues, and unpredictable shipping patterns, we moved up to New Jersey; but my parents remained off-island subscribers to the synagogue, and continued to receive the congregation's newsletter three times per year.

With each update, we learned of the congregation's continued growth. In 1983, the synagogue commemorated the 150th anniversary of its sanctuary's completion with an island-wide celebration. Reform movement president Alexander Schindler came to speak during the event, as did Dr. Edward Wilmot Blyden III (namesake and great-grandson of the St. Thomas–born African nationalist), Columbia University African-American Studies professor Hollis Lynch, and Norma Levitt, President of the National Federation of Temple Sisterhoods. Letters of congratulations were sent from descendants of the island's Sephardic families in Panama and the United States, and the synagogue received notes of acknowledgment from local, American, and foreign dignitaries, including Israeli President Yitzhak Navon; even American President Ronald Reagan sent his official regards.[2] Relkin and synagogue president Monroe Abrams, meanwhile, updated the congregation's historical pamphlet for the occasion by adding a new introduction and several professional-looking color photographs, retypesetting the text, and printing the entire venture on glossy paper.[3] The gala weekend included such diverse elements as religious services attended by several island politicians and clergy, a banquet and ball at one of the local luxury hotels, one day's free admission for all island residents at a local underwater aquarium, the dedication of a congregation-sponsored scholarship to the College of the Virgin Islands, and a special postal cancellation stamp.

Three years later, Rabbi Relkin sent me a copy of the new pamphlet as a gift for my Bar Mitzvah. I kept it as a reminder of my own past, occasionally taking it out to look at the pictures and fantasize about returning to see the exotic community it portrayed.

That opportunity came in 1994, during my junior year of college. Having taken majors in music and religious studies, I aimed to go abroad to conduct fieldwork for my senior thesis. My initial plans for studying the Jewish community in Prague fell through; then my parents suggested I look into returning to St. Thomas. Thus, with some trepidation, I initiated contact with the synagogue for the first time in over sixteen years. The response I received was overwhelming: The new rabbi, Bradd Boxman, told me I had approached them at the perfect time. The congregation was in its planning stages for an international celebration in honor of its 1996 bicentennial, and was looking to hire a professional historian to write and document its history. I could help this person by conducting initial research on the synagogue.

In this way, I became readmitted into the flow of St. Thomas's Jewish history. Over the course of the next few years, through several extended stays on the island, I became active in congregational life: leading music in services, conducting interviews, acting as a substitute Hebrew school teacher, giving tours of the synagogue, attending major congregational events, going to services, washing gravestones in the Jewish cemeteries, and relishing my interactions with congregants of all backgrounds, all while spending significant periods of time each weekday in the back of the public library poring through microfilm. Time passed, and slowly I was allowed to grow into the historian they had initially sought elsewhere. This was the fulfillment of a dream for me. Outwardly, I was trying to uncover the layers of St. Thomas history that had been buried by the island's often fragile economy and significant population shifts. Privately, however, I was embarking on a quest to understand my *own* past, left behind over a decade and a half earlier. I had been a member of this community too; and I took on as my own the heritage that the congregation was trying to revitalize. Dead individuals who I had never known, and with whom I probably shared little, eventually became endeared figures to me; and I, like all the other current congregants, was their spiritual descendant.

In the fall of 1995, I compiled and assembled a museum of Virgin Islands Jewish history based on my researches, to be housed in the back foyer of the synagogue and dedicated to the memory of a prominent congregant. The ceremony, to take place on September 15, was also intended to kick off the congregation's bicentennial year. Once again, however, the island's historic legacy took over: An afternoon curfew imposed on the day of the dedication forced us to cancel the event and prepare for a hurricane heading our way. By six o'clock the next morning, the island had been laid to waste. All plans were pushed back by months, as the St. Thomas population once again took time to regroup and rebuild. I stayed for the next two days to help with the initial cleanup. Ultimately, however, I was encouraged by congregants to take tourist status, complete the return trip on my plane ticket, and leave the island.

I came back two months later to dedicate the museum anew, and celebrate the beginning of a beautiful and well-regarded bicentennial. Prominent personalities such as Supreme Court Justice Ruth Bader Ginsburg, writer Maya Angelou, and Nobel laureate Elie Wiesel came to speak to island-wide audiences over the following year; and violinist Yitzhak Perlman gave a well-attended performance. A historic exhibition of early Camille Pissarro works, long in production, was successfully shown from late 1996 into early 1997. The congregation sponsored the training of teachers to introduce the Anti-Defamation League's "A World of Difference" curriculum into the island's public schools. And, in a symbolic connection with its earliest congregants, the synagogue researched and held an "authentic" Western Sephardic religious service, in the hopes of recreating the experiences that had first brought the instituiton into existence two centuries before.

I was able to attend only a few of the events; but when I *was* on the island, I felt as if I had rejoined family. It is likely, I thought, that the warmth with which I was received had to do with our common past—through the experiences we had had together in the previous couple years, through my own childhood presence in the community, and through our common affiliation with an aged, spiritual institution that operated within a unique religious environment. Through this realization, I came to understand that in writing the synagogue's history, I was also redefining present-day identity: not only my own, but that of the entire congregation.

Since then, the synagogue has continued to take pains to preserve its past as a part of its present. Thanks to knowledgeable, enthusiastic congregants, the synagogue's oldest papers have been preserved, and the rest of the synagogue's materials have been arranged into an archive for future scholars to explore. At the turn of the twenty-first century, moreover, the synagogue underwent another major renovation, in part to replaster the crumbling inner walls uncovered in the 1970s. To celebrate, the congregation held a rededication ceremony in March 2002 that consciously re-enacted the original dedication ceremony from September 1833. Not only was history preserved, but a certain ethnic identity was reinforced and projected to the island and the world.

Thus, the Jewish community of St. Thomas, which has changed so many times since the first settlers in the seventeenth and eighteenth centuries, continues to display a cumulative identity. Living a life both exotic and mundane, the congregants recognize their place as Jews in St. Thomas by looking to their spiritual forebears; yet simultaneously, they *practice* their identity by taking on modern conventions in the present. Both appropriately and ironically, my own story (and this resulting history) serves as a clear example.

I close by juxtaposing the stories of two of the congregation's candelabra in a manner that might help explain the ways St. Thomas's Jewish community perceives its heritage at the start of the twenty-first century. Both are housed within the St. Thomas synagogue building. Their comparative meaning to both congregants and visitors, however, provides significant insight.

The first, a seven-branch candelabrum mentioned in the introduction to this book, was purchased for a considerable sum in the 1970s by a prominent Eastern European–descended St. Thomas Jewish family. According to local lore, the seller had assured the family that the candelabrum had been constructed in Cordoba, Spain, in the eleventh century—long viewed as the "Golden Age" for Sephardic Jewry. The family acquired the item and subsequently donated it to the synagogue to symbolize the congregation's origins. Since the sanctuary's 1974 renovation, the candelabrum has remained a cherished congregational artifact, prominently mounted for all to see during services, tastefully included in the congregation's historical pamphlet and pointed out during most sanctuary tours. The authenticity of the item has never been verified, though the bolts used to hold it together lay some doubt on the seller's claims. Yet such issues are in many ways irrelevant: The congregation looks to it as a site of collective memory, both as Jews and as members of the

St. Thomas Hebrew Congregation. The culture that had been wiped out by the Spanish Inquisition, it implies, lives on in the founding and maintenance of this congregation.

In contrast, the second candelabrum—a nine-branched *hanukkiah*—was first mentioned in chapter 1, and mirrors the history presented in this book. It was created in Amsterdam in the late eighteenth century, as a copy of a brass candelabrum donated to the Sephardic synagogue there by a prominent congregant over a century and a half earlier. The Amsterdam congregation sent the lamp to the synagogue in St. Eustatius sometime during the 1770s, engraved in Hebrew with the congregation's name and the date. Presumably, the artifact came over to St. Thomas around the turn of the nineteenth century, possibly with the migration that led to *Beracha Ve-Shalom*'s founding. From there, it was likely handed down over several generations. David Cardoze Jr. had it in his possession through the early part of the twentieth century, and he in turn gave it to his spiritual successor, Moses De Castro Sasso, for safe keeping. After holding onto the lamp for several decades, Sasso subsequently donated it to the local Fort Christian museum, where it remained in storage for decades. The item came to light during a cursory search there in 1995 for any objects that might be appropriate for the synagogue's new museum. Granted on long-term loan to the congregation, the lamp went on display in the Johnny Weibel Museum of St. Thomas Jewish History, badly oxidized and missing its *shamash* oil well, but otherwise complete. It, too, is a source of great pride, and represents the heritage of the congregation; as of this writing, however, it did not figure as prominently in the synagogue's public image.

Displayed only a few yards away from each other, these objects can be seen as representing two sides of the Hebrew Congregation's identity: On the one hand, paying fealty to an imagined past, reflecting communal memories inherent in the contemporary popular Jewish-American narrative of Sephardic history; and on the other hand, quietly serving as tangible proof of a long legacy of adaptation, innovation, conflict, and change. In many ways, one cannot exist without the other on the island, for they are equally rich in their significance, and equally important in maintaining the community's sense of history, culture, and continuity.

NOTES

List of Abbreviations

Periodicals

AI:	*Les Archives Israélites de France*
PAJHS:	*Publications of the American Jewish Historical Society*
AJH:	*American Jewish History*
AJA:	*American Jewish Archives*
VIDN:	*Daily News of the Virgin Islands/Virgin Islands Daily News*
FFW:	*First Fruits of the West*
JC:	*Jewish Chronicle of London*
NYT:	*New York Times*
Occident:	*The Occident and American Jewish Advocate*
RDAG:	*Royal Danish American Gazette*
STH:	*St. Thomas Herald*
STMN:	*St. Thomas Mail Notes*
STT:	*St. Thomas Times*
Tidende:	*Sanct Thomæ Tidende*
VOJ:	*The Voice of Jacob*

Archival Materials

Borger Eder: Rigsarkivet, Danske Vestindiske Lokalarkiv, St. Thomas og St. Jan, Guvernement mm. 1757–1909. Borger Eder [Burgher Briefs], 1815–1909.

Matrikul: Rigsarkivet, Danske Vestindiske Lokalarkiv, St. Thomas og St. Jan, Guvernement mm. 1757–1909. Matrikul [tax lists].

SACO: Shearith Israel Archives, New York, N.Y. Clerk's Office Correspondence, 1927–1931. Box 8(a), Folders 1–2: Letters regarding Rev. Dr. Henry Pereira Mendes's visit to St. Thomas.

STBDM1: St. Thomas Hebrew Congregation Protocols. Births (1786–1845), Deaths (1792–1826), Marriages (1841–1869), Confirmations (1843–1865), and Marriage Contracts (1843–1925). Microfilm copy in possession of St. Thomas Hebrew Congregation, Charlotte Amalie, St. Thomas, U.S. Virgin Islands.

STBDM2: St. Thomas Hebrew Congregation Protocol Book: Births, Deaths and Marriages, 1852–1954. In possession of St. Thomas Hebrew Congregation, St. Thomas, U.S. Virgin Islands.

STHCA: St. Thomas Hebrew Congregation Archives. Charlotte Amalie, St. Thomas, U.S. Virgin Islands.

Invitation (pages xiii–xviii)

1. Campbell 1942, 161.

Introduction (pages xix–xxvi)

1. Marcus 1964 [1953], 3.
2. Ibid., 32.
3. Ibid.
4. During my time on St. Thomas, for example, a referendum to build casinos on St. Croix was stalled in the legislature due in part to a debate over the meaning and significance of the terms "native" and "aboriginal." In another case, an island senator with strong ties to the Nation of Islam vociferously invoked the unfounded discourse associated with that organization asserting Jewish dominance of the slave trade while opposing a bill honoring the synagogue on its two hundredth anniversary. On a more personal level: During a tour of the synagogue I gave to a group of local island children, I found myself answering many questions on Jewish history, including a query as to "what tribe" I was from. These and many other examples show the importance of history to the local population.
5. At a synagogue-sponsored community seder, meanwhile, much emphasis was given to the common historical experience of both blacks and Jews, including the use of a special *Haggadah* created for such a purpose by the Anti-Defamation League.
6. For more on collective memory, see Halbwachs 1991 and Connerton 1992.
7. For an interesting discussion of the difficulty in finding source material for Caribbean Jewish communities, see Krohn 1993; admittedly, his arguments are only partially applicable to St. Thomas.
8. For an example of how these records also revealed much about the St. Croix Jewish community, see Cohen 1997a. These records comprise a significant amount of the St. Thomas material kept at the American Jewish Archives in Cincinnati.

Chapter 1: Gathering (pages 1–18)

1. While Columbus is documented to have sailed by St. Thomas on this voyage, he actually sustained contact with the inhabitants of St. Croix. For more on this episode, see Highfield 1995.
2. For a detailed discussion of the period of Danish West India Company rule in the Danish West Indies, see Westergaard 1917.
3. For more, see Cohen 1991 (on Surinam); Emmanuel 1957 and Emmanuel and Emmanuel 1970 (Curaçao); Andrade 1941, Arbell 2001, and August 1989 (Jamaica); Samuel 1936 and Shilstone 1988 [1957?] (Barbados). Other studies have dealt with the more general movement of Jews to the Caribbean region, including Cohen 1976 and 1983 (covering the British sphere); and Yerushalmi 1982 and Israel 1989 (covering the Dutch sphere).
   It is also significant to note that the Recife Jewish community was expelled in 1654, when the island was conquered by Portugal.
4. Krarup 1893–1894 (translated, edited, and illustrated in Paiewonsky 1992, 151–229); also recounted in Westergaard 1917, 57–66; and Friedman 1922.
5. See Paiewonsky 1959.
6. See Paiewonsky 1959; Westergaaard 1917, 210, n. 43. Vass is mentioned in the St. Thomas tax lists for 1755, 1756, and 1758 as one of the head servants for a plantation owner, possibly named J. J. Schafilisky de Muckadell (*Matrikul*).
7. Rigsarkiv, *Kancelli*, Vestindiske Sager St. Thomas og St. Jan: 1699–1745.
8. *Matrikul.* It is possible that Correa had owned the plantation before 1755, since tax records only go back to that year. What is known, however, is that Correa "disappeared" (likely left the island) by 1758, and the plantation was transferred to the widow of a non-Jewish merchant.
9. Paiewonsky 1959 mentions an Elias family that lived on the island in the late seventeenth century; there is, however, no evidence of their religious identity save an intriguing (and perhaps deceptive) name.
10. This is according to research conducted by Eva Lawaetz (see Loker 1991, 308–309). In my own researches through what I thought to be the same materials at the Copenhagen Rigsarkiv, I was unable to find any material that confirmed Lawaetz's claims.
11. Few sources on eighteenth- and nineteenth-century St. Croix Jewry have been published, and comprise mainly passing entries in larger works (such as Loker 1991, 308–309, Emmanuel and Emmanuel 1970, 836, and Rosenbloom 1960, 17, 123–24). Unpublished works such as Smith 1996—which looks at the St. Croix Jewish cemetery—and Cohen 1997—which analyzes the relationship between the Jewish communities of St. Croix and St. Thomas during this time—are helpful, though hard to access and somewhat narrow in scope.
12. See Kaplan 1982, 200–203. Significantly, while the synagogues in Amsterdam and Recife, Brazil, required that "members live openly as Jews for a set period of time

before being eligible for congregational leadership positions," Curaçao apparently had no such requirement (Benjamin 2001, 95).

13. Hurst 1996, 110–11.

14. Several sources, such as Barka 1996, assert that the French attempted set up a colony unsuccessfully on the island in the 1620s.

15. For a significantly more detailed account of St. Eustatius and the other Dutch West Indian islands during this time period, see Goslinga 1979, 80–86.

16. I present the following as a summary of St. Eustatius Jewish history. For somewhat more involved retellings, see Emmanuel and Emmanuel 1970, 518–27, and Hartog 1976.

17. van Grol 1982 [1934], 343.

18. Emmanuel and Emmanuel 1970, 518.

19. Hartog 1976, 2; Emmanuel and Emmanuel 1970, 519.

20. Hartog 1976, 3.

21. Compiled from "Poll Tax List of Citizens and Families and Slaves," Algemeen Rijsarchief, 1st Section, the Hague, Netherlands. (On display at the St. Eustatius Historical Foundation Museum, Oranjestad, St. Eustatius).

22. Letters, Chamber of Amsterdam to Governor I. Faesch, February 23, 1737, and November 21, 1739. State Archives, The Hague, 341—West India Company, 474. Quoted in Hartog 1976, 5.

23. Emmanuel and Emmanuel 1970, 520, 1068; Fuks-Mansfield 1989, 166.

24. [Schaw] 1939, 137–38.

25. Emmanuel and Emmanuel 1970, 522.

26. *RDAG*, September 23, 1772. Evidence shows that Monsieur de Georgé was a citizen in absentia on St. Eustatius in 1781; but he died in St. Croix on May 7, 1794 (St. Thomas Hebrew Congregation death records, 1794–1826). Lime, incidentally, is a prime ingredient for mortar.

27. At port, the ships cleared out the bricks and replaced them with desirable locally produced goods for transport back to their destination. Barka describes this phenomenon in a short discussion about the construction of the warehouses in the Lower Town (Barka 1996, 227).

28. This is a traditional orientation for a synagogue, symbolically pointing in the direction of Jerusalem.

29. The *hanukkiah* was a replica of a well-regarded original donated to the Amsterdam congregation in the 1620s.

30. This is an estimate based on the number of Jewish men rounded up by the British during the siege. Hartog 1976, 11.

31. Hurst 1996, 109.

32. Mundy 1830, v. 2, p. 8. Quoted in Tuchman 1988, 96.

33. For a minutely detailed account of this episode, see Hurst 1996, especially 125–82.

34. *The Parlimentary History of England from the Earliest Period to the Year 1803*, v. 22, col. 222 (henceforth *Parliamentary History*).

35. Tuchman 1988, 97.

36. A reproduction of one of these inventories, enumerating the estate of Jewish merchant Elias Gomez (and signed February 7, 1781), is on display at the St. Eustatius Historical Foundation Museum.

37. Contrary to a popular story, Rodney kept the island's structures intact. All powers involved knew the inherent value of the island's infrastructure, and would not do something so counterproductive as to destroy it. The island's records, however, are a completely different issue. Rodney gutted Statia's archives for evidence of trade with the French and Americans, and subsequently lost the papers en route to England. (Conversation with Mr. Ellis Lopes, St. Eustatius Historical Foundation, St. Eustatius Historical Foundation Museum, April 22, 1996).

38. Hurst 1996, 132.

39. *Parliamentary History*, col. 225.

40. Ibid., col. 719.

41. Ibid., cols. 225–26.

42. *Massachusetts Spy*, May 1781. AJA.

43. Emmanuel claims that the British shipped the remaining Jews to Antigua, but presents no source (Emmanuel and Emmanuel 1970, 524). I find nothing that corroborates this assertion.

44. General Vaughn later claimed that he sent the imprisoned Jews a ship "to carry them to St. Thomas, at their own request." After he found out they instead went to St. Kitts, Vaughn says he sent a ship to take them back to St. Eustatius, where he restored the Jews to property (*Parlimentary History*, col. 782). Based on the rest of the testimony, certain elements of this story are false, or true but out of context (the property restored to Samuel Hoheb, for example, was an empty house and a small bag of money overlooked in a dresser drawer [Ibid., col. 1023]); other allegations, however, cannot be proven nor disproven.

45. Hurst 1996, 142–43.

46. *Parliamentary History*, col. 1023.

47. Tuchman 1988, 105. It is worth mentioning that a month and a half later, the French ambushed this convoy and took control of twenty-two ships. Only eleven ever made it back to England (Hurst 1996, 166–73).

48. Hurst 1996, 153–97.

49. Woods 1992, 91. It is worth speculating that these merchants (save Benjamin, who is recorded as living in Dronningens Quarter) lived on or near the street bordering the Jewish cemetery, known today as "Jøde Gade" or "Jew Street."

50. This is complicated somewhat because it seems St. Thomas began using a different system for recording and assessing taxpayers in 1783.

51. Emmanuel and Emmanuel 1970, 1066–67.

52. St. Eustatius Historical Foundation Museum.

53. *Parliamentary History*, cols. 1023–26.

54. See also Emmanuel and Emmanuel 1970, 1061, #14.

55. Ibid., 527, 1066–67.
56. Hartog 1976, 16.
57. This section will deal only with Jewish conditions on St. Domingue after 1789. For more information on the Jewish communities of St. Domingue before the French Revolution, see Arbell 2001: 301–309 and Garrigus 2001.
58. Knight 1990, 365. It is worth noting the dramatic decrease in the efficiency of sugar production. One possibility for this, noted by several historians (including Ott), may be the extreme cruelty with which plantation owners treated their slaves.
59. Emmanuel and Emmanuel 1970, 829; *Matrikul,* 1792; St. Thomas Census, 1846.
60. Constructed from several sources: Ott 1973, 90; *Matrikul,* 1795–1810; journal of Monsanto family history, in the possession of Beatrice Anderson, 12–13; St. Thomas Census, 1846. Based on this timeline, it appears that Moses Pomié's wife gave birth to a daughter, Abigail, around this time. Abigail was eventually sent to France for her education, where she later married Samuel Lopes Dubec, another prominent St. Thomas merchant.
61. Corcos 1971: col. 895. The name is supposed to be a combination of the first letters of the Hebrew phrase: "*Yavo'u V'Yishtachavu L'Fanecha.*"
62. Letter from A. M. DaCosta to Lucien Wolff, 22 March 1901. Lucien Wolff Collection, B20 COS. University College of London, Manuscripts collection.
63. Ibid.
64. Monaco 1998, 383, n. 31.
65. Stories about Moses Elias Levy characterize him as a Jew of radical opinions and actions. His grandson relates two stories during his time in England:

> In London, in the midst of a Sunday [church] service, he arose and in a loud voice addressed the congregation thus: "This is idolatry. Christianity is paganism; it is an evolution from the 50 Gods of Rome to the 5, etc., etc." When the astonished congregation had recovered its equanimity he was seized and expelled. He was not prosecuted.
>
> On another occasion in London he smashed the window plate of a bookseller and seized Tom Paine's works, tearing them up. He was arrested and fined. He declined to pay a farthing. He said, 'I did my duty; I would be compromising with wrong if I paid for doing right.' Friends of his came forward and arranged matters.
>
> The London 'Times' the day after the occurrence had an article headed, "A Jew did what a Christian ought to have done."

Source ibid. We know he removed the "Yuly" from his name both through his grandson's recollections ("My grandfather dropped the Yulee when 20 to 23 years old." Letter from A. M. DaCosta to Lucien Wolff, July 5, 1901, source ibid.) and through St. Thomas tax lists, which first list him in 1806 as Moses Levy. Possibly, this helped him to supplant the cruelty of the sultans, who had allowed his ancestors this name in the first place.

66. "Tax-paying" in this case is defined as individuals or families who owned either slaves or land, and could thus be taxed according to government regulation.

67. *Matrikul*, 1795. Elias Sarquy's presence is known through the 1846 census.

68. In 1685, Jews in the Danish colonies received permission to practice their religion privately. There was really no need for a formal place of worship until the population expanded in the 1790s.

69. Photographs of the old grating on the cemetery gate show its opening date as 5510, corresponding to the common year 1750 (Johnny Weibel Museum of St. Thomas Jewish History, St. Thomas).

70. *Matrikul*, 1781–1782. These two lists are organized by geographic quarter, and show that those taxpayers with clearly Jewish names lived either in Kronprindsens Quarter (the westernmost quarter, within sight of the cemetery), or Dronningens Quarter ("Queen's Quarter," just to the east of Kronprindsens Quarter). Kongens Quarter ("King's Quarter," to the east of Dronningens Quarter; home to Fort Christian and the Danish Lutheran Church) had no clearly Jewish residents.

71. Emmanuel 1957, 60–61. According to Emmanuel, Curaçao's Hebre itself took after similar societies founded by the communities of Amsterdam in 1639 and London in 1665. Moreover, Curaçao's society was significantly more extensive than that of St. Thomas, including subsidiary societies named the *Cabranim* (gravediggers), *Hesed Ve Emeth* (which bathed the deceased before burial), *Anse Hesed* (which transported bodies from plantations to the Jewish cemetery in the city), *Habodat Akodes* (which supplemented *Anse Hesed*), and *Mishpat Habanot* (a group of women who prepared women for burial, in addition to serving as midwives and keepers of the ritual bath) (Emmanuel 1957, 62–73).

72. Records of the Hebrew Congregation of St. Thomas, Deaths, 1792–1826, Death record #4. It is likely that Serano was son of David and Hannah Serano, who died in Curaçao on December 27, 1758, and August 27, 1756, respectively (Emmanuel 1957, 525). The secretary possibly was Abraham Julien, a French-born Jew; the records, after all, are written in French.

73. *AI* 3 (1842): 532.

74. St. Thomas Panteprotokol, 1793–1806; National Archives II, College Park, Maryland; Document Group 55, Box 1999–2003.

75. This indicates at least twenty-one male congregants, and probably more.

76. Elazar 1992, 23.

77. There is a strong possibility that the St. Thomas Congregation created this position in full knowledge of New York's *Shearith Israel* action six years earlier. At that time, the New York congregation changed the official title *parnas* to "President," likely in reference to the country's leadership (Sarna 1992, 38).

78. St. Thomas 1796 Bylaws, Article 12.

79. These "honors" also included a compulsory contribution to the synagogue. In the

case of being called up to the Torah, for example, the contribution was "no less than one half Royal." Thus, the president's decision had more than just honorary repercussions. Ibid., Article 18.

80. Ibid., Article 15.

81. Ibid., Articles 10, 11, 22.

82. Ibid., Article 23 (translated by the author from the Portuguese).

Chapter 2: Growth: 1791–1831 (pages 19–42)

1. Dookhan 1994 [1974], 96.

2. Ibid., 136.

3. Based on tax records, no Jew owned property outside of the town (i.e., a plantation).

4. At this time, Altona was a part of the Danish empire.

5. More often than not, these measurements indicated the areas of the buildings on each lot, and not the actual areas of the lots themselves.

6. 1796 Bylaws, *Kahal Kadosh Beracha VeShalom.* National Archives II. College Park, Maryland. Document Group 55, Box 1999–2003, St. Thomas Panteprotokol 1801–1803. [Herein 1796 Bylaws].

7. *Matrikul,* 1797–1802.

8. Synagogue bylaws, 1802. National Archives II. College Park, Maryland, Document Group 55, Box 1999–2003, St. Thomas Panteprotokol, 1801–1803. [Herein 1802 Bylaws].

9. Emmanuel and Emmanuel 1970, 586–612.

10. It is possible that the wording in both sets of bylaws was exactly the same, since the documents were apparently written originally in Portuguese. I only had access to official English translations of both.

11. 1796 Bylaws, Article 24.

12. *Matrikul,* 1803. The actual listing mentioned two different properties, and combined the total area for tax purposes. In 1803, there was an increase in the congregation's land holdings. Since the Jewish burial ground's buildings had amounted to 300 square alen (approx. 1,200 square feet) in the past, the additional amount (166 square alen, or 664 square feet) appears to have indicated an additional building, presumably the synagogue. This is borne out with the land tax listings from the next year. The item, "Jødernes Synagogue" received its own entry, with an area of 186 square alen (744 square feet). These, unfortunately, were the only years that contained data on the structure, since the first synagogue burned down in 1804.

13. 1802 bylaws. Although *Occident* 12: 58 states that Reverend Isaac Lopes served the St. Thomas congregation for seven years corresponding to 1800 to 1807, it appears this account (given at Lopes's death in 1854) may be off a few years.

14. Nissen 1838, 1804 entry.
15. *Occident* 12: 58. Reverend Lopes's obituary states that he officiated at St. Thomas for seven years, although specifics are lacking. There is only one year—1805— which mentions him in the tax lists (where he paid 14.09 rigsdalers tax on 451 square alen of property).
16. According to Nissen, a fireproof store cost ten to fourteen thousand Danish rigsdalers to build. Most materials had to be imported or otherwise obtained at a decent expense, while wood remained plentiful on the island.
17. Nissen 1838, 1806 entry.
18. Ibid. The building had stone rubble masonry walls and a brick roof.
19. Although Levy is credited as a St. Thomas native, his birth is not registered in the synagogue protocols.
20. Marcus 1989, vol. 1, 364–70; "David Yulee, Ex-Senator from Florida" *Tidende,* 5 February 1873: 1.
21. On August 6, 1811. For more, see Evans 1988, Meade 2001 [1943].
22. Ironically, these relatives would forever obscure Judah Benjamin's origins. Three and a half months after Judah's birth to Philip and Rebecca, their cousins Emanuel and Esther Benjamin gave birth to a son in St. Thomas, also named Judah. This second Judah Benjamin, who did not rise to great American political prominence, has misled biographers, and caused Judah P. Benjamin's gravestone in England to erroneously include "St. Thomas" as his place of birth.
23. Significantly, however, Benjamin did not finish his studies at Yale, and seems to have left under mysterious circumstances. See Oren 2001, 6–8.
24. *Matrikul,* 1810, 1813.
25. A more literal translation is "Shit Street."
26. St. Thomas Recorder of Deeds Office, Book X, folio 43, #4.
27. *St. Thomas Gazette,* 23 November 1812; 25 March 1813.
28. Ibid., 13 December 1813.
29. Ibid., 27 December 1813; Rigsarkiv, *Danske Vestindiske Lokalarkiv,* St. Thomas og St. Jan Guvernement mm. 1757–1909 Testamenteprotokol 1815–1827: 13–14.
30. These trips usually required notice in the local papers along with ample opportunities for residents to settle their accounts before the merchant left. To Europe, voyage time itself was over a month in each direction, depending upon the time of year and the trade winds.
31. The store of Hannah Piza, for example, operated from the 1830s to the 1860s (Guiterman [1971]). Other times, women were listed along with their husbands in the city's tax lists, such as "Madame" Sarquy, listed under her husband Elias in 1807.
32. Classic examples of this include Meriam Ezra and Rachel Pomié during the 1820s to 1830s, and the frequent widows listed in the St. Thomas *Matrikul* during the early 1800s.
33. Nissen 1838, 1815 entry.

34. *Tidende,* 19 April 1815.

35. Nissen 1838, 1791 entry. It is worth passing mention that the early bedtime, in addition to granting merchants plenty of time to rest before returning to work the next morning, helped limit exposure to moonlight, which popular science saw as harmful at the time.

36. Hall 1992, 96.

37. Based on *Tidende,* 20 March 1852, which notes the continuous presence of a cock pit. Cockfighting was a popular sport among whites throughout the eighteenth century (Hall 1992, 120).

38. One more memorable exchange is printed—complaint and response—in the *Tidende* of 10 November, 1817: Nathan Hart prints: "Whereas Iael Hart, my wife, has eloped from my Bed and Board. This is to forbid all Persons from harbouring or treating her on my account, as I will not pay any Debt or Debts caused by her after this date [October 29, 1817]." Yael responds with a couplet: "Nathan wo'nt pay my debts, oh! what an Elf,/ Who expects him to pay for me, when he can't for himself."

39. The most colorful example of this comes on July 8, 1813, when Isaac Athias reveals that he gave his runaway slave Joseph the nickname of "Purim" (*St. Thomas Gazette,* 8 July 1813). See Hall 1992, 93–95.

40. See the story of Nathan Levy later in this chapter.

41. *Tidende,* 7 March 1816: 4. Marriage of Mr. Rodrigues to Miss Rebecca Levy; Emmanuel 1957, 429–30. Emmanuel claims, through evidence of an 1817 wedding contract signed in Christiansted, St. Croix, that Pinto was the spiritual leader of the St. Croix Jewish community before coming over to St. Thomas. More likely, however, Pinto was stationed on St. Thomas, and included Jewish religious activity on St. Croix in his duties.

42. M. E. Montefiore, who sold texiles at his shop on #30 Dronningens Gade in 1822 (*Tidende,* 22 March 1822: 1).

43. The masonic lodges were affiliated by nationality, and organized through a hierarchy that placed the king at the top (as Grand Master). Each local lodge met and worshiped in a building called a "Temple"; all activities behind the Temple's pillars were regarded as confidential. Part of freemasonry's appeal to Jews probably arose because the order followed certain traditions with semitic origins, such as an adherence to a quasi-Hebraic concept of the calendar (that is, the belief that God created the world 3760 years before the birth of Jesus). Another part came through an idealistic base in masonic doctrine that embraced a universalist philosophy.

44. Marcus 1989, vol. 1, 571–74.

45. Woods 1993.

46. Ibid.

47. "Founding Members of Harmonic Lodge 356 E. C.," in ibid.

48. "Roll of Masters," in ibid.
49. Ibid.
50. *Tidende*, 11 August 1818: 3. This date is in some dispute, and it appears that Levy's appointment was a complex and troubling issue. Marcus simply lists his political career as American Representative in St. Thomas as lasting from 1818 to 1836 (1989, 57–74). Blau and Baron claim his consulship lasted from 1820 to 1832 (1963a). The *Tidende*, a week after making its announcement, recalled the note because of miscommunication and lack of recognition on the part of the Danish government. On March 30, 1821, the *Tidende* mentions Levy as vice consul. To those who find the line of debate significant, therefore, this subject warrants further research.
51. Blau and Baron 1963a.
52. Ibid., 327.
53. St. Thomas Recorder of Deeds Office, Public Works Book "A."
54. *Tidende*, 17 May 1822; 23 July 1822.
55. It is tempting to make the connection between St. Thomas and Copenhagen, where the synagogue also lies on Crystal Gade. Unfortunately, the connection does not ring true: the Chief Rabbi of Copenhagen, Abraham Alexander Wolff, took the first steps toward building the present structure in 1828, six years after this reference to the St. Thomas street's name change (Bamberger 1983, 62).
56. Most of this description is extrapolated from the article that appeared in the *Tidende* 23 July 1823: 4.
57. This and all other quotations referring to the 1823 synagogue dedication are from ibid.
58. S. D., "The Late E. H. Lindo." *JC*, 23 June 1865: 2.
59. *Tidende* 30 January 1817: 4; 13 February 1817: 3.
60. *Tidende*, 22 November 1826: 1.
61. *Tidende*, 25 November 1826: 1.
62. *Tidende*, 27 December 1827: 1. The letters to the chief rabbis have not yet been found, nor the letter to the King of Denmark. All this has been extrapolated from the *Tidende* advertisement.
63. *Tidende*, 16 February 1831.
64. Nissen 1838, 1832 entry. He described the instrument (which he spells "Gombee") as "a small barrel the bottom of which being taken out a goat skin is drawn over the rim," which may have born some similarity to Manuel, Bilby, and Largey's more contemporary definition as "the square-frame drum used in this music, which is also used by Maroons in some communities" (Manuel, Bilby, and Largey 1995, 251).
65. Nissen 1838, 1832 entry.
66. Most prominent among these was Alexander De Castro, who, though illiterate, became one of the richest men on St. Thomas.

67. "Mr. Editor!" *Tidende*, 14 January 1832: 4; Nissen 1838: 1832 entry; alternately, the name of the merchant on whose property originated the Old Year's Night fire could be Mr. Hill, as mentioned in the *Tidende* account.

68. This and all other quotations about the fire are from "Mr. Editor!"

69. "Christmas breezes" is a local name for the stronger-than-usual trade winds that cool the island from the middle of December through January.

70. Presumably, there was time to retrieve the Torahs from the building before the fire engulfed it. There is, however, no definite evidence to this effect save the one St. Thomas Torah that lists the date 1771 on its handles (and it is worth speculating that this Torah could have come over from Curaçao after the fire).

71. Nissen 1838, 1832 entry.

Chapter 3: Rebuilding: 1831–1833 (pages 43–50)

1. "David Yulee, Ex-Senator from Florida," *Tidende*, 5 February 1873: 1. Perhaps most prominent of these was Jewish lumber merchant and philosophical idealist Moses Elias Levy. Continuing his mission to create a homeland for the Jews in the United States, Levy used the fire as an opportunity to move his interests to Florida. He eventually bought a large tract of land on the state's western coast; while it never became a Jewish state, Levy's land eventually gained its own political identity as a state county, which continues to bear his name. According to the cited account, Levy bought up the land from the U.S. government, which was attempting to sell Florida real estate to cover its debt from the Seminole War.

2. Rigsarkiv, *Danske Vestindiske Lokalarkiv,* St. Thomas og St. Jan Guvernement mm. 1757–1909, Kommandantskab, Referatprotokol 1832, #607.

3. Nissen 1838, 1832 entry.

4. *Tidende,* 11 January 1832: 4, col. 3.

5. Gjessing and Maclean 1987, 21.

6. Ibid.

7. Nissen 1838, 1837 entry. Note that all prices are in rigsdalers, which used the same symbol ("$") as American currency. Houses probably cost somewhat less.

8. See Woods 1992, 10.

9. Bricks were also popular for gravestone foundations, perhaps because fewer were needed to make a solid structure.

10. *Tidende,* 28 April 1832: 2.

11. *Tidende,* 6 April 1833; Emmanuel and Emmanuel 1970. An appeal to New York was likely because the two synagogues remained in adequate contact with each other; Amsterdam, as a center of Sephardic Jewry in Europe, seemed a highly likely collection location as well.

12. *Tidende,* 6 Apr 1833. The irregular dollar amounts are the result of several forms

of currency that commonly appeared on the island. The wardens, for example, gave in pieces of eight (1.625 pieces equalled $1). While account lists show the rest of the contributions in dollar amounts, the common donations in multiples of two dollars may also indicate translated pieces-of-eight donations.

13. Ibid.

14. Ibid.

15. *Tidende*, 19 December 1832, 2.

16. Ibid.

17. Paiewonsky 1959. Michael Paiewonsky (Isidor's son) asserts that the same architect designed the Continental Building on Nørre Gade (Woods 1992, 157, n. 8, communicated through Kurt Fischer), though I have been able to find no evidence either corroborating or disproving the story. The original plans are missing, the architect's name is unknown, and nothing in the synagogue's design marks it as particularly French.

18. *Tidende*, 6 April 1833; Hall 1992, 90–93.

19. *Tidende*, 6 April 1833. The lime was probably obtained through a procedure of drying and crushing coral.

20. Such a mix was common on St. Thomas, serving as mortar for the Episcopal Church on the island as well.

21. *Tidende*, 30 March 1833: 1; 3 April 1833: 1; 6 April 1833: 1.

22. *Tidende*, 17 April 1833: 2–3. Barbados's previous synagogue had been destroyed in an 1831 hurricane. Its replacement, according to Wilfred S. Samuel, was particularly remarkable, since the congregation at that time numbered about thirty persons (Samuel 1936, 108).

23. *Tidende*, 14 September 1833: 2.

24. Ibid.

25. The following description is based on the author's observations of the present building (which is little changed from the original), supplemented by a conversation with Frederik Gjessing, who studies the synagogue's architecture. See also Gjessing and Maclean 1987, 60–61, and Woods 1992, 64–65.

26. Complete with the outer courtyard, the edifice bore a structural resemblance to the synagogues of Amsterdam and Curaçao. Placed on irregularly shaped plots of land, the synagogues still managed to face in the traditional eastward direction through such design.

27. Confirmation of this layout, outside of observations of the present building, can be seen in a layout of the city's buildings drafted by a Mr. Hingelberg for taxation purposes in 1836 to 1837 (photocopies in possession of Katina Coulianos, Charlotte Amalie, St. Thomas). The synagogue appears on Plan No. 11, dated November 1836. The columns, incidentally, consisted of a wooden core surrounded by special rounded bricks and then coated with plaster.

28. *Tebah* and *Ahal* are Hebrew, Western Sephardic terms for the reader's desk and holy ark respectively. Also used in Curaçao.

29. This feature also appears in the old Sephardic congregations of London, Amsterdam, New York, and Curaçao, among others.
30. For comparison with other contemporary synagogue layouts in Europe and the New World, see Goldman 2000, 38–77.
31. *Tidende*, 6 April 1833: 1. Though the material of the lamps is not mentioned in the *Tidende* account, all the lamps in the synagogue today are made of bronze.
32. Both quotations are published in *Tidende*, 14 September 1833, 2–3. The latter quotation is from Psalms 118:24.
33. It is quite possible these "priests" were in fact *kohanim*, individuals identified by the Jewish community as having descended from the priests who tended the Great Temple in Jerusalem. Such an identity would have been appropriate for their role in the ceremony.
34. This and all other quotations from the ceremony are from *Tidende*, 14 September 1833, 2–3.

Chapter 4: A Battle of Reforms: 1833–1848 (pages 51–86)

1. Parry, Sherlock, and Maingot 1987, 172.
2. Knight 1990, 365.
3. Hall 1992, 90.
4. By 1835, for example, free-coloreds outnumbered white residents three to one (Ibid., 180).
5. Nissen 1838, 1837 entry.
6. Petersen 1837–1840(?).
7. Although marriage is a strong component of Christian belief, every attempt to enforce the idea among the population—from the work of missionaries in the eighteenth and nineteenth centuries, to the concerns of the U.S. government in 1920, to the ridiculed missionary "Parade of the Married" during the first half of the twentieth century, to a 1990s television advertising campaign against teen pregnancy—failed miserably despite strong church attendance (Colby 1940).
8. Hall 1992, 83–84, 175–76.
9. Although the Jews comprised about 22 percent of the white population, they only made up about 3.3 percent of the entire Charlotte Amalie population (Nissen 1838, 1837 entry).
10. Rigsarkiv, *Danske Vestindiske Lokalarkiv*, Menighedernes Indberetninger om Fødte, Viede og Døde pa St. Thomas.
11. Above the entrance to the Altona cemetery is a sign that reads "Beit HaChayim, 5596." This Hebrew year corresponds with the Gregorian year 1836. Death records for the congregation are missing between 1826 and 1852.
12. Rigasrkiv, *Danske Vestindiske Lokalarkiv*, St. Thomas og St. Jan Guvernement mm. 1757–1909, Testamenteprotokol, 1828–1841, 158a–160b.
13. Occasionally, the testator would donate to other synagogues as well. Emanuel

Alvares Correa gave sixteen dollars to the Curaçao synagogue (Rigsarkiv, *Dansk Vestindiske Lokalarkiv*, St. Thomas Byføgedarkiv, Eksekutor og Konkursboer, 1778–1868, V); and Moise C. Lopes Dubec, Jr., donated a sum to his synagogue in Bordeaux (ibid., VI).

14. Interview with David Stanley Sasso, June 8, 1994.
15. Such as the cemetery at the Cambridge (Massachusetts) Episcopal Church, in which only former pastors and presidents of Harvard University receive their own table.
16. The following descriptions are based on both written and oral accounts, as well as the author's personal experience with Hurricanes Luis and Marilyn in September 1995.
17. The eye of a hurricane contains some of the lowest sustained atmospheric pressures on Earth, going below 27.50″ (931 millibars) in the strongest storms. See, for example, http://www.aoml.noaa.gov/hrd/hurdat/andreweasy.html.
18. Within the Virgin Islands, the rhythm over the last century is somewhat erratic: Major storms hit the islands in 1916, 1928, 1989 (Hugo), 1995 (Marilyn), and 1996 (Bertha).
19. More recently, authorities moved the date back a month to June 25.
20. See *Tidende*, 27 July 1821, for example. Today, the island observes the holiday by shutting down government offices and holding a single pan-religious service (*VIDNews*, June 26, 1994, p. 1, for example).
21. *Tidende*, 26 October 1872, for example.
22. *Tidende*, 2 August 1837.
23. *Tidende*, 16 August 1837: 2. This time, the collection was at the store of Mr. Charles Lopes Dubec, a Bordeaux native.
24. Ibid.
25. *Tidende*, 27 December 1837.
26. Which, at the time, was around $1,000 per year.
27. Obituary of S. E. L. Maduro, *Tidende*, 26 January, 1867: 2–3.
28. Information on S. E. L. Maduro is from ibid., and Emmanuel and Emmanuel 1970, 343–45.
29. *Hymnal for the Hebrew Congregation B. V. S. & G. H.*, 1942, 1964; both in possession of Katina Coulianos, St. Thomas.
30. Obituary of Mr. E. A. Correa, *Tidende*, 10 January 1838: 2, col. 3.
31. *Tidende*, 4 September 1818: 4.
32. STBDM 1.
33. Rigsarkiv, *Danske Vestindiske Lokalarkiv*, St. Thomas Byføgedarkiv, Eksekutor og Konkursboer, 1778–1868, V, Cor-Dec. Altona and Hamburg were both Danish possessions before they moved into German hands. Correa may have chosen Altona for practical purposes. When his children grew up and presumably entered into business on St. Thomas, the cost of a Burgher Brief for them as residents would be substantially reduced.
34. Ibid.

35. Ibid.
36. Not a single reference in the *Tidende* between 1816 and 1838 links him to any facet of synagogue life.
37. Rigsarkiv, *Danske Vestindiske Lokalarkiv*, St. Thomas Byføgedarkiv, Eksekutor og Konkursboer, 1778–1868, V, Cor-Dec., Letter from Rachel Correa to J. H. Osorio, July 27, 1838.
38. Ibid.
39. Ibid.
40. Ibid., Letter to O. G. C. Degetau from Bahnsen, Marshall and Osorio, November 3, 1838.
41. Ibid., Letter from O. G. C. Degetau to Executors of Correa will, July 28, 1838.
42. Ibid.
43. Ibid. Letter to O. G. C. Degetau from Bahnsen, Marshall, and Osorio, November 3, 1838.
44. The subject of Reform in Judaism is far too large to discuss in great detail here. Several books have been written on the subject, probably the most comprehensive of which is Meyer 1988.
45. Most of the information in this section comes from Steven Singer's illuminating article "Jewish Religious Thought in Early Victorian London" (Singer 1985). Although other historians argue that English reform came as a direct result from German reform, I find Singer's argument particularly compelling, especially in the context of St. Thomas reform.
46. Ibid., 186.
47. Ibid., 207.
48. English was also the primary language of the *Tidende*.
49. Dookhan 1994 [1974], 102.
50. St. Thomas, however, did not publicly refer to their philosophy as "neo-Karatism," as the British reformers did; rather, they simply led their lives according to the same principles.
51. Emmanuel and Emmanuel 1970, 344.
52. *Tidende*, 30 December 1840: 2.
53. Combining Carillon's seal on Hannah de Sola's confirmation certificate (STBDM 1: "Benyamin ben Aharon haCohen"), and the signature "A. C. Carillon [Aharon ben K'moharar Binyamin HaCohen]" on the rabbinical diploma of soon-to-be minister of Curaçao Aaron Mendes Chumaceiro (Emmanuel and Emmanuel 1970, 485). *Studia Rosenthaliana*, 10, no. 1 (July 1986): 77–79 (Dutch), 83–84 (English), makes mention of an "Amsterdam printer and writer" named A. C. Carillon, who wrote a pamphlet criticizing the Dutch Jews and Dutch government for their inaction during the Damascus blood libel incident in 1840. This may be the same person.
54. *Tidende*, 24 June 1840: 2.
55. *Tidende*, 3 October 1840: 2.

56. Several contemporary accounts take note of Carillon's English deficiencies. See introduction to Carillon 1845; see also *Occident* 1: 54.

57. *Occident* 1: 347–48; Carillon 1845.

58. This year is difficult to gauge. The next reference to Carillon after the announcement of his speech is on January 10, 1842, soon after which he goes up to New York (Pool and Pool 1955, 189). The only direct evidence that he remained there during 1841 is contained in a letter from David Woolf Marks to Isaac Leeser and the *Occident and American Jewish Advocate*, which states that in 1843, the congregation "receive[d] back the Rev. Mr. Carillon, who had made an application to be re-engaged." Through this I determine that Carillon spent at least several months with the congregation before leaving it for New York City.

59. See Lieberles 1987.

60. *Tidende*, 10 January 1842.

61. It is worth noting here that pseudonyms were used commonly in nineteenth-century St. Thomas to mask the identities of newspaper editorialists. Presumably parallel to similar practices in Europe and the United States, such actions allowed for the free and public exchange of ideas while at the same time providing some form of protection for those with controversial ideas—even in small societies such as St. Thomas.

62. *Tidende*, 19 and 22 January 1842.

63. *VOJ* 2, no. 45; Pool and Pool 1955, 189.

64. Meyer 1988, 171–75.

65. Ibid., 176.

66. Petuchowsky 1968, 66–68. *AI* 2 (1841): 535–37, gave the first book of this series a glowing review, stating that "[t]he changes brought to this Ritual have been done with wisdom and discernment."

67. *AI* 2 (1841): 535–37.

68. *Occident* 2: 53. The West London Synagogue's form of liturgy, Wolff added, seemed to be the best choice for the Jewish Sunday school he intended to open shortly.

69. Ibid., 54.

70. Ibid.

71. Interestingly, there is evidence that the congregation intended to introduce an organ to the service, even though the West London synagogue disapproved of the practice. Nothing ever came of this intention. (*AI* 3: 532).

72. *Tidende*, 16 August 1843.

73. See subscription lists for *Archives Israélites* 2 (1841); and *Voice of Jacob* 3 (1843). To give an idea of the importance of the Caribbean Jewish community to these periodicals, the latter example lists almost as many subscribers in Jamaica as in London. (Though, to be fair, the Jamaican Jews ordered considerably fewer copies.)

74. *Tidende*, 22 February 1843: 2.

75. *Occident* 1: 346. The advertisements read: "Notice: Needed for the synagogue at St. Thomas (Danish Antilles), a man who can take over the functions of officiating minister, in the same style and according to the same principles as the new synagogue established in London for the British Jews, under the name of West London Synagogue. Please address, for information on the subject, Mr. Rev. D. W. Marks, 51 Burten Street, Burten Crescent, London." (Translated from *AI* 3:592.)

76. *Occident* 2: 54.

77. *AI* 3:592.

78. Combining *Occident* 2: 54; 3: 358. The salary is estimated through another want-ad by the Synagogue in 1853 (*AI*, May 1853), which offers $1,200 per year, and the *Occident*'s report of Carillon's settlement in 1845 (3: 358), which was twice that.

79. *Occident* 2: 55.

80. *Occident* 1: 347.

81. Ibid., 348.

82. *VOJ* 2: 207.

83. Ibid., 192.

84. *Occident* 1: 348.

85. For more detail, see *VOJ* 2: 207; 3: 94.

86. *VOJ* 2: 207.

87. *Occident* 1: 347.

88. The laws concerning confirmation comprise articles fourteen through seventeen of the Royal decree of March 29, 1814. These exist in a full English translation in Bamberger 1983: 50–57. The phrase quoted here is from page 55, §14.

89. Ibid., 56, §17.

90. This is the popular understanding. The Charleston Reformed Society of Israelites, which began in 1825, had an individual confirmation ceremony in their prayerbook (which came out around the same time), though there seems to be no evidence that this ceremony was ever used (Meyer 1988: 232). The *Occident*, meanwhile, printed a poem entitled "Lines to a Young Friend on His Confirmation," which the magazine claims dates to 1839 (*Occident* 5: 187), though any evidence surrounding this poem's subject is lacking.

91. *VOJ* 2: 207; 3: 13.

92. *Tidende*, 16 August 1843: 2 (Emphasis mine).

93. Ibid.

94. Ibid.; *Tidende*, 19 August 1943: 2.

95. 1802 By-Laws, Article 1.

96. *VOJ* 3: 29.

97. Miriam, Rebecca, and Alexander Wolff were Aron Wolff's children; Miriam Cappé was his daughter-in-law, married to his son Daniel.

98. STBDM1.

99. *VOJ* 3: 45; *Occident* 1: 512. See also "St. Thomas Confirmations," typescript by

Malcolm H. Stern, American Jewish Archives. Original confirmation certificates exist in fragments at the Maryland Jewish Historical Society, and on microfilm at the St. Thomas Hebrew Congregation (STBDM1).

100. *VOJ* 3: 13.

101. Singer 1985, 194; Petuchowski 1968, 66–67.

102. *VOJ* 3:13.

103. Ibid., 94.

104. Ibid., 162.

105. Ibid., 150; see also *FFW* 1, no. 4 (May 1844): 178, where Aron Wolff writes: "The Congregation is at peace. . . . There is a better observance of the Sabbath—only ten stores now remaining open . . ."

106. *VOJ* 3: 199. Letter dated May 25, 1844.

107. Emmanuel and Emmanuel 1970, 343–44.

108. Obituary of S. E. L. Maduro, *Tidende*, 26 January 1867: 2–3.

109. Guiterman [1971], 18; *VOJ* 3: 199.

110. See letter of "A Silent Observer," in *Tidende*, 17 July 1844: 2; for a more detailed description of his later offenses, see letter from "ELDAD" in the *Kingston Despatch*, 6 August 1845.

111. That many teachers supported Carillon's reforms is evident through an advertisement by F. D. Petit in the *Tidende* of 24 July 1844: 2, which assures subscribers of the Sunday School that their education will continue, and subsequently opens the door for potential teachers to apply for their positions. On the break-off group's activities: see *Tidende*, 5 October 1844: 2, response to "One of Your Subscribers."

112. Guiterman [1971], 18.

113. *Tidende*, 17 July 1844: 2. Letter from "A SILENT OBSERVER."

114. *VOJ* 4, no. 85 (4 October 1844): 5.

115. *Tidende*, 2 October 1844: 3.

116. *Tidende*, 5 October 1844: 2.

117. Reverend Moses N. Nathan was instrumental in settling the score with Carillon's suit. See *Occident* 3: 358; *JC* 1: 255; *JC* 2, no. 1 (17 October 1845).

118. *VOJ* 4: 223, 230, 238, 245; 5: 29, 37, 46, 98, 121, 144–45, 171, 187. *Occident* 2: 514 states that Carillon was minister of Spanishtown, Jamaica, in 1845, but this is true only to the extent that he presided over the consecration of a new synagogue building there.

119. *VOJ* n.s. 1, no. 4 (6 November 1846): 28. He may have moved back to St. Thomas for a short time, judging from a letter of his published in the *Tidende* of 11 October 1849: 2, col. 1; but this is the last known of him.

120. Emmanuel and Emmanuel 1970, 343–44.

121. *VOJ* 4: 39.

122. *Tidende*, 28 November 1866.

123. Today, this congregation is known as the Western Synagogue. The name of the congregation had nothing to do with its regional affiliation, nor its members, but rather its geographical location (in Denmark Court).

124. *JC*, 18 May 1883: 9.

125. "Sermon Delivered in the Synagogue Kingston Jamaica on Shabbat Teshuva, 5598 [1838]." University of Southampton Archives, MS 116/104, AJ 258/3, pp. 1–2.

126. *VOJ* 2: 183.

127. *FFW* 1, no. 2 (March 1844): 66. Attributed only to the editors of the magazine. However, from the tone of the piece, it is very likely that Nathan penned this alone.

128. *VOJ* 4: 39–40.

129. Ibid., 119.

130. Ibid., 148; *Occident* 3: 57. Reverend A. A. Wolff bore no relation to St. Thomas's Aron Wolff.

131. Proclamation of 29 March 1814, Article 10 (Bamberger 1983, 53).

132. *VOJ* 4: 148.

133. *Tidende*, 5 April 1845.

134. *Tidende*, 22 March 1845: 2.

135. The Jews gathered over $1,500 through this effort (*Occident* 3: 164).

136. *VOJ* 5: 82.

137. *Tidende*, 22 March 1845: 2.

138. *Occident* 3: 358.

139. STBDM1; "St. Thomas Confirmations," typescript of originals by Rabbi Malcolm Stern, in American Jewish Archives.

140. Shavuot, the holiday celebrating the Jews' receipt of the Torah at Mount Sinai, is now the traditional time of the year to hold confirmation ceremonies in American synagogues that uphold the ritual.

141. *VOJ* n.s. 1, no. 6 (4 December 1846): 45. This was by no means Nathan's last confirmation. Another thirteen children were confirmed on a Friday evening in the middle of Passover, 1847, where "no Seppharim was taken out, nor was there any oath or promise administered" (*Occident* 5: 215).

142. *Occident* 5: 215.

143. *VOJ* 5: 82; *JC* 2, no. 9 (6 February 1846). The other members of the committee were Aron Wolff, Sigismund Rothschild, Emanuel Charles Mendes Da Costa, and J. H. Osorio.

144. *Tidende*, 24 January 1846: 1.

145. *Occident* 5: 379.

146. "Code of Laws" 1848, §2, 8, 25.

147. These included electing representatives, buying or selling synagogue property, electing a minister, and raising the minister's salary (§3).

148. *Occident* 5: 215.

149. Notably, this printer—C. Sherman, at 19 St. James St.—was the same printer who published Isaac Leeser's *Occident*.

Chapter 5: Development: 1848–1867 (pages 87–111)

1. Hall 1992, 208–11.
2. In all probability, the most affected urban population, besides the slaves themselves, were a group known as "spinsters." Unmarried women who had outlived their legacies and had no husbands with whom to establish businesses, they often received income by renting out their house slaves to do occasional work. After emancipation, these women had to rely more heavily on charity.
3. Letter from M. B. Simmonds to Reverend Isaac Leeser, 3 February 1848. St. Thomas Synagogue Archives, Charlotte Amalie, St. Thomas. Original in collection of Mr. Robert Marcus, Springfield, Virginia.
4. Sharfman 1988, 222–25; *Occident* 5: 117, 211. Israel at this point was too far away for the fruit to arrive intact in the United States.
5. *Tidende,* 3 October 1840: 2.
6. STBDM1, Birth #549; *Occident* 5: 58.
7. *Tidende,* 12 January 1850: 2.
8. Psalms 127:1. Translation adapted from *JPS.* Simmonds's house is to the north of the synagogue, behind Denmark Hill, on an estate called Fairview; his plaque was still clearly visible at the start of the twenty-first century.
9. *Tidende,* 17 July 1850: 3.
10. *Tidende,* 25 November 1849: 2; 8 June 1850: 2.
11. *Occident* 7: 479; 8: June issue.
12. Matthew Bagg, "St. Thomas, Santa Cruz, and Porto Rico in 1851 and 1852." Typescript manuscript, New York Public Library, 18–19.
13. Hall 1992, 209.
14. See, for example, *Tidende,* 7 October 1849: 2.
15. See, for example, *Tidende,* 13 December 1851.
16. *Tidende,* 20, 24, and 27 March 1852.
17. *Tidende,* 5 January 1853: 2.
18. *Occident* 10: 415.
19. *Occident* 11: 428.
20. *Tidende,* 20 February 1856: 2.
21. *AI* 14: 240, 300, 360; *Occident* 11: 79.
22. *Occident* 14: 188.
23. Ibid.
24. *Tidende,* 12 January 1856: 2.
25. I make this assertion based on a positive attitude held toward him by one of the pro-minister letter writers, the difficulties he faced in achieving a Hebrew

Benevolent Association, and the board's general inaction after the next bout of writing (*Occident* 14: 349–50).

26. *Tidende,* 20 February 1856: 2.

27. Ibid.

28. *Tidende,* 24 May 1856: 2.

29. *Tidende,* 8 March 1856: 3.

30. *Occident* 14: 349–50.

31. *Tidende,* 15 March 1856: 2.

32. *Occident* 14: 349–50.

33. Ibid.

34. Emmanuel 1973, 9, 14. Coro is a small port city on the northern coast of Venezuela situated about fifty miles south of Curaçao.

35. Many of the St. Thomas Jewish family names in the 1860s appear on the known list of Coro Jews from this time, including Delvalle, Senior, Pereira, Namias De Crasto, and Curiel (Ibid., 11). Because of the finite number of Jewish names that circulated in the Caribbean, however, this may prove little.

36. *Tidende,* 21 November 1857: 2.

37. *Tidende,* 25 November 1857: 2.

38. *Tidende,* 26 January 1867: 2–3. This account, taken from Maduro's obituary, states that Chumaceiro conferred the honorary title in 1858. However, because it also states that this occurred when "the Chief Rabbi of Curaçao first visited [St.Thomas]," and since there is no evidence that Chumaceiro visited the island in 1858, I include it here.

39. *Occident* 16: 312; *Tidende,* 2 December 1857.

40. *Occident* 18: 196.

41. Unfortunately, this building was destroyed by German bombs in 1941.

42. *Tidende,* 8 February 1862: 2, col. 3.

43. *Occident* 18: 196.

44. Ibid.

45. *Tidende,* 15 February 1862: 2, col. 3; 26 February 1862: 3, col. 1.

46. *Occident* 18: 196.

47. Ibid.

48. *Occident* 19: 95; *Tidende,* 3 April 1861: 2.

49. *Occident* 19: 142–43. The benefit raised $557.48.

50. *Tidende,* 19 June 1861. Penha's intentions become clearer still when combined with a later advertisement for his school that appeared in Spanish—a language used extremely rarely in the pages of the *Tidende*—and targeted the Jewish community of the island (*Tidende,* 12 March 1862: 4).

51. *Tidende,* 13 March 1861: 2; 13 July, 10 August, 17 August, 28 August, and 2 October 1861; 28 May 1862.

52. Case of Myers v. Maduro, in American Jewish Historical Society, Curaçao Docu-

ments [Microfilm I-112], Roll #1. Note that this source is a translation of the original Danish text, which is buried somewhere in the Rigsarkiv. Though misplaced in the *AJHS* microfilm, and only 85 to 90 percent complete, it is clearly identifiable as a St. Thomas document. Accompanying documents that would further elucidate the case are missing from the microfilm. The accusations are not specified in the available text.

53. This and all other references to Myers v. Maduro are from ibid., unless otherwise notated.

54. Ibid., 4–5.

55. *Tidende*, 8 February 1862: 2, col. 2.

56. *Occident* 19: 382–83.

57. Ibid.: 383–84.

58. *AJHS*, Curaçao documents [Microfilm I-112], roll #1, Myers v. Maduros: 7.

59. *Tidende*, 1 February 1862: 3.

60. *Tidende*, 5 February 1862: 2. Pretto reveals himself as "Israelite" in *Tidende*, 15 February 1862: 2, col. 1.

61. *Tidende*, 8 February 1862: 2–3.

62. *Tidende*, 15 February 1862: 2.

63. *Tidende*, 19 February 1862: 2. D'Azevedo writes: "Mr. A. then informed me that Dr. Pretto demanded satisfaction [often used to mean a duel], to which I replied that I was ready to give it."

64. One account (*Tidende*, 29 March 1862: 3) calls this Chumaceiro's third visit to St. Thomas. I can find no documentary evidence that supports this claim, however.

65. *Tidende*, 26 March 1862: 3.

66. *Occident* 20: 96; *Tidende*, 26 March 1862: 2; STBDM1; STBDM2.

67. Translation taken directly from *Tidende*, 29 March 1862: 3, col. 2.

68. *Tidende*, 29 March 1862: 3, col. 2.

69. *Tidende*, 2 April 1862: 2, col. 2.

70. *Tidende*, 2 August 1862: 3.

71. *Tidende*, 3 September 1862: 2.

72. *Occident*, 20, Supplement.

73. Ibid., 430.

74. Letter from the Hebrew Congregation B. v. S. & G. H. to Governor Wilhelm L. Birch, 24 May 1967. AJA Microfilm #380; *Tidende*, 17 January 1863: 2.

75. *Tidende*, 3 December 1862: 2, 3; 6 December 1862: 4.

76. *Occident* 10: 558–63; *AI* 1853: 298.

77. *AI* 1854: 269. This translates to about $3,000 American.

78. *Occident* 16: 505. *Occident* 11: 233 notes that Jews are leaving Jamaica, thus creating a dwindling community by the time Nathan had arrived in 1863.

79. *Tidende*, 5 September 1863: 3.

80. *Tidende*, 12 September 1863: 3.

81. While not explicitly allowed in the synagogue's 1848 bylaws, the allowance of non-voting members as observers in the meetings of the voting community appeared to have been common practice at that time (Ibid.).

82. Ibid.

83. *Occident* 21: 568. *Tidende,* 2 October 1863; 24 October 1863; 28 October 1863: 3.

84. *Tidende,* 12 December 1863: 3; *Occident* 22, 110–20; "Form of Special Service" 1864.

85. *AJA* Microfilm #380, Part I.

86. Letter from Moses B. Simmonds to "the Presidency," 16 December 1863. *AJA* Microfilm #380.

87. *Tidende,* 17 July 1850: 2.

88. The final word on this issue actually did not come until three years later, in a letter dated 27 December 1866. (From communication dated 1 April 1867, Hebrew Congregation B. v. S. & G. H. to Governor of St. Thomas; *AJA* Microfilm #380).

89. See, for example, *Tidende,* 11 October 1864. Note that both Simmonds and Reverend Nathan were trustees of the Savings Bank at the same time; see also *Tidende,* 28 February 1863; 15 November 1865.

90. This statement is based on the 1863 Synagogue Board, which consisted of Benjamin Delvalle (president), age 53; David Cardoze, Jr. (Vice president), age 39; Alexander Levy (treasurer), age 31; Eugene Petit (representative), age 48; and Moses De Sola (representative), age 28 (*Occident* 21: 40. Ages are compiled from synagogue marriage, birth, and death records, and may be off by one year).

91. *Occident* 22: 285–87. In attcking the Jewish hegemony in Curaçao, *Shemah Yisrael* resorted to familiar anti-Semitic techniques. Most effectively, the newspaper quoted sections of "old" Hebrew liturgy and presented them to the outside community as secret tracts of world domination.

92. *Occident* 22: 285–87; 23: 135.

93. Letter from forty-five members of the congregation to the BvSvGH Board of Representatives, September 1865. From *AJA* Microfilm #380.

94. *JC,* 9 February 1866: 2.

95. Letter from forty-five members of the congregation to the BvSvGH Board of Representatives, September , 1865. From *AJA* Microfilm #380.

96. Letter from Reverend M. N. Nathan to Chamberlain L. Rothe, 8 November 1865. *AJA* Microfilm #380.

97. Letter from Moses De Sola to "The Honorable Presidency of St. Thomas and St. Johns," 27 November 1865. *AJA* Microfilm #380.

98. Letter from M. N. Nathan to Moses De Sola, Esq., 26 September 1865. *AJA* Microfilm #380.

99. *JC,* 6 October 1865: 7.

100. *JC,* 8 December 1865: 6.

101. *JC,* 9 February 1866: 2.
102. Cardoze's father was David Cardoze, Sr., the minister who beat out S. E. L. Maduro for the top position in Curaçao in 1844 to 1845. There is no reason to believe that any residual feelings resentment existed between the younger Cardoze and Maduro—or, for that matter, that any residual feelings existed at all.
103. See, for example, letters from David Cardoze, Jr., to the St. Thomas governor, 12 January and 18 October 1866. *AJA* Microfilm #380. The government generally responded to the notes, but only to defer the decision or to bounce it to another official.
104. *Occident* 24: 431. The *Tidende* simply has no information or account of the confirmation.
105. *Tidende,* 28 November 1866: 2.
106. *Tidende,* 12 December 1866; *JC,* 22 February 1867.
107. *Tidende,* 8 January 1867.
108. *Tidende,* 26 January 1867: 2–3.

Chapter 6: The Hebrew Reformed Congregation: 1867–1875 (pages 112–41)

1. The ages of two of the seceders—Alex Nones and J. L. Penha—cannot be determined through available sources, though it is not hard to believe that they fell around the average. The other approximate ages, culled through marriage, birth, and 1870 census records, are as follows: Moses De Sola, 32; M. R. A. Correa, 29; M. C. D'Azevedo, 35; Emanuel C. Osorio, 25; Alfred Nones, 30; M. Osorio, 29; J. H. Lindo, 29; Jacob Lindo, 46; M. Myerston, 26; Samuel Joseph, 42; A. D. De Jongh, 26.
2. Letter from M. N. Nathan to David Cardoze, Jr., 20 February 1867. *AJA* Microfilm #380.
3. Letter from Jacob Lindo to the Synagogue Board, 21 February 1867. *AJA* Microfilm #380.
4. Letter from Synagogue Board to Jacob Lindo, 21 February 1867. *AJA* Microfilm #380.
5. Letter from Jacob Lindo to the Synagogue Board #2, 21 February 1867, *AJA* Microfilm #380.
6. Letter from J. H. Lindo, Jacob Lindo, A. Da Costa Gomez, M. Myerston, E. C. Osorio, J. H. Moron, Ad. Nones, Joseph Fidanque, Alex Nones, M. R. A. Correa, M. Osorio, and Samuel Joseph to the BvSvGH, Board of Representatives, 26 February 1867. *AJA* Microfilm #380.
7. Letter from fourteen Congregants to the BvSvGH, Board of Representatives, 14 March 1867. *AJA* Microfilm #380. The three other congregants who signed the 26 February missive—A. Da Costa Gomez, J. H. Moron, and Joseph Fi-

danque—probably frequented the same group, but officially joined the seceders later. Da Costa Gomez's family is listed in the 1870 census as "Hebrew Reformed," and Reformed Congregation birth and marriage records register the Moron and Fidanque families as participants and members.

8. Ibid.

9. A. D. De Jongh to Isaac Leeser, *Occident* 25: 131–36.

10. New Virgin Island Colonial Laws were enacted in 1852 and 1863. For more, see Dookhan 1994 [1974]: 203–13.

11. Letter from fourteen Congregants to the BvSvGH, Board of Representatives, 14 March 1867. AJA Microfilm #380.

12. Letter from Hebrew Reformed Congregation to Presidency of St. Thomas, 10 April 1867. AJA microfilm #380.

13. From letter by A. D. De Jongh, *Occident* 25: 131–36.

14. Letter from A. D. De Jongh to Isaac Leeser, *Israelite* 14, no. 14 (4 October 1867): 5.

15. Letter from Hebrew Reformed Congregation to Presidency of St. Thomas and St. John. 1 April 1867. AJA Microfilm #380. For more on this congregation, see Lieberles 1987.

16. "Discourse of Mr. Jacob Lindo," in *Occident* 25: 134.

17. *Tidende*, 11 September 1867.

18. *Occident* 25: 132–34.

19. Letter from HRC to Presidency of St. Thomas and St. Johns, 1 April 1867. AJA Microfilm #380.

20. Letter from BvSvGH to Presidency of St. Thomas and St. Johns, 1 April 1867. AJA Microfilm #380.

21. *Occident* 25: 136.

22. Mentioned in D. W. Marks letter to "M. de Sola, Esq, and others," 14 May 1867. AJA Microfilm #380.

23. In other words, no such letter appeared in the *Jewish Chronicle.*

24. *Occident* 25: 131.

25. *Israelite* 14, no. 1 (5 July 1867).

26. *Israelite* 14, no. 14: 5.

27. Letter from D. W. Marks to the Wardens of the Hebrew Reformed Congregation, no date (appears to be a hastily copied letter). AJA Microfilm #380.

28. Ibid.

29. *Tidende*, 23 June 1869: 3, col. 1 (English translation of a letter from Presidency of St. Thomas and St. Johns to Wardens of Hebrew Reformed Congregation, 3 April 1867.) See also Letter from Hebrew Reformed Congregation to Minister of the Interior, Copenhagen, 6 August 1868 [AJA Microfilm #380] and *Israelite* 14, no. 13 (27 September 1867): 6.

30. Osorio's approximate age based on St. Thomas census of 1846.

31. BvSvGH wedding records, #19, 34, 36, 85. Weddings #34 and 36 were performed

in St. Croix and Coro, Venezuela, respectively. In #85, Osorio performed the ceremony "in consequence of the Hazan's disposition."

32. *Israelite* 14, no. 13 (27 September 1867): 6.

33. Letter from Hebrew Reformed Congregation *Beth Elohim* to the Honorable Presidency of St. Thomas and St. Johns, 20 June 1867. *AJA* Microfilm #380.

34. Letter from Board of BvSvGH to M. Rosenbaum, 4 July 1867. *AJA* Microfilm #380; *JC*, 3 November 1871: 4–5 (in article entitled "St. Thomas").

35. Letter from Board of BvSvGH to Governor-General Ludwig Birch, 27 May 1867. *AJA* Microfilm #380.

36. *Tidende*, 28 September 1867: 3.

37. *Tidende*, 24 July 1867.

38. 29 October through 13 November 1867. For more on this fearsome turn of events, see Watlington and Lincoln, comps., 1997.

39. *Harper's Weekly*, 28 December 1867: 829 (reprinted in Watlington and Lincoln, comps., 13).

40. *Israelite* 14, no. 27 (10 January 1868).

41. *Occident* 25: 462.

42. The full text of this prayer is well worth the read, and constitutes in this author's opinion a deeply effective example of modern Jewish rhetoric. It can be found in *Occident* 26: 455–57.

43. *Israelite* 14, no. 27 (10 January 1868).

44. *Israelite* 14, no. 26 (3 January 1868): 5.

45. Ibid.

46. Ibid.

47. *Tidende*, 30 November 1867: 3.

48. Ibid., p. 2; *Israelite* 14, no. 26 (3 January 1868): 5.

49. *Tidende*, 10 January 1868. David Cardoze, Jr. (president of BvSvGH), hosted the meeting. Jacob Jessurun Lindo (vice president of the HRC) was the chair.

50. *Tidende*, 7 December 1867; STBDM2 (Marriage #1867–60).

51. Rules and Regulations for the Govenment of the Hebrew Reformed Congregation (*Beth Elohim*), 1868. (Herein HRC Bylaws)

52. Ibid. The cover page has a handwritten address, "To His Excellency the Governor General of the Danish WI Possessions." If microfilming procedure reflects organization, these rules were stored along with the other synagogue regulations.

53. *Israelite* 14, no. 50 (19 June 1868): 6.

54. Purchase deed of the Cemetery of the Hebrew Reformed Congregation, St. Thomas. In *AJA* Microfilm #380.

55. HRC Bylaws, Article XX. The existing records of the Hebrew Reform Congregation include births and marriages, but no deaths; nor does the *Tidende* record a burial ceremony in the Hebrew Reformed Congregation.

56. *JC*, 3 November 1871, 5.

57. The seal consisted entirely of text. It was round, and read "Hebrew Reformed

Congregation ° St. Thomas" around the circumference, with the Hebrew Inscription *K"K Beth Elohim* across the middle (Rigsarkiv, Vestindiske Lokalarkiv, Menighedernes Indberetninger om Fødte, Viede og Døde Pa St. Thomas og St. Jan).

58. Births, Marriages and Deaths of the Reformed Synagogue (ibid.).

59. Letter from Council of Administration of the Hebrew Reformed Congregation to the Minister of the Interior, Copenhagen, 6 August 1868. *AJA* Microfilm #380.

60. Ibid.; Letter from Hebrew Reformed Congregation Council of Administration to Minister of the Interior, Copenhagen, 25 August 1869. *AJA* Microfilm #380.

61. *Tidende*, 7 February 1868; *JC*, 13 November 1871: 4–5, (in longer article called "St. Thomas.")

62. Both quotations from *Tidende*, 16 June 1869: 2, col. 1 (from minutes of the Colonial Council meeting of 8 June 1867); see also *Tidende*, 24 December 1870: 3.

63. This did not hamper his religious affiliation. In 1869, when the King's birthday fell on a Saturday, Cappé moved the planned fireworks celebration to Sunday. *Tidende*, 20 February 1869.

64. *Israelite* 16, no. 10 (10 September 1869).

65. *Tidende*, 12 April 1869. I have found no response to this letter, so I cannot assess the effectiveness of this protest.

66. Letter from "PRY," *Tidende*, 8 October 1869: 2–3; see also *Tidende*, 4 January 1871: 2–3; 18 January 1871: 1, col. 3; 17 January 1872: 1. Notably, H. Hjernö, a non-Jew, introduced this referendum to the council in late 1870.

67. One of these announcements has been reprinted in full in Philipson 1967, 289–91.

68. Ibid., 191.

69. *Tidende*, 26 June 1869. Cardoze co-officiated in the ritual with acting Worshipful Master Dr. Daniel Pretto, whose was present along with several members of the Masonic Lodge, to mark Wolff's Masonic associations.

70. *Tidende*, 23 June 1869: 2–3.

71. Ibid., 2.

72. Letter from Hebrew Reformed Congregation "Beth Elohim" to the Governor of the Danish West Indies, 24 April 1872. *AJA* Microfilm #380.

73. *Shtetlach* is the plural of the more familiar *shtetl*.

74. *Tidende*, 15 June 1870: 2, col. 1.

75. Ibid.

76. *Tidende*, 20 July 1870: 2.

77. *Tidende*, 20 August 1870: 2–3. Original appears in French.

78. For examples, see *Tidende*, 19 August 1871: 2; 20 March 1872: 3; 10 July 1872: 2.

79. There is no evidence to pinpoint exactly when Nathan resigned from the post.

80. Rubin 1983, 152–53. Nathan received an initial request to give an audition sermon, but he did not get the job.

81. *JC*, 3 November 1871: 4–5.

82. In addition to his application to Charleston, Nathan also received an invitation

from New York's *Shearith Israel*—which at the time was searching for a minister—to come as a guest lecturer for six weeks in 1869. Contrary to the account given in Pool and Pool 1955, 191, Nathan postponed the invitation due to precarious health (*Tidende*, 13 March 1869: 3). The New York synagogue acquiesced, keeping its invitation open. There is no evidence that Nathan ever fulfilled the agreement.

83. STBDM2 (#1869–62); *Tidende*, 30 October 1869: 2, col. 1.

84. Letter from Hebrew Reformed Congregation to the Governor of St. Thomas, 24 April 1872. *AJA* Microfilm #380.

85. *JC*, 15 September 1871: 4.

86. E. N. Martinez obituary, *JC*, 31 March 1911: 33; *Tidende*, 21 February 1872: 2; *Tidende*, 6 March 1872.

87. Letter from the Board of BvSvGH to Governor of the DWI, 23 August 1872. *AJA* Microfilm #380.

88. *Tidende*, 13 May 1871: 2.

89. Term taken from *JC*, 3 November 1871: 4–5.

90. Ibid.

91. *Tidende*, 22 April 1871: 2.

92. *Tidende*, 10 May 1871: 4.

93. *Tidende*, 20 May 1871. Queen's Street, also known as Main Street, was a highly desirable area to live, and combined with the list of Nathan's possessions, showed Nathan as a man very well-off.

94. *JC*, 13 October 1871 (from article titled "Our Brethren in the Colonies").

95. Letter from Reverend E. N. Martinez to H. Hjernö, 23 April 1872. National Archives, RG 55, Entry 998, Box 2230: Municipal Councils & Commissions, School Commission or School Board.

96. *Tidende*, 7 June 1871: 2.

97. *JC*, 15 September 1871: 4 ("Good News From St. Thomas"). There are no known male births registered by the Reformed Congregation that correspond even roughly to this date.

98. Ibid.

99. See letter from Benjamin Delvalle to Governor F. Bolle, 12 April 1872. *AJA* Microfilm #380.

100. Dookhan 1994 [1974], 220–21.

101. Ibid., 223.

102. Ibid., 245.

103. *Israelite* 16, no. 13 (1 October 1869).

104. Ibid.; Communication from Board of BvSvGH to the Governor of the DWI, 23 August 1872. *AJA* Microfilm #380; Communication from Board of BvSvGH to Governor of the DWI, 19 December 1873. *AJA* Microfilm #380.

105. This is apparent through birth records, which lists his two daughters (born in 1869 and 1870 respectively) together. STBDM2 (#1869–220, 1869–220a).

106. Communication from Board of BvSvGH to Governor of the DWI, 23 August 1872. AJA Microfilm #380.
107. Rigsarkiv, *Danske Vestindiske Lokalarkiv.* Records of the Hebrew Reformed Congregation. These notes continued until 3 July 1882.
108. Communication from Board of BvSvGH to Governor of the D. W. I. Possessions, 11 June 1873. AJA Microfilm #380.
109. Communication from Board of BvSvGH to Governor of the D. W. I. Possessions, 19 December 1873. AJA Microfilm #380.
110. STBDM1.
111. "Code of Laws for the Government of the Hebrew Congregation Blessing and Peace and Acts of Piety in the Islands of St. Thomas." 1875, 2 (herein 1875 Bylaws).
112. 1848 Bylaws §1.
113. 1875 Bylaws §1.
114. Ibid., §27; as in the 1848 bylaws, this prohibition did not include "family worship"; elimination of the fine is particularly clear, since the rest of section 18— denoting different fines for different infractions—remains almost exactly the same as its 1848 incarnation.
115. Ibid., §15.
116. Ibid., §41.
117. Ibid., §30.
118. See HRC bylaws, Article XIII. Choirs had sung in the synagogue's sanctuary before, yet only in the Reformed Congregation were they an official, named entity within the congregation's organizational structure.
119. 1875 Bylaws §25.
120. *STT,* 29 July 1876: 2; Fidanque et al. 1977, 74–77.
121. I was unable to find Wolff's gravestone during a trip to the Ball's Pond cemetery (7 January 1996). Although Wolff's burial appeared on a list of burials compiled by David Jacobs (personal communication), a long search through nearly every grave in the area revealed nothing. At the very least, this shows that Wolff's gravestone was unremarkable.
122. *Tidende,* 13 July 1872.
123. Communication from Per Nielsen, January 1996, Copenhagen, Denmark.
124. Rachel Wolff Obituary, *STT,* 12 February 1879, 2, col. 2.
125. The only possible exception to this was the *Israelite,* which served as the voice of the Reform movement on St. Thomas. Yet even in this publication, there were no direct attacks on Reverend Nathan throughout the controversy.
126. "St. Thomas," *JC* (3 November 1871): 4–5. The correspondent may well have been one of Nathan's supporters on St. Thomas. Yet regardless of who wrote the article, it still shows the positive projected image of the minister in the world outside of St. Thomas.
127. *JC,* 18 May 1883: 9.

128. Ibid.

129. Ibid.

130. Ibid. The three representatives were Reverend A. Löwy, Mr. Walter Josephs, and Mr. F. D. Mocatta. While the account of Nathan's funeral does not hint at the total number of attendees, the number of prominent attendees mentioned suggests that there was a considerable turnout for Nathan's burial.

131. Ibid.

132. Only part of this inscription is readable. The rest has been eroded beyond recognition.

133. Personal observation, Ball's Pond cemetery, London, 7 January 1996.

134. Fidanque et al. 1977, 73–83. Fidanque claims erroneously that Martinez was reader at St. Thomas from 1872 to 1878.

135. *JC,* 31 March 1911: 33.

136. E. N. Martinez gravestone, Golders Green cemetery (London, England). I am grateful to Mr. David Jacobs for photographing this gravestone for me and taking down its inscription in both English and Hebrew.

137. *JC,* 31 March 1911: 33.

138. According to genealogist Josette Goldish, J. L. Penha moved to Curaçao, and Moses De Sola may have moved to Panama. The others are yet to be chronicled (personal communication).

Chapter 7: Changing of the Guard: 1875–1914 (pages 142–63)

1. Dookhan 1994 [1974], 245.

2. 1870 St. Thomas Census.

3. Borger Eder.

4. *STT,* 2 January 1875: 2; 1870 St. Thomas Census. The name references in these two citations are very close, but not exact. The only Piza on the island who corresponds to D. M. Piza in the 1870 census is David Piza, listed as a merchant with no middle initial. I assume these two entries designate the same person.

5. *STT,* 24 March 1875; 1870 St. Thomas Census. Again, this connection between the names in these two sources is likely, not iron-clad: the advertisement for the concert in the *Times* refers only to a "Professor Levy." Although the 1870 St. Thomas census lists Levy's occupation as a "Professor," there is still a little room for doubt. According to baptismal records for All Saints Church in Charlotte Amalie, Levy and his wife had at least one child: Mannette Azelia, born May 24, 1870 and baptized two months later.

6. *STT,* 10 July 1875. Bright's disease is a form of nephritis.

7. *STT,* 15 January 1876.

8. *STT,* 15 March 1876. Rothschild died on March 14.

9. *STT,* 3 June 1876. The 1870 census claims Jacobs as a St. Croix native.

10. *STT*, 4 January 1879.

11. This is a conjecture based on some supporting evidence. Assuming that the married couple would desire a copy of their marriage certificate, it is probable that the ones kept on file are duplicates. There is one example of this from 1840, held in the collection of Emita Levy, New York City.

12. STBDM2, STBDM1. Clearly, this new role did not come from the government, as Cardoze already had all the power he needed to officiate at Jewish life-cycle ceremonies.

13. STBDM2; *STT*, 29 July 1876: 2, col. 2.

14. Throughout most of St. Thomas's period of Danish rule, the colonial government required all new births to be registered with a religious institution. Copies of these records were then collected quarterly and used by the government to obtain a picture of the religious nature of the populace. From the look of the standardized baptismal form the government sent out to gather this information, it is likely that there was an acute awareness of the lax marriage habits of the island. In addition to the name, date, and gender spaces, the form also called for the names and religions of each parent, as well as an indication of whether or not the birth was "legitimate." Different churches held different definitions for legitimacy; it is notable, however, that all save the synagogue recorded such births commonly. Recognizing their roles as recorders of the newborn population, the churches thus kept a relatively vivid picture of the islanders' socio-sexual tendencies. The analysis in this section is based on personal research done in the collected birth records of the religious congregations on St. Thomas, submitted to the government quarterly between 1867 and 1880 (Rigsarkiv, *Danske Vestindiske Lokalarkiv*, Menighedernes Indbereitner). Most of the records were written on pre-printed baptism forms that included, among other information, the religions of all parents involved. This allowed the compilation of an accurate list during this period.

    In order to place the list in perspective, I cross-checked the names with lists of self-identified Jews from the 1870 and 1880 censuses, as well as the synagogue's birth, marriage, and death records. This gave some form of identity to thirty-four of the references. My observations are based on these findings.

    I must also note here that despite great care taken in trying to make names as accurate as possible, there is a good chance that one or several of the following non-Jewish names may be incorrect. This comes from several factors: messy scribes' handwriting, variable orthography (or a dearth of orthographic skill), and the author's (and scribes') lack of familiarity with many of the names involved. I take responsibility for all errors and request clemency for the time being.

15. As with Alexander DeCastro, it was possible for children of these unions to go to other islands for their livelihood. Thus, the non-Jewish Monsanto families could have come from Curaçao originally, or some other such island.

16. There are some other possibilities, but not enough information exists either to

confirm or deny such allegations. Delvalle is the only person with a documented marriage at the time of his "out" child's birth.

17. 1880 St. Thomas Census.

18. STBDM2.

19. The baby girl born to Hebrew Reform Congregation member Semmy Henriquez Moron and his (presumably non-Jewish) wife Anna Petronella Moron was accepted into All Saints Church in 1872, during the controversy over Jewish Reform on the island.

20. Maria (born April 21, 1873; baptized June 16), and Theodore (born April 16, 1878; baptized July 17).

21. Arthur Wellington (born October 17, 1878; baptized December 26), and Alfonso (born December 9, 1879; baptized July 4, 1880).

22. *STT*, 23 March 1881: 1.

23. For a more detailed description of these riots, see Dookhan 1994 [1974], 227–31.

24. See Ibid., chapter 13, for more information.

25. See, for example, articles in *STT*, 24 January 1881: 3, col. 1; 24 September 1881: 2, col. 2–3.

26. See, for example, the series of articles entitled "St. Thomas: A Port of Necessity," which ran in the *St. Thomas Herald* in October and November of 1882.

27. 1880 St. Thomas Census. Notably, the records for this census, taken from microfilm in the Von Scholten Collection at the Enid M. Baa Public library in Charlotte Amalie, are incomplete. However, the existing records still provide information on 144 Jews on the island—enough of a sample, in this author's opinion, to calculate averages with some confidence. The calculated average age for the 1880 population, according to the available information, is 29.03.

28. Synagogue Protocol Births.

29. For example, *STT*, 8 March 1876 (Fast of Esther); 8 September 1880 (Rosh Hashanah); 15 September 1880 (Yom Kippur); *STH*, 3 October 1883: 2 (Rosh Hashanah).

30. *STT*, 25 September 1875; *STH*, 8 March 1882: 4–5, "Persecution of the Jews in Russia"; many of these articles were taken from *The Jewish Week*.

31. *STT*, 22 December 1880. Rabbi Gottheil was the influential preacher of New York's Temple Emanu-El.

32. *STH*, 28 July 1883: 2–3; *STT*, 23 April 23, 1881: 3; *STT*, 1 May 1880: 3, respectively.

33. *STH*, 27 September 1882: 2. For other accounts of high holiday services, see *STT*, 8 and 15 September 1880; 1 October 1881.

34. *STH*, 3 October 1883: 2.

35. STBDM2. Here, I focused on birthdates in order to determine numbers of births. Thus, if a birth in Panama occured in 1890, and was entered into the protocol in 1891, I still counted the birth in the statistics for 1890.

36. *STT*, 1 July 1879: 2, col. 2.

37. *Tidende*, 6 June 1896.

38. "Golden Wedding Celebration," *STT*, 19 May 1900: 2.
39. "Hymns to be sung on the occasion of Revd. & Mrs. D. Cardoze's 'Golden Wedding.'" STHCA, DG 1, Series 3, Folder 2. The hymn was comprised of five numbered verses: 1. "We now offer our thanks / To the great Almighty King / For having spared our cherished ones / To witness this event." 2. "This grand auspicious day / A blessing from on high / With grateful happy, thankful hearts / Unitedly we pray." 3. "Protected by thy boundless love / We humbly entreat thee / To give them renewed strength / And shield them from harm." 4. "O thou! Divine Supreme / Accept our fervent prayer / And spare our treasured Parents / To us for many years." 5. "O thou! Eternal God / Grant us continued mercies / That we may cheer their declining years / And complete our filial love."
40. Ibid.
41. 1901 St. Thomas Census.
42. Dookhan 1994 [1974], 221.
43. Ibid., 237.
44. See McCollough 1977, 17–241.
45. St. Thomas Recorder of Deeds Records, Book UU: 200, #5 (1874).
46. Borger Eder, 6 June 1854.
47. *Tidende*, 9 June 1858; STBDM2. Joshua is buried in the new Jewish cemetery under a stone engraved Jos. A. Levien.
48. *Tidende*, 8 April 1857.
49. St. Thomas Recorder of Deeds Office, Book MM: 307, #2.
50. In September 1857, Joseph Levien provided information to help catch a thief on the island. After receiving a posted reward of $50.00, Levien split it between the Moravian Church and the Hebrew Benevolent Society (*Tidende*, 3 October 1857).
51. St. Thomas Recorder of Deeds Office, Book UU: 200, #5.
52. Levin Obituary, *VIDN*, 3 December 1934. The exact year of Israel Levin's arrival is obscured by his own accounts in the censuses: The 1880 census states his arrival twelve years earlier, in 1868. In the 1901 census, however, Levin calls 1872 the year of his landing on St. Thomas. Because his name does not appear in the 1870 census (which, to the best of my knowledge, is complete), I would opt for the second date.

    Oral traditions abound surrounding Israel Levin's arrival on St. Thomas. Ralph M. Paiewonsky, former governor of the Virgin Islands and descendant of a prominent twentieth-century Jewish family on St. Thomas, prints this version of the story as handed down to him: "Oral tradition has it . . . that as a religious man [Israel Levin] ate nothing but kosher food. . . . Accordingly, on the long sea trip from Hamburg to St. Thomas, which took about twenty-one days at the time, it is reputed that he ate nothing but bread and sardines. His abstinence, together with the rigors of the Atlantic crossing, so weakened his constitution that he was duly thankful to God for placing him on solid land once more. It had been Levin's intention to proceed from St. Thomas by means of an interconnecting trading ship to Brazil, where he had no relatives. But he was so seasick that he decided to go no farther than St. Thomas" (Paiewonsky 1990, 12). Notably, Paiewonsky incorrectly remembers Israel Levin's first name as Isaac.

53. Although the plaque at I. Levin's store claims that the shop existed "Since 1875," evidence suggests that Israel Levin's shop was not independent at that time. Levin has no record of receiving a Burgher Brief, allowing him to open a new business. Further, Levin did not advertise as "I. Levin" in the *St. Thomas Times* or the *St. Thomas Herald*, two prominent late-nineteenth century St. Thomas newspapers. This would lead me to believe that Levin took over a pre-existing business—presumably Joseph Levien's—an action that did not require a Burgher Brief.

54. As noted earlier, Reverend Wolff bore no relation to departed prominent St. Thomian Aron Wolff.

55. I assert this because Victoria's wedding announcement (see next footnote) is the first time this name appears. "Sarah" is not used on Victoria's birth record, nor does it appear on any of the legitimation or deeding records from the 1850s. Further, a conversion customarily requires that the converted take on a Hebrew name—for which Sarah qualifies. Notably, she remained known on the island as "Victoria." The last based on communication with Katina Coulianos, great-granddaughter of Victoria and Israel Levin.

56. *STT,* 29 September 1879: 2.

57. *Lightbourne's Mail Notes,* 27 March 1896.

58. Paiewonsky 1990, 9, 12. See also Israel Levin's letter to the *Tidende,* 22 March 1905: 3, col. 3.

59. *Tidende,* 18 March 1905: 2, col. 4.

60. *Tidende,* 22 March 1905: 3, col. 3.

61. 1901 St. Thomas Census. According to popular legend, Max Eleazar Trepuk did not acquire his last name until he married Paris-born Mathilde Antoinette Trepuk in the 1890s.

62. Paiewonsky 1990, 14. Synagogue birth records suggest that Jacob was the second son in the family. His brother Moses is listed in the birth records as being twenty-nine at the birth of his son Benjamin on September 18, 1898. If this is correct, then he would be older than Jacob, who was born between April and August 1870.

63. 1901 St. Thomas Census; Paiewonsky 1990: 18. There is no positive evidence to prove that Jacob married in Lithuania. However, the lack of a marriage record in St. Thomas provides a strong argument.

64. Borger Eder, 1896.

65. 1901 St. Thomas Census. The entry lists them both as "Clerk."

66. STBDM2.

67. The Frankels' son's marriage record lists him as originating from Colon. This combined with a lack of records for the family on St. Thomas likely means that the entire family moved to Colon. Neither is buried on the island.

68. Moses Paiewonsky is an interesting case. His earliest record in St. Thomas is the

birth of his son Benjamin on September 18, 1898 (Benjamin died three weeks later). His wife's Sephardic name—Isabella Brandao—suggests that he had been in the Caribbean for a while, possibly Curaçao, Venezuela, or Brazil, where families with these names still lived.

69. 1901 St. Thomas Census; Paiewonsky 1990, 18.

70. STBDM2.

71. Paiewonsky 1990, 21.

72. Ibid., 19.

73. Two newspaper accounts place the celebration on different days: *Lightbourne's Mail Notes* pegs the date as December 31, 1913 (Saturday, 3 January 1914: 2); *The Bulletin* refers to January 1, 1914 (2 January 1914: 2). In this case, I would be more likely to believe the former account, as the writer was a good friend of the Reverend, and also because other articles in the latter paper refer to December 31 ("Watchnight") as "yesterday."

74. This and all following details about the ninetieth birthday celebration are taken from *The Bulletin*, Friday, 2 January 1914: 2; *Lightbourne's Mail Notes*, 3 January 1914: 2–3; and *Tidende*, 3 January 1914: 2.

75. *Lightbourne's Mail Notes*, 17 June 1914: 2.

76. The following paragraph is compiled from four accounts: *The Bulletin*, 17 June 1914: 2; *Lightbourne's Mail Notes*, 17 June 1914: 2; *Tidende*, 17 June 1914: 4; 20 June 1914: 3.

77. *St. Thomas Bulletin*, 29 June 1914: 2. According to Paiewonsky 1959: "In 1914, [Sasso] returned to St. Thomas to see his aged mother. Rabbi Cardoze, from his sick bed, pleaded with him to stay. No other person was available to head up the Jewish Synagogue which was so poor at the time that the Congregation could not afford to import a Rabbi. Young Moses D., who had always been [a] very religious youngster, answered the call." This story has been difficult for me to verify, though it appeared in Paiewonsky's tourist pamphlet while Sasso was still in the pulpit.

Chapter 8: Struggle: 1914–1946 (pages 164–94)

1. To its credit, the local paper at least made efforts to sustain optimism to the very end. In January 1913, the *Tidende* reprinted a *Scientific American* article on the canal, and proudly pointed out that: "In a map showing the relationship and sailing lines to the Canal it is worthy of note that St. Thomas is the only island in the West Indies named on the map, which shows the island prominently on the route from principal ports from which vessels will take their course to the great waterway."

2. *Tidende*, 18 April 1914: 2, col. 1. Most trading nations still retained a nominal presence in St. Thomas. During this time, the shrinking population and waning trade allowed some individuals to attain multiple consulships at once, collecting appointments as preceeding consuls left.

3. Interview with Isidor Paiewonsky, 29 April 1996. Another account in the 11 October issue of *Lightborn's Mail Notes* states that the roof ended up on top of another house.

4. Interview with Isidor Paiewonsky, 29 April 1996.

5. *Lightborn's Mail Notes*, 11 and 12 October 1916.

6. *Tidende*, 11 October 1916: 2: "The roof of Talitha Kumi and Bakkedal damaged, the Synagogue also."

7. The true extent of damage to the synagogue's roof is not easy to ascertain. Though numerous reports from members of the synagogue lament the state of the structure's roof for the next several years, Danish as-built drawings from 1919 do not show any evident damage. Possibly, Tyge Hvass, the artist who created the as-builts, decided to overlook the damage in favor of posterity. Hvass's expedition was sponsored by the Danish government as a kind of "final look" at the old colonies, and such damage did not portray the building as the Danes remembered it (see Bradley and Rezende, comps., 1987).

8. "Rabbi Sasso Recalls When . . ." *VIDN*, 3 April 1967: 51.

9. Report of the Joint Commission 1920.

10. STBDM2 Death Record. Funeral announcement and route: *STMN*, 16 July 1920: 2. Other details compiled from aspects of St. Thomas funerals as described by Isidor Paiewonsky and a photograph of a Jewish funeral (probably that of Benjamin Levin) from the 1920s or 1930s in possession of Katina Coulianos, St. Thomas, USVI.

11. Interview with Isidor Paiewonsky, 29 April 1996.

12. Ibid.

13. Isidor Paiewonsky, sermon at St. Thomas Synagogue, December 1992.

14. Ibid.

15. STBDM2. Index #1923–96. There is no indication of how Paiewonsky blessed the couple, or which prayers he used.

16. See letter of 22 March 1925, from Rev. H. Pereira Mendes to Rev. David de Sola Pool. SACO, Folder 1: Mendes Jubilee, 1927 [consisting of letters from 1922–1926]): "Sometimes I want to rehearse . . . some ritual . . . 'but no prayer books!' except the Kipur [and] festival books in my book-case!" Mendes in the same letter did mention that one or two prayer books did exist, but since they contained the German ritual, and not the Sephardic one, they did the congregation little good.

17. Letter from Mendes to Pool, 8 February 1925. SACO.

18. Letter from Mendes to Pool, 17 November 1922. SACO.

19. Pool and Pool 1955, 193–94; Pool 1938, 4.

20. The question of what would have happened had Mendes come to St. Thomas is interesting to ponder. Perhaps the decimation of Jewish knowledge on the island would have never occurred.

21. Pool and Pool 1955, 194.

22. Quotation taken from Ibid., 201.

23. Ibid., 195.

24. STBDM2. Rosalie's parents were Samuel and Rachel Piza. Samuel was a partner in the firm of Piza, Robles & Co., which still operated on St. Thomas when Reverend and Mrs. Mendes visited in 1924 to 1925.

25. Letter from Mendes to David and Tamar de Sola Pool, 21 November 1923. SACO.

26. Letter from Board of Representatives of the St. Thomas Hebrew Congregaton to Rev. Dr. Henry Pereira Mendes, 6 August 1924. St. Thomas Synagogue Archives: Document Group 1, Series 5: "Henry Pereira Mendes Visit: 1924–1925."

27. Letter from Mendes to David and Tamar de Sola Pool, 21 November 1923. SACO. It is worth mentioning here that Reverend Mendes, following a social custom of the time, referred to his wife as "Cousin," or "Coz." Such style of appellation was commonplace: Rose Hertz, wife of British Chief Rabbi Joseph H. Hertz, referred to her husband as "Father," and other occurrences from the era abound.

28. Ibid.

29. Letter from Mendes to Pool, 9 January 1924: "If I could afford it, I could go to Central America and the West Indies, for it so happens that Cousin Rosalie's relatives in some places and mine in others would facilitate matters." SACO.

30. Pool and Pool 1955, 196.

31. Letter from Mendes to Pool, 23 October 1923. SACO.

32. "A Sketch of Dr. Mendes' Activities." *STMN*, 13 December 1924: 2.

33. *STMN*, 15 December 1924: 1.

34. "A Sketch of Dr. Mendes' Activities." *STMN*, 13 December 1924: 2.

35. Letter from Mendes to Pool, 22 March 1925. SACO.

36. Ralph and Isidor Paiewonsky were by this time attending a private boarding school in the states.

37. Reverend Mendes set a minimum age of twenty for the class, citing Deut. 1 as his source: "referring to the affair of the mergalim, it calls those who at that episode were under twenty 'those who do not know the right hand from the left',—under the age of responsibility." To this group, he added one seventeen-year-old who was especially mature, and one fifteen-year-old girl, "only because I leave soon." Letter from Mendes to Rev. Dr. Joseph H. Hertz, 26 March 1925. Southampton University Library, Archives and Manuscripts. MS 175 24/3. Papers of Joseph H. Hertz.

38. "The Jews of St. Thomas," *The Bulletin*, 11 March 1925: 3. The play was a combination of two Purim presentations Mendes had written earlier for the *Shearith Israel* Sunday School.

39. Ibid.

40. *American Israelite*, May 1925 (unspecified date): "A Historic Congregation"; STHCA, DG 1, Series 5.

41. Letter from Mendes to Pool, 16 February 1925. SACO.

42. Letter from Mendes to Pool, 4 January 1925. SACO.

43. Letter from Mendes to Pool, 20 February 1925. SACO. "I wrote to you about the lecture, we had a good number, fifty-sixty people, possibly more; of the congregation a good half of all members, but alas, how many does that mean? the rest were Christians, whites and blacks."

44. Ibid.

45. Letter from Mendes to Pool, 19 February 1925. SACO.

46. Ibid.

47. Letter from Mendes to Pool, 14 March 1925. SACO.

48. "The Jews of St. Thomas," *The Bulletin*, 11 March 1925: 3.

49. Letter from Pool to Mendes, 23 March 1925. SACO.

50. Letter from Mendes to Pool, 11 April 1925. SACO.

51. Alton Augustus Adams (1889–1987) was himself both a local and international celebrity. As the only black bandmaster in the U.S. Navy, Adams had recently earned fame by undertaking an eight- or nine-month tour of the United States Eastern seaboard with his band (presumably the same band that played for Reverend Mendes's celebration). He also composed the territory's anthem, "The Virgin Islands March." For more on Adams, see Clague 1998.

52. "Hebrews Honor Pastor," *The Bulletin*, 14 April 1925: 3.

53. "Spanish & Portugese Synagogue," *The Bulletin*, 2 June 1925. Quoted from Mendes's speech.

54. Ibid. The account in the paper includes only: "there is only one God!" However, since the *Shema* was a traditional affirmation prayer during such ceremonies, it is justifiable to believe that Mendes recited the whole sentence. The quality of the Reverend's voice can be ascertained from the correspondent's misinterpretation of the prayer as "the penuried war cry of the Hebrews."

55. Ibid.

56. Fragment of paper recounting a synagogue board meeting; no date. STHCA, DG 1, Series 5. I choose this time for the meeting because of Mendes's comment in his letter to David de Sola Pool of 9 June: "As I wrote you, they have organized for actual work for the interests of the religion and the synagogue." He places this comment in between Sunday's consecration and his wife's birthday on 7 June. Possibly, this means that the meeting took place on Sunday morning, 7 June.

57. "Rev. Dr. Mendes Leaving," *The Bulletin*, Monday, 13 July 1925.

58. The corresponding two lines in the original song read: "The past is gone, but memory gives // one clinging thought: the future lives." (Kennedy 1893).

59. Letter from the Rev. And Mrs. Mendes to Pool, 22 July 1925.

60. Ibid.

61. This is not to say that the Virgin Islands has always had an antagonistic relationship with the United States. Early on, the residents of St. Thomas seemed eager to please the American government. When President Warren Harding died in

August 1923, all the major religious institutions on the island (including the syn-agogue) held non-denominational memorial services for him. One paper even printed the words: "Remember to Attend Memorial Service on Friday" atop one of their news pages (*The Emancipator*, 8 August 1923: 2). Such practices lessened with the succeeding years, as the population began to feel increasingly disenfran-chised.

62. Dookhan 1994 [1974], 275–76.

63. U.S. Department of the Interior, "The Virgin Islands of the United States," 1932.

64. First quotation taken from *VIDN*, 3 April 1931; second taken from "Caveat Emp-tor," editorial in *VIDN*, 4 April 1931.

65. Letter from Moses Sasso to Rev. Henry Pereira Mendes, 10 October 1934. STHCA, Sasso correspondence.

66. Dookhan 1994 [1974], 278–81.

67. Watson 1934.

68. I suggest that the two were married so their children would be seen as legitimate, and thus entered in the synagogue's register.

69. To this day, descendants of these unions take leadership roles in the synagogue, even after several generations of Jewish females marrying non-Jewish males. Else Levin Siggelkow's daughter Franzi, for example, married Greek ship captain Costas Coulianos; their daughter Katina married American Douglas Sell. In all cases, the women have remained active within synagogue life, with Katina be-coming synagogue president in May 2001.

70. It should be noted here that the synagogue's standard for affirming Jewish iden-tity differed from Biblical tenets, which required only that children be born to a Jewish mother.

71. This is taken from notations in the BvSvGH list of births (STBDM2).

72. *VIDN*, Tuesday, 3 December 1930: 5, col. 2–3. All further descriptions of the wedding come from this source as well.

73. Primary among this evidence is that the boys were not circumcised until 1933.

74. As per letter from Moses Sasso to Rev. Dr. Henry Pereira Mendes, 10 October 1934.

75. STBDM2.

76. The lyrics for the first verse of this hymn are: "Oh God, to Thee my voice I raise / And prostrate at Thy throne, / I lift my heart to sing Thy praise / To Thee my God alone" (taken from the Hebrew Congregation's 1964 hymnal).

77. Interview with David Stanley Sasso, 8 June 1994.

78. "The Observation Tower," *The Daily News*, 8 October 1930: 3.

79. Interview with David Stanley Sasso. The early morning start of a service also came up during an interview with Gladys De Castro and Elaine Robles (11 July 1994), but since they mentioned it in the context of "regular" services, such evi-dence is inconclusive.

80. David S. Sasso, personal remembrances, typed manuscript. STHCA.

81. Interview with David Stanley Sasso.

82. Franzi Coulianos, St. Thomas Sisterhood meeting, 24 April 1992. Videotape taken by Gary Rosenthal.

83. Ibid.

84. Interview with Amalia Mylner, 23 June 1994.

85. "Our Common Foe," *VIDN*, 5 July 1939: 3, 4.

86. Morris De Castro, "Address of Acting Governor Morris De Castro delivered at the thanksgiving service at the Synagogue on July 2, '39." *St. Thomas Daily News,* 6 July 1939: 3.

87. Perl 1992, 7–8.

88. Ibid., 8–10.

89. Alland 1940.

90. Campbell's subsequent work was called *St. Thomas Negroes—A Study of Personality and Culture* (Campbell 1943).

91. Campbell 1942, 161, n. °.

92. Ibid., 161.

93. Ibid., 163.

94. Ibid., 164.

95. Ibid., 165. Campbell's explanation that "These persons represent the fruit of unions between Jewish men and colored women," has little support after 1867. See analysis in the previous chapter.

96. Ibid., 166.

Chapter 9: A Revival from America: 1946–1967 (pages 195–220)

1. Orlins 1969, 7, 89.

2. Colby 1940.

3. Ibid.; Orlins 1969, 89.

4. "In the Wake of the Buccaneers: A Visit to St. Thomas in the Virgin Islands." RG 48, #13 and "The Old Danish Sugar Bowl," RG 48, #14. US National Archives II.

5. Alland 1940, Part Two (5 April): 6.

6. Compiled from Wales 1971, Kimelman 1989, and Schouten 1991.

7. Schouten 1991.

8. According to Paiewonsky (1990, 68–69), Kessler's entry into more general alcohol production during World War II (as opposed to rum production) forced him out of business once the war ended, because alcohol manufacturers in the States began producing such items more cheaply and efficiently. As to his legal issues, Kessler was one of twenty-three defendants ("three corporations and twenty individuals") accused by the Office of Price Administration in 1945 of "a conspiracy to sell liquor at prices exceeding those allowed under OPA regulations, and [con-

cealing] the overcharges" (*NYT*, 8 December 1944: 17, col. 6); I do not know the outcome of this charge.

9. "St. Thomas Hotel" 1958.

10. Interview with David Stanley Sasso, 8 June 1994.

11. Ibid.

12. When attendance actually became "mixed" is difficult to determine through oral histories. Paul Hoffman recalled the synagogue seated men at the near side and women at the far side as an attempt to "respect [the old Sephardic] traditions" (interview with Hoffman, 1 May 1996). Others simply say that gender segregation ended in the 1950s (Sisterhood Meeting, 24 April 1992).

13. This practice continued well into the 1960s, as evidenced by *The Hebrew Congregation B. V. S. & G. H.* 1964.

14. Interview with David Stanley Sasso, 8 June 1994.

15. "Native Governor Urged," *NYT*, 19 October 1949: 18, col. 4.

16. "Islands Governor Named," *NYT*, 1 March 1950: 3, col. 2.

17. Births, STBDM2.

18. "De Castro, Morris" 1950, 115; Alland 1940; Part 2 (5 April) 7. This account is more anecdotal than the *Current Biography* account, and I treat it as such (although it is worth noting that Alland's information probably came at least in some respects from a personal interview with Morris De Castro). In dealing with discrepancies in dates, I will use those from *Current Biography*.

19. "De Castro, Morris" 1950, 115.

20. "In Memoriam: Morris F. De Castro 1902–1966." Memorial booklet used at his funeral, 10 December 1966. STHCA.

21. "Virgin Islands: New Broom," *Time Magazine*, 5? March 1950: 27.

22. Ibid.

23. *VIDN*, 11 March 1950: 1.

24. *VIDN*, 22 March 1950: 2.

25. "Over 6000 People Attend Colorful Inaugural Ceremony Here," *VIDN*, 25 March 1950: 1, 4.

26. "Inaugural Address of Morris F. De. Castro, Gov. of the V. I," *VIDN*, 27 March 1950: 2.

27. Louchheim 1950.

28. The exact date of the Virgin Islands Development Board's founding varies in different sources. Louchheim (1950) implies that it began during the first year of the De Castro administration, in 1950. Orlins (1969, 93–94) gives the date as 1948. Dookhan (1994 [1974], 286) places the date (clearly incorrectly) at 1952. For a detailed account of the Virgin Isle Hotel, its development and its operating history, see Kimelman [1997?], 77–158.

29. Interview with Ambassador Henry Kimelman, 1 June 1996.

30. Virgin Isle Hotel advertisement, *NYT*, 10 December 1950, Sect. 10: 32.

31. Ibid.

32. Ambassador Henry Kimelman quoted a survey to me during our interview that showed the Virgin Isle Hotel's impact on the Virgin Islands as twenty times General Motors's impact on the United States.

33. Statistics taken from the Virgin Islands Tourist Board *Annual Report,* as presented by Orlins 1969, 108.

34. One of the Virgin Isle's most colorful and morally ambiguous promotions capitalized upon St. Thomas's liberal divorce law. According to *New York Times* travel reporter Leon A. Mawson, the hotel offered a "two-way proposal—a special rate for honeymooners and a special rate for persons coming to St. Thomas for a six-week divorce. Honeymooners can have twelve days with room, breakfast and dinner for two for $298; candidates for divorce can get room, breakfast and dinner for one for $498 for six weeks" (Mawson 1951).

35. The Virgin Isle Hotel also affected the island's population in another way: During construction, the need for inexpensive, menial (or somewhat skilled) labor brought many hundreds (if not thousands) of people over from the British Leeward islands, thus creating a poor black underclass on St. Thomas. This condition is important to understand and deserves due mention. In the context of the Jewish community, however, it is peripheral.

36. I take the term "resident tourists" from Orlins 1969.

37. Ibid., 322–23.

38. Interview with Norma Levin, 12 April 1996.

39. Interview with Kimelman, as well as communications with other congregants.

40. Interview with Paul Hoffman, 1 May 1996.

41. Paiewonsky 1990, 27.

42. Interview with Norma Levin.

43. Interview with Paul Hoffman.

44. Interview with Henry Kimelman.

45. Notably, there is at least one instance of a girl going through a similar training process and ceremony at this time: Rabbi Sasso's daughter, Emmeline Joy (also his only biological child), had her own confirmation ceremony on July 10, 1953 (see program "Hymns Used at the Confirmation Service of Emmeline Joy Sasso," STHCA). A notation on the program states: "*1st* confirmation service held in St. Thomas," suggesting that this ceremony was not a common one. It seems that the primary reason girls did not receive "Bar Mitzvah" equivalents was that there were almost no girls of the appropriate age (about thirteen or fourteen) on St. Thomas during the 1950s.

46. *VIDN,* 29 March 1958: 1, 4. Admittedly, the price for the *seder* was relatively steep: $7.50 for adults and $5.00 for children in 1958 (similar in price to a day's car rental at the time).

47. Ibid.

48. Ibid.

49. Interview with Norma Levin.

50. Ibid.

51. Program, "Annual Community Passover Seder," 16 April 1965. STHCA. This claim is an extrapolation, though one that seems rather plausible.

52. The Sisterhood continues to sponsor the community *seder* each year. In 1996, the last time I attended, the *seder* took place at the Frenchman's Reef Hotel in St. Thomas and attracted about four hundred people, including islanders, members of the local clergy, and tourists who came down to the island specifically for the event.

53. *VIDN*, 29 July 1955: 1; 5 August 1955: 2, 4; 14 September 1955.

54. "Rabbi Bernard Heller, 77, Dies; A Scholar, Author and Teacher," *NYT*, 7 May 1976: 4, 18:1.

55. Paiewonsky 1990, 52.

56. *CCAR Yearbook*, vv. 68–77 (1958–1966).

57. Letter from Morris F. De Castro to Rabbi Samuel Markowitz, 25 August 1966: "Dr. Heller has no connection whatever with the congregation. He never had. He is not here." STHCA Box 9, Series: Board, B. Minutes 1966–1978.

58. Marcus 1953, 5–21 (St. Thomas, 20–21).

59. Harman 1958.

60. Dreis 1958.

61. Ibid.

62. Interview with Isidor Paiewonsky.

63. Paiewonsky 1959, Preface.

64. Wouk also decided to settle in "paradise" on a whim. According to accounts, the author convinced his wife Sarah "to make the move with the help of a batch of martinis and a stack of Harry Belafonte records one wintry night." The Wouks lived on St. Thomas between 1958 and 1964 in a hillside house along a road known as "Skyline Drive" (Zink 1997). Increasingly religious (Wouk's statement of faith *This is My God* came out in 1959), the author and his family were responsible for bringing a Hebrew teacher onto the island to educate his sons and the synagogue's youth (Paiewonsky 1959, 1959 entry). Herman Wouk's experiences on St. Thomas also inspired his novel *Don't Stop the Carnival* (1965).

65. Application for inclusion, Synagogue Sisterhood of St. Thomas to National Federation of Temple Sisterhoods, 27 March 1959. In Women of Reform Judaism Archive, *AJA*.

66. Ibid.

67. American Sephardic transliteration tended to use "gn" for silent or aspirated letters. Thus, a more "standard" transliteration for Sasso's title would be *Ne'im Zemirot Yisrael.*

68. Orlins 1969, 106. This number is particularly impressive because the island's airport was still not large enough to accommodate jet airplanes.

69. Extrapolating from Ibid., 104.

70. Ibid., 93–94.

71. Interview with Hoffman.

72. Ibid.

73. Paiewonsky 1990, 89–90; "Virgin Isle Hotel Sold," *NYT*, 4 July 1960: 21, col. 1.

74. Paiewonsky 1990.

75. Ibid., 7–178.

76. Moses Sasso, "Inaugural Prayer at the Inauguration of Governor Ralph Paiewonsky" unpub. typescript, dated 5 April 1960. *AJA*.

77. Paiewonsky 1990, 44–45.

78. "Governor's Father Succumbs; Was 78," *VIDN*, 15 July 1963: 1, 9, 11.

79. While there is only one major descendant of the German-Jewish St. Thomas families—Franzi Siggelkow—her story is significant among these other histories. Siggelkow met and married Costas Coulianos, a non-Jewish Greek sea captain. Commerce kept the couple on St. Thomas. They continued to value their ties with the Jewish community, remained familiar faces in the synagogue, and made sure to raise their children in the Jewish faith.

80. Program for Sasso's fiftieth Anniversary, 1 July 1964, STHCA.

81. "Rabbi Celebrates 50th Year," *VIDN*, 2 July 1964: 1, 16.

82. "Rabbi Moses De Castro Sasso Honored on 50th Anniversary." Clipping of unmarked English-language Canal Zone newspaper, early July 1964. STHCA Box 9.

83. Ibid.

84. Letter from the Board of Representatives to Rabbi Moses D. Sasso, 17 August 1966. STHCA, Box 9.

85. *VIDN*, 24 January 1966: 3.

86. *VIDN*, 1 February 1966: 1.

87. *VIDN*, 3 February 1966.

88. Letter from the Board of Representatives to Rabbi Moses D. Sasso, 17 August 1966. STHCA, Box 9.

89. Letter from Morris F. De Castro to Rabbi Malcolm Stern, 30 October 1966. STHCA, Box 9.

90. This was illustrated particularly well by one incident in which a female member of the congregation was asked to light the Sabbath candles during Friday evening services. Upon coming to the pulpit, however, the woman revealed that she did not know the blessing. This enraged the rabbi, who later insisted that anyone asked to kindle the Sabbath lights rehearse the blessing in front of him first. Memo from Rabbi Samuel Markowitz to Morris De Castro, 28 October 1966. STHCA, Box 9.

91. See, for example, "Procedure for Sabbat Eve Services November 4, 1966." STHCA, Box 9.

92. Letter from the Henry L. Kimelman Foundation to Morris De Castro, 9 November 1966. STHCA, Box 10.

93. "In Memoriam: Morris De Castro, 1902–1966." Program for De Castro's memorial service. STHCA.

Epilogue (pages 221–26)

1. Namely Rabbis Joseph Karasick and Stephen Schafer, as well as congregants Harvey and Mitzi Henne.
2. It is worth noting, however, that due to a typing error, the letter was addressed to the "Hewbrew Congregation."
3. Relkin and Abrams 1983.

BIBLIOGRAPHY

Andrade, Jacob A. P. M. 1941. *A Record of the Jews of Jamaica from the English Conquest to the Present Time.* Kingston, Jamaica: The Jamaica Times, Ltd.

Alland, Alexander. 1940. "The Jews of the Virgin Islands: A History of the Islands and Candid Biographies of Outstanding Jews Born There." *The American Hebrew*, 29 March: 5, 12, 13, 16; 5 April: 6–7; 26 April: 5, 12, 13; 17 May: 5, 12.

Arbell, Mordecai. 1994. "La Historia de la Familia Lopez Penha." In *Presencia Judia en Santo Domingo,* ed. Alfonso Lockwood. Santo Domingo, Dominican Republic: n. p.

———. 2000. *The Portuguese Jews of Jamaica.* Mona, Jamaica: Canoe Press.

———. 2001. "Jewish Settlements in the French Colonies in the Caribbean (Martinique, Guadeloupe, Haiti, Cayenne) and the 'Black Code.'" In *The Jews and the Expansion of Europe to the West, 1450 to 1800,* ed. Paolo Bernardini and Norman Fiering, 287–314, Vol. 2 of the European Expansion and Global Interaction Series. New York: Berghahn Books.

August, Thomas. 1989. "Family Structure and Jewish Continuity in Jamaica Since 1655." *American Jewish Archives* 41, no. 1: 27–42.

Bahloul, Joëlle. 1996. *The Architecture of Memory: A Jewish-Muslim Household in Colonial Algeria, 1937–1962.* Cambridge: Cambridge University Press.

Bamberger, Ib Nathan. 1983. *The Viking Jews: A History of the Jews of Denmark.* New York: Shengold Publishers.

Barka, Norman F. 1996. "Citizens of St. Eustatius, 1781: A Historical and Archaeological Study." *The Lesser Antilles in the Age of European Expansion,* ed. Robert L. Paquette and Stanley L. Engerman, 223–38. Gainesville: University Press of Florida.

Barnet, Lionel D., ed. 1940–1993. *Bevis Marks Records.* 4 vv. Oxford, England: Oxford University Press.

Benjamin, Alan F. 2001. *Jews of the Dutch Caribbean: Exploring Ethnic Identity on Curaçao.* New York: Routledge.

Bernardini, Paolo, and Norman Fiering, eds. 2001. *The Jews and the Expansion of Europe to the West, 1450 to 1800.* Vol. 2 of the European Expansion and Global Interaction Series New York: Berghahn Books.

Bijlsma, Roelof. 1982. "David de Is. C. Nassy, Author of the *Essai Historique sur Surinam.*" Tr. Maria J. L. van Yperen. In *Dutch Authors in West Indian History: An Historiographical Selection,* ed. M. A. P. Meilink-Roelofsz, 27–37. Translation Series 21. The Hague: Martinus Nijhoff.

Blau, Joseph, and Salo Baron. 1963. *The Jews of the United States, 1790–1840*. New York: Columbia University Press.

———. 1963a. "Nathan Levy's Difficulties in St. Thomas, 1820–1830." In *The Jews of the United States, 1790–1840*, ed. Joseph Blau and Salo Baron, 325–27.New York: Columbia University Press.

Boyer, William. 1983. *America's Virgin Islands*. Durham, N.C.: Carolina Academic Press.

Bradley, Betsy and Elizabeth Rezende, comps. 1987. *Captured in Time, 1919: St. Thomas, St. John, St. Croix*. St. Croix, U.S. Virgin Islands: Island Perspectives.

Brettell, Richard R. 1996. "Camille Pissarro and St. Thomas: The Story of an Exhibition." In *Camille Pissarro in the Caribbean, 1850–1855: Drawings from the Collection at Olana*, ed. Richard Brettell, Karen Zukowski, and Joachim Pissaro, 8–17. St. Thomas, U.S. Virgin Islands: Hebrew Congregation of St. Thomas.

Bro-Jørgensen, J. O. 1966. *Dansk Vestindien indtil 1755*. vol. 1 of *Vore gamle Tropekolonier*. Denmark: Fremad.

Campbell, Albert A. 1942. "A Note on the Jewish community of St. Thomas, U.S. Virgin Islands." *Jewish Social Studies* 4: 161–66.

———. 1943. *St. Thomas Negroes—A Study of Personality and Culture*. Evanston, Ill.: American Psychological Association, Psychological Monographs. J. F. Dashiell, ed. v. 55, #5.

Carillon, A. C., and B. C. Carillon. 1836. "Leerede over Spreuken Salomons, Cap. 2. Vervaardigd voor de Godsdienstige Inwijding." Amsterdam: Carillon.

Carillon, Benjamin C. 1845. *Sermon Delivered at the Spanish and Portuguese Synagogue on Sunday Evening, the 2nd March, 1845*. 2nd ed. Kingston, Jamaica: R. J. de Cordova.

Carstens, J. L. 1997. *St. Thomas in Early Danish Times*. Tr. and ed. by Arnold Highfield. St. Croix, U.S.V.I.: Virgin Islands Humanities Council.

Clague, Mark. 1998. "Instruments of Identity: Alton Augustus Adams Sr., the Navy Band of the Virgin Islands, and the Sounds of Social Change." *Black Music Research Journal* 18, no. 1–2: 21–65.

Code of Laws for the Government of the Hebrew Congregation Blessing and Peace and Acts of Piety in the Island of St. Thomas. 1875. New York: Industrial School of the Hebrew Orphan Asylum.

Code of Laws for the Government of the Israelite Congregation in the Island of St. Thomas. 1848. Philadelphia: C. Sherman.

Cohen, Judah. 1997a. "Satellite of a Satellite: The Jewish Community of St. Croix and its Relationship with the Jewish Community of St. Thomas." Unpublished paper presented at the Annual Meeting of Virgin Islands Historians, Christiansted, St. Croix, 18 January.

———. 1997b. "A Matter of Trust: A Taxonomy of Anthropological Source Documents." Unpub. Term Paper, Harvard University.

Cohen, Robert. 1976. "Jewish Demography in the Eighteenth Century: A Study of London, the West Indies, and Early America." Ph. D. Thesis, Brandeis University.

———. 1983. "Early Caribbean Jewry: A Demographic Perspective." *Jewish Social Studies* 45: 123–34.

———. 1991. *Jews in Another Environment: Surinam in the Second Half of the Eighteenth Century.* New York: E. J. Brill.

Colby, Merle. 1940. *The Virgin Islands: A Profile in Pictures.* New York: Duell, Sloan and Pearce.

Connerton, Paul. 1992. *How Societies Remember.* New York: Cambridge University Press.

Creque, Darwin. 1968. *The U. S. Virgins and the Eastern Caribbean.* Philadelphia: Whitmore Publishing Co.

Davis, David Brion. 1994. "The Slave Trade and the Jews." *New York Review of Books* 41, no. 21 (22 December): 14–16.

"De Castro, Morris." 1950. *Current Biography,* 115.

Dookhan, Isaac. 1994 [1974]. *A History of the Virgin Islands of the United States.* Mona, Jamaica: Canoe Press.

Dreis, Harry. 1958. "Jewish Historical Development in the Virgin Islands." St. Thomas, n.p.

Dunn, Richard S. 1973. *Sugar and Slaves: The Rise of the Planter Class in the English West Indies, 1624–1713.* New York: W. W. Norton.

Elazar, Daniel J. 1992. "The Constitutional Documents of Contemporary Jewry: An Introduction to the Field." In *A Double Bond: The Constitutional Documents of American Jewry,* ed. Jonathan D. Sarna Elazar and Rela G. Monson. New York: University Press of America.

Elazar, Daniel J., Jonathan D. Sarna, and Rela G. Monson, eds. 1992. *A Double Bond: The Constitutional Documents of American Jewry.* New York: University Press of America.

"Eldad." Letter to the Editor. *Kingston Despatch,* 6 August 1845.

Emmanuel, Isaac S. 1957. *Precious Stones of the Jews of Curaçao.* New York: Bloch Publishing Company.

———. 1973. *The Jews of Coro, Venezuela.* Cincinnati: American Jewish Archives.

Emmanuel, Isaac S., and Suzanne Emmanuel. 1970. *History of the Jews of the Netherlands Antilles.* Cincinnati: American Jewish Archives.

Evans, Eli N. 1988. *Judah P. Benjamin: The Jewish Confederate.* New York: Free Press.

Faber, Eli. 1992. *A Time for Planting: The First Migration, 1654–1820.* Vol. 1 of the Jewish People in America Series. Baltimore: The Johns Hopkins University Press.

———. 1998. *Jews, Slaves and the Slave Trade: Setting the Record Straight.* New York: New York University Press.

Fidanque, E. Alvin. 1970. "Glimpses of the Past: Jews and Panama." *The American Sephardi* 4, no. 1–2: 37–48.

Fidanque, E. Alvin (Bill), Ralph De Lima Valencia, Eugene Sasso Maduro, Eleanor D. L. Perkins, and Joseph Melamed. 1977. *Kol Shearith Israel: A Hundred Years of Jewish Life in Panama, 1876–1976.* Panama City, Panama: Kol Shearith Israel.

Finestein, Israel. 1992. "Jewish Emancipationists in Victorian England." In *Assimilation and Community,* ed. Jonathan Frankel and Steven J. Zipperstein. New York: Cambridge University Press.

Fishman, Ken. 1980. *Paradise.* New York: Dell Publishing.

"Form of Special Service Held in the Synagogue, St. Thomas, W. I. 1863." 1864(?). St. Thomas, W. I.: Tidende Office. [Published account of memorial service for King Frederik VII.]

Friedman, Lee M. 1922. "Gabriel Milan, the Jewish Governor of St. Thomas." *Publications of the American Jewish Historical Society* 28: 213–21.

Fuks-Mansfield, R. G. 1989. *De Sefardim in Amsterdam tot 1795.* Hollandse Studiën 23. Hilversum, Netherlands: Uitgeverij Verloren.

Garrigus, John D. "New Christians/'New Whites': Sephardic Jews, Free People of Color, and Citizenship in French Saint-Domingue, 1760–1789." In *The Jews and the Expansion of Europe to the West, 1450 to 1800,* ed. Paolo Bernardini and Norman Fiering, 314–32. Vol. 2 of the European Expansion and Global Interaction Series. New York: Berghahn Books.

Gjessing, Frederik C., and William P. Maclean. 1987. *Historic Buildings of St. Thomas and St. John.* London: The Macmillan Press.

Goldman, Karla. 2000. *Beyond the Synagogue Gallery: Finding a Place for Women in American Judaism.* Cambridge: Harvard University Press.

Goslinga, Cornelius Ch. 1979. *A Short History of the Netherlands Antilles and Surinam.* Boston: M. Nijhoff.

van Grol, G. J. 1982 [1934]. "Historical Foundation of the Political Organization of the Netherlands Windward and Leeward Islands." Tr. Maria J. L. van Yperen. In *Dutch Authors in West Indian History: An Historiographical Selection,* ed. M. A. P. Meilink-Roelofsz. Translation Series 21. The Hague: Martinus Nijhoff.

Gross, Nachum, ed. 1975. *Economic History of the Jews.* Jerusalem: Keter Publishing House Jerurusalem, Ltd.

Guiterman, Vida Lindo. [1971]. *Joshua Piza and His Descendants.* Manuscript, microfilm copy in possession of the author.

Halbwachs, Maurice. 1992. *On Collective Memory.* Lewis A. Coser, trans. and ed. Chicago: University of Chicago Press.

Hall, Neville A. T. 1992. *Slave Society in the Danish West Indies, St. Thomas, St. John and St. Croix.* B. W. Higman, ed. Jamaica: The University of the West Indies Press.

Harman, Jeanne Perkins. 1958. "St. Thomas—Its Heritage from a Rich Past," *New York Times,* 13 July, Sect. 11, 35: 1.

―――. 1961. *The Virgins: Magic Islands.* New York: Appleton-Century-Crofts, Inc.

Hartog, Johannes. 1976. *The Jews and St. Eustatius: the Eighteenth Century Jewish Congregation Honen Dalim and Description of the Old Cemetery.* St. Maarten,

Netherlands Antilles: Theodor Maxwell Pandt in cooperation with Windward Islands Bank.

The Hebrew Congregation B. V. S. & G. H. [Hymnal]. 1964. Charlotte Amalie [St. Thomas, USVI]: [St. Thomas Hebrew Congregation].

Highfield, Arnold R. 1995. *St. Croix 1493: An Encounter of Two Worlds.* U.S. Virgin Islands: Virgin Islands Humanities Council.

Hobhouse, Henry. 1985. *Seeds of Change: Five Plants that Transformed Mankind.* New York: Harper and Rowe.

Hobsbawm, Eric. 1983. "Introduction: Inventing Tradition." In *The Invention of Tradition,* eds. Hobsbawm and Terrence Ranger, 1–14. Cambridge: Cambridge University Press.

Holsoe, Svend E., and John H. McCollum, eds. 1993. *The Danish Presence and Legacy in the Virgin Islands.* Frederiksted, U.S.V.I.: St. Croix Landmarks Society.

Holzberg, Carol. 1987. *Minorities and Power in a Black Society: The Jewish Community of Jamaica.* Lanham, Md.: The North-South Publishing Co.

Hurst, Ronald. 1996. *The Golden Rock: An Episode of the American War of Independence.* Annapolis, Md.: Naval Institute Press.

Israel, Jonathan I. 1989. *European Jewry in the Age of Mercantilism 1550–1750.* 2nd ed. Oxford: Clarendon Press.

Jarvis, J. Antonio. 1938. *A Brief History of the Virgin Islands.* St. Thomas, U.S.V.I.: The Art Shop.

Jarvis, J. Antonio, and Rufus Martin. 1948. *Virgin Islands Picture Book.* Philadelphia: Dorrance & Co.

Kaplan, Yosef. 1982. "The Curaçao and Amsterdam Jewish Communities in the 17th and 18th Centuries." *American Jewish History* 72, no. 2: 193–211.

Karner, Frances P. 1969. *The Sephardics of Curaçao: A Study of Socio-Cultural Patterns in Flux.* Assen: Van Gorcum.

Karp, Abraham A. 1987. "Overview: the Synagogue in America." In *The American Synagogue: A Sanctuary Transformed,* ed. Jack Wertheimer. New York: Cambridge University Press, 1987.

Kennedy, Harry. 1893. "Say 'Au Revoir' but not 'Goodbye.'" New York: Kennedy Publishing House.

Kimelman, Henry L. [1997?]. *Living the American Dream: The Life and Times of Henry L. Kimelman.* New York: Vincent Lee Publishing, Inc.

Kimelman, John. 1989. "Frances Kessler dead at 90." *Virgin Islands Daily News,* 14 April: 3, 12.

Knight, Franklin. 1990. *The Caribbean: The Genesis of a Fragmented Nationalism.* 2nd ed. New York: Oxford University Press.

Kohn, S. Joshua. 1964. "David Naar of Trenton, New Jersey." *American Jewish Historical Quarterly* 53, no. 4: 373–95.

Krarup, Janus Frederik. 1893–1894. "Gabriel Milan og Somme af hans Samtid." *Personalhistorisk Tidsskrift* 3, no. 2: 102–30; no. 3: 1–51.

Krohn, Franklin B. 1993. "The Search for the Elusive Caribbean Jews." *American Jewish Archives* 45, no. 2: 146–56.

Larsen, Jens. 1950. *Virgin Islands Story.* Philadelphia: Muhlenberg Press.

Levy, Emma Fidanque. 1992. "The Fidanques: Symbols of the Continuity of the Sephardic Tradition in America." *American Jewish Archives* 44, no. 1: 179–207.

Lewis, Gordon K. 1972. *The Virgin Islands.* Evanston, Ill.: Northwestern University Press.

Lieberles, Robert. 1987. "Conflict Over Reforms: The Case of Congregation Beth Elohim, Charleston, South Carolina." In *The American Synagogue: A Sanctuary Transformed,* ed. Jack Wertheimer, 274–96. Hanover, N.H.: Brandeis University Press.

Lockwood, Alfonso, ed. 1994. *Presencia Judia en Santo Domingo.* Santo Domingo, D.R.: n. p.

Loker, Zvi. 1981–1982. "An Eighteenth-Century Plan to Invade Jamaica; Isaac Yeshurun Sasportas-French Patriot or Jewish Radical Idealist?" *Transactions of the Jewish Historical Society of England* 28: 132–44.

———. 1986. "Conversos and Conversions in the Caribbean Colonies and Socioreligious Problems of the Jewish Settlers." In *Proceedings on the Ninth World Jewish Congress of Jewish Studies,* Div. B, Vol. 3: The History of the Jewish People: 205–12.

———. 1991. *Jews in the Caribbean.* Jerusalem: Misgav Yerushalayim.

Louchheim, Aline B. "St. Thomas Opening." *New York Times,* 10 December, 1950. Sect. 10:17, col. 7.

Macmillan, Allister, ed. 1911. *The West Indies Illustrated: Historical and Descriptive Commercial and Industrial Facts, Figures, & Resources.* London: W. H. L. Collingridge.

Mawson, Leon A. 1951. "Virgin Isles Side Trip." *New York Times,* 15 April, 1951. Sec. 10:3, col. 7.

Manuel, Peter L., Kenneth Bilby, and Michael Largey. 1995. *Caribbean Currents: Caribbean Music from Rumba to Reggae.* Philadelphia: Temple University Press.

Marcus, Jacob R. 1953. "The West India and South America Expedition of the American Jewish Archives." *American Jewish Archives* 5, no. 1: 5–21.

———. 1964 [1953]. *How to Write the History of an American Jewish Community.* Cincinnati: American Jewish Archives.

———. 1970. *The Colonial American Jew, 1492–1776.* 3 vols. Detroit: Wayne State University Press.

———. 1989. *United States Jewry, 1776–1985.* Vol. 2. Detroit: Wayne State University Press.

Margolinsky, Jul. 1965. "299 Epitaphs from the Jewish Cemetery in St.Thomas, W.I. 1837–1916." Copenhagen.

Martin, Tony. 1994. "Jews to Trinidad." *The Journal of Caribbean History* 28, no. 2: 244–57.

McCollough, David. 1977. *The Path between the Seas: The Creation of the Panama Canal 1870–1914.* New York: Simon and Schuster.

Meade, Robert Douthat. 2001 [1943]. *Judah P. Benjamin: Confederate Statesman.* Baton Rouge: Louisiana State University Press.

Meyer, Michael A. 1988. *Response to Modernity: A History of the Reform Movement in Judaism.* New York: Oxford University Press.

Monaco, Chris. 1998. "Moses E. Levy of Florida: A Jewish Abolitionist Abroad." *American Jewish History* 86, no. 4: 377–96.

Mundy, Lieutenant General George B. 1830. *The Life and Correspondence of the Late Admiral Rodney.* London.

Nissen, Johann Peter. 1838. *Remembrances of a 46 Years' Residence in the Island of St. Thomas.* Nazareth, Penn.: Senseman and Co.

Nørregaard, George. 1966. *Dansk Vestindien 1880–1917.* Vol. 4 of *Vore gamle tropekolonier.* Denmark: Fremad.

Oren, Daniel. 2001. *Joining the Club: A History of Jews and Yale.* Rev. ed. New Haven: Yale University Press.

Orlins, Martin Garson. 1969. "The Impact of Tourism on the Virgin Islands of the United States." Ph. D. diss. Columbia University.

Ott, Thomas O. 1973. *The Haitian Revolution, 1789–1804.* Knoxville: University of Tennessee Press.

Paiewonsky, Isidor. 1959. *Jewish Historical Developments in the Virgin Islands.* St. Thomas: n.p.

———. 1989. *Eyewitness Accounts of Slavery in the Danish West Indies.* New York: Fordham University Press.

———. 1992. *The Burning of a Pirate Ship La Trompeuse in the Harbour of St. Thomas July 31, 1683 and Other Tales.* New York: Fordham University Press.

Paiewonsky, Ralph, with Isaac Dookhan. 1990. *Memoirs of a Governor: A Man for the People.* New York: New York University Press.

Paquette, Robert L., and Stanley L. Engerman, eds. 1996. *The Lesser Antilles in the Age of European Expansion.* Gainesville: University Press of Florida.

The Parliamentary History of England from the Earliest Period to the Year 1803. 1814. London: T. C. Hansard. Vol. 22, cols. 218–62, 769–85, 1023–26.

Parry, J. H., Philip Sherlock, and Anthony Maingot. 1987. *A Short History of the West Indies.* 4th ed. London: Macmillan.

Perl, William R. 1992. "The Holocaust and the Lost Caribbean Paradise." *The Freeman:* 7–10.

Petersen, C. P. R. 1837–1840(?). *Lovlexicon eiller Alphabetisk Repertorium over den danske Lovgivning og de dertil henhørende offentlige Actstykker.* Copenhagen.

Petuchowski, Jakob. 1968. *Prayerbook Reform in Europe.* New York: The World Union for Progressive Judaism, Ltd.

Philipson, David. 1967. *The Reform Movement in America.* 2nd ed. New York: Ktav.

Plaut, W. Gunther. 1963. *The Rise of Reform Judaism.* New York: The World Union for Progressive Judaism, Ltd.

Pool, David de Sola. 1938. *H. Pereira Mendes: A Biography.* New York: n. p.

Pool, David de Sola, and Tamar de Sola Pool. 1955. *Portrait of Shearith Israel 1654 – 1954: An Old Faith in the New World.* New York: Columbia University Press.

Postal, Bernard, and Malcolm H. Stern. 1974?. *American Airlines Tourist's Guide to Jewish History in the Caribbean.* New York: American Airlines.

Relkin, Stanley T., and Monty R. Abrams. 1983. "A Short History of the Hebrew Congregation of St. Thomas." St. Thomas, U.S.V.I.: n. p. [NB: An update of Paiewonsky 1959].

"Report of the Joint Commission: Virgin Islands." 1920. *Congressional Record,* January 1920, Document no. 734.

Rosenbloom, Joseph R. 1960. *A Biographical Dictionary of Early American Jews.* Louisville: University of Kentucky Press.

Roth, Cecil. 1964. *History of the Jews in England.* 3rd ed. New York: Oxford University Press.

Rovner, Ruth. 1994. "St. Thomas Congregation Prepares for its Bicentennial." *Metro-West Jewish News,* 13 January: 46.

Rubin, Saul Jacob. 1983. *Third to None: The Age of Savannah Jewry, 1733–1983.* Savannah, Ga.: S. J. Rubin.

Rules and Regulations for the Government of the Hebrew Reformed Congregation (Beth Elohim). 1868. New York: Egbert, Bourne & Co.

"St. Thomas Hotel." 1958. *New York Times,* 8 August: Sect. 2: 15, Col. 3.

St. Thomas Times, Almanac and Popular Mercantile Advertised for the Year 1879. 1879. St. Thomas, W. I. [USVI]: St. Thomas Times.

Salomon, H. P. 1970. "The Fidanques: Hidalgos of Faith." *The American Sephardi* 4, nos. 1–2: 15–36.

Samuel, Wilfred S. 1936. "A Review of the Jewish Colonists of Barbados in the Year 1680." London: Purnell & Sons. [NB: Slightly expanded reprint of Samuel's essay in *Publications of the Jewish Historical Society of England* 13: 1–114.]

Sarna, Jonathan D. 1992. "What is American about the Constitutional Documents of American Jewry?" In *A Double Bond: The Constitutional Documents of American Jewry,* ed. Daniel J. Elazar, Jonathan D. Sarna, and Rela G. Monson, 35–55. New York: University Press of America.

[Schaw, Janet]. 1939. *Journal of a Lady of Quality, Being the Narrative of a Journey from Scotland to the West Indies, North Carolina, and Portugal, in the Years 1774 to 1776.* Evangeline Walker Andrews, ed. New Haven: Yale University Press.

Schlesinger, Benjamin. 1967. "The Jews of Jamaica: A Historical View." *Caribbean Quarterly* 13, no. 1: 46–53.

Schouten, Fredreka. 1991. "Development Pioneer Kessler Dies at 94." *Virgin Islands Daily News,* 9 July: 1, 2.

Scott, Julius S. 1996. "Crisscrossing Empires: Ships, Sailors, and Resistance in the

Lesser Antilles in the Eighteenth Century." In *The Lesser Antilles in the Age of European Expansion,* ed. Robert L. Paquette and Stanley L. Engerman, 128–43. Gainesville: University Press of Florida.

Sharfman, I. Harold. 1988. *The First Rabbi: Origins of Conflict Between Orthodox and Reform: Jewish Polemic Warfare in Pre-Civil War America: A Biographical History.* Malibu, Calif.: J. Simon/Pangloss Press.

Shilstone, Eustace M. 1988 [1957?]. *Monumental Inscriptions in the Jewish Synagogue at Bridgetown, Barbados: With Historical Notes from 1630.* Barbados: Roberts Stationery. [NB: Two previous editions apparently published simultaneously(?) around 1957. One was published in London by the Jewish Historical Society of England, and the other was published in New York by the American Jewish Historical Society.]

Singer, Steven. 1985. "Jewish Religious Thought in Early Victorian England." *AJS Review* 10, no. 2: 181–211.

Smith, Verona. 1996. "An Inquiry into the History of the Jewish Community and the Jewish Cemetery in Christiansted, St. Croix." Unpublished Term Paper.

Skrubbeltrang, Fridlev. 1966. *Dansk Vestindien 1846–1880.* Vol. 3 of *Vore gamle tropekolonier.* Denmark: Fremad.

Stern, Malcolm H. 1991. *First American Jewish Families.* 3rd rev. ed. Baltimore: Ottenheimer.

Tansill, Charles. 1932. *The Purchase of the Danish West Indies.* Baltimore: The Johns Hopkins University Press.

Taylor, Charles. 1888. *Leaflets from the Danish West Indies.* London: William Dawson and Sons.

Tuchman, Barbara. 1988. *The First Salute.* New York: Knopf.

Tyson, George F., and Arnold R. Highfield, eds. 1994a. *The Danish West Indian Slave Trade: Virgin Islands Perspectives.* St. Croix, U.S.V.I.: Virgin Islands Humanities Council.

———. 1994b. *The Kamina Folk: Slavery and Slave Life in the Danish West Indies.* U.S. Virgin Islands: Virgin Islands Humanity Council.

Vibæk, Jens. 1966. *Dansk Vestindien 1755–1848.* Vol. 2 of *Vore gamle tropekolonier.* Denmark: Fremad.

U.S. Department of the Interior. 1932. *The Virgin Islands of the United States.* Washington, D.C.: U.S. Department of the Interior. (April).

Watlington, Roy A., and Shirley H. Lincoln, comps. 1997. *Disaster and Disruption in 1867: Hurricane, Earthquake, and Tsunami in the Danish West Indies.* [St. Thomas, V.I.]: University of the Virgin Islands.

Wales, Jane. 1971. "Portrait of an Island Lady: Frances Kessler," *Virgin Islands Daily News,* 20 January: 10.

Watson, Douglas. 1934. "Letter to the Editor." *Young Israel* 27, no. 2: 17.

Westergaard, Waldemar. 1917. *The Danish West Indies Under Company Rule.* New York: Macmillan.

Willis, Jean Louise. 1963. "The Trade between North America and the Danish West Indies, 1756–1807, with Special Reference to St. Croix." Ph. D. thesis, Columbia University.

Woods, Edith deJongh. 1992. *The Royal Three Quarters of the Town of Charlotte Amalie.* St. Thomas: MAPes MONDe editore.

Woods, John D. M. 1993. "A Short History of the Harmonic Lodge 356 E. C." In *Harmonic Lodge 356 E. C. 175th Anniversary.* Commemorative booklet. St. Thomas, U.S.V.I.: n. p. Unpaged.

Wouk, Herman. 1965. *Don't Stop the Carnival.* New York: Doubleday.

Yerushalmi, Yosef. 1982. "Between Amsterdam and New Amsterdam: The Place of Curaçao and the Caribbean in Early Modern Jewish History." *American Jewish History* 72, no. 2: 172–92.

York, Nina, trans. 1986. *Islands of Beauty and Bounty: A Historical Profile of the Danish West Indies.* [Excerpt from the Danish work DANMARK]. St. Croix, U.S.V.I.: Nina York.

Zink, Jack. 1997. "Buffett and Wouk Take 'Carnival' to the Stage." *The Tampa Tribune,* 9 April: 3.

Archival Material

American Jewish Historical Society, New York, N.Y.

Microfilm I-112. Curaçao Documents. 4 reels.
Box °I-139. Barbados Jewish Community.

Bancroft Library, University of California at Berkeley

BANC MSS Z-A 1: Documents relating to the Danish West Indies, 1655–1819.

Congregation Shearith Israel, New York City

Clerk's Office Correspondence, 1927–1931. Box 8(a), Folders 1–2: Letters regarding Rev. Dr. Henry Pereira Mendes's visit to St. Thomas.

Von Scholten Collection, Enid M. Baa Public Library, St. Thomas,
U.S. Virgin Islands

Virgin Islands Census: 1841, 1846, 1860, 1870, 1880, 1901 (on microfilm).

Gemeentearchief Amsterdam, Netherlands

PA 334, #706: Letters in St. Eustatius
PA 334, #1028A: Documents regarding Mordechay Pareira
PA 334, #1039: Documents regarding the family of Shalom Delvalle

Jacob Rader Marcus Center of the American Jewish Archives, Cincinnati, Ohio

Microfilm Role #380. "Correspondence between the Hebrew Congregation and the Danish Colonial Gov't, 1865–1916."
Women of Reform Judaism Collection.

National Archives II, College Park, Maryland

DOCUMENT GROUP 55: RECORDS OF THE DANISH WEST INDIES

"Kvartels Rapporter til Finansministeriet. Copies of Quarterly Statistical Reports to the Ministry of Finance Concerning Births, Deaths, and Marriages in the St. Thomas–St. Jan Administrative District, Including Reports Received from Various Churches in the District for Baptisms, Marriages, and Burials, 1882, 1895, 1903, 1916."
Boxes 1999–2003: Panteprotocol, 1793–1806.

RECORD GROUP 48: FILMS OF THE DEPARTMENT OF THE INTERIOR

#13: "In the Wake of the Buccaneers: A Visit to St. Thomas in the Virgin Islands."
#14: "The Old Danish Sugar Bowl."

Private Collection, Robert Marcus, Springfield, Virginia

Letter from M. B. Simmonds to Isaac Leeser, 3 February 1848.

Rigsarkivet (Danish National Archives), Copenhagen, Denmark

DANSKE VESTINDISKE LOKALARKIV

St. Thomas og St. Jan guvernement mm. 1757–1909.

Borger Eder (Burgher Briefs): 1815–1857, 1858–1909.
Kommandantskab
  Referatprotokol, 1832.
St. Thomas Byføged
  Eksekutor og Konkursboer 1778–1868: V, VI, XIX.
  Matrikul (Tax lists): 1755–1813.
  Testamenteprotokol: 1815–1827, 1828–1841.
  Menighedernes Indberetninger om Fødte, Viede og Døde pa St. Thomas og
  St. Jan.

Kancelli: Vestindiske sager 1699–1771

Vestindiske aabne Breve og Missiver: 1773–1799.

St. Thomas Recorder of Deeds Office, Charlotte Amalie, St. Thomas,
U.S. Virgin Islands

Various records associated with real estate dealings of members of the St. Thomas
  Jewish community.

St. Thomas Hebrew Congregation, Charlotte Amalie, St. Thomas,
U.S. Virgin Islands

Selected Archives of Materials before 1967, including:

Box 1: Series: Religious Leaders.
Box 2: Series: Auxiliary Associations. B. Sisterhood.
Box 9: Series: Board. B. Minutes 1966–1978.
Box 13: Synagogue Bulletins.
Box 15: Series: Cemetery.
Box 17: Constitutions.
Box 22: Series: Events.
Box 45: Series: Membership. 1966.

Materials not kept in the archive:

Protocol Book of Births, Deaths, and Marriages for K. K. BvSvGH. 1852–1973.
Assorted records, 1794–1826. Including births, deaths, marriages, marriage certificates (*ketubot*), and confirmation records. Kept on microfilm.

University College of London, Manuscripts Collection, London, England

Lucien Wolf Collection, B20.

University of Southampton Archives and Manuscripts, Southampton, England

MS 116/104, AJ 258/3: Sermon given by Rev. Moses N. Nathan, Shabbat Tshuvah, 1838.
MS 175, 24/3: Papers of Joseph Herman Hertz

Periodicals (dates denote years searched)

Archives Israélites (Paris), 1850–1854, 1869–1872
CCAR Yearbook, 1958–1966
The Emancipator (St. Thomas), 1921–1928
First Fruits of the West (Kingston, Jamaica), 1844–1845
Israelite (Cincinnati), 1867–1868
Lightbourne's Mail Notes (St. Thomas), 1895–1896, 1914
London Jewish Chronicle, 1844–1846, 1865–1867
New York Times, 1920–1960, plus assorted dates
Occident and American Jewish Advocate (Philadelphia), 1843–1869
Royal Danish American Gazette (St. Croix), 1770–1776, 1789–1802
Sanct Thomæ Tidende (St. Thomas), 1815–1875, 1896, 1900, 1913–1916
St. Thomas Gazette, 1807–1815
St. Thomas Herald, 1882–1884
St. Thomas Mail Notes, 1918–1925
St. Thomas Times, 1875–1881
L'Univers Israélite, 1850–1870 (Selective)
Virgin Islands Daily News, 1930– (Selected years)
Voice of Jacob (London), 1840–1846

Interviews

Murray Blackman, 16 August 1999
Katina Coulianos, 4 June 1994
Gladys De Castro, 11 July 1994 (with Elaine Robles)
Harvey Henne, 6 June 1994
Paul Hoffman, 1 May 1996
Henry L. Kimelman, 1 June 1996 [telephone]
Norma Levin, 12 April 1996

Emma Fidanque Levy, 22 August 1994

Amalia Mylner, 23 June 1994

Isidor Paiewonsky, 14 July 1994; 29 April 1996

Elaine Robles, 11 July 1994 (with Gladys De Castro)

David Stanley Sasso, 6 June 1994 [with Clementine Kaufman]; 8 June 1994; 12 April 1995 [conducted by Bradd H. Boxman]

Carol Weinberger, 18 July 1994

Edith and John Mendes Woods, 17 April 1996

Other Materials

St. Thomas Hebrew Congregation Sisterhood Luncheon. Discussion of Personal Histories: Franzi Coulianos, Gladys De Castro, Clara Moron, Elaine Robles. 24 April 1992. Videotaped by Gary Rosenthal.

Isidor Paiewonsky, Sermon at St. Thomas Hebrew Congregation. December 1992. Videotaped by Donald Pomerantz.

"Ralph M. Paiewonsky. Memoirs of a Governor: A Man for the People." Radio broadcast, WSTA (St. Thomas), 1991. Tape recording in possession of author.

INDEX

A Note on Names: All persons with the same last name are listed together in this index regardless of familial or religious affiliations. Those individuals who have received special attention in the text (such as Moses Sasso) will be listed separately.

Abendanone (family), 7, 14
Abbitt, Rev. Raymond, 219
Adams, Alton Augustus, 179, 265n51
Adams, John Quincy, 33
Adjuntos, 23, 24
Adon Olam (Lord Over All), hymn, 72, 187
Ahal (Holy Ark), 48, 49, 162, 187, 188
Allan, Rev. W. O., 129
Alland, Alexander, 192, 268n18
Allgemeine Zeitung des Judenthums, 71
Alliance Israélite Universelle, 129, 131, 134
All Saints Church. *See* Episcopal Church
Altona (Germany/Denmark), xvi, 20, 60, 234n4, 241n33
American Hebrew, 192
American International Academy, 216
American Jewish Archives, 208
Amsterdam (Netherlands), 2, 6, 39, 45, 229n12, 238n11, 240n29; reform in, 68
Angelou, Maya, 224
Anglicanism. *See* Episcopal Church
Anglo-Jewish Association, London, 139
Anti-Defamation League, 224
Antigua, 231n43
apprenticeships, business, 29
Archives Isralites de France, Les, 91
Arecibo, Puerto Rico, 155–56
Artom, Dr. Benjamin, 171
Aruba, xvii
Ashenheim, Dr. Lewis, 80
Athias (family), 32; Isaac, 236n39
Aux Cayes. *See* Haiti; St. Domingue

Baa, Enid M., 208
Bahnsen, S., 61
Baiz, 32; David, 88

Balls Pond Cemetery. *See under* cemeteries
Baltimore, Maryland, 33
baptisms, Christian, 147–49, 258n14
Barbados, xvii, xxii, 2, 28, 33, 47, 95, 115, 154, 170
Bar Mitzvah, 189, 205–6
Baruch HaBa/Aba, hymn, 49, 211, 215
Bayne, 198, 204; Benjamin, 197; Irene, 206
Benjamin 7, 32; Emanuel, 28, 29, 235n22; Esther, 28, 235n22; Jacob, 75; Judah, 235n22; Judah Philip, 28, 152, 192, 235n22–23; Philip, 28, 235n22; Rebecca, 28; Solomon, 10
Benlisa: Clara, 150; Esther, 150; Rachel, 150; Zipporah, 150
Beracha VeShalom. See Synagogue, St. Thomas
Berents, Melchior, 2
Beth Elohim. See Hebrew Reformed Congregation (*Beth Elohim*)
Bevis Marks (London Spanish and Portuguese Synagogue), 170
births, legitimate and illegitimate, 146–50, 258n14
Bismark, Otto von, 152
Blackman, Rabbi Murray, 219
Bluebeard's Castle Hotel, 197
Blyden: Edward Wilmot, xvii; Edward Wilmot, III, 222
B'nai Brith, Sasso-Cardoze Lodge #2488, 217, 218
Boston, Massachusetts, 6, 197, 221
Boxman, Rabbi Bradd, 223
Brandao, Isabella (wife of Moses Paiewonsky), 261n68

Brand Corps, St. Thomas, 41
bricks, as form of construction, 44–45, 238n9
Bright's disease, 144, 257n6
British occupation of St. Thomas. *See* occupation, British
Buenos Aires, Argentina, 144, 172
Bulletin, The, 161
Burgher Brief, 29, 38, 241n33, 261n53
Burgher Council of the Danish West Indies, 91
burial rites, Jewish, 55
Burial Society (*Gemilut Hasadim*), 15, 17, 23
Burke, M.P. Edmund, 8
Busby, Catherine, 156
by-laws, congregational: Curaçao, 1786, 21–24; Hebrew Reformed Congregation, 1868, 124, 135, 137; 1796, 16–18, 22; 1802, 21–24, 31, 74; 1848, 84–86, 92, 113–15, 117, 126, 135, 247n149, 250n81, 256n114; 1875, 133, 135–38

Campbell, Albert A., xv, 192–93, 267n95
Cappé: Aaron, 150; August, 150; Judah, 46, 60, 97, 126, 131, 254n63; Miriam, 244n97
Captain Kidd, 2
Caracas. *See* Venezuela
Cardoze, David Jr., 109, 135, 144, 169, 211, 226, 250n90, 254n69; acting reader under Rev. Nathan, 127–28, 130; death of, 162–63; Golden Wedding celebration, 153–54, 260n39; and Moses Sasso, 168, 262n77; ninetieth birthday of, 161–62, 262n73; as reader, 143, 145, 152, 258n12
Cardoze: David Sr., 251n102; Grace, 147; Moses, 153; Rachel, 153
Carillon, Rev. Aaron Cohen, 66, 242n53
Carillon, Rev. Benjamin Cohen, xv, xvii, 59, 84, 85, 90, 91, 93, 94, 245n118; breach of contract suit against the synagogue, 78, 245n117; first time in St. Thomas pulpit, 66–69; minister in Jamaica, 78–79, 245n118; seal,

242n53; second time in St. Thomas pulpit, 71–78, 243n58
Carioca Rum, 197
Catholic Church, 25, 26, 148, 149, 150
cemeteries, xxiv; London, Balls Pond, 140–41, 256n121; London, Golders Green, 141; St. Croix, 229n11; St. Croix, Moravian, 88; St. Thomas, Altona (new), 35, 53, 240n11; St. Thomas, Hebrew Reformed Congregation, 124–5; St. Thomas, Savan (old), 14–15, 35, 233n69
Census of 1870, St. Thomas, 143, 149, 150
Charleston, South Carolina, xvi, 28, 68, 130, 254n82
Charlotte Amalie, St. Thomas, 12, 37; after the 1831 fire, 43; culture, 51–52; decline of, 142; fires in (*see* fires); economy, 51; emancipation in, 88; growth of, 15, 19; harbor, 142–43; Jews as percentage of the local population, 240n9; Sunday activities, 31. *See also* St. Thomas
Chase Manhattan Bank, 212
choir: in main Synagogue, 49–50, 65, 76, 137, 256n118; in Hebrew Reformed Congregation, 124
Christian VII (king of Denmark), 15
Christiansted, St. Croix, 88
cholera, 110, 121
Chumaceiro, Rev. Aaron Mendes, 94–95, 100–102, 242n53, 248n38, 249n64
circumcision, 132
Civil War, U.S., 28
cockfighting, 31
Cohen D'Azevedo, 32; Benjamin, 100
collections, financial: to build new synagogue, 44–45; for Jewish orphans in Russia and Poland, 129; for "Repair Fund," 175
College of the Virgin Islands, 223
Colonial Council of St. Thomas and St. Johns, 126, 150
Colonial Law, Danish, 115, 135
Columbia College, 197
Columbus, Christopher, 1
Commandant Gade, 41, 116, 155

Committee of the Society of Hebrew Literature (London), 139

confirmation: as a religious practice, 72–73, 244n90; in twentieth century, 189, 269n45; under Carillon, 72–73, 74–75; under Nathan, 83–84, 110, 246n141, 251n104

conversion: to Christianity, 61–63, 106; to Judaism, 157

Copenhagen (Denmark), 24, 39, 86, 157, 237n55

Correa: Abraham, 60; Emanuel Alvares (eighteenth century), 3, 229n8, 240n13; Emanuel Alvarez (nineteenth century), 46, 60–63; Gabriel, 60, 97; Judith, 60; Moses (Maurice), 60–63; M. R. A., 251n1; Rachel, 60–63

Correa, Bahnsen & Company, 60

Cortissos, Deborah Simha, 75

Costa Rica, xviii, 143, 146, 163, 168; Alajuela, 146

cotton, 19

Coulianos: Costas, 271n79; Franzi [*see* Siggelkow, Franzi (Coulianos)]

Crystal Gade, 35, 41, 46, 52, 165, 167, 205, 237n55. *See also* Skidengade

Cuba, 51

Curaçao, xvi, xvii, xxii, 45, 93, 94, 100, 109, 145, 229n12, 238n70; birthplace of David Cardoze, Jr., 115, 128; Burial Society, 15, 233n71; emigrants to St. Thomas, xviii, 21, 20, 109, 143; influence on 1803 St. Thomas Synagogue by-laws, 21–24; and S. E. L. Maduro, 58, 76, 79, 95; M. H. Myers in, 99; *Mikveh Israel*, 21, 107; as model for St. Thomas Jews, 18; Reformers in, 107, 115, 250n91; St. Thomas religious leaders from, 32, 58; and St. Eustatius, 5, 6, 7. *See also* by-laws, congregational; cemeteries

Curiel (family), 248n35

Da Costa, 146; Elias Charles Mendes, 33, 246n143; Jacob M., 138

Da Costa Gomez, 166; A., 251n7

Daily News of the Virgin Islands, 206, 217

Damascus Blood Libel (1840), 66–67, 242n53

Danish Lutheran Church. *See* Lutheran Church, Danish

Davis, Rabbi Daniel L., 219

Davis, Jefferson, 28

D'Azevedo, 29; Benjamin, 126, 249n63; Isaac, 49; Captain Moses, 41, 46; M. C., 251n1; Rachel Cohen 112–13

D'Azevedo & Robles, 29

de Casseres, Samuel de Josias, 21

De Castro, Alexander, 146, 237n66, 258n15

De Castro, 146, 161, 187; David, 61; David M., 161, 166, 167; David Maduro, 200–201; Hannah, 200; Jacob, 46, 52

De Castro, Morris Fidanque, xvi, 192, 211, 213, 215, 217, 218–19; acting governor of the Virgin Islands, 191, 200; death of, 218–19; governor of the Virgin Islands, 201–2, 203, 204, personal history, 200–202; president of St. Thomas Hebrew Congregation, 179, 218

DeCordova, Esq., 45

Degetau, O. G. C., 61–63

De Jongh, Abraham D., 117, 118, 123–24, 251n1

De la Motta (family), 7

De Leon, 7, 14, 32; Isaac, 3, 14

de Lesseps, Ferdinand, 134, 154, 164

Delvalle, 146; Benjamin S., 133, 250n91; David, 147, 258n16; Henry H., 147; Mr. & Mrs. Jacob B., 153; R. E., 148; Salomon J., 149

De Meza: Esther, 74; Raphael, 47; Rebecca Rosabelle, 147

Denmark, xxiv, 1–2, 14, 128, 165, 209; freemasonry in, 32; government, 120

Denmark Court Synagogue, London, 79, 246n123

De Pinna, Elias, 29

De Sola: Hannah, 242n53; J. H., 45; Moses, 107, 109, 116, 250n90, 251n1, 279n138

de Solas, Isaac and Jacob, 10

Dineÿra, Jacob, 21
D'Oliveyra: Alexandrine, 149; Jacob, 100;
    Leah, 149; Ludvic B., 149; Rachel, 100
Dookhan, Isaac, 19
Dreis, Harry, 209–10
Dronningens Quarter, Charlotte Amalie.
    See Queens Quarter, Charlotte Amalie
Dutch Reformed Church, 26, 90, 129, 148

E. & B. Lindo & Co., 29
earthquakes, 20, 122–23
"Ein Keloheinu" (hymn), 187
Elias (family), 229n9
"El Porvenir," 107
England, 27, 151; Bath, 139; Bristol, 139;
    freemasonry in, 32; Manchester, 171.
    See also London
Episcopal Church, 25, 148, 149, 150,
    257n5, 259n19
ethnicity, accumulative, xxii–xxiv
Evelyn: Alfred, 184; Laura, 185
Ezekiel (prophet), 101
Ezra, Meriam, 47, 235n32

Fidanque: J., Jr., 76; Jacob, 152; Joseph,
    251n7
"fireproofs," 26, 27, 41, 43–44
fires, in Charlotte Amalie, 25–27, 41–42,
    43, 46, 238nn67–70
First Fruits of the West, 80
Fishman, Elliot, 198, 204, 205
Flax, Eliza, 155
floating dock, in St. Thomas, 120–21, 142
Florida, xxiii
France, xvi, 27, 40, 115, 143, 151;
    Bordeaux, 2, 38, 241n23; Paris, 138;
    reform in, 68
Frankel, 161, 261n67; Abraham, 159–60;
    Zacharias, 64
Franks, Jacob, 2
Frederick VI (king of Denmark), 36,
    38–39
Frederick VII (king of Denmark), 46, 105
Frederiksted, St. Croix, 87
"free-coloreds" (also "free blacks"), 40, 52,
    146
freemasonry. *See* Masonic Lodge
French Revolution, 11–12

Galveston, Texas, 104
"Gaza Strip," 205
Geiger, Abraham, 64
Gemilut Hasadim, See Burial Society
    (Gemilut Hasadim)
Georgé, Salomon de, 7, 230n26
Gibraltar, 13
Ginsburg, Ruth Bader, 224
Comez, Elias, 231n36
Goodman & Pretto, 28
Gottheil, Rev. Gustav, 152
Government Hill, St. Thomas, 204
Great Synagogue, London, 96
gumbe (drum), 40

HaGomel (Prayer), 89, 122
Haiti, 13, 158, 160. *See also* St. Domingue
Halman, 161; Maria, 148; Moses, 147;
    Samuel B., 148
Hamburg (Germany), xvi, 2, 45, 157, 172,
    184, 241n33
hanukkah lamp, 7, 230n29
Harding, Warren, 265n61
Harmonic Lodge 356 E. C., 33, 88, 179,
    189
Harper, Edward, 219
Harper's Weekly, 121
Hart, Nathan and Yael, 236n38
Hascamoth. See by-laws, congregational,
    1802
Haskalah movement, 127
Hastie, Gov. William, 200, 201
Hazan, See Reader
Hebre, See Burial Society *(Gemilut
    Hasadim)*
Hebrew Benevolent Association/Society,
    93, 97, 123, 260n50
Hebrew Reformed Congregation *(Beth
    Elohim)*, 112–38, 144, 155; births,
    125, 253n55, 255n97; by-laws *(see* by-
    laws, congregational); deaths, 253n55;
    marriages, 118–19, 123–24, 128, 134,
    253n55; recognition by Danish Colo-
    nial Government, 125, 130–31; seal,
    253n57
Hebrew Union College, 208
Heller: Rabbi Bernard, 207–8, 270n57;
    Edith (Paiewonsky), 208

Henne, Harvey and Mitzi, 272n1
Henry, James, Esq., 88
Hertz, Joseph H. and Rose, 264n27
High Holidays, 142, 187–89
Hispaniola, 11
Hitler, Adolf, 189–91
Hoffman, Paul, 205, 212
Hoheb, 7, 10, 32; Benjamin, 15, 20;
    Rachel, 73; Samuel, 9, 11, 15, 33, 60,
    231n44
Holland. *See* Netherlands
Holst, Elaine, 185
Holy Ark. See *Ahal*
Honen Dalim Congregation, St. Eustatius,
    5, 7
Hoover, Herbert, 182–3
hurricanes, xvii, 6, 20, 55–60, 133, 166,
    222, 241nn16–18; in 1837, 58; in 1867,
    121–22, 125; in 1871, 133; in 1916,
    166; in 1996, 224; liturgy for, 58–59
Hurricane Supplication Day, 57,
    241nn19–20
Hurricane Thanksgiving Day, 57–59, 105,
    20, 121
Hvass, Tyge, 263n7

"I. Levin," 157, 261n53
Intermarriage (Jewish/Non-Jewish), 148,
    184–85, 193, 214–15, 266n69
Israelite, 117, 119, 123, 124, 256n125

Jacobs, Eleanora, 144, 257n9
Jamaica, xvii, 2, 47, 59, 115, 170, 172;
    Kingston, 26, 75, 79, 80, 102, 104; and
    Meyer H. Myers, 95, 102; Montego
    Bay, 78, 170, 171; and Moses Nathan,
    81, 105, 249n78; Spanish Town, 78, 82,
    245n118; subscribers to *Voice of Jacob*,
    243n73
Jewish Chronicle of London, xxv, 78, 91,
    108, 109, 117, 133, 139
Jewish Social Studies, 192–93
Jewish Theological Seminary, 172
Jewish Week, 259n30
"Jew Street." *See* Jøde Gade
Jøde Gade, 15, 231n49
"Joint Subscriptions of the Jewish and
    Christians of St. Thomas in aid of the
Jewish Orphans of Poland and Russia,"
    128–29
Jos. M. Monsanto & Co., 29
Joseph, Samuel, 251n1
Josephus Flavius, 60
Julien: Abraham, 12, 14, 89, 233n72;
    Hannah, 43; Judith, 60; Rachel, 12, 14

Karasick, Rabbi Joseph, 272n1
Kennedy, Harry, 181
Kennedy, John F., 213
Kessler, 204, 205; Frances, 197, 206, 210;
    Sidney, 197–98, 203, 212, 267n8
ketubah (marriage contract), 118, 186,
    258n11
Kidd, Captain. *See* Captain Kidd
Kimelman, Henry, 198, 204, 205
Kipur. *See* High Holidays
Knights of Leopold, 126
Knights of the Dannebrog, 46, 138, 144
kohanim (priests), 240n33
Kol Shearith Israel. See under Panama
Kreke, Marilyn, 206, 210
Kronprindsens Quarter, Charlotte Amalie,
    10, 26

Lamb: Adele 148; Albert, 148; Alexander,
    148; James, 148; Rachel (Moron?),
    148; Regina, 148; William Charles, 148
Lange, Ludorisca, 149
Lauderdale Road Synagogue, 140
Leeser, Rev. Isaac, 71, 84, 87, 88, 102–3,
    117–18, 245n58, 247n149
Leffmann, Emilie, 155; Moses, 155
Lehman, Gov. Herbert H., 172
leisure time, increased for Americans after
    World War II, 195–96
Leon, Esther Anita, 148; M., 148
Levi, 166; Herman, 149; Joseph, 144;
    Willie, 188
Levien: Alice Eugenie, 156; Joseph, 116,
    154–57, 260n50, 261n53; Joshua, 155,
    260n47; Leo, 155, 156; (Sarah) Victoria
    Elizabeth, 149, 154, 261n55
Levin, 161, 178, 189, 206; Benjamin,
    263n10; Leah Else (Siggelkow), 184,
    189, 190, 214; Sarah Victoria Elizabeth
    (*see* Levien); Zorach, 159

Levin, Israel, 156–59, 184, 214, 260n62; as "Israel Leon," 156; death, 189; early years on St. Thomas, 156–57, 260n52; at services in St. Thomas synagogue, 168, 170. *See also* "I. Levin"

Levy, 7; Abraham, 58; Alexander, 250n90; Benjamin, 47, 73; Clothilde, 144, 148; David (*see* Levy-Yulee, David); Hannah, 27; Leon, 29; Manette Azelia, 148, 257n5; Moses Elias, 14, 27–28, 29, 43, 232n65, 238n1; Nathan, 33–34, 53, 237n50; Sylvain, 116, 143–44, 148, 257n5

Levy and Benjamin, 29

Levy Maduro: Isaac, 145; Judith, 146; Judith (wife of Samuel Elias), 144. *See also* Maduro

Levy Maduro, Samuel Elias, 58, 79, 101, 115, 144; background, 58; in Curaçao, 76, 77, 79, 251n102; death, 110–11, 112; named Negnim Zemirot Yisrael, 95; reader in St. Thomas, 89, 91, 93, 109

Levy-Yulee, David, xv, 27–28, 152

Levy-Yuly, Elijah, 13

Lindo, 32, 146; Abraham Alfred Jessurun, 146; Benjamin, 29; Clara Jessurun, 145; Elias H., xvi, 29, 33, 37; Isaac, 33, 49–50; Jacob Jessurun, 112–13, 116, 117, 118, 251n1; J. H., 251n1

Lightbourne's Mail Notes, 161, 163

Lion, A. A., 20

Lithuania, 159

Liverpool, England, 69, 79; Old Hebrew Congregation in, 80

London, England, xvi, 2, 18, 33, 39, 55, 158, 170; London Sephardim donations to St. Thomas Synagogue, 45, 47; Rev. E. N. Martinez in, 140–41; Rev. Moses Nathan in, 79, 139–40; reform in, 68; Shaaré Tikvah Schools of, 131; subscribers to *Voice of Jacob*, 243n73. *See also* cemeteries

London Jews' Free School, 79

Lopes, 20, 32

Lopes Dubec, 20, 32; Charles, 241n23; Louis, 28; Moise C., Jr., 240n13; Samuel, 232n60

Lopez: Isaac, 3; Rev. Isaac 26, 234n13, 235n15

"Lord Over All" (Hymn), 153

Louchheim, Aline, 202

L'Ouverture, Toussaint, 12–13

Lucas, Henrietta, 147

Lutheran Church, Danish, 25, 54–55, 211

Lynch, Hollis, 222

Maduro, 77, 146; Jacob, 98, 99; Mordecai, 98. *See also* Levy Maduro

Mahamad/Mahamade, creation of, 16, 23–24

malaria, 20

Maracaibo. *See* Venezuela

Marcus, Jacob Rader, xix-xx, xxiv

Marks, Rev. David Woolf, 69–71, 116, 117, 140; consulted for St. Thomas religious leader, 70–71, 243n58, 244n75; student of Rev. Moses Nathan, 79, 139, 140

marriage, 29, 52–54, 240n7; common-law, 148; and Jews, 53–54, 118, 145, 193, 214–15

Martinique, xvii

Masonic Lodge, xvii, 32–33, 126, 129, 163, 236n43, 254n69. *See also* Harmonic Lodge 356 E. C.

Markowitz, Rabbi Samuel H., 218, 219, 271n90

Marshall, John, 61

Martinez, Rev. Elias Nunes, 131–35, 138, 140–41, 175

matzah, 17, 88, 207

Meara, Mashod, 76–77

Mears: David Leon, 14; Hannah, 14; Samson, 14

mehitza. *See* separation

Melbourne, Australia, 96

Memory, Collective, xxiii

Mendelssohn, Moses, 68

Mendes, Rev. Henry Pereira, xxv, 164, 170–82, 184, 187, 193, 263nn16, 18, 264n38, 265nn54, 56; biographical background, 171–73; consecration class, 175, 180, 181; correspondence with Moses Sasso, 183; decision to

come to St. Thomas, 173–74; departure from St. Thomas, 181–82
Mendes: Isaac H. Abendana, 174; Rosalie Piza, 181, 264n24
Mendes Monsanto (family), 32
Mercantilism, 51–52, 120, 126–27
Methodist Church, 156
Miami, 196
Milan, Gabriel, xvii, 2
Mocatta, Moses, 70
Mohel, 125
Molina, Anna Viera de, 11
Monsanto, 146, 147, 232n60; Esther, 149; Jos. M., 29; Jacob Mendes, 46
Montefiore, 32; Sir Moses, 96, 152
Montefiore Hospital, New York, 172
Moravian Church, 25, 148, 260n50
"Moreinu Rab," 98–100
Morocco, 13–14; Essaouira, 13; Mogador, 13
Moron, 161, 166, 187, 206; Anna Petronella, 259n19; Enrique, 217; Isaac H., 126.; J. H., 251n7; Olga Rachel Henriques, 184; Semmy Henriquez, 259n19
mosquitos, 20
Moulay Abd-Allah, 13
Moulay Yazid, 13
Muhammad b. Abd-Allah, Sultan, 13
Mühlenfels, Frederik Baltharzar von, 15
Musaph service, 75–76
Music, xiv, 115, 173, 223; Organ, 198, 243n71. *See also* choir
Myers: Rev. E. M., 96; Rev. J. H., 96; Rev. M. H., 96
Myers, Meyer H., xvii, 95–102, 103, 104, 126; confrontation with uncle, 97–98; departure for Jamica, 102; granted title "Morenu Rab," 98; suit against Maduro, 248n52; and visit from Aaron Menndes Chumaceiro, 100–102; visit to Curaçao and subsequent controversy, 99–100
Myerston, M., 251n1
Mylner, Svend (husband of Amalia Paiewonsky), 190, 215

Naar: Judge David, xv, 47, 152; Joshua, 21
Naimas De Crasto (family name), 248n35

Nathan, Rev. Moses Nathan, xv, xvii, 75–76, 79–86, 88, 89, 90, 91, 93, 103–32, 134, 137, 139–40, 245n117, 254nn79–82, 256nn125–26; on board of Savings Bank, 250n89; confirmations, 83–84, death of, 257n130; editor of *First Fruits of the West*, 80, 246n127; first tenure on St. Thomas, 79–86; and the Hebrew Reformed Congregation, 112–20, 123–28, 130; in Jamaica, 75, 81, 104, 249n78; preparing David Cardoze, Jr. as reader in St. Thomas, 130; role in forging 1848 St. Thomas synagogue by-laws, 84–86
National Federation of Temple Sisterhoods (UAHC), 210–11; Norma Levitt, president of NFTS in 1983, 222
Navon, Yitzhak, 223
Nazis, 189–91
"Negnim Zemirot Yisrael," 95, 162, 211
Netherlands, 2, 4, 7. *See also* Amsterdam
Nevis, xvii, xxii, 170
New Orleans, 89, 104
New York Board of Jewish Ministers, 172
New York City, xviii, 138, 197, 215, 217, 243n58; port, xvi, 6; Sephardic population in, 15, 18, 45 (see also *Shearith Israel*); source for various products, 55, 69, 88, 124; Temple Emanu-El, 107; tourism origin, 195
New York Federation of Reform Synagogues, 219
New York Times, 198, 202
New York University, 172, 213
Nissen, Johann Peter, 26, 27, 30, 31, 44, 53, 235n16
Noah, biblical figure, 121
Noah, Mordecai Manuel, 34
Nones: Alex., 251n1; Alfred, 120, 126, 131, 134, 251n1
Nunes: Julius, 149; Lucien A., 149

Occident and American Jewish Advocate, xxv, 90, 92, 243n58, 247n149; and confirmations, 110, 244n90; and the Hebrew Reformed Congregation, 117, 118; rabbinic want ad in, 91, 102–3

occupation, British: in 1801–1802, 20–21; in 1807–1815, 27–30
Ochoa, Dolorita, 149
Old Year's Night, 40–41
O'Reilly, Joseph, 33
"Orthodox" title, 68, 74, 77, 107, 108, 109
Osorio: Betsy Bertha, 119, 123; Emanuel Correa, 112, 134, 251n1; Jacob Haim, 61, 76, 91, 92, 123, 246n143; Jacob Haim, performing weddings, 118–19, 252n31; Moses, 128, 251n1
Oster, Sol H., 217

Paiewonsky, 161, 178, 189, 206; Alice, 185; Amalia (Mylner), 185, 190, 191, 215; Anna, 160, 217; Benjamin, 170, 261nn62, 68; David, 160; Esther Rachel/Ethel, 159, 184, 185, 189; Isaac, 160, 162, 166, 169, 170, 214, 217; Isabella, 160; Jacob, 159, 170, 184, 185–86, 261nn62, 63; Lena (Kushner), 185–86; Moses, 160, 261nn62, 68; Paulina (Puritz), 166, 185, 214; Rachel, 160; Rebecca (Kirchner), 160, 214; Wolf, 160
Paiewonsky, Isidor, 162, 166, 169, 264n36; rewriting the St. Thomas Hebrew Congregation's history (1959), 209–10
Paiewonsky, Raphael (Ralph) Moses, 160, 170, 215, 260n52, 264n36; governor of U.S. Virgin Islands, xvi, 213–14; marriage to cousin of Bernard Heller, 208
Panama, 146, 170, 172, 215; Colon, 146, 160, 170, 261n67; greetings from, xxiii, 162, 222; *Kol Shearith Israel*, 138, 146; migration to, xviii, 134–35, 143, 167, 201; rise as a desirable area, 134
Panama Canal, 134, 151, 154, 164, 165, 167, 181, 262n1
Pan American World Airways, 195–96
Pareira, 32
Parnas-Presidente position, 23
Passover, 117, 178–79, 206–7; community seder, 269n46, 270n52
Pearson, Paul M., 183
Peneke, Mr., 27

Penha, J. L., 97, 126, 248n50, 251n1, 257n138
Pereira (family), 248n35
Petit, 178; Abigail, 38; David, 38; Esther, 37–38; Eugene (nineteenth century), 250n90; Eugene (twentieth century), 192; F. D., 245n111; Hannah, 38; Isaac, 37–38; Isaac, Jr., 38; Joseph, I, 37; Joseph, II, 38; Moses, 37; Rachel Monsanto Pomié, 38–40; Rebecca, 38; Samuel, 38
Perlman, Yitzhak, 224
Philadelphia, Pennsylvania, 6, 84, 86, 88
Pinto, Abraham Jessurun, 32, 36, 236n41
Pissarro: Aaron, 40; Abraham Gabriel Frederick, 38–40, 46; Jacob Camille, xv, 14, 40, 192, 224; Joseph Gabriel, 38; Moses, 39; Rachel Monsanto/Manzana Pomié Petit, 38–40
Piza, 146; David M., 143, 257n4; Hannah, 235n31; Jeudah, 77; Rev. Joshua, 89; Moses, 77; Samuel and Rachel, 264n24; Rosalie Rebecca, 172
plantations, 19
Pomié, 12–13, 32; Abigail, 232n60; Moses Monsanto/Manzana 12, 14, 38; Rachel Monsanto 38, 235n32
Pollack, Jacob, 8–9
Pool, Rev. David de Sola, 164, 170, 172, 175, 176, 177
Pretto, 146; Abraham Elias, 98; Daniel [*see* Pretto Henriquez (family), Daniel]
Pretto Henriquez: Daniel, 98, 99–100, 249n63, 254n69; David, 54–55, 74; Rachel, 54
Princip, Gavrilo, 165
privateers, 20
Prohibition, 197
protocols, synagogue. *See* Synagogue, St. Thomas, birth/death/marriage records
Providence, Rhode Island, 6
pseudonyms, for newspaper editorialists, 243n61
Puerto Rico, 1, 195–96, 197, 215, 221
Purim, 100, 176–78, 222, 264n38; name given to slave, 236n39

Puritz: Alfred, 185; Paulina (*see* Paiewonsky, Paulina); Sadie, 185

Queens Quarter, Charlotte Amalie, 26, 28,
41, 231n49
Queen's Street/Main Street, Charlotte
Amalie, 131, 255n93

Ratclif, M., 147
Reader (*Hazan*), 58, 66, 109; in by-laws, 23
Reader's Desk, See *Tebah*
Reagan, Ronald, 223
Recife (Brazil), 2, 12, 229n3
Redemption of a child from illegitimacy,
156
"Reformers," 68–69, 75, 81, 94, 109
Reform Judaism, xxii, 64, 242n44; Ameri-
can, 106, 197, 198; British, 64–65, 68–
69, 75, 78, 80–81, 88, 106, 242n50; in
Curaçao, 65, 250n91; German, 64–68,
75, 78, 79; in St. Thomas, 65–86,
106–41, 207, 210 (*see also* by-laws,
congregations, cemeteries, Hebrew
Reformed Congregation)
"Reform Sephardic" Practice, 199, 216
Relkin, Rabbi Stanley, 223
Robles: Elaine, 210; Elias Athias, 163,
165–66; Esther Athias (Watson), 186;
Esther Consuelo Cardoze, 168; Jacob,
10; Joseph Athias, 168; Rosa Athias,
169, 186; Samuel J., 28, 29
Rodney, George Brydges, 4, 7–11, 231n37
Roosevelt, Franklin D., 183
Rosette, Abraham, 2
Rosh HaShanah. *See* High Holidays
Ross, Jeanette, 148
Rothschild: Emil, 138; Sigismund, 58, 89,
138, 246n143; Sigismund, death of,
257n8
Royal Mail Steam Packet Company, 154
rubble masonry, 44–45
rum, 41, 197
Russia: Jews in, 128–29, 152; Russians
misdirected to St. Thomas, 158

St. Croix, xvi, 7, 20, 28, 43, 47, 90, 133,
150, 229n1, 252n31, 257n9; agricultural economy of, 19, 51, 87; Jewish
community in, xvii, 3, 88, 236n41; riots
in, 151; status as part of the Virgin
Islands, 1, 2
St. Domingue, 11–13, 14, 19, 21, 38. *See
also* Haiti
St. Eustatius, xviii, 3–11, 14, 19, 143,
144; attacked by the British, xvii, 4,
7–10; history, 4–5; emigration of
Jews to St. Thomas, 20, 21; Jewish
community in, xxii, 3–7, 8–10
St. John/St. Johns, 1, 3, 51, 150
St. Kitts, 9, 231n44
St. Lucia, 100
St. Thomas: Fort Christian Museum, 226;
as "Little Paris" 165; Organic Act
(1936), 183; religious revival on, 90;
Revised Organic Act (1954), 213;
Savings Bank, 165; as shipping entre-
pôt, 34; size of Jewish population in,
52, 154; transfer of, from Denmark
to United States, 166–67
St. Thomas Choral Society, 211
St. Thomas Commercial Academy, 97
St. Thomas Community Band, 185
St. Thomas Gazette, 30
St. Thomas Hebrew Congregation. *See*
Synagogue, St. Thomas
St. Thomas Herald, 142, 152, 157
St. Thomas Times, 152, 157
Samas/Samos. See Sexton (*Samos*)
Sanct Thomae Tidende, 30, 91, 110, 129;
accounts of synagogue events, 36, 43,
73, 105; B. C. Carillon in, 68–69, 78;
death announcements, 38, 52, 54; dis-
seminator of international news, 34,
47; editorialists, 92; Hebrew Reformed
Congregation, 120, 128; local observa-
tions, 90; M. H. Myers in, 99; organ for
advertisements, 31; and rebuilding of
synagogue, 45, 47; synagogue schism
detailed in, 77
San Diego, California, 218
Santo Domingo, xvi, 6, 160
Sao Tomé, 209
Sarquy, 32; Elias, 13, 14, 20, 26, 29, 89,
233n67, 235n31; "Madame," 235n31

Sasso, 146, 161, 187; Abraham, 153, 160; David Stanley, 187; Elias, 148; Ellen, 148; Emmeline Joy, 215, 269n45; Ernest, 215; Judah, 76; Julianna, 148; Leah, 148; Rebecca, 160

Sasso, Moses De Castro, 185, 189, 190, 194, 196, 198, 205, 226; appointment as reader, 168; as assistant reader, 163, 165, 166, 168; background, 167–68; and David Cardoze, 262n77; honored at Community Seder, 206; honored on fiftieth year with congregation, 215–16; honored on forty-fifth year with congregation, 211–12; marriage to Esther Watson,186–87; marriage to Rosa Athias Robles, 169, 186, 187; officiant at gubernatorial inaugurations, 202, 213; officiating over marriages, 186; provided regular salary, 199; as Rabbi Emeritus, 217, 219; relationship with Henry Pereira Mendes, 164, 173, 174, 175, 179, 180, 182, 183, 184; retirement, 218; training boys for Bar Mitzvah, 205–6

Schafer, Rabbi Stephen, 272n1

Schiffer, Jacques, 192

Schindler, Alexander, 222

Schon, August, 41

schools, secular, 126, 132

Scientific American, 262n1

seder. See Passover

Sefer/Sepher. See Torah

Senior (family), 248n35

separation, between men and women during Jewish worship, 48, 199, 268n12

Serano, David, 15, 233n72

Sexton (*Samos*), 17, 23, 188

Shattuck, Jared, 28

Shavuot, 83, 180, 246n140

Shearith Israel (New York Spanish and Portuguese Synagogue), 69, 233n77, 240n29; aiding St. Thomas synagogue, 7, 176–78, 238n11, ; and B. C. Carillon, 69; and Moses Nathan, 254n82; and Henry Pereira Mendes, xxv, 170, 171, 176–78, 264n38

Shpetner, Kate, 204–5, 206, 210–11

Shrewsbury (ship), 9

Siggelkow: Eugene August "Franz," 184, 189; Franzi (Coulianos), 189, 206, 271n79; Gertrude, 189; Leah Else (see Levin)

Simchat Torah, 110

Simmonds, Morris B., xvii, 67, 247n8, 250n89; background, 88–89; conversion to Unitarianism, xvii, 106, 149; refusal to pay synagogue-imposed taxes, 105

Singer, Steven, 64–65, 242n45

Skidengade, 28, 32, 35. *See also* Crystal Gade

slavery, 10, 11, 19–20, 31, 150; emancipation, 51, 87–88, 151

smallpox, 20, 122

sohet (slaughterer), 23

Solomon: Moses, 79; Mrs. Jerome, 210

Sonthonax, Léger, 12

spinsters, 247n2

Statia. *See* St. Eustatius

Sterner, Harold, 202

sugar, 11, 19, 51

Sukkot (Feast of Tabernacles), 74, 83; citrons for, 247n4

Surinam, 2, 15, 67

"Sweet Singer of Israel." *See* "Negnim Zemirot Yisrael"

"Synagogue Hill," xiii, 143, 163

Synagogue, St. Thomas: as *Beracha VeShalom*, 15–18; author's associations with, 221–25; birth/death/marriage records, 53, 145, 151, 152, 185; by-laws, xxv (*see also* by-laws, congregational); consecration class, 175, 180; damaged roof of, 122, 175, 263n7; 1823 Consecration, 35–37; 1832 Cornerstone Dedication, 46; 1833 Consecration, 47–50; financial crisis, 125–26; gift shop, xx; as historically significant site, 208–10; historiography of, 209–10, 223; identity issues, xiv, xxii–xxiv, 225–26; Johnny Weibel Museum of St. Thomas Jewish History, 224, 226; land holdings, 234n12; marriages in,

130, 135, 185; 1974 Rededication, 221;
1983 150th Anniversary of Sanctuary,
222–3; 1996 Bicentennial, 224; 2002
Rededication, 225; rabbinic searches,
70–71, 91–92, 217–19, 244n78; religious school, 72, 73–74, 76, 77, 84, 92,
97, 132, 144, 175, 181, 222, 223; secessions, 77–86, 114–20; taxation, 103,
104–6, 114, 119–20; tourists in, xiii,
222; transition to American Reform
congregation, 210–11, 217–20; vestry,
103; Women's Club/Sisterhood, 206–7,
210–11, 270n52
Synod, 1872, 132; Leipzig, 1869, 127, 130

Talmud, 64–65, 68, 71
Tebah (Holy Ark), 48, 49
Thomas, Rev. Howard E., 190
tidal wave, 123
Tidende. See Sanct Thomae Tidende
Time Magazine, 201
Torah, 7, 18, 36, 47, 60, 69, 83, 137, 180,
187, 188, 233n79, 238n70
Tortola, 150, 155
tourism, 195–96, 200, 207, 208, 212–14;
Virgin Islands Tourist Development
Board, 203, 268n28; V.I. Department
of Tourism and Trade, 212
Touro, Judah, 104
trade. *See* mercantilism
Trepuk: Mariette, 184; Mathilde A.,
261n61; Max E., 159, 161, 166, 184,
185, 189, 261n61
Truman, Harry S, 200

Union of American Hebrew Congrega-
tions, 217, 219
Union Prayer Book, 199, 219; Rabbi's
Manual, 205
Unitarianism, 106, 149
United Grand Lodge of England, 32
United States, 27, 151; attitude of St.
Thomas toward, 166–67, 182–83,
265n61; Department of the Interior,
196; purchase of Danish West Indies,
133, 166–67
Unna, Salomon Joseph, 2

Vass, Emanuel, 2
Vaughn, John, 9, 231n44
Venezuela, xvi, xviii, 93–94, 112, 143;
Barcelona, 88, 126; Caracas, 45, 47, 89,
170; Coro, 93, 248nn34–35, 252n31;
Maracaibo, 45
V.I. Distillers, 197
Virgin Islands Tourist Development
Board. *See* tourism
Virgin Isle Hotel, 202–4, 206, 216,
269nn32–35; purchase by the Hilton
Corporation, 212
Voice of Jacob, xxv, 70, 72, 74–76, 78, 81
von Rosenørn, 46
von Scholten, Casimir, 33
von Scholten, Peter, 45, 82, 83, 84, 87, 90,
147

Washington, D.C., 213, 215
Watson: Esther (Robles), 186, 215;
Gladys, 185; John Douglas, 186;
Walter C., 215; Walter I., 186
Weinberger, Carol, 214
Welcome, Isaac, 10
Westerman, George W., 216
West London Synagogue, 69–71, 74,
117–18, 244n75; attempts to use
liturgy in St. Thomas, 70, 116, 118,
137, 243n68; cemetery (*see* ceme-
teries, London, Balls Pond); liturgy
of, xv, 69–70, 72, 75, 81, 116, 243n66;
and Moses Nathan, xvii, 139–40. *See
also* Marks, Rev. David Woolf
White, John Frank, 184
Wiesel, Elie, 224
Wills, 55, 61–63
Wise, Isaac Mayer, 117
Witkin, Rabbi Nathan, 215
Wolff, 32; Alexander, 244n97; Rev. Alexan-
der Aaron (Chief Rabbi of Copen-
hagen), 82, 96, 157, 237n55; Daniel,
244n97; Elias, 112–13, 128; Julius, 73;
Miriam, 244n97; Rachel, 138–39;
Rebecca, 244n97
Wolff, Aron, xvi, 45, 46, 73, 89, 91, 112,
128, 243n68, 246n143; defender of
Jewish law in Danish West Indies

Wolff, Aron, (continued)
90; in London, 126, 138; officer of
St. Thomas Hebrew Congregation, 39;
reporting on synagogue activities,
66–67, 72, 76, 245n105; synagogue
school director, 88
women: right to vote in synagogue elections, 124; role in mercantile industry,
29–30

Women's Club. *See under* Synagogue,
St. Thomas
World War I, 165
Wouk, Herman, xvi, 195, 210, 270n64

Yale College, 28, 235n23
yellow fever, 20, 122, 155, 201
Yom Kippur. *See* High Holidays
Yulee, David Levy. *See* Levy-Yulee, David